S0-AQJ-804

Collected Papers on the Jacobite Risings

Rupert C. Jarvis

Collected Papers on the Jacobite Risings

Volume II

Manchester University Press
Barnes & Noble Inc, New York

© 1972 RUPERT CHARLES JARVIS

Published by the University of Manchester at
THE UNIVERSITY PRESS
316–324 Oxford Road, Manchester M13 9NR

UK ISBN 0 7190 0488 8

U.S.A.

BARNES & NOBLE INC
105 Fifth Avenue, New York, N.Y. 10003

US ISBN 0 389 04572 1

942.071
J38c

157517

Printed in Great Britain by
Butler & Tanner Ltd, Frome and London

Contents

		Page
Preface		vii
Acknowledgements		xiii
References		xv

IV *Communication*

13	News	3
14	Intelligence	37
15	Espionage	70
16	Propaganda	110

V *Controversy*

17	Fugitive histories of the Forty-five	143
18	Fielding and the Forty-five	169
19	The *True Patriot*	189
20	London	212

VI *Courts*

21	The Manchester constables, 1745	237
22	The Carlisle trials, 1746	255
23	Trial proceedings	277
24	The administration of the anti-catholic laws	303

| | Index | 327 |

Preface

History is a true record of what happened, how people lived and died,
what they did and said.
An epic theme merely distorts the record.

I, Claudius

The first volume of this collection contained a dozen papers,
divided under three topics: military, constitutional and local
affairs. This concluding volume contains another dozen papers,
likewise presented under three topics: communication, controversy and courts. They have also this in common, namely, that
neither volume attempts to record an epic. 'An epic merely
distorts the record.'

Professor G. R. Elton, on the contrary, in his latest admirable
contribution to historiography, *Political History: Principles and
Practice*, sums up and defends the traditional task of the historian
as precisely that of presenting an epic—of telling a story. He then
throws down the gauntlet to sociological historians and mere
quantifiers and others who, by *not* telling a story, have consequently fallen from grace. He goes on to say that those who can
muster no interest for the active political life of past societies have
no sense of history at all.

It is, however, precisely out of a sense of history, out of a keen
interest in the active life of a past society—an interest in what
people actually did, and particularly what *ordinary* people did
locally—that the papers republished in this and the preceding
volume have often deliberately refrained from 'telling a story' as
such. It may be, perhaps, that a story comes through, but if it
does it is no part of the primary intention. No subject could have
been chosen which of itself is essentially an epic, which apparently
absolutely demands the form of 'a story that is told', than any
account of the jacobite risings. However, notwithstanding this
traditional method of handling—or rather, perhaps, because of it
—the emphasis here has been not at all upon 'telling the story'—
not at all upon the *linear* narrative—but rather upon a closer
examination into what was being done by ordinary people, and

particularly by those people who were far too ordinary to find a place in the oft-told story. And this involves an analysis in depth of a number of *local* situations. This is illustrated by the fact that in the first volume there were, in that account of the last desperate throws of the Stuarts, only two references in the index under 'Stuart': one was to an officer in the Liverpool militia and the other to Alan Breck. There was no reference in the index to 'Moidart, the Seven Men of', but—in contrast—there were more than ninety references to the 'Lieutenancy', under more than thirty various sub-headings. Or again, there were no fewer than sixty references to 'Local officials', divided between bailiffs, bellmen, churchwardens and constables (high and petty)—eighteen various sub-headings. Doubtless the story, *as a story*, could easily enough be told without bringing in the local bailiff who had to provide for horse-hire and riding charges and was left to procure the straw for the king's forces; the bellman who had to 'cry' in the streets the arrival of the invaders into the town; the church-warden who recorded the baptism of Mary—daughter of a rebel passing; the parish constable who paid six pence for 'a gill of wine' for a dragoon's child that died and four shillings for its coffin.

None the less, it was they, the local officials, who *at the time* were facing the main impact of the invasion, who were taking the main active part in England—and probably the only active part— in at least one aspect of the past society that Professor Elton appears to be speaking about. Thus, with the mere narrative, as a narrative, safely tucked away—with no obligation to find a story to tell—with no ' "Nantes, over the sea from" to "Skye, over the sea to" '—one is able to indulge more fully one's interest in the actual life of ordinary people in that past society. Thus, by ignoring the primacy of chronology, one is better able to study the real structure of past life, in its various and varying signifi-cances. In any case, it is inevitable that in this structural analysis the time factor is necessarily at something of a discount.

Dr Marshall, in a sympathetic reference to this aspect of these present papers, in Professor Harold Perkin's *History: an Introduc-tion for the Intending Student* (pp. 108–11), has been kind enough to say, with regard to this 'work on the frontier of knowledge' (as he says), with specific reference to the jacobite risings in local and regional history, that the scholarship of Mr Jarvis has made the subject fit into [certain] categories most effectively . . . by showing how people in those areas reacted to the Scot's arms; the county gentry, the militiamen, the parish officers, the religious groupings, even the journalists . . . Mr Jarvis explores in detail. In so doing he shows us how the county was held together at the time of crisis by the thinnest of administrative tape.

I have indeed at least attempted to discover and relate a continuity of theme—a 'story', if you like to say it that way—in successive situations, rather than to repeat once more the almost ritual recital of personal incidents.

All this Mr Jarvis has managed to adumbrate, basing his researches largely on local records. Running through all his published work is a sustained story, a developing narrative, the stuff of history; yet he has also added to our knowledge of military, legal, administrative history. Yet how much more interesting is his material than a dreary recital of administrative and legal functions! We learn not what people were supposed to do, but what they *did*.

And what has been so much neglected in 'history' is not only 'what people did', but what *ordinary* people did *locally*. Not that the sources relied upon here are in fact mainly local or regional. Even before the days of Marshall McLuhan we were teaching that certain record media can produce only the conditioned message. One might instance, in this regard, the case of 'Captain' Bradstreet, detailed in paper No. 15 as one of four characters to illustrate the theme of espionage during the last rising, as one of the modes of communication. In 1755 *The Life and Uncommon Adventures* of Dudley Bradstreet appeared in Dublin, a piece of picaresque reminiscence fairly characteristic of the genre of that day. It was therefore, as one might expect, full of pimps and prostitutes, low life and high. Bradstreet included among a variety of other well spiced fare a circumstantial account of himself as a government confidential agent, sent out from London to spy out the invading jacobite army. He tells a story of the immensely significant part he took—as a double agent—in the much discussed and much disputed decision at Derby on that critical day, 5th December 1745. His story, however, is not in itself inherently very probable, but Bradstreet included, as a hallmark of its authenticity, what purported to be the actual text (so far as he could remember it) of certain letters he claimed to have written to the secretary of state and also to the king himself after his services to the crown had been ill requited. Because, however, this story was found wedged in between an account of himself as a pimp in a regular 'Place of Pleasure' and another of himself as a pimp working on a freelance basis, his version of himself as a confidential government agent—notwithstanding the claimed corroboration of the letters—was not taken too seriously.

In 1929, however, a new editor contemplating a new edition went searching the Reading Room of the British Museum, doubtless for a reference to any earlier editions of the *Life and Uncommon Adventures*. Although the (printed) general catalogue of printed books did not throw up anything for 'Bradstreet', the (printed) catalogue of 'additional' manuscripts did. This particular catalogue (or 'list') has a valuable characteristic which those who know it very much value. Its printed index of the manuscripts contains a precise reference to those personal names, place names and other features that are contained in the manuscripts themselves but which do not, however, appear in the printed list. This index did in fact produce a number of references to the name of Captain Bradstreet. The fact that a number of them turned out to relate to an altogether different Captain Bradstreet and his doings in the British army in North America was moderately disappointing; others of them, however, did in fact refer to Dudley Bradstreet, the government spy of the Forty-five. These latter turned out to be none other than the very letters, now among the correspondence of the duke of Newcastle, which Bradstreet had produced as evidence of his credibility in his *Life and Uncommon Adventures*. Facsimiles of the British Museum letters were accordingly reproduced by the editor of the 1929 edition, and these authentic texts coincided, near enough, with the versions Bradstreet had produced from memory. The letters, then, were genuine after all, and this unexpected corroboration entirely rehabilitated Captain Bradstreet, the government spy, who after serving so well had himself been so ill served by an ungrateful ministry. Even Alister and Henrietta Tayler, usually so scholarly in their approach, now accepted him as 'the spy who was usually well informed' (and incidentally quoted him approvingly—although from a mis-cited source).

This is not the place to expatiate—as pedants will—upon the distinction between those manuscripts that have full archival value and those that do not, for that is an arid field. Archives (when the word in this context is exactly used) denotes those records that accrued naturally to an administration in the course of its own affairs; which did not merely report those affairs, but were actually *part of them*; and which came to be retained in the administration's own custody for its own purpose, and not for any other. In this realization, clearly one should search not only the version of the 'Captain' telling his own story; not only—it is a fine point—the *records* collected together in the British Museum, but also, surely, the *archives* of the situation accrued in the Public Record Office. There should, for example, if Bradstreet's story is true, be a letter 'standing on the file' from a Lancashire curate who got caught up with the invading army, a letter addressed from Standish in December to the secretary of state at the instance of this intrepid spy. The document, however, is not to be found in its proper place—that is to say, in bundle 76 of the state papers, domestic, for the period concerned, namely, the first fortnight in December. In fact it is merely misplaced—because it is misdated.

Arthur Agarde, a late Tudor archivist still revered by the modern followers of his craft, once said that there is a threefold hurt, 'that may bring wrack to records: fire, water, rats and mice—and misplacing'. Certainly misplacing can bring 'wrack to records' as final as the 'hurt' of fire and water, rats and mice. In this particular instance, however, if informed search did not discover the curate's letter in its own place, serendipity disclosed it in its (misdated) misplacement.

That too was genuine. Dudley Bradstreet, the government spy, seemed now, therefore, completely confirmed in his recent rehabilitation, being now satisfactorily documented from each of the three classes of documentary source distinguished by the research historian: firstly, from *chronicle* sources (Bradstreet's own *Life and Uncommon Adventures*); secondly, from the sources of *collected* records (the duke of Newcastle's correspondence collected in the British Museum); and thirdly—the final accolade—from accredited *archives* (the state papers in the Public Record Office). What now could shake the reputation of 'Captain' Dudley Bradstreet, the government spy?

Alas for Dudley Bradstreet, there are other items in the archival series—still in their proper archival 'place'—items, however, that provide quite a different version. It would not be fair to anticipate here, but they tell quite another story, and exit the honest agent. Exit the self-styled 'Captain'. Exit the trustworthy spy.

The point is, therefore, that it is not just a matter of *records*: it is a matter of *which* records.

Acknowledgements

Thanks are owing to the editors of the *Bulletin of the John Rylands Library*, *The Modern Language Review*, *Notes and Queries*, the *Transactions* of the Lancashire and Cheshire Antiquarian Society and the Cumberland and Westmorland Antiquarian and Archaeological Society, and the Cumberland County Council, for permission to republish matter which has earlier appeared in their publications; to the Carlisle Public Library, the Clerk to the Lieutenancy of the City of London, the Corporation of London Record Office and the Guildhall Library Muniment Room, to Earl Fitzwilliam and his trustees of the Wentworth Woodhouse Settled Estates, the University of Nottingham (Department of Manuscripts) and the City of York Library, for authority to quote from unpublished sources; and to the Bodleian Library, the Joint Archives Committee for the Counties of Cumberland and Westmorland and the City of Carlisle, the University of Nottingham (Department of Manuscripts), Yale and the City of York Library for special facilities received.

Part of the paper on London and the Forty-five was originally delivered as the inaugural George Eades Memorial Lecture at the City Literary Institute under the aegis of the London and Middlesex Archaeological Society, and I am accordingly indebted for consent to reproduce. Also, I am pleased to express in particular my gratitude to the Leverhulme Research Trustees, who made it possible to undertake a study of unpublished manuscript sources. Thanks are owing also to the libraries and record repositories more generally for the unfailing assistance one has come to expect. To take for granted, however, the unstinting help given personally by the librarians and archivists and their assistants, indicated by the notes, could be taken either as something of a compliment—or as downright ingratitude.

References

Add. MSS	BM: Additional manuscripts.
Army route books	PRO: WO 5 (Out-letters: Marching orders: General).
Astle MSS	BM: Add. MSS 34712.
BM	British Museum.
Cab. minutes	Add. MSS 33004 (1739–45).
Carlisle MSS	H.MSS.C. 42, *Fifteenth Report*, appendix VI (1897).
Ches. sess. doc.	Cheshire (quarter) sessions documents; Cheshire County Record Office, Chester.
Clarke nb	Notebook of Baron Charles Clarke; Tullie House, Carlisle (quoted by courtesy of Carlisle Public Library).
CM	*The Chester Miscellany, being A Collection of Pieces* . . . Chester, 1750.
Cope Inq.	*The Report of the Proceedings and Opinion of the Board of Officers in the Examination into the Conduct Behaviour and Proceedings of Lieut-General Sir John Cope* . . . London, 1749.
Culloden Pp.	H. R. Duff, *Culloden Papers* (1815).
Cumb. LMB	Cumberland lieutenancy minute book; Joint Record Office, Carlisle.
Cumb. QSMB	Cumberland quarter sessions minute book; Joint Record Office, Carlisle.
Cumb. QSR	Cumberland quarter sessions records; Joint Record Office, Carlisle.
Customs	Customs outport letter-books (69–84); Custom House, London.
CW2	*Transactions*, second series, Cumberland and Westmorland Antiquarian and Archaeological Society.
Egerton MSS	BM: Egerton manuscripts.

Egmont	*Egmont Diary*. H.MSS.C. *Sixteenth Report* (3 vols), (1920–3).
Fitzherbert MSS	H.MSS.C. 32, *Thirteenth Report*, appendix VI (1893).
GM	*Gentleman's Magazine* (London), vol. XV = 1745, vol. XVI = 1746.
Guildhall MSS	Guildhall Library Muniment Room, London.
Hardwick MSS	BM: Add. MSS 35888 (other volumes specifically cited).
Hoghton MSS	Hoghton manuscripts; Lancashire County Record Office, Preston.
H.MSS.C.	Historical Manuscripts Commission.
Jarvis, *Jac. Risings*	R. C. Jarvis, *The Jacobite Risings of 1715 and 1745* (1954).
Kenyon MSS	H.MSS.C. 35, *Fourteenth Report*, appendix IV (1894).
Lancs CRO	Lancashire County Record Office, Preston.
Lancs CRO: PR	Lancs CRO: Parish records.
Lancs QSR	Lancaster quarter sessions records; Lancs CRO.
LCAS	*Transactions*, Lancashire and Cheshire Antiquarian Society.
L. Lon. MB	Court of lieutenancy, London, minute books of the commissioners, Corporation of London Record Office (quoted by courtesy of the Clerk to the Lieutenancy).
Lonsdale MSS	H.MSS.C. 33, *Thirteenth Report*, appendix VII (1893).
MLB	Malton letter-books: Wentworth Woodhouse MSS; Sheffield Public Library. Quoted with the permission of Earl Fitzwilliam and his Trustees of the Wentworth Woodhouse Settled Estates.
MM	*Whitworth's Manchester Magazine* (1745), continued as *The Manchester Magazine* (1746).
Newcastle MSS	BM: Add. MSS 32705 (other volumes specifically cited).
Pelham–Holles MSS	Pelham–Holles manuscripts; University of Nottingham, Newcastle MSS, 'Scottish Affairs (1)'.
PRO	Public Record Office.
Repertories	Repertories of the Court of Aldermen, City

	of London; Corporation of London Record Office.
Rydal MSS	H.MSS.C. 25, *Twelfth Report*, appendix VII (le Fleming) (1890).
S & A	Sir Bruce Gordon and Jean Gordon Arnot, *The Prisoners of the '45*, three vols, Scottish History Society, third series, 13–15 (1928–9).
SP Dom.	PRO: State papers, domestic, George II: SP 36 [bundle]/[number].
SP Dom. Mil.	PRO: State papers, domestic, military: SP 41/–.
SP Scot.	PRO: State papers, Scotland, second series: SP 54 [bundle]/[number].
Stowe MSS	BM: Stowe manuscripts.
TLB	Tweeddale letter-book: PRO: State papers, Scotland, SP 55/13 (1742–6).
WO	PRO: War Office papers.
WO Estabs.	PRO: War Office Establishments: WO 24.
York Guildhall	City of York records, York Guildhall.

IV *Communication*

13 *News*

During the autumn of 1944 there appeared in the periodical press[1] an essay, addressed to an historian in the twenty-first century—to a conscientious investigator, patiently inquiring into the history of the present, an historian careful for the feeling and the tone of a period as well as for accuracy in military detail. In comparing—and perhaps contrasting—that spring with that autumn the essayist remarked with regard to the D-day landings that since the spring 'fortune has attended our arms. We are nearer by a measurable step to what in Europe will be—or will be called—peace.' Then the essayist in the present went on to remind the historian of the next century of what is so often overlooked, namely, 'Though you, from the vantage point of the future, can measure that step, and relate it to the whole journey, remember that we cannot.'[2] At this distance, of course, we for our part may be tempted to see the invasion of 1745 as a march leading southwards only as far as Derby, and the return as being only the next step on the way to Culloden. But they of those days saw it not at all that way. The historian, therefore, inquiring into the history of those times, 'careful for their feeling and their tone, as well as for their military events', may for his part now be able to measure each step in relation to the whole, but he must remember that the men of those days could not. It is from this angle, therefore, that the day-to-day columns of contemporary news-sheets seem to be a much neglected source in relation to local events and local reactions—'feeling and tone' if the essayist wishes—particularly as regards the Forty-five. They can be a much needed corrective, for they check that backwards-looking fallacy to which all historians are prone.

The notes and references are on pages 32–6

In any case, much has been written about the Forty-five, both by way of history and romance—many think *too* much. The rising has been studied by jacobite and whig alike, from journals, memoirs, diaries, and histories written by actual participants; from various family papers, letters, and the indictments and proceedings at the trials; but not, it seems, apart from a few scissors-and-paste-pot jobs at the time, from the day-to-day columns of the news-sheets of the period. This, perhaps, is something of a pity, for although the newspaper accounts may often be inaccurate or misleading as to detail, they do reproduce in the main a truer general picture of local conditions and reactions than that drawn by the more familiar histories. The confusion locally, for instance, the general amazement at the advance, indeed the terror in anticipation during the course of the excursion into England, is easier to recapture from the day-to-day news than from any of the more formal pages of the histories. This is precisely because the histories, memoirs and similar accounts were written, naturally enough, in retrospect, whereas the news-sheets, on the contrary, were written obviously without the advantage of knowing what the ultimate result of the rising was going to be. They have all the merits of a breathless serial, when at each contribution it cannot be known what exactly the next instalment may bring.

The *Gazettes* and newspapers were of course about the only source available to the compilers of the earliest narratives of the rising, that is to say, such works as those by Samuel Boyse, the Dublin eccentric, Andrew Henderson, whom Secretary Murray called the 'little ignorant scholl master', John Marchant, whom Andrew Lang dismissed rather too contemptuously, I think, Rapin's Continuator, and certain of the anonymous chronicles.[3]

Indeed, only by recognizing the reliance which these early compilers placed on the *Gazettes* can we account for some of the errors and omissions, otherwise quite inexplicable, which were repeated even in much later editions, long after it had become possible to correct them. For example, in the early stages the official bulletins in the *London Gazette* had been none too informative. In fact the very first item of firm news of Charles Edward's landing in the west[4] was tucked away in an inner page of the *Gazette*, wedged—not to say hidden—in between an account from the Hague of a minor cavalry brush between a

Dutch detachment and some Hanoverian horse, and an account from the Admiralty Office that Vice-Admiral Martin had brought some French ships into Plymouth Sound.[5]

After landing firstly at Eriskay in the Isles on 23rd July (old style) and at Loch nan Uamh on the mainland on the 25th, Charles Edward moved up Loch Shiel to Glenfinnan, raised his standard there on 19th August, marched up the Great Glen, crossed the Corrieyairack Pass and marched southwards to be in Perth by 4th September.

Although of course the facts were fully known—in due course —in London,[6] no official bulletin whatsoever was issued through the *Gazette*, nor was any reference whatsoever made to any military movements until 14th September, when a communique was printed stating that the clans were actually in possession of Perth.[7] It so happened that an early compiler in London was getting together a serial history of the rising for *The Museum*, a periodical which Robert Dodsley commenced during the course of the rising.[8] The first instalment of this history appeared in the very first issue, that dated 29th March 1746. This account took Cope on 'a long and fatiguing march over the mountains to Inverness', but continues that

the rebels gave him the slip and instead of marching through the Pass of Corryeroch they took the way over the mountains, and the first news heard of them was that they had taken Perth.

It is a reasonable assumption that the compiler of this serial history was working at this stage, with little more than the file of the *London Gazette* at his elbow, for, noticing the more or less unaccountable gap in the *Gazettes* already referred to, and working presumably in haste, he did not trouble to refer to any other source of information but merely transferred this hiatus in the *Gazettes* bodily into his own history. From its somewhat ephemeral setting in Dodsley's periodical this error found its way into the *Compleat And Authentick History* and likewise into the Manchester printed history ascribed to James Ray, the Whitehaven gipsy.[10]

Since those early days, however, the *Gazettes* and provincial news-sheets have fallen out of favour. During the first half of the eighteenth century the provincial press was at an interesting stage in its development. With the commencement of daily newspapers in London,[11] the cost in the country of a subscription to a London paper increased considerably. It was now definitely expensive, bearing in mind the increased numbers the subscription had to cover, and the additional stamp duty (and carriage). Behind this margin of additional cost the provincial press sought to establish itself. As the jacobite faction was stronger in the country than it was in town, many of the provincial weeklies had a marked jacobite leaning. Manchester, however, for all its jacobitism had at the time only Whitworth's whig *Manchester Magazine*.

As regards the actual news the provincial weeklies published about this time, it will be found that the local papers then were not local in the same sense they are today. In fact, their function was not so much to collect and print local news as it was to give local circulation to news obtained from the wider world.[12] One feels, nevertheless, that one would like to see certain of the issues in particular of some of the papers from the towns more or less on the line of march. It is, however, immensely to be regretted that no 1745 copy is known to exist of the Whitehaven *Weekly Courant*, nor of Thomas Cotton's *Kendal Courant*, nor of Thomas Ashburner's Kendal *Weekly Mercury*.[13] Ashburner's other journal, *The Agreeable Miscellany; or Something to Please Every Man's Taste* was certainly running from 13th May 1749 until 26th October 1750, and during this period he reproduced at fortnightly intervals Henderson's whig *History*,[14] with slight variations and additions. This, however, was not strictly contemporary. The Whitehaven *Weekly Courant* is known to have been in existence in 1736, and *The Kendal Weekly Mercury* in 1742; No. 1 of the *Kendal Courant* was dated 1st January 1731; but whether any one of these papers was being published in 1745 is an open question. The *Carlisle Journal* did not commence until as late as 1798. It is interesting, therefore, to note that when quarter sessions ordered the clerk of the peace during the 1740s to place an advertisement in the newspapers, either with regard to some public announcement or to let some contract, or invite a tender, it was ordered to be placed 'in the Newcastle papers'. For example, when 'the Causey at the South end of Priestbeck Bridge was out of Repair and ought to be repaired', it was ordered that 'the Clerk of the

Peace do forthwith advertise in two New Castle Papers the letting of the said Causey to be repaired';[15] or when tenders were invited in 1747 for the transport of the baggage of the king's army, it was in the Newcastle papers that the advertisement was to be inserted.[16] This evidence seems to favour the view that the Whitehaven and Kendal papers had discontinued by this time, or at least that they did not circulate in the county generally, or in the northern parts in particular.

The reference to the 'two New Castle Papers' must presumably have been to the Thompsons' *Newcastle Journal* and William Cuthbert's *Newcastle Gazette*.[17] Although copies of the former survive in Newcastle from 1739 to 1742, there is unfortunately for our present purpose a break until the run from 1746 to 1758. As regards the *Gazette*, although odd copies survive in respect of 1744, the only copy surviving covering any part of the rising (so far as I know) is an odd copy for 5th February 1746. Although the York *Gazette* ran throughout the rising, the only copy known (in York Minster) is dated 1741. The York *Journal* probably commenced in November of 1745 and there are some surviving copies in York public library. The Derby *Mercury*, unlike its Kendal namesake, has contrived to survive, with copies from 1732 onwards in Derby library.

An association between the Lancashire local press and the rising is to be found at Preston. According to tradition, Charles Edward lodged there in the premises long occupied as the offices of the *Preston Journal* in the entry to Strait Shambles, formerly known as Mitre Court. Moon's *True British Courant* or *Preston Journal* probably made its first appearance in the very year of the rising, but Smith's *Preston Journal* had certainly been somewhat earlier in the field. For the rest of Lancashire, Blackburn, Bolton, Bury, Lancaster, Prescot and even Warrington were as yet without their local newspaper, the last named notwithstanding its fine record in the previous century in the matter of the printed word.

So far as Manchester is concerned, its first newspaper, Roger Adams' *Manchester Weekly Journal*, established in 1719(?), had already met its demise seven years later. John Berry's weekly, the *Lancashire Journal*, commenced in 1738, proved to be even shorter lived. There was, however, Whitworth's *Manchester Magazine*, already mentioned, successor to *Whitworth's Manchester Gazette* and precursor of *Whitworth's Manchester Advertiser and Weekly Magazine*. Robert Whitworth's press was noteworthy in the rising in that the jacobites upon their arrival in Manchester compelled Whitworth's apprentice, one Thomas Bradbury by name, who had apparently been left more or less in charge 'in the absence of his master', as the paper tactfully put it,[18] 'to print a treasonable Paper which they called a Manifesto and likewise an Advertisement'. The apprentice, presumably to prove that his service in this had been rendered against his will, consented to be a witness against the Manchester men at their trials.[19]

Chester for a dozen years past had had its local press, *The Chester Weekly Courant*, then being produced by Elizabeth Adams, widow of Roger Adams, who earlier had been responsible for the *Manchester Journal*. Throughout the rising the *Chester Courant*, unlike Robert Whitworth's *Manchester Magazine*, was able to keep up publication without a break.[20] I say 'unlike the *Manchester Magazine*' because although it is commonly known that Whitworth left his press just before the arrival of the jacobites in Manchester, and although his press was used by them to print some treasonable manifestoes, it has not, I think, been recognized that he missed printing two particular issues, that for 3rd December 1745 and that for the 10th.[21] Although a number of Chester *Courants* are known and variously distributed, there is none now in the editor's files at Chester earlier than 1749. I think the absence of these old issues from the editorial files, notwithstanding the extraordinary unbroken sequence of the paper, even to the present day, can be accounted for in this way. In 1750 Elizabeth Adams published a little work entitled *The Chester Miscellany*.[22] She opened its preface with a note of apology—'the Editors are only the Printers of a Country Newspaper'.[23] It appears 'that frequent Applications having been from Time to Time made for particular Numbers of past *Courants*, which it was impossible for them to oblige their Friends with', the editors were induced to make a collection of extracts covering a number of years, and to publish this selection in the form of a pocket volume. This little work, containing amongst other items some accounts 'carefully extracted from the London and other newspapers',[24] would form a readable history of 'the Insurrection of the Scots, AD 1745', 'a sort of compendious but Impartial History of that Extraordinary Affair'.[25] It seems, then, that the *Courant* offices ran out of stock of the issues published during the course of the rising, having met a demand from those who wanted them mainly as souvenirs of the times. Not being able to oblige even their friends, as Elizabeth Adams says, they were presumably reduced to their own file copy only. These sole remaining file copies they almost certainly used as the printers' 'copy' for setting up the *Chester Miscellany* in 1750, and hence of the *Courants* of the period none is now extant.[26]

However, the provincial news-sheets in general took their earliest news of the rising from such journals as the *London Gazette*, the *General Evening Post*, *St James's Evening Post*, *The General Advertiser*, *The London Evening Post*, Fielding's *True Patriot*, and of course the official *London Gazette*, the Scottish items being largely borrowed from the *Caledonian Mercury* or the *Edinburgh Evening Courant*.

Certainly they were stirring times and there was much to report. The jacobite force crossed the Esk into England on 8th November: Carlisle capitulated—town and castle—on the 15th. Moving south from Carlisle they consisted of four bodies; firstly, there was the advance guard of horse under Lord Elcho and Lord Pitsligo; secondly came the van proper under Lord George Murray, consisting of the so-called Athol brigade, the Ogilvies, and John Roy Stuart's and Glenbucket's men; thirdly came the main body, the rest of the army, highland and lowland, under Charles Edward himself; and lastly came the baggage and artillery under the duke of Perth,[27] guarded by his own regiment. The horse guards moved off first from Carlisle, and were in Penrith on 18th November, passing on at once to Lowther House on the 19th and 20th. On the 20th and 21st they were at Kendal. The van under Lord George, who gave the horse two days' start, left Carlisle on the 20th, making Penrith that night; they were at Shap on the 21st, Kendal on the 22nd, and caught up the horse at Burton just outside the Lancashire border on the 23rd. Charles Edward brought the main body out of Carlisle on the 21st, stayed at Penrith two nights, and at Kendal two nights, and entered Lancaster on the 25th. Meanwhile the baggage and cannon could not manage the direct road, and left Carlisle by way of the eastward road to Warwick Bridge. It arrived at Penrith on the 22nd. Still avoiding the direct Shap road, it took the parallel course by way of Orton on the 23rd, Kendal on the 24th, to join up with the main body at Lancaster on the 25th. Lord George Murray and the van, together with the horse, had already occupied Lancaster on the 24th. Leaving the main body again at Lancaster, the van occupied Garstang on the 25th, Preston on the 26th, and waited at Preston on the 27th also in order to enable the main body and cannon to come up. The whole force was at Preston on the 27th and Wigan on the 28th, with some horse thrown out to places such as Leigh and Manchester. Manchester was occupied on the 29th, and the artillery marched in on the 30th, on which day the horse were occupying Stockport and outlying places. On 1st December the horse marched out through Sale to Altrincham, and the foot to Macclesfield. For reasons too well known to enter into here,[28] Lord George Murray and the van and horse bore off to Congleton, and completely out-manoeuvring Cumberland, turned away again for Ashbourne, where the van were again ahead of the main body, and the whole force re-united at Derby on Wednesday, 4th December. The whole force remained at Derby on the 5th, and the much discussed retreat was commenced on Friday the 6th. They were at Ashbourne that night, and at Leek, Macclesfield, Manchester, Wigan and Preston on successive nights. They remained at Preston on both the 11th and the 12th, at Lancaster on the 13th and 14th, and were in Kendal again by the 15th and 16th; they crossed Shap on the 17th, fought the rear-guard action at Clifton and made Penrith by the 18th, and were at Carlisle once more on the 19th. They re-crossed the Esk to make their return to Scotland on 20th December—it is usual to say, on Charles Edward's birthday.

As might be supposed, some at least of the reports of this advance and retreat that found currency through the press were far removed from actual facts. Especially is this so when the reports do not originate from the actual seat of operations. On the other hand, many of the reports are correct to a surprising degree. Also, it often happens that even when a report is obviously unlikely in itself, it can, by easy and often interesting stages, be traced back to a plain statement of fact. As an example of this, we might take the reports, which at one time or another were widely current, that the jacobite army had suffered some reverse at Preston. The story took various forms. The rebels had withdrawn—*to* Preston. The rebels had returned—*from* Preston. The rebels were now surrounded and were about to be defeated —*at* Preston. Perhaps rumour had some sort of lingering memory of Hamilton in 1648, or of Mackintosh in 1715. One version, towards the end of November, had it that the jacobites had retreated before they actually reached Preston; they had returned to Carlisle—had in fact already retreated almost out of England. It was reported in the *St James's Evening Post*, 23rd–26th November, that:

an advance Party of the Rebels arrived at Lancaster last Saturday [23rd November] and proclaimed the Pretender there: but towards the Evening it was said that there was an Account that they were returned to Carlisle.

A similar report was published in the *Daily Advertiser*, and was repeated as late as 3rd December, in the *True Patriot*. If this were in fact the case there seemed every reason to believe the report which accompanied it to the effect that 'the Ribble-Bridge in Lancashire is broken down to retard the March of the Rebels southwards'. The appearance of the jacobites in Manchester, how-ever, dispelled all doubts that might still remain as to whether or not they had retreated from about Preston. But after Derby the stories revived. The invaders were understood now to be in a bad way. They were, according to the story, 'in so bad a Condition that they must in a few Days lay down their Arms and submit'. This information—from Chester—was dated 7th December (*St James's*, 7th–10th December). But rumour seemed determined still that it should be at Preston again that the Scots should come to grief. Therefore the old batch of stories, adjusted to suit the cir-cumstances of the retreat, took a new lease of life. There was, for instance, information from Chester dated 16th December which still managed to combine the old retreat to Preston with the breaking down of the Ribble Bridge.

We have Accounts that the Rebels are now surrounded at Preston by the King's Army: that a Party of Wades Horse[29] on Friday last [13th December] stopped them at or near Garstang ten miles from

Preston, and drove them back into the said Town, where the Duke's Army arrived on Saturday Night. The Rebels have blown up Ribble-Bridge, fix'd some cannon on Preston Steeple, and are entrench'd close by the Town; and we hope and expect every Moment to hear of their Reduction, being informed the Attack would be made this Morning.

(*St James's*, 17th–19th December)

It seems that further information, tending apparently to confirm this news that the jacobites had been forced back to Preston and were surrounded there, arrived in London during the next few days. Some at least of the papers, although reporting this, advised caution, the more so because this particular crop of rumours seemed all to arrive from about Chester, whereas north Lancashire had quite another story. I quote from the *London Courant*:

It may not be amiss to inform our Readers that by Wednesday's Post [the 18th] was received several Letters from Chester and other Places near it containing an Account of the King's Troops coming up with the Highland Rebels, and their entrenching themselves at Preston: but as these Letters were dated the 16th, and as we had Letters from Preston directly dated the Evening before, which gave quite another Relation, and that the Rebels were actually marched towards Lancaster, we did not think proper to amuse[30] our Readers with those Reports.

Incidentally, to that particular piece of editorial discretion the *True Patriot* made the somewhat cutting observation that the editor 'should show his judgment by omitting most of the Article which he prints' (24th December).

What, then, was the real source and origin of all these stories of the Preston retreat? Let us go back to an early and quite accurate report published in November, based apparently upon information from a man from north Lancashire 'just arriv'd at Warrington'. This particular account made it clear that the jacobite army had in fact advanced southwards just beyond Preston, and had then withdrawn—but withdrawn only as far as the town of Preston itself. I quote the *London Evening Post* of 28th–30th November:

A Person of undoubted credit is just arrived here [Warrington] and brings an Account that about 2,000 of the Rebels were this Day on their March from Garstang to Preston; and that Evening a Party of them were advanc'd on this Side Preston but intended to return into that Town.

The ensuing confusion both in the north, and in the capital, as to whether the jacobites were now marching northwards or southwards was clarified by a letter from Manchester two days later:

I have just time to inform you that the whole Army of the Rebells have pass'd over Ribble Bridge in their way to here. After which they were review'd in Harding Heath by the Duke of Perth, the Lord Pitsligo and other chiefs.

The writer goes on that he could give no certain account of their numbers. Ribble Bridge had not been broken down to impede their progress. They themselves, so the report went, had broken it down as soon as they had passed over it, with what motive was not recorded (*ibid.* 28th–30th November). Those reports, then, of the defeat of the jacobite army in Lancashire, or alternatively of their retreat to Carlisle, derived in the first instance from a report of their withdrawal from the Ribble Bridge to Preston town. The news of this withdrawal led naturally to an assumption that the bridge had been broken down. When later it was found that the jacobites were in fact south of the Ribble, the report that the bridge had been broken was still credited but the work of destruction had to be ascribed to the jacobites themselves.

What, then, are the facts behind this manoeuvre of Ribble Bridge? Actually the facts as initially reported were quite accurate. Other sources are, of course, available from which the facts of the case can be established or checked. One of the clan narratives, after recording that the clansmen went out of the town of Preston, goes on to say that they 'crossed the bridge and quarter'd a great many of the men on that side of the water'. This narrative refers to a highland fear that Preston had in the past been so 'fatale to the Scots that they would never get beyond it'. This was clearly a reference to 1648 and 1715. Lord George Murray therefore marched some of the men beyond Preston this time, if only to 'evade the freet', as the clan narrative said, that is, to break the spell, or lay the old bogey.[31] What Murray of Broughton said confirms this. 'There were few if any of them [the highlanders] ignorant of what their predecessors had suffered.' Therefore Lord George marched some of them actually beyond Preston if only to evade any superstition, and 'to convince them that the Town should not be their *ne plus ultra* for a third time'.[32] Lord Elcho, who commanded the advance guard, would naturally have more regard to the sheer tactical situation. He merely says Lord George 'march'd and took possession of Ribble Bridge a mile beyond Preston'.[33] There can be little doubt that even if Lord George did not know the details of how in 1648 Cromwell, after his brilliant march from the south, fell unexpectedly upon Preston from the east, he would be strategist and tactician enough to see the need there was for holding the approaches, and particularly the Ribble Bridge. His move, then, was probably dictated by the sheer military necessity of the case. But, a highlander himself, he knew 'the superstitions of the Highlanders in such matters', as he himself said (in his private papers), to fall in 'with their humours', even though 'these things may seem of no consequence'.[34] He seized the opportunity to 'evade the freet'. Much of this laying the bogey of Preston can be obtained from the better known sources, but I do not recollect any references in the contemporary histories—nor indeed in any of the later ones—to the fact that this turning back to Preston after the 'token' march beyond gave rise to a rumour of the retreat and the defeat of the whole jacobite army. Indeed, even while Manchester was occupied there were, as we have seen, accounts current to the effect that the jacobites had already retreated almost out of England altogether.

Already in September, just after Prestonpans and before the jacobites were anywhere near the Border, it was reported in Chester[35] that the Stuart standard had already been raised in Manchester, a story which Whitworth promptly and indignantly denied. The accusation had been made, he said, only to bring Manchester into bad odour, and to make the town suspected by the government.[36] On the whole there did not seem any grounds for concern in England until the second week in November, when the jacobites were learned to be before Carlisle. A letter was received in Chester, dated, 'Preston, Nov. 10. Half an Hour past 11', which said, 'We have just this Moment receiv'd an Express that the Rebels are encamped two Miles behind Carlisle; this may be depended on for fact.' The letter continues, 'Since the above we have receiv'd another Express which informs us that the Rebels have actually laid Seige to Carlisle, which I am afraid will not hold out long' (*Chester Courant*, 13th November). Indeed, Carlisle was no sooner invested than much of the north-west was already thinking apparently in terms of evacuation. News from Lancaster as early as 10th November was to the effect that 'The People in General at this Town have sent away their most valuable effects, and many families are in Desperation to avoid the Rebels' (*London Evening Post*, 12th–14th November). By the 17th, Carlisle, town and castle, had capitulated, for Wade, on the other side of the Pennines, had been forced to turn back to Newcastle, being 'impeded by the great Quantity of Snow that had fallen' (*London Gazette*, 19th November). This surrender of the only fortress on the route—although admittedly a pretty poor one —'cast a great Damp on People's Spirits' (*Chester Courant*, 20th November).

After the fall of Carlisle the news from Lancaster was that 'they had received Intelligence from Kendal that Lord George Murray and two thousand foot demanded Quarters at Lancaster for Saturday' (the 23rd) (*London Evening Post*, 23rd–26th November). But by Saturday the invaders had not arrived. They had, however, 'sent some of their Quarter-Masters to a place called Burton, which is but 8 Miles from hence, to demand Quarters for 100 Horse and 8000 Foot which will arrive there this evening' (the 23rd) (*ibid.* 23rd–26th November). The most precise count—not necessarily the most correct—was made over Eamont Bridge,[37] two miles south of Penrith, and was hurried to London forthwith. It reads:

Monday Morning	18th.	100 Horse.
Thursday —	21st.	840 Horse and Foot.
Same Day		500 Ditto.
Same Day		300 Ditto.
Same Day		300 Ditto.
Friday —	22nd.	100 Ditto.
Same Day		2746 Ditto.
		4886
	Left in Carlisle	120
		5006

Sixty Carriages with 16 pieces of Cannon.

(*St James's Evening Post*, 28th–30th November)

The secretary of state addressed a letter to lords lieutenant 'giving an account of the Rebels'; the letter went on 'that a Considerable Body of Forces were marching towards the north under the Command of General Huske, specifying also that the Laws in this Case being deficient, his Majesty's Friends were desired to assemble and concert Measures for raising Forces'[38] (*General Evening Post* and *Manchester Magazine*, 24th September). General meetings of 'the Gentry, Clergy &c.' of the counties were accordingly called. So far as Cheshire is concerned we learn that the nobility and gentry of the county assembled at Chester Castle and entered upon measures to raise and maintain a body of men numbering 2,500. Many gentlemen subscribed a year's income of their estates. The bishop[39] subscribed £200 and Sir Robert Grosvenor[40] gave £2,000 and promised as much more when required (*Gentleman's Magazine*, vol. xv (October 1745), p. 554).

The earl of Warrington[41] also was most active:

> They write from Dunham Massey in Cheshire, the seat of the Earl of Warrington that his Lordship has furnished all his tenants with Arms and Ammunition who have sign'd their names to be ready on the first notice to defend the Religion and Liberties of their Country.
> (*Manchester Magazine*, 8th October)

The following from the next week's issue furnishes an interesting sidelight on practice on estates.

> We hear that the Right Hon. the Earl of Warrington hath signify'd to all his tenants in Cheshire & Lancashire that several Regiments of Soldiers are to be forthwith raised in these Counties by his Majesty's Orders, to serve against the Rebels & for Defence of the Country, & that his Lordship assures all his tenants, who will on this Occasion serve as a Soldier that if any Life or Lives should happen to fall out of their Leases in such Service, his Lordship will add another Life or Lives in the room of those so lost, without any fine or consideration whatsoever.[42]   (*Manchester Magazine*, 15th October)

The county militia was accordingly raised, and later there was information that the earl of Warrington together with Lord Cholmondely[43] marched the Cheshire and Staffordshire militia into Frodsham, accompanied by Lord Herbert's[44] newly raised regiment (*St James's*, 10th–12th December). Six hundred of the county militia are said to have entered Chester under the command of Sir Willoughby Ashton, Bart., and Peter Leicester, Esq., 'followed by a great number of Gentlemen, being ordered here by the Lord Lieutenant of the County to defend the City in case the rebels make this way' (*ibid.* 7th–10th December).

The story of the capture of Manchester by a chevalier's sergeant, his mistress and a drum, even though well known, is too good a story to let pass without at least some sort of reference. At least it provided some much needed light relief for the newspapers of the day. Most of them had it, in all its detail—except of course the *London Gazette*, which even then had too much official decorum to make a reference to anything so unofficial as a mistress.[45]

Whitehall, December 1st.
By Advice from Lancashire of the 29th, the main Body of the Rebels lay at Wigan and Leigh upon the 28th. That after-noon a Party of them came to Manchester, beat up for Volunteers for the Rebels, enlisted several Papists and Nonjurors, and offer'd Five Guineas a Man to any that would enter: Those that took the Money had White Cockades given them, and marched about the Town with the Drummer and Sergeant. The Party above order'd Quarters to be prepared for 10,000 Men who were to come thither the next Day.
(*London Gazette*, 30th November–3rd December)

The liberal estimate of ten thousand was probably an official effort to arouse the public at large from the general apathy into which it was feared to have fallen. The *London Evening Post* also (30th November–3rd December) mentions 'two Highlanders beating up for Volunteers' and the offer of five guineas a time. The *St James's Evening Post*, however, appearing the same day as the two journals already mentioned, insisted apparently not only upon having the sergeant's mistress on the stage, but upon having her there in true pantomime style, in male attire. The information is addressed from Halifax:

Our Express has brought Advice from Manchester that a Sergeant with a Drummer and a Woman in Man's Cloaths, came to that Town about Four O'Clock last Thursday Afternoon [i.e. the 28th] and beat up for the Pretender, and before seven that Night (as was said) above forty had enlisted themselves: and at Midnight came in there a great Number of Highlanders belonging to the Rebell Army. Our Town [i.e. Halifax] is now in the greatest Confusion upon Advice of Part of the Rebels coming towards Rochdale we see families continually passing that have deserted their Dwellings: the Roads are quite full.

There was, however, in the same issue intelligence from Manchester direct:

The Bell-Man is now going thro' the Town, [it says.] In my Opinion the Rebels will make all possible haste thro' Derbyshire. The Parties of Highlanders came in this Morning [i.e. the 29th] and they have fixed upon Mr. Deninsons (*sic*) for the Pretender's Quarters. At Two O'Clock several Thousands came in: a great many of them are poor diminutive creatures,[46] but there are many strong stout Men amongst the Guards and Officers. They have ordered the Bells to ring. The Bell-Man is going with Orders for us to illuminate our Houses which must be done. At Three O'Clock the Pretender march'd by my Door in a Highland Dress on foot, surrounded by a Highland Guard, and no Musick but a pair of bag-pipes with him.

The official communique of the 1st and 2nd still conveyed a measure of uncertainty as to the route beyond Manchester—to the south or into the west,

Upon the 29th the main Body moved towards Manchester. A Party of them arrived there at Ten in the Morning, examined the best houses, and fix'd upon one for the Pretender's Son's Quarters. . . . About two in the Afternoon another Party arrived there with the Pretender's Son, who marched on Foot in a Highland Dress, surrounded by a Body of Highlanders, and was proclaimed. The Bellman went round the Town again to order the Houses to be illuminated. That Night some of them gave out that their Route was for Chester, and others reported that they should march for Knutsford through Middlewich and Nantwich into Wales.

(*London Gazette*, 30th November–3rd December)

In reading these contemporary news-sheets one catches here and there a glimpse of some of the difficulties there must have been in getting letters and information through from the towns and cities either to the duke of Cumberland or to Wade, or even to the government in London. According to the *London Evening Post* of 26th–28th November, even by 24th November (when the main body was no farther south than Kendal and the advance party only at Lancaster) the post office at Preston was already shut down. Two days later, by the 26th, when the army was at

Preston, it was reported that 'an anonymous letter has been sent to the Postmaster here [i.e. at Manchester] telling him his Letters would be stopt this Night' (*St James's*, 28th–30th November). This was on the 26th. It is interesting, in this connection, to compare an entry in Beppy Byrom's journal:

[November] 27th. the post-master is gone to London to-day, we suppose to secure the money from falling into the hands of the Rebels.[47]

With this sort of interruption, communication must sometimes have become somewhat difficult.[48] Little wonder then that when communications were a little more normal a letter from Manchester, dated 11th December, closed with the words:

I am sure that Marshal Wade will be at Kendal before the Rebells; but I heartily wish he may. I have wrote two or three Letters before to you: but as all our Posts are stopt was obliged to burn them.

(*St James's*, 12th–14th December)

When news was despatched by express it was often very difficult for the express riders to get through.[49] For instance, news of the entry into Preston is contained in 'a Letter from Northallerton from a Gentleman who went Express from Bolton to General Wentworth'.

I got about 30 Miles, he said, that night to General Wentworth; and after riding 78 Miles the next Day met with him at Ten O'Clock at night at Ferry Hill near Durham, where all the Foot were encamp'd.

(*London Evening Post*, 30th November–3rd December,
and *St James's*, same date)

An appreciation of this type of difficulty gives a new meaning to certain entries in the constables' account for Manchester:[50]

	£	s.	d.
On Account of expenses for Expresses	00	10	06
For Horses standing ready, and for Corn for the Horses standing by	00	02	06

At the time the main jacobite body was as far south as Macclesfield, newspaper information does not seem to have been very good, if the London papers are to be believed, for a letter was printed as from Chester saying the invaders had been at

Manchester 'ever since Friday' (the 29th) and were now expected at Chester 'every Day'.

> We are in expectation of the Rebels giving us a Visit every Day for they have been at Manchester ever since Friday: where they were received with ringing of Bells, Illuminations, &c. They also beat up for Volunteers and proclaimed the Pretender. If they come to Chester the Accommodation they will meet with will be Fire and Sword: for the Castle and the City are determined to fight it out to the last Extremity. Ligonier is very near them, so that we expect every Hour to hear of an Engagement. Their coming here will occasion their being so hemmed in that it will be impossible for them to get out without being destroy'd; for the Duke of Cumberland has sent us word that he will be with us in a Day or two if the City can hold out so long. We have Advice that on Sunday Morning the Lord Elcho with 400 Men enter'd Altringham and demanded Provisions and Quarters for 10,000 Men. According to custom they went to the Excise Officer and demanded the Accounts, and levied a month's Excise upon the Inhabitants, which they obliged to pay directly upon pain of military execution.   (*St James's*, 2nd–5th December)

The account continues to the effect that the army, after levying the excise, marched on to Knutsford, 'proclaim'd the Pretender at the Market Cross', and gave out that they 'were marching in all haste to give Battle to his Royal Highness the Duke' (*ibid.*). The local press says, however, that 'they had given out they would call at Knotsford, but they were prevented by a Report that 2,000 of the King's Troops were there'—a proof, it says, 'that their Intelligence was not always good' (*Manchester Magazine*, 24th December). Nevertheless, some of the reports of their progress are rather curious as to the information and intelligence credited to the jacobites. For example, in this part of Cheshire:

> In their Way to Macclesfield they call'd on Col. Lees of Adlington,[51] where they demanded such a particular Number of Muskets, Pistols &c. and six French Horns, and mentioned the particular Rooms they were in.   (*Manchester Magazine*, 24th December)

Certainly the *Gazette* remarks that 'the Party which lay at Altringham were very solicitous to know what Number of the King's forces there was at Knotsford.[52] (*London Gazette Extraordinary*, 5th December). The *Gazette* reports also:

They press'd, or rather took away, all the Horses they could meet with about Manchester before they crossed the Mersey, and obliged several Gentlemen who had sent their Horses out of the Way, to send for them back.   (*Ibid.*)

I quote as an example an advertisement of a gentleman attempting to regain possession of his old bay mare:

Taken, the 1st Instant, from Peter Leadbeater, Junior, near Buckley-Hill, in Cheshire, by a Party of the Rebels—A Dark full aged Bay Mare, 14 Hands high, somewhat thick shoulders, a big black Main and Tail, a few White hairs in her forehead, &c., bare place under her Wind-pipe, very near her jaws, all black hoggs. Whoever gives account of her to Peter Leadbeater . . . shall be rewarded: or if sold to any Countryman on Notice to the [above] and Delivery of the said Mare to Peter Leadbeater shall have that Money repaid.

                              (*Manchester Magazine*, 24th December)

With the invading force rumoured to be somewhere between 9,000 and 16,000 men, and wild men at that, it is not very surprising that the civilian population in the towns on the anticipated route were early thinking in terms of dispersal of goods and evacuation of personnel. On 27th November information from Stockport was to the effect that 'all the principal Inhabitants were retired with their best effects[53] from Manchester' (*St James's*, 28th–30th November, and *London Evening Post*, same date). Another account says that whole families were to be seen continually passing who had left their dwellings. 'The roads are quite full' (*St James's*, 30th November–2nd December). The *General Advertiser* had it:

From Liverpool we hear that the Appearance of the Rebels cause a great Hurry[54] amongst them; they have drawn all their Shipping out of the Docks into the channel on board which they are putting their most valuable Effects and have sent their Wives and families over the River into Worral.

Reports such as these enable us to see in another light such entries as the following in the Constable's Account of the Manor of Manchester:

1745. Nov. 25.   Pd. Bellman for crying
                 agt. Beding being   00 : 01 : 00[55]
                 remov'd out of Town

So far as Chester was concerned, it seems to have suffered from the disadvantage that the people within the city wanted to get out for safety's sake, while those outside wanted for the same reason to get in. Clearly Chester regarded itself as in the way of the route for Wales. There was much confusion in consequence. Here again, in the account selected, there is doubtless some exaggeration, but with the motive of studying 'the feeling and tone' of the period as well as establishing the military facts,[56] one need not apologize for introducing it. It was dated from Chester on Saturday 23rd November. The advance guard had not as yet entered Lancashire.

We are in great confusion here. Several Families on the one hand are returning out of the Town, and the Inhabitants of the Suburbs on the other are bringing their Bedding and Effects into the Town. Trade is absolutely at a Stop, and I believe most of the Shopkeepers will shut up very soon. The Gateways are bricking up and on Monday night [the 25th] there will be no entrance into the City but by two small wickets, one on the Bridge and the other at the East Gate. They are using all imaginable Despatch to put the Castle into the best Posture of Defence so short a Time will allow. . . . Great Plenty of Provisions are coming into the Town from all Parts, there being an Order from the Mayor to provide a sufficient Quantity for a Fortnight.[57]

(*London Evening Post*, 23rd–26th November)

According to an item of news in the *General Advertiser*, the people of Chester were 'in the utmost consternation for fear of a visit from the Rebels'. Incidentally that journal went on to say that 'just now Advice is arrived, that the Rebels in marching over a boggy part of that Country were retarded by a Sinking of their Artillery'. The news-sheets provide a reference also to the find of '14 Bullets', dating from the Civil War.

Chester 30th November

In digging about the walls there were found 14 Bullets each about 40 lbs. weight, supposed to have been there since the time our Castle was besieged by Oliver Cromwell, who though he had 20,000 men under his command, spent twenty weeks before it, when the garrison consisted of only 800 men. As to the Rebels,[58] [the account goes on hopefully] they are at present at Manchester between the two Armies, that of the Duke being 10 miles nearer than Marshal Wade.

(*London Evening Post*, 30th November–3rd December)

By the first days of December it was reported that 'the Gentry and all the Heads of this City are gone away, and all Manner of Trade stopp'd, the Shops in general have been shut up this fortnight past' (*St James's*, 2nd–5th December). If it were stated on 25th November that 'most of the shopmen will shut up very soon' (*London Evening Post*, 23rd–26th November), it could scarcely have been true on 2nd December that 'the Shops in general have been shut up this fortnight past', so it is likely enough therefore that not 'all the Heads of the City' were gone with the gentry away. But the following week *St James's Evening Post* was still able to reproduce another graphic picture from Chester.

To tell you of our Calamity is more than I can express, for above this month past little or no Business has been done in the City, Our Wheat is still in many Places unsow'd, and the industrious Poor are now starving for Want of Employment, our Shops are shut up every Day as Sundays: in a Word, if this Country is not soon rid of the Rebels all Provisions will be so dear that few will be able to get Money to purchase common Necessities.[59]

(*St James's*, 7th–10th December)

But a few days before this London had had another version. An account sent out of Chester by another correspondent said that they within no longer had any complaint. The castle was in so good a condition for defence 'that we are no longer in any pain about the Rebels. They may come when they like, and be sure of a warm welcome' (*London Evening Post*, 3rd–5th December). Indeed, not only could Chester now look after itself, but it could send supplies to support the duke of Cumberland. According to the *Chester Courant* it could at the end of November send as many as twenty-three waggons and carts from the castle loaded with provisions and ammunition to meet the army at Stone (*Chester Courant*, 4th December). (*CM* 56.)

It was commonly reported in the capital that

It is said that the Rebels expected to have Chester delivered to them at their Approach: but thank God they are Disappointed.

'Before they have approached' was the cutting comment of the *True Patriot* (3rd December). However, letters now from Cheshire advised that the gates of the city were opened again and trade was now being carried on as usual 'since the Rebels took the Route to Derby and Nottingham'. Also a number of stragglers from the jacobite column, who had been taken up by the country people were brought into Chester and thrown into the castle for safe custody[60] (*St James's*, 5th–7th December).

When spies or prisoners were thus brought in, it occasioned great excitement, and their wild appearance and strange dress caused much curiosity. When the first Scotsmen were brought in, Chester learned, apparently with amazement, that they 'had no breeches, nor stockings that came up to the Knees, but a short Kind of petticoat about a Foot deep which they call a Fillibeg, which is all the Highlanders wear in their own Country' (*Chester Courant*, 18th December). (*CM* 63.) There was some excitement in the City earlier on when two spies were brought in and committed to the gaol. The story, as reported, was that these two spies, coming on well in advance of the van, had arrived in Chester

to deliver a Letter to a Person of Distinction's House, but was not at Home, and had received a disagreeable Answer from his Son: that thereupon one of them who seemed to be the Principal, said he knew nothing of the contents, that he was a Grocer in Cumberland, and his name Pattison, and went away to an Inn; where it being observed that the Man who was with him inadvertently call'd him My Lord, they were both taken up and committed.[61]

The *St James's Evening Post* closed this account with a conjecture:

As it is mention'd in some Letters that the Marquis of Tullibardine disappeared of a sudden after the taking of Carlisle, it is not impossible that his Lordship may be secured in the shape of a Grocer.

(23rd–26th November)

Tullibardine[62]—'the High minded Moray, the Exiled, the dear' of *Waverley*—had earlier been reported killed at the siege of Carlisle, and Fielding's *True Patriot* put this later story of 'Tullibardine in the shape of a Grocer' in its proper light by commenting:

We hope his Lordship will not regain his Liberty as easily as he returned to Life, after his having been killed by the Historians of last week.

(*True Patriot*, 3rd December)

One of the prisoners taken up and brought into Chester told a curious tale of how he came to be involved in the rising. He said 'he was a Servant to one Mr. V[augha]n[63] a Monmouthshire Gentleman, who took him out with him pretending a visit to some of his Acquaintances, but instead thereof went with him directly into the Rebellion' (*Chester Courant*, 18th December). (*CM* 63–64.) Other prisoners, including 'two officers called serjeants', were brought into Chester during the first week in December by a party of Sowle's Regiment,[64] having been taken at Whalley, and others taken at Stone in Staffordshire apparently as late as 14th December (*St James's*, 7th–10th and 17th–19th December). These prisoners who were held at Chester were later, some of them, sent to York to stand their trial. There is a curious account in *Whitworth's Manchester Magazine* about their journey through Manchester *en route*. Forty-nine of these prisoners, including a woman and eight or ten of the Manchester volunteers, arrived from Chester in three waggons and a cart. They were guarded by about fifty of Wade's Horse,[65] and were lodged in the Exchange. Next morning they left for York at about seven o'clock, in the manner in which they came.

They most of them were very chearful. They had a good deal of Money given them upon the Road in this town [Manchester]. Some of them threw Halfpence out of the change-windows to the Boys in the street.

(*Manchester Magazine*, 5th and 19th August 1746)

With regard to the retreat of the jacobites, the details of Thomas Siddal's return to Manchester are, of course, well known,[66] but I may perhaps be excused for quoting them from a mutilated copy of the *Manchester Magazine*. When the main body was at Macclesfield a party of the Manchester volunteers went through Altrincham, where they stayed some time, and decided to proceed via Stretford, but found Crossford Bridge again down. They were therefore forced to go to Stockport, 'where a considerable Body lay that Night'.

On Saturday Night [7th December] four of the Manchester Rebels came to Stockport, and having given the Watch the Slip, who fired at them and shot one of their Horses, they got over the Ford. The Rebels were very much enraged when they came to Stockport on this Account, and threatened to burn the Town, and did cut several Persons with their Swords. They seized upon Mr. Elcock an Attorney, Mr. Osborn, Mr. Robinson a Grocer, Mr. Bower a Mercer, one Lee, and the Constable, whom they took with them to Manchester, where by proper Application they were all discharg'd, except the Constable, about whose Neck they put a Halter when at Stockport, and threatened to hang him; both he and many others thought they would have been as good as their Word. The four Rebels above mentioned came to Manchester that Night, and one of them supposed to be Thomas Siddal the Barber narrowly escaped being seized at the upper End of Market street-lane. He was forc'd to gallop down the street and through the Ackers Gates, and in the Square he quit his Horse.[67]

The above is quoted from a fragment of a copy of Robert Whitworth's *Manchester Magazine*, undated but undoubtedly of 24th December.[68]

So far as concerns the matter of jacobite depredations and outrages in the country, most know the story of the march through the north-west from the pages of the *History*, ascribed to James Ray[69] largely because Ray was himself a north-countryman; he claimed to have been an eye-witness of most of what he reported, he was later a volunteer with Cumberland's army, and his *History* was printed in Manchester at the house of Robert Whitworth. 'Ray's' *History* is eloquent of the depredations and outrages practised by the jacobites in their passage through the country. A study of contemporary news-sheets, however, will show that much of Ray's testimony is not to be accepted too easily, and if actually true is not always representative. For himself, Ray was writing (what he *did* write) probably at a time when he felt that something ought to be done to justify or perhaps to offset the unhappy reputation Cumberland had acquired in the north. In the main it is true to say that most of the reports in the press of various outrages are either too vague to be real testimony, or else too obviously second-hand to be accepted as reliable evidence. The general tone of the reports from the actual scenes themselves are tolerant and temperate, and almost without exception they report great restraint on the part of the invaders. The following is an account of certain plundering in Manchester:

What we heard yesterday is confirmed to-day of their being at Manchester, where they are plundering unmercifully without Exception. Major Grey's House was begun to be rifled this Morning;

Mr. Horton of Chatterton, the late Sheriff of Lancashire, has suffered very much; Mr. Justice Duckinfield's House is entirely plundered, and one of his servants put to his Oath to make Discoveries.

(*St James's*, 17th–19th December)

But this account of the depredations in Lancashire will be found to have originated in Yorkshire.

More representative, I think, are the reports quite frequently occurring that broadly speaking the conduct of the invaders, surprisingly, was exemplary. Even the *True Patriot* had to admit the almost complete absence of personal outrage or assault. 'The few Outrages on our Women are to be wondered at,' it advises on 21st December. 'In Lancashire a small Party of them overtook a very pretty young Woman on Horseback whom they robbed of her Money and Horse, without even offering to salute her.' Or again, 'They took no money out of the Town, but the Excise' (*London Evening Post*, 10th–12th December). Or the more precise version of the same report: 'They Collected no Contributions except the Excise on Malt, Ale, Candles, Leather, Etc.' (*St James's*, 3rd–5th December). Although there was doubt and confusion—as there was doubtless intended to be doubt and confusion—in the press reports about the Mersey bridges and the intended route south,[70] there was no doubt whatsoever about the practice—and the intended practice—of collecting locally the public moneys due.[71]

Extract of a Letter from Preston, dated 24th November at 6 in the Evening.

A Gentleman who left Lancaster at three O'Clock is just come here and says that about Twelve a Quarter Master of the Rebells with Twelve Men came into that Town and demanded Billets an Hour after. About Two O'Clock Lord Elcho at the head of 200 Foot entered the Town, and drew up in the Market Place. They issued out Orders for all Publick Money to be paid To-morrow at Twelve O'Clock.

(*St James's*, 26th–28th November)

In the English counties it was principally the excise that came in for collection. The official bulletin as to Preston reads as follows:

Whitehall,
November 28th.

By advices of the 26th from Manchester there is an Account that six Quarter Masters belonging to the Rebells came into Preston at

Eleven O'Clock that Day . . . They have proclaimed the Pretender in every Market Town and have levied the Excise.

(*London Gazette*, 26th–30th November)

A later bulletin referring to the occupation of Manchester went into greater detail:

> Whitehall,
> December 1st.
>
> By Advices from Lancashire of the 29th a Party of them came to Manchester. By their Order the Bellman went round the Town to give Notices to all Persons belonging to Excise, Innkeepers, etc., forthwith to appear to bring their last Acquittances and Rolls and all ready Cash they have in their Houses belonging to the Government upon Pain of Military Execution.
>
> (*London Gazette*, 30th November–3rd December)

An unofficial version records that the bellman summoned not only 'Innkeepers, etc.' but 'all Persons that pay any kind of Excise' (*St James's Evening Post*, 30th November–3rd December). We are informed a day or two later that this included 'the Excise on Malt, Ale, Candles, Leather, etc.', and that 'they gave a Receipt as part to the 8th Dec.' (*ibid.* 3rd–5th December; see also *London Evening Post*, same date). The *London Evening Post* records furthermore that 'they took no money of the Town, but the Excise for six weeks' (10th–12th December).

Henry Fielding early on had given all and sundry very clearly to understand from the columns of the *True Patriot* what life would be like when the rebels arrived. Houses are burnt, bodies of men, women and children lying about in the streets, scarce anyone dare stir out save priests and highlanders.[72] Women are being fought for and outraged. This is jacobite rule, 'with all the fury which rape, zeal, lust and wanton fierceness could inspire into the bloody hearts of Popish priestly bigots and barbarians'— (*True Patriot*, 19th November). This was all somewhat premature, however. Fielding is describing this in anticipation. It is only 19th November as yet, and the dreaded jacobites had not yet arrived. When they did arrive it was not to endorse Fielding's prophecies. But Fielding was regarded as, and was in fact, something of a ministerial mouthpiece, and some at least felt safe in taking their cue from him.

Our general Accounts from the North [says *St James's*] are full of Complaints of the Cruelty of the Rebells, having taken several People away with them Prisoners. And from Lancaster we hear that they hang'd up three Inhabitants of their Town.

(17th–19th December)

Referring to the progress southwards, the *General Advertiser* gave accounts of all sorts of outrages. 'In short,' it summed up, 'they appear to be nothing but a ragged crew of Miscreants who commit every Outrage without regard to Law and Decency.' Even Fielding—by this time somewhat converted from his earlier bias—felt he had to retort:

If they are such a ragged crew as here represented, the greater shame it is to the Militia of those Parts to suffer such Outrages to be committed on them with Impunity.

(*True Patriot*, 3rd December)

The *True Patriot*, then, first in the field in the atrocity-mongering business, was at least honest enough to admit (when 'the Bandits arriv'd once more safe in their own neighbourhood, after an Expedition which is not to be parallel'd in History') that so far as outrages were concerned, it had been editorially mistaken, for the invaders had been, surprising as it may seem, restrained and orderly—even in retreat.

As the Loss they suffered [said the *True Patriot* in retrospect] hath been much less than they could have reasonably promised themselves, so have the cruelties they have committed fallen altogether short of what might have been apprehended from such a Rabble, especially when incensed with Disappointment.

(31st December)

An incident, I have no doubt typical, is reported from about Wigan. The invaders had apparently 'borrowed' a cart, and later abandoned it again at Hindley. One of the inhabitants there took upon himself to look after this cart, and inserted the following advertisement in the *Manchester Magazine* (14th January 1745 [1746]):

Whoever has lost, or has had forcibly taken from him (by those shabby, scabby, scratchy, lowly, shitten Rebels) A tolerable good cart, and wheels, which were taken up and are still kept in Hindley, two Miles distant from Wigan, let him repair to William March or Robert

Gorton, in Hindley aforesaid, and give a just Description of the Same: And if they appear to be theirs, may have them restored upon paying for taking up, and the Charge of this Advertisement.

This good-humoured tolerance was much in evidence. More moderate opinion seems to have admitted that some number of the relatively few incidents complained of derived in the first instance from the local people attempting to over-reach the highlanders or taking advantage of their lack of English. In such cases some of the incidents were not without their own comedy:

There are some which seem to have affected a kind of Humour. One of these fellows sold his Horse to a poor Countryman for 10s. which was not the Tenth Part of its value; but as soon as he had touched the Money, instead of delivering the Horse, he told the Purchaser he was a damn'd Rogue to take Advantage of a poor Straggler's Ignorance of Horse Flesh, and immediately rode off with both Money and Beast. Another having sold his Plaid for a Crown told the Person who bought it he should have occasion to wear it in his Journey Home, but he would be sure to surrender it if ever he saw him in the Highlands.
(*True Patriot*, 31st December)

The last word on the matter probably was said by the official announcement which appeared in the *London Gazette*:

The Rebells behaved tolerably well in the March Southward.
(*London Gazette Extraordinary*, 12th January 1746)

In many of the newspaper reports and comments this refreshing turn of humour, even where one might perhaps least expect to find it, is, one might think, in the best English tradition. Particularly is this so in Fielding's short-lived *True Patriot*. It will be remembered that Fielding promised in his new paper 'to provide the public a better entertainment than it hath lately been dieted with' (*True Patriot*, No. 1, 5th November 1745). But if it did not quite live up to its early promise, its humour and irony at least were unrivalled. The *True Patriot* delighted in extracting reports from a number of journals—or better still, a number of reports from the same journal—and republishing them side by side, asking some ironical or sarcastic question. 'These two accounts,' it once said, holding them up for comparison, 'differ in so many circumstances of their Relation that it may be much

Morning, 31—Their Artillery thats come in here three Field peeces and 8 on the Road . . .

3 a Clock after Noon—This Moment I went to see the train of Artillery wch consisted of 12 Small Field Pieces in all they Sai will be 16, a very poor guard with them and the Baggage Carriages wch were Drawn by 3 and some by 2 Horses a peece.[106]

Or again:

This Computation was made by Counting what has passed at Eamont Bridge, which is south of Penrith and a considerable River where they cou'd be exactly counted and adding this by what came into Penrith next Day and was intercepted at Fallow Field Bridge at the North end of Penrith over a very small Brook where it is difficult to give a truer account of the Numbers.[107]

Not surprisingly, this intelligence was very promptly relayed, fanned out and siphoned off, mainly through the postmasters, to Brough,[108] Warrington,[109] Boroughbridge,[110] Raby Castle,[111] Byram,[112] Newcastle,[113] and other centres.[114] Another account professes to divide up the invaders not only between horse and foot but also between (1) 'Lusty tall and Stout Men'; (2) 'Middle aged and Middle sized men'; (3) 'Old men and boys'; and (4), 'The Lame sick and feeble'. This version, however, was rightly discounted—the informer had too much to say for himself.[115]

Nor were generalizations acceptable where more precise information was available. When Bryce Blair at Annan receives a piece of generalized information from a forward correspondent he passes it on, but says, 'I have wrote to him to know what particular Information He has of this, but have not got his answer'.[116] Attitudes were very creditably critical. Advance quartermasters demanded quarters at Dumfries for 5,000 foot, 1,000 horse, but the postmaster, in forwarding the information, comments, 'but we do not believe there are so many of them', and added a postscript: 'We don't believe the Highlanders to be near the Number they give out.'[117]

Not only were efforts made to check the reported facts, but steps could be taken to authenticate reporters. Useful information from 'A Gentleman . . . who came a good part of the Road with the Highlanders from Edin^r', closes with the remark, 'Youll please send this to your Brother at Whitehaven, *he knows the hand.*' The letter has a footnote: 'This Letter came from Dumfries to a Gentleman of this Town whose Brother is a merchant in Whitehaven, but I know not from whom it came.'[118]

In any case, what was needed was objective facts, not subjective impressions. It is significant that when Alexander Spencer, writing from the Westmorland–Lancashire boundary, once expressed his fears rather than the facts, he said, 'I hope your Grace will put no stress upon this furder than my own fears, as I am now continually on Horseback; I shall give your grace a just Account to morow night.'[119] There is also much advance information as to the habits and practice of the insurgent force: they go 'in quest of Horses and have imprest a good many, and We apprehend there will be parties sent for that purpose'.[120] The Dumfries postmaster says, 'The Country should be advertis'd [i.e. the neighbourhood should be advised in advance] to keep good Cattle [i.e. horses] and Cariages out of their Hands', by which 'their progress will be retarded'.[121] Bryce Blair of Annan warns that 'Small parties on Horseback Have Gone over the Country in search of Horses'.[122] The postmaster of Penrith, reporting direct to the postmaster-general, said,

They march with droves of Black Cattle and Sheep, Waggons of Biscake and Cheese wch they sit down at Noon to eat. At Night and Morning get a little Oat Meal wch they buy up at their own price or take away wherever they can get it, and Constantly Carry it in Leather Bag at their Side. . . . They March always by day break and sooner when they have the benefit of the Moon. They main Body encamps every Night: the Officers go to the Towns or Houses. The Baggage Guard is reliev'd every day and consists of about 300.[123]

An account from Appleby (via Barnard Castle) says that 'they pay for everything and are very civil'.[124] The postmaster at Lancaster says on Friday the 22nd that they will be at Kendal tonight and 'propose to be at Lanc[r] Satterday tomorrow'. However, he gathered that 'the Country should not suffer in the least by them' and this 'puts us all in great spirits'.[125] Another account at the same time from Kendal, via Lancaster, said 'we are all very well and does not in the least fear the Rebells as they are so civil. We have taken care of all the papers and other Valuable Effects and has taken an Inventory of all Merchandise Goods &c'.[126]

Information from Penrith passed through the postmaster at Brough, to the effect that 'all publick [money] demanded under pain of Military Execution'—not only had they received the Excise but they called also for the post office moneys. 'I have been Twice Called upon,' said the postmaster, 'for the post office Accts here. They talk high but I have agreed to wait upon their Principal or Even thier Prince him Self before I can Settle.'[127] Or again, from Lancaster, 'The Bellman is caused by the Quartermaster to go about Town ordering all Moneys belonging to the Government to be paid by noon.'[128]

Occasionally the advice was altogether more directive, specific directions, for example, of how exactly to deploy any local troops against the invading force. The following two letters were both dated in the early part of November:

All the advice I can give you is that if you have any armed forces as most other countries have, to make use of it by dividing it into small parties who may fire from every hedge to keep the rebels from separating from their main body to pillage and plunder.[129]

The other reads:

All the Light Horse of the County should follow close and destroy them among the hedges and when going in stragling partys. The country should pluck up Spirit and keep themselves in Bodies upon the hills and in passes and Knab them whenever they find them. It would be right to cause write these and like circumstances to every place.[130]

One was from the general officer commanding to the mayor and corporation; the other was from a local postmaster to anyone on the route. It seems not to matter much which one is which.

It is a remarkable fact that when the text of these fugitive and ephemeral letters are now compared—from the somewhat unlikely repositories in which they now lie—there is hardly a single instance of identifiable exaggeration; the same basic facts are often reported in those exciting times, and repeated and re-repeated, and remain absolutely factual in every word. One might reasonably conclude, therefore, that not only in timeliness but also in accuracy the information and intelligence furnished to the ministry in London, the deputy lieutenants and lords lieutenants and the regular forces, was good both in quantity and quality and also in its regularity; that both the standing and the hurriedly improvised machinery worked both promptly and well, and this notwithstanding the current local difficulties—the frequent references to the snow on the roads and the seasonal difficulties over the hills. In other words, the information and intelligence made available by the country to the military and civil government at the time was of a quantity and quality beyond the standard any establishment in the circumstances had any right to expect.

Notes

1 See Paper 1, volume I.

2 1 Geo. I, stat. 2, cap. 54; and 11 Geo. I, cap. 26.

3 In the lord chancellor's notes on the Cope Inquiry (see Paper 1, volume I); he 'noted' that this was the fact. Hardwick MSS, f. 10.

4 See below.

5 See Paper 4, volume I.

6 See below.

7 SP Dom. 73/9 (or 18). (Curiously enough, the letter is mis-dated, 'Carlisle November 2, 1744'—but endorsed, 'Carlisle Nov. 2, 1745'.)

8 SP Dom. 73/21 enc.

9 *Ibid.*

10 *Ibid.*

11 *Ibid.* 73/36.

12 *Ibid.* 73/38 enc.

13 Hardwick MSS, f. 31.

14 SP Dom. 73/46 enc.

15 *Ibid.* 73/46 enc. (or 143).

16 *Ibid.* 73/46 enc. (or 144).

17 *Ibid.* 73/37 (or 112).

18 *Ibid.*

19 *Ibid.* 73/18 (or 40).

20 *Ibid.* 73/46 (or 145).

21 *Ibid.* 73/65, enc. 6 (and 78 or 240).

22 *Ibid.* 65, enc. 4.

23 *Ibid.* 65, enc. 5.

24 *Ibid.* 73/42 (or 130).

25 *Ibid.* 74/77 enc. (or 234).

26 *Ibid.* 77 enc. (or 232).

27 *Ibid.* 78 enc. (or 239).

28 *Ibid.* 99 enc. (or 299–300).

29 *Ibid.* 78.

30 *Ibid.* 106 (or 326).

31 *Ibid.* 113 (or 350).

32 *Ibid.* 129 (or 399).

33 *Ibid.* 146 enc. (or 431–2) and endorsements, and Hardwick MSS, f. 43.

34 *Ibid.* 74/11 (or 29).

35 *Ibid.* 52 (or 149–50).

36 *Ibid.* 55 (or 156).

37 *Ibid.* 55 (or 157).

38 *Ibid.* endorsement.

39 *Ibid.* 55 (or 160).

40 *Ibid.* endorsement.

41 *Ibid.* 55 (or 166).

42 *Ibid.* 74 (or 207).

43 *Ibid.* 74 (or 209).

44 *Ibid.* 74 (or 212).

45 *Ibid.* 74 (or 209).

46 See Paper 10, volume I.

47 See Paper 9, volume I.

48 See, for example, Custom 85/71A (8 May 1689).

49 See Add. MSS 33050, ff. 130–93, for the Excise and Add. MSS 24900, ff. 32–45, for the Customs.

50 I.e. churchwarden, parish constable, overseer of the poor, etc. Thomas Pattinson, postmaster of Carlisle, however, appears to have served local office in the capacity of surveyor of the highways—a rational enough combination (Jarvis, *Jac. Risings*, 387).

51 And incidentally usually also exempt from liability to the land tax.

52 9 Anne, cap. 11 (10 in Ruffhead), see 17.

53 Newcastle MSS, 32705, f. 211.

54 9 Anne, cap. 11 (10 in Ruffhead), sec. 40. See also *Report from the Secret Committee on the Post Office*, House of Commons, 1844, 582, pp. 8 and 12.

55 The order was 'that no Person [was to] be permitted to go with Post Horses on the several roads' through the north of England 'without a Pass or Order from the Post Office'. Newcastle MSS (cab. minutes), f. 89.

56 Newcastle MSS (cab. minutes), f. 95.

57 Newcastle MSS, f. 211.

58 MLB, ii, 270.

59 SP Dom. 69/40.

60 I.e. the roads crossing the road to Edinburgh from London, SP Dom. 73/27 and TLB (1742–59), f. 131.

61 Newcastle MSS (cab. minutes), f. 95.

62 Jointly with the earl of Leicester.

63 See, for example, the early accounts of Prestonpans coming south by this route (SP Dom. 68/107, 120 etc.).

64 This being before the General Turnpike Act of 1766–7 (7 Geo. III, cap. 40).

65 See Paper 5, volume I.

66 SP Dom. 68/120.

67 *Ibid.* 73/47 (or 150).
68 *Ibid.* 65 (or 207).
69 *Ibid.* 75/5 (or 15–16).
70 *Ibid.* 73/38.
71 *Ibid.* 73/46 enc.
72 *Ibid.* 73/65 (or 208 or 240).
73 *Ibid.* 73/80 (or 245).
74 Newcastle MSS, f. 429.
75 SP Dom. 73/79 (or 244) [intercalated].
76 *Ibid.* 73/65 (or 208).
77 The latter is annotated: 'Mr Baty is a clergyman who live in the uttermost Limit of the English Side.'
78 SP Dom. 73/65 (or 209).
79 *Ibid.* 73/118 (or 345).
80 *Ibid.* 73/21 (or 80).
81 *Ibid.* 73/47 (or 150).
82 *Ibid.* 73/47 (or 151).
83 *Ibid.* 73/65 enc.
84 *Ibid.* 74/68 (or 188–90) and 74 (or 212) and 81 (or 232).
85 *Ibid.* 73/26 (or 81).
86 *Ibid.* 73/65 (or 207-10).
87 *Ibid.* 73/78 (or 238).
88 Presumably captain Roger Wilson, Westmorland militia.
89 SP Dom. 73/80 (or 245).
90 *Ibid.* 74/52 (or 150 or 141).
91 *Ibid.* 52 (or 149 or 137).
92 *Ibid.* 74/1 enc. (or 8).
93 *Ibid.* 74/40 (or 119).
94 *Ibid.* 74/55 (or 157).
95 *Ibid.* 74/55 (or 160).
96 *Ibid.* 74/55 (or 150 and 161–3).
97 *Ibid.* 74/83 (or 238).
98 *Ibid.* 74/68 (or 188–9).
99 *Ibid.* 74/1 enc. (or 8).
100 *Ibid.*
101 *Ibid.* 74/63 (or 181).
102 SP Dom. 74/10 (or 27).
103 See Paper 11, volume I.
104 SP Dom. 74/10 enc. (or 27).
105 *Ibid.* 73/65 enc.
106 SP Dom. 74/61 (or 137) and Newcastle MSS, f. 377. Also forwarded to secretary of state by Lord Lonsdale, 74/79 (or 226), and also printed as a single sheet and forwarded by Wade on 23rd November, SP Dom. 74/74 (or 211).
107 SP Dom. 74/93 (or 268).
108 *Ibid.* 74/93 (or 269).

[109] *Ibid.* 74/93 (or 271).
[110] *Ibid.* 74/93 (or 272).
[111] *Ibid.* 74/93 (or 273).
[112] *Ibid.* 74/79 (or 226) and 74/93 (or 268).
[113] *Ibid.* 74/74 (or 211).
[114] Newcastle MSS, f. 377.
[115] Hardwick MSS, f. 55.
[116] SP Dom. 73/26 (or 81).
[117] *Ibid.* 73/65 (or 209) and 73/78 (or 237).
[118] *Ibid.* 73/65 enc. (or 208).
[119] *Ibid.* 74/56 (or 158).
[120] *Ibid.* 73/65 (or 208).
[121] *Ibid.* 73/65 (or 209).
[122] *Ibid.* 73/78 (or 24).
[123] *Ibid.* 73/93 (or 276) and 73/99 enc. (or 297).
[124] *Ibid.* 73/99 enc.
[125] *Ibid.* 74/63 (or 181).
[126] *Ibid.*
[127] *Ibid.* 74/68 (or 190).
[128] *Ibid.* 74/85 (or 250). See Paper 9, volume I.
[129] Hoghton MSS, Wade to Lancaster, 6th November.
[130] Postmaster, Dumfries: SP Dom. 73/65 or (209) 8th November.

15 *Espionage*

It is not intended in this present paper to consider the general character of espionage during the Forty-five, nor to attempt any conclusion (nor even to point the direction of any conclusion) as to the efficacy or otherwise of espionage on either one side or the other. It is not intended to pass any part of its practice under any general or closely critical review; but rather to do no more than examine the details of a few specific instances—representative cases, perhaps—to illustrate the general context in which spying, or alleged spying, was conducted during the course of the rising. The professional military in the mid-eighteenth century had the habit of giving pretty short shrift, of course, to any spy caught actually in the field in the run-of-the-mill way. Michael Hughes, a London volunteer—an old Bluecoat boy—enlisted in Bligh's regiment and went north with it to Culloden. He says in his *Narrative*, casually enough, that a spy was caught at the Bridge of Don and hanged, 'and there ordered to hang for several Days'.[1] The general run of that type of victim, in the nature of the case, leaves no story.

In some at least of other cases, part of the essential story (if not the whole of it) may possibly be recorded. Often a little slice of the story—if not a big slice of it—may already be known from narrative sources or else be recoverable from the state papers, the trial proceedings, the manuscripts of the secretary of state or the lord chancellor's correspondence. To this—or these—may often enough be added the odd reference or odd references from local records, the quarter-sessions rolls and so forth. Thus, one may be able to reconstruct the 'particular instance papers' (so to speak) of a specific spy, or accused spy, and thus be able to state a whole case history. Furthermore, specific case histories may be selected in relation to particular types of case, selected (that is to say) specifically because they illustrate similar or contrasting backgrounds, according to the aim one has set oneself. It is proposed here to take four reconstructed selected case histories.

The first of these relates to a man who by reason of some odd coincidence, plus possibly a minor indiscretion, found himself caught up in espionage accusations; he is taken, indicted and then by some means or other manages to slip through the net and is then (officially) heard of no more. Such a case is that of Richard Jackson, a Manchester merchant or tradesman who in the late summer and autumn of 1745 was operating, by way of business, on both sides of the border. At the time when the battle of Prestonpans was hot news on the border, Jackson had just returned from the Scottish side and addressed a letter to a man at Brampton on the other, by the name of Campbell, a name—to some, at least—suspicious of itself. The letter was therefore not delivered to Campbell but to the justices, and it was found that the man from Manchester had referred to Charles Edward, not as the 'pretender', but as the 'prince', whereupon the man from Manchester found himself in a load of trouble.

The second case history refers to one which in its opening stages closely resembles the first, but had an altogether different ending. The probability is that the subject of this case, John Henderson, a writer (variously described as of Edinburgh, of Castlemains and of Lochmaben), was not in the first instance a spy at all, as ordinarily understood. Again, it was almost accidentally that he found himself indicted for espionage. He was committed to Carlisle castle and later the jacobites, finding the prisoner charged with being a jacobite spy, naturally released him when they took the castle—*and enlisted him*. It may very well have been no more than ordinary gratitude to his deliverers that he served them now, but in serving them he certainly was able to turn the tables on his late captors. He became literally the guard of his guards. But fate was fickle and Carlisle was in due course retaken, so that the turned tables turned once more. Henderson, too, was retaken, but not to stand his trial for the original charge of espionage—it was simpler now to charge him with treason. In either case the penalty was the same—death—and Henderson's was one of the first heads to be spiked over the gate of Carlisle.

The third case history is the curious story of the go-between who got the message through from Charles Edward's cronies, immediately after they crossed the border into England, to the earl of Barrymore's place on the Welsh border, Barrymore being by now the acknowledged leader of the English jacobite faction. The case has all the makings of a good modern spy story, for with skill they landed the sprats in the case, but with all their consummate arts the whales slipped through their net.

The fourth case history again runs parallel with the current vogue in spy scenarios. In the first scene the spy comes in from just-about-nowhere-at-all; only one thing is certain, he had something of a smutty past, and moves thereafter confidently amongst the highest in the ministry (just like that!). Scene: where the money is handed over, no questions (*almost* no questions) asked. Scene: where the gold is buried; scene: where an unsuspecting fellow traveller is handed over as a counter-spy; scene: with the cloak and dagger; scene: where the agent becomes double agent; scene: where the agent/double agent saves his country. End of drama. Epilogue: scene: where hero is denounced as double-double-spy; disclaimed by the highest in the ministry; appeal to king's royal person—saved country and hasn't even been paid his expenses. And now, at last, the whole truth can be disclosed (!) partly. Agent/double agent/hero tells his own story!—full of fashionable name-dropping, plus all the other characteristics the pop literature of that time demanded. The name is Dudley Bradstreet.

The first of these case histories, then, is that of Richard Jackson, a Manchester man who moved about—ostensibly by way of his ordinary business—on both sides of the border. He was known to have been on the Scottish side the weekend of Prestonpans and then to have crossed over into Cumberland and to have addressed a particular letter to a David Campbell, of Brampton. This David Campbell was known to be a one-time jacobite and, indeed, to have been 'out' in the Fifteen. Jackson had sent this letter to a Carlisle attorney to be forwarded to Campbell at Brampton. The attorney, however, professed to know that Campbell 'was a suspicious character and that he was in the Rebellion in 1715'. Instead, therefore, of forwarding the letter direct to Campbell he took it to Thomas Pattinson at Carlisle, who opened it, but whether he opened it in his capacity of postmaster, deputy mayor or justice of the peace is not quite clear. The letter was, indeed, of interest; not only on account of Campbell but also on account of Jackson. It contained a brief account of the battle of Preston-pans (fought the previous Saturday), and not only referred in specific terms to 'the victory', but furthermore to 'the prince' rather than to 'the pretender'. What is even more, it appeared to give some suspicious directions to Campbell about 'going where you promised' and then sending a special messenger, when 'I will come to you'.

'It being pretty late in the Evening' when the letter came to hand in Carlisle, the deputy mayor, Chancellor Waugh and the commandant met the following morning. They knew that Camp-bell had been 'out' in 1715, and it looked as though Jackson was already 'out' again in 1745. Not one of the three examining magistrates however, knew anything more about this Jackson. Nonetheless, they learned from 'a Gentleman that lately lived at Brampton', where Campbell and Jackson traded, that Jackson 'was a Manchester Trader and a Suspicious character as to his Loyalty'. On the basis of this information the chancellor 'imme-diately acquainted all the Justices and the D[eputy] Lieut[enant]s that were then in Town' and 'made out Warrants [and] sent the High Constable in Quest of both'. Campbell, the veteran of the Fifteen, was found, three days after the jacobite victory of Prestonpans, innocently enough 'Drinking Tea with some Ladys near home in Brampton' and, 'without any Warrant executed upon him', he went in directly to Carlisle. There he was examined the same day by the recorder and no less than five other magis-trates. Campbell was shown part, but part only, of the inter-cepted letter intended for him, and he readily identified the hand-writing as that of Jackson. In this letter, after the account of Prestonpans, Jackson said,

[I] must Beg you'l Delay no time in goeing where you promised me, and Beg you'l send a Special Messenger to me at home [to let me know[2]] how you go on, and I will come to you. I shall be at Home in 4 or 5 Days, and I am. Sir. . . .[3]

Campbell was specifically questioned as to whether he had ever made any 'appointment with any person whatsoever to go from Home to any place'. This he resolutely denied. He admitted knowing Jackson, 'but never had any Intercourse with him further than drinking a Glass with him when he came to Brampton at his Entertain ments of his Chapmen &c buying goods and getting Bill of Exchange from him'. Pressed further as to Jackson's movements, he professed not to know anything about his present whereabouts. The high constable of the ward,[4] however, apprehended him in Whitehaven[5] and brought him forthwith to Carlisle, where he too was examined next day, also by the recorder and five other justices.

Jackson testified that he was a Manchester trader who travelled in materials of various descriptions (including fustians)—but 'cutts nothing himself or deals in any goods by Retale'. On Thursday, 19th September, he had been in Brampton in Cumberland attempting to do business with David Campbell, with whom he had earlier had some business relations and whom, in any case, he knew to be a Scotsman. The only business he had done with Campbell that day, however, was to lend him £30. When the intercepted letter was produced, he did not deny writing it. Although some of the phrasing might *seem* complicated, the explanation was quite simple. He had loaned Campbell £30 on a mere note of hand and no security; he had been willing to let him have further money, but subject to reasonable security. If Campbell could obtain such security where he implied he could, and let him know in Manchester, he (Jackson) would return to transact the business. In confirmation of this story Jackson produced Campbell's signed acknowledgement of the loan of £30. It was all quite innocent. So far as the rest of the letter was concerned, Prestonpans was fought on Saturday, 21st September, and the news had run across the border. He (Jackson) was in Dumfries next day, on Sunday the 22nd—by way of business—'when two Gentlemen arrived who was at the Field of Battle . . .' and gave a realistic account of the 'Compleat Victory'. Jackson thereupon left for England and wrote from Wigton in Cumberland to Campbell at Brampton on Monday the 23rd the letter which had been intercepted, about the loan and the further security. In this same letter he gave to Campbell, as a piece of hot news, the version of Prestonpans taken to Dumfries by the 'two Gentle-men . . . who was at the Field of Battle'; but, he concluded, 'I have not the time to give you the particulars'. It was in this brief account that Jackson had used the expression 'prince' (query: repeated the expression of 'the two Gentlemen'): 'as soon as Light appeared in the Morning the Battle began, when each Gave a General Discharge, and the Prince's Forces Lay Down their Guns and Broke in upon them'. Asked why he had used the expression 'the Prince', he replied 'that the using the Expression *The Prince* in his Letter was only through haste, having heard him call'd so in Scotland, where some give him that Title, some the bold Adventurer, some the Pretender'.[6]

Campbell was recalled the same day; he did not deny the loan and the receipt, but he did deny that any further sum or any further security had been broached; and, furthermore, he had made no promise to go anywhere.

After they had been separately examined, they were brought together and when Face to Face, both stood to what they had said.[7]

The justices were in a quandary. Obviously Campbell, who had been 'out' in the Fifteen, was the man to be watched, although 'there was no Suspicion of [his] having Stirred from Home'. Obviously, too, Jackson was a suspicious character, looking upon Prestonpans as a 'Compleat Victory' and using the term 'prince' instead of 'pretender', notwithstanding that everything else seems capable of a perfectly innocent construction. There did seem to the justices a great likelihood that Jackson might be using some verifiable business interest as a cover story to facilitate his moving about on both sides of the border at precisely this critical junc-ture. He might very well be a representative of the Manchester faction of English jacobites maintaining liaison with the insurgent force, with Campbell a link in the chain. Indeed, it *could* very well be that Campbell was a reluctant veteran of the Fifteen, with Jackson urging him, cajoling him—even blackmailing him—into re-activating his latent jacobite principles. The justices before whom the examinations of Campbell and Jackson had been taken were some of the most distinguished—and the most active—in Cumberland. Apart from Richard Gilpin, the recorder, and John Waugh, the chancellor, there were Jerome Tullie, deputy lieutenant; Joseph Dacre, in command of the Cumberland and Westmorland light horse; Montague Farrer, deputy lieutenant and captain of one of the companies of the Cumberland militia, moved into Carlisle for the defence of the city; John Barnard Gilpin, in command of the invalid company in the castle; and Thomas Pattinson, alderman, deputy mayor, postmaster and positive Boo-bah of Carlisle.

They all agreed that 'there was no further proof', yet they were all satisfied 'that something in Favour of the Rebells was intended by the Letter'. The obvious course seemed to be to charge them both 'upon suspicion of Treason' and confine them in the county gaol to stand their trial at the next sessions. But—on second thoughts—if they were confined 'here in the County jail, if the Rebells come this Way [it] would only be forcing them into [the rebels'] Service'.[8] In the outcome, both were charged 'upon suspicion of High Treason' to appear at the Epiphany sessions and admitted to bail. Campbell was bound in his own security for £500, plus £100 from four other sureties (£25 each), namely Richard Bell, Francis Jackson, John Armstrong and John Dean, all of Brampton, 'Four Substantial Neighbours', who, incidentally, all declared their own 'Beliefs of his Innocence and that he has not been from Home for some Months'. For Jackson's part, he seemed to be unable to find any security but his own. Peter How of Whitehaven,[9] 'a merchant of Great Business' there, a keen justice, the receiver-general for Cumberland and Westmorland in 1743 (and later a member of the grand jury at the Carlisle trials), wrote to the Carlisle justices that Jackson had been personally known to him for some years as 'a pretty great dealer and has the character of an honest man'. Unless something could be 'proved pretty full against him' it did not seem likely that he would enter any traitorous design. Jackson was willing to take the statutory oaths. There were several tradesmen locally in Carlisle who 'deal with him, are in his Debt, and declared they have no fear of losing their Money by being bound'; but 'they apprehended it would hurt their Credit and affect their Business if they should be known to have any concern with a Person whom there was reason to be suspect of Disaffection to his Majesty's Person and Government'.

Jackson eventually found as sureties John Davinson of Carlisle and another for £10 each, and a man named Parrot of Warwick for £50. In the circumstances the justices decided to admit him to bail on these and his own additional recognizance of £1,000, which was forthcoming. Standing on the recognizance file of the quarter-sessions records for the following Epiphany there is a memorandum on which there is a note against Campbell's name, saying, 'Respited, Campbell being a prisoner of the King'. There is, however, no record among the quarter-sessions rolls of any indictment or verdict against him, but it is at least possible that Campbell was proceeded against at the assizes. The case of Richard Jackson, 'of Manchester, Merchant', however, is even more vague. Jackson did not surrender to his bail at the Cockermouth sessions on 15th January and his own and the other sureties were therefore forfeit. There is a somewhat enigmatic memorandum about the bondsmen on the recognizance file, written by Chancellor Waugh to Thomas Simpson, the clerk of the peace. Waugh says, 'I am not clear in the least, but they are to the best of my remembrance. I cannot tell at present where they are. Do your best for the public good.'[10] This Richard Jackson 'of Manchester, Merchant' may be the same Richard Jackson 'of the Manchester Regiment' who turns up later in Lancaster gaol—but he is a shadowy character. Seton and Arnot, in their standard work *The Prisoners of the '45*, say of him after Lancaster gaol, 'His disposal is unknown'.

The conclusion, therefore, of case history number one is still, 'disposal unknown'.

Our second case history is that of John Henderson, writer to the signet, of Edinburgh or Lochmaben. After Prestonpans Cope's shattered troops—such as survived—fell back, as is generally known, upon Lauder and Berwick. It is not so generally known that others of them—including elements of Lascelles' regiment, the 47th foot—found themselves in Carlisle. About a month after the action, towards the end of October, two soldiers of Lascelles' regiment, quartered in the 'Red Lion' at Carlisle, made the acquaintance of a suspicious character then staying at that house. John Henderson, apparently an educated Scotsman, 'made some enquiries of his Landlord and Some Others' as to the 'Number of Cannon, men and Provisions were in the . . . Town of Carlisle, and Several other Suspitious Questions about the Strength of the Garrison'.[11] It seems likely that the landlord of the 'Red Lion' stalled the questions by suggesting he ask some of the soldiers quartered in the house. Henderson, on his own admission, questioned two soldiers of Lascelles' regiment. One of them testified that Henderson asked him to take him for a walk round the ramparts, and then suggested they should go and talk more privately in another room. In the other room Henderson then inquired after the total number of men in garrison in the town, the number of cannon in the castle, and the quantity of provisions and other stores laid up in the town. From this both soldiers concluded that Henderson was a spy sent forward to obtain military intelligence. According to Lascelles' man, Henderson got little enough encouragement and no information:

The said John Henderson enquired of this Informant what Number of Cannon were in the Castle and upon the Ramparts of Carlisle to which this Informant replied enough to kill all the High Landers. He then enquired what stores of Provision were laid Up in the Town to which this Informant answer'd that there was sufficient to last long enough, and then enquired what Number of Men were in Garrison upon which this Informant answered there were so many that he could not tell the Number. He then enquired what Number of Men were in the Castle this Informant thereupon told him he did not know not having been permitted to go to the Castle. He enquired what provisions were laid in there, upon which this Informant told him he did not know but had heard and believed that a Sufficient Quantity was laid up there and further saith that he this Deponent suspecting him to be a Spy, refused to hold any further Conversation wth Him.[12]

Henderson appears to have sought out another soldier, likewise from Lascelles' regiment, whom he told he had left Edinburgh on 17th October and 'that he came to sell 12 Cattell', and said also that his companion was his servant.[13] It was alleged that in the course of further conversation he had said that when he had gone to Edinburgh and was stopped at the west port by the occupying jacobites, 'upon his telling them who he was and that He was acquainted with some of the officers . . . they permitted Him to go into Edinburgh and further . . . he was afterwards permitted to view them in Camp'.[14] When this soldier at the 'Red Lion' gave Henderson his account of the battle of Preston-

question'd whether they both intend the same fact' (*True Patriot*, 10th December). In another instance one of the newspapers reports that some local worthy had been good enough to open his cellar to a section of the local militia. The paper announced that this good deed 'comforted them and inspired them'. But the particular body of the militia which received this comfort and inspiration does not, unfortunately, seem to have done so very well in the military task allotted to it, which occasioned the remark as regards the free beer they consumed, 'by the courage it inspir'd we conclude (at least hope) he gave them only *small* beer'.

Or again—less elegantly, perhaps—the *Daily Advertiser* reported, 'We hear that the Rebells are very much affected with the bloody Flux': to which the *True Patriot* added, 'A Distemper which may probably increase upon them if General Hawley should be able to come up with them' (*ibid.*). As a matter of fact, Hawley was able to come up with them—after they had waited for him. But that was at Falkirk, and that is part of another story.

Another example—this from the *True Patriot* of 5th November. A unit of the trained bands, the eighteenth century equivalent of the home guard, was stationed at a point, charged with the duty of stopping all vehicles and examining them with a view to preventing the passage of any arms. In pursuit of this duty, the guard stopped a hackney coach, which as a matter of fact contained four young ladies. The guard inquired whether there were any arms within. The ladies replied there were not. The zealous guard however opened the coach door to satisfy himself in that regard.

'Well, sir! Do you see any Arms?'

'No, Madam,' answered the Centinel, 'I see nothing but legs.'

Talking of coaches reminds one of another story. A number of the newspapers got hold of a story about the romantic-sounding person 'Miss Jenny Cameron—the young pretender's mistress'.[73] Firstly, it is necessary to say that the 'Miss Jenny Cameron—the young pretender's mistress' is a somewhat mythical personage in any case—notwithstanding that Sophy Western in *Tom Jones* was mistaken for her by the landlord of the inn. Secondly, it might be remarked that the stories of this most elusive lady divide themselves into three categories: one, she was Charles Edward's mistress; two, she was not Charles Edward's mistress—being then nearly fifty years of age—but by that time she had been nearly everyone else's; and three, that tradition avers that her home was in Morven, and lilies of her sowing still bloom on the machair at Acharn on Loch Ari Innes near the beautiful Loch Ahiae.

One makes one's choice according to taste. But mostly it is a case of penny coloured and tuppence lurid. The taste and choice of most of the newspapers will not greatly surprise one. However, after 'Miss Jenny Cameron—the young pretender's mistress' had had a good run for her money the *St James's Evening Post* reported[74] that she had been brought by the jacobites to England in a coach and six. The *General Advertiser* at once went one better and reported that the news had been received in a letter dated 17th December from Burton near Kendal 'that the Coach in which road the Young Pretender's Favourite Miss Jenny Cameron and Mrs Murray[75] broke down near that Place and that the country People rose, and seiz'd the two ladies with some of the Rebels'.

Attaching to the story just about the importance it merited, Fielding's *True Patriot* was content to cap it with the comment: 'It is a great Neglect in the Pretender, either as a Lover or a General, to leave his Baggage with so slender a Guard.'[76]

Notes

[1] *Menander's Mirror. Times Lit. Sup.*, 14th October 1944.

[2] Reprinted: Charles Morgan, *Reflections in a Mirror*, second ser. (1945), 168.

[3] See Paper 17.

[4] All this announcement said was merely that it was reported that some strangers had landed in Scotland from France, 'one of whom from the general report, and from several concurring circumstances, there is the greatest reason to belief, is the Pretender's son'.

[5] *London Gazette*, 13th–17th August 1745.

[6] See in particular SP Scot. 25/106.

[7] *London Gazette*, 10th–14th September 1745.

[8] See Paper 17.

[9] *Museum*, 29th March 1746 or vol. i, 27.

[10] See Paper 17.

[11] Samuel Buckley's *London Courant* (sold by E. Mallett). No. 1, dated Wednesday, 11th March 1702. There was also a thrice-weekly edition.

[12] It is recorded, for instance, of John Berry's *Lancashire Journal* (1738–1741?) that it contained 'very little local news'; of Lancashire newspapers in 1738–9, that 'there is, after the fashion of the time, very little local news, the object of these early journals being to tell the people what is going on at a distance'; of Adams' *Manchester Weekly Journal* (1719–26) also it was said, 'Of local news concerning Manchester and Lancashire there is none.' The most cursory glance at the old files will confirm that this was ordinarily so.

[13] G. A. Cranfield, *Hand-list of English Provincial Newspapers and Periodicals, 1700–1760*, pp. 10 and 23.

[14] See Paper 17.

[15] Cumb. QSMB, Epiphany (Cockermouth), 14th January, 1740–1.

[16] *Ibid.* 14th January 1746–7.

[17] Cranfield, *op. cit.*, 14–15.

[18] *MM*, 24th December 1745; and Timperley, *Dictionary of Printers*, 673.

[19] *Compleat History of the Trials*, N.D. [1746], 144; *MM*, 2nd September 1746.

[20] This can be demonstrated from the *CM* (*vide infra*) if we correct certain errors as to dates, e.g. 25th November 1745 should read 27th November (p. 53) and 18th November should read 18th December (p. 60).

[21] This is a reasonable assumption. No. 460 is dated 19th November. Stockport has a copy numbered 461 and dated 26th November. No. 462 is dated 17th December and contains the statement that 'we have not published any news for a fortnight'. The fragment referred to in LCAS, vol. xli, 128, is presumably No. 463 dated 24th December (both the Manchester and Stockport copies are imperfect). Hence 3rd and 10th December were presumably without issues.

[22] THE CHESTER MISCELLANY/being A/Collection/of Several *Pieces* both in/*Prose* and *Verse*/which were in the *Chester Courant*/from *January* 1745 to *May* 1750 [line : Quotation : double line] *Chester*:/Printed by and for Eliz. Adams . . . . . MDCCL.

[23] *Ibid.* preface iii.

[24] Not all the extracts, however, were made as carefully as here implied. That Cope, before Prestonpans, landed at *Durham*—in error for *Dunbar*—will deceive no one. (From *Chester Courant*, 2nd October 1745.) But other errors are less obvious. Dates sometimes require careful checking.

[25] *CM*, preface iii–iv.

[26] The late Mr Charles Cooper, former editor, concurred with me in this assumption. Extracts cited in the present paper are taken from the *CM*.

[27] A 'duke' of jacobite creation.

[28] See Paper 4, vol. I.

[29] Later the 3rd (Prince of Wales') Dragoon Guards.

[30] I.e. distract.

[31] 'Journal and Memoir of the Young Pretender's Expedition'. *Lockhart Papers*, ii, 457.

[32] *Murray Mem.*, 246.

[33] *A Short Account*, 326.

34 See also K. Tomasson, *The Jacobite General* (1958), 97 (quoting Lord George Murray's unpublished notes).

35 The *MM* was on sale in Chester 'at the Black Bear'.

36 *MM*, 1st October 1945.

37 See next Paper.

38 See Paper 5, vol. I.

39 Samuel Peploe (b. 1668: cons. 1726: d. 1752). Was vicar of Preston in 1715, and an ardent Whig. On 13th October 1745 he preached a sermon in the cathedral, afterwards published under the title, *Popish Idolatory a Strong Reason why Protestants should Steadily Oppose the Present Rebellion.*

40 (1695–1755) M.P. for Chester 1733–55. Father of the first earl Grosvenor, grandfather of the first marquis of Westminster.

41 George Booth, Lord Delamere, and last earl of Warrington (in that creation). The earldom became extinct in 1758, and the barony in 1770.

42 One is reminded of the terms of an act passed after the rising in 1715, 'And for the further Encouragement of becoming Zeal & Bravery in his Majesty's and the Country's Service against the said Pretender and his Adherents; Be it also further enacted by the Authority aforesaid, that if it shall happen any Subject of Great Britain having Lands or Estate in Scotland held Waird of the Crown, or of any Subject Superior there, as well, Vassal as Sub-Vassal, to be killed in his Majesty's Service against the said Pretender or his adherents . . . the Heir of every such Person or Persons shall be and is hereby enacted & ordained to be free of the Duties & Casualties of Waird Relief & Marriage For & on Account of the said Pretender or his adherents . . . the Heir of every such Person such Lands & Estate.' (1 Geo. I, stat. 2, cap. 20, sec. vii.)

43 George, 3rd earl of Cholmondeley (1703–70), Walpole's son-in-law, and late lord privy seal.

44 Henry, Lord Herbert (1734–94), later tenth earl of Pembroke, son of Henry, the ninth earl (1693–1751). The regiment raised in 1745 was disbanded in 1746. The fact that Lord Herbert was only eleven years of age at the time would not prevent a regiment being raised in his name.

45 An apparently contemporary ballad identifies the sergeant's trull as 'Long Preston Peggy', who picked up with Sergeant Dickson at Preston, having gone there solely to see the jacobite force pass. The ballad commences:

> Long Preston Peggy to Proud Preston went.
> To see the Scotch Rebels it was her intent.

It has been touched up and published in *Palatine Note-book*, i (1881), 66–7.

46 See Paper 23, pp. 297–300.

47 Byrom, *Remains*, II, ii, 386.

48 But see next Paper.

49 We know from other sources that among the expresses so employed was the ex-dragoon John Shaw of John Shaw's (Manchester), later to achieve local fame in another connection. (*Constables' Accounts*, ii (1743–76), 22.)

[50] *Constables' Accounts*, ii (1743–76), 23.

[51] Charles Legh of Adlington (d. 1781), s. of John Legh of Adlington.

[52] Lord Elcho himself said his own and Lord Pitsligo's Horse entered Altrincham on the 1st but were ordered next day to join the main army, i.e. on the Macclesfield road. Elcho, *A Short Account*, 333–4. The *Gazette* said that a party of horse came to Altrincham 'by Break of Day and bespoke Quarters for a Body of Foot, which arrived there about Ten'. (*London Gazette Ex.*, 5th December.)

[53] One recalls a reference in Walpole's Letters which says that the towns on the route were left more or less desolate, and 'the people hide and bury their effects, even to their pewter'. (Walpole to Mann, 29th November 1745, ii, 55.) (The pewter might of course be requisitioned for moulding bullets. As to the moulding of bullets, particularly in Manchester, see Paper 21.)

[54] I.e. confusion.

[55] *Constables' Accounts*, iii (1743–76), 21.

[56] See Paper 4, vol. I.

[57] *St James's* of the same date says, 'Our Trade is in a Measure quite stopped, and every Family has orders to prepare a Fortnight's Provisions.'

[58] The passage will be found borrowed verbatim by Marchant, *History of the Present Rebellion*, 1746, pp. 191–2.

[59] A parallel passage in Thucydides naturally comes to mind. He says of the evacuees:

They brought their wives and children and all their household furniture into the city. Deep was their trouble and discontent at abandoning their houses, and at having to change their habits of life and to bid farewell to what each regarded as his native city. When they arrived few had houses of their own to go to or could find an asylum with friends or relatives. Many took up their quarters in the towers of the walls or wherever else they could. For when they were all come in the city proved too small to hold them. All this while great attention was being given to the war; the allies were being mustered and an armament of a hundred ships equipped. (*History of the Peloponnesian War*, ii, §16–17.)

[60] See Paper 12, vol. I.

[61] See Paper 15, pp. 82–94.

[62] The marquis of Tullibardine was the eldest surviving son of the first duke of Athol, and hence the elder brother of James the reigning whig second duke, and himself jacobite titular duke (and elder brother of Lord George Murray, jacobite lieutenant general). He was out in the '15 and in '19 and was attainted by parliament, in consequence of which the family honours and estates were settled on remoter heirs.

[63] 'Mr Vaughan from Wales' joined at Preston the same day as Townley and Councillor Morgan. Murray, *op. cit.*, 246.

[64] Colonel Robinson Sowle's Regiment, the 3rd Foot (later the Royal Devonshire Regt.).

[65] Later the 3rd (Prince of Wales') Dragoon Guards.

[66] Cf. *Kenyon MSS*, 482–6, and Beatrice Stott, *James Dawson and Thomas Syddal*, in LCAS, xliv (1929), 9.

[67] See LCAS, vol. lvi, 128.

[68] The passage cited appears also at Marchant, pp. 204–5.

[69] See Paper 17.

[70] See Paper 4, vol. I.

[71] See Paper 9, vol. I.

[72] See Paper 19, pp. 194 and 209.

[73] There was an extensive pamphlet literature on this particular subject: *A Brief Account of the Life and Family of Miss Jennie Cameron* (1746. Printed for T. Gardner. 64 pp.): (*Scots Magazine*, vii (August 1746), p. 400, *London Magazine* (September 1746), 537, and *Gentleman's Magazine*, xvi (August 1746), p. 44): *The Life and Adventures of Miss Jennie Cameron, The Reputed Mistress of the Deputy Pretender*: [Archibald Arbuthnot], *Memoirs of the Remarkable Life and Surprizing Adventures of Miss Jennie Cameron* (published originally in twelve weekly nos.). All fictitious. (See also A. Graeme, *Jenny Cameron, Mystery Woman of the '45: Too Many Jean Camerons, Scots Magazine*, April 1931, pp. 17–28.)

[74] 14th–17th December 1745.

[75] Wife of John Murray of Broughton, secretary to Charles Edward.

[76] 24th December 1745.

14 *Intelligence*

At the outbreak of the Forty-five the government's very first move was to order the commander-in-chief in Scotland, in most peremptory terms, to march into the highlands with all available troops with all available speed. This had two objectives: one, to distribute to the friendly clans the arms they needed to defend themselves; and two, to ferret out and defeat the insurgent clans at the very seat of the insurrection.[1] The first was a political, the second a military issue.

On the political issue, the civil leaders of state, both in Edinburgh and in London, the lord president, the lord justice-clerk, the lord advocate, the solicitor and the secretaries of state, were all satisfied on two points. (*a*) That as a result of the Disarming Act[2] the friendly (whig) clans had disarmed themselves in compliance with the law; the unfriendly (jacobite) clans, however, had defied the law—and defeated it: they had unlawfully retained their arms and were now in insurrection. And (*b*) that the friendly clans, still loyal to the government, would certainly 'come out' in the government's defence—and their own—if only they had the arms to do so. On the military issue—marching north—Cope, as a soldier, was naturally much concerned about front and flank reconnoitring *en route*, moving as he would be with untried troops through a difficult terrain. He was, however, categorically assured that he could rely upon enlisting on his route sufficient auxiliaries by way of local friendly clansmen willing and eager to reconnoitre his front and scout his flanks in the admittedly difficult country.

In the result Cope discovered, when it was too late, that on the political side the whig chiefs would not accept the arms he had 'lugged north' for them; he could not prevail upon them to accept them on any terms. He therefore found himself in a situation far from the capital, and far from safety, in which he not only could not distribute the arms to the friendly clans, he could not even defend them from the unfriendly. He had therefore to return them south, necessarily under a sufficient military guard, a guard that he could ill spare in that critical situation. On the military side, Cope had undertaken the march on the firm 'intelligence' from the civil authorities that he would be able to recruit auxiliaries as he marched northwards through the friendly clans.[3] Here again he was misled. No clansmen whatsoever could be recruited *en route*, except the few in Athol, who deserted at the first opportunity with their arms. The 'friendly' clans, too, were unfriendly. Information and intelligence at ministerial level, therefore, both political and military, whether from Edinburgh or London, turned out to be bad.

After Prestonpans, when the jacobite army moved south from Edinburgh, Wade lay at Newcastle with a superior regular government force. He was uncertain of the route by which the invaders would approach England: by way of Newcastle, east of the Pennines and direct for London, or by way of Carlisle, west of the Pennines through catholic Lancashire and possibly for Wales and the west, where a landing from France was confidently expected. His marchings and counter-marchings were abortive, and in the result he failed to prevent the invasion. In London the diplomatic and general intelligence was not good. In Newcastle, however good the civil information,[4] the military intelligence was bad.

A few weeks later, when the invaders halted for a brief rest in Manchester, the duke of Cumberland at Coventry and neighbouring places was still uncertain whether the invaders were making for Derby and London or for Chester and the west. Upon the receipt of what Cumberland took to be good intelligence, he moved sharply across to counter a dart to the west—but was mistaken—and thereby left the enemy the open road to London. His military anticipation may not have been very good, but his military intelligence was clearly bad.[5]

The matter of intelligence generally during the rising seems never to have been fully inquired into. The prevailing practice of taking the history of the rising almost unexceptionally in narrative form militates against any adequate consideration of themes of this character. In any examination of this topic one could consider the type of intelligence, for example, at the level of long-term international diplomacy and court intrigue in the chancelleries of Europe, or at the other extreme one could consider short-term, down-to-earth, day-to-day pieces of information coming in, by one route and another, to the military officers in the field or the civil offices in Edinburgh and London. One could, indeed, take any one of a number of aspects of intelligence. It is proposed in this present paper, however, to consider information and intelligence merely at the grass roots, that is to say, to consider, in the south-western counties in Scotland and the north-western counties in England, both the quasi-official and the unofficial networks, both the regular and the *ad hoc* machinery (if the term 'machinery' does not too much imply something specifically designed for the job), by which such information and intelligence was initially gathered up, and how it was later passed along the line until it reached the location where action on it could be taken.

It is not necessary perhaps, for the purpose of this present paper, to distinguish always between information on the one hand and intelligence on the other. In this context it might be said that the essentials of gathering information are to collect quickly, and to transmit promptly, accurate statements regarding particular significant occurrences or facts. Intelligence, however, requires something more: it requires a prompt mental apprehension of a current intention or a future probability, as distinct from a mere awareness of a report of a past or present fact—plus the quick realization of where exactly this must be communicated in order that timely action may be taken; that is to say, intelligence in this sense requires a quick grasp of the essential likelihood inherent in an immediate situation. For example, on Saturday, 2nd November, a countryman making his way up upper Tweeddale brought the news that the provost of Peebles 'had got a Message . . . to prepare Meat, drink and Lodging that Evening for 1800 Men':[6] this was *information*. It was, however, soon grasped that the troops from Dalkeith for Kelso (and Coldstream or Wooller) *might* be making for Newcastle and the eastern route, necessarily for

London; if, however, bodies were peeling off at Peebles or Selkirk, then they were necessarily making for Carlisle and the western route, either (*a*) to pass later by way of Brough over Stainmore, merely to by-pass Wade at Newcastle; or (*b*), to pass through Lancashire for Wales and (possibly) a French invasion in the west; or (*c*), for London by the longer route. If one of these three must necessarily be the case, then the forward elements of the insurgent force at Kelso would have to turn for Carlisle by way of Jedburgh and Langholm, and the mid-way troops by way of Selkirk. This is *intelligence*.

It is intended, however, to look at the gathering and forwarding of mere information, as such, as well as that of intelligence thus narrowly defined. It might be as well, perhaps, to consider firstly the mere sequence of this information and intelligence gathering and forwarding, both on the Scottish and on the English side of the border; secondly, to consider the potential and the actuality of the governmental machinery available for such gathering and forwarding; and thirdly, to examine in detail specific examples of the measures taken in the first instance to secure absolute accuracy, or at least as much accuracy as was reasonably possible in the circumstances; the steps taken to funnel such accurate intelligence promptly to a definite point on the regular network; the promptitude and regularity with which such 'service' in general worked; and lastly the methods intelligently adopted to siphon material off to other interested parties without any delay to the original despatch.

As regards the earlier and Scottish side, Prestonpans was fought on 21st September. It was not, however, until a month later that there was any real sign of an intention to invade England. Certainly it was talked of in Edinburgh that the army would move south at the end of October. This was known in Dumfries, for example, on the 31st as a piece of firm information, 'taken from a Letter [the postmaster] saw, that came . . . from Edinburgh that Day'. But in a postscript to a letter addressed to Carlisle he said, 'a person is just arrived from thence with an Account that the Army of the Rebels' had in fact 'marched to Dalkeith on Thursday'. The provost of Dumfries followed that with a letter on Friday night (1st November), which arrived at Carlisle next day, to the effect that a Dumfries gentleman who had left Edinburgh Thursday mid-day had just arrived bringing the more precise information that 'the Baggage, Artillery, Ammunition &c were upon Wagons and Carts going to Dalkeith, and that the whole Army were in Motion', preparing to march towards Kelso. It is to be noted that the march was stated to be *towards Kelso*. As further intelligence was expected that day, the provost promised an express upon any confirmation. Chancellor Waugh at Carlisle thereupon wrote to Dumfries asking for 'an Account of whatever he receives, *whether it be conformed or Not*'. He then sent an express forward to Selkirk 'for Intelligence from that Side' and communicated the facts, as at present known, to the secretary of state in London.[7] It is to be noted that it was *to Selkirk* that this forward express was directed.

On Sunday morning, 3rd November, certain information came to Moffat by a Galloway man who was returning from Stirling. He brought the news that French arms, ammunition and baggage, from the landing at Montrose, were coming south and that although General Blakeney had sallied out from Stirling and had taken some prisoners, yet the supplies had crossed the Forth, accompanied by twenty-four French engineers.[8] More importantly, however, on the Saturday two men, going from Dumfries to Edinburgh, were making their way from Moffat over into upper Tweeddale, and when they were 'about 3 Miles from the Crock [inn]' they met a countryman making for Annandale. The countryman said that at Peebles, just before he came away, 'the Provost had got a Message sent him by the Rebels to prepare Meat, drink and Lodging that Evening for 1800 Men'. Furthermore, 'that great preparations were also that Night making at Broughton', the seat of John Murray of Broughton, secretary to Charles Edward, on the road between the 'Crock' and Selkirk, 'where some persons of distinction were arrived escorted by 60 Horse'. On hearing this news, one of the two Dumfries men turned back for Dumfries, but the other continued towards Edinburgh. At ten o'clock on Sunday morning the former was overtaken at Moffat by another express riding south from Peebles. The Dumfries man who had ridden on 'had taken the opportunity of writing a Letter, that [the express] might call on him at Moffat'.

And there that Express told him he left Peebles about Two a Clock Sabbath Morning and that the above mentioned 1800 Men with 150 Carts with Baggage Ammunition &c were come there on the Saturday Night and a little before he left the Town a larger Body came up which he was informed were to number 4,000 Men.[9]

John Graham, 'the man at Moffat', seems immediately to have seen the point. If the insurgents had moved off: Dalkeith–Lauder–Coldstream (and Wooller), they would be bound for Newcastle. If they moved: Dalkeith–Lauder–Kelso, the route would be ambiguous. But if any of the insurgents were now peeling off at Peebles for Moffat, or Selkirk for Hawick, then the Kelso move was merely intended to deceive; the whole exercise must therefore be necessarily intended for Carlisle. John Graham at Moffat immediately despatched an express across to Wade at Newcastle—although realizing that an express from Moffat might not be able to get through on the Scottish side of the border, with the insurgents ranging the country some way to the east—and others to both the provosts of Dumfries and Annan. The intelligence, and its significance, was now fairly on the network. George Bell, the provost of Dumfries, immediately passed it on to Carlisle with a request to Chancellor Waugh to communicate it to the mayor and governor there, and to repeat it to Wade at Newcastle 'in case the [Moffat] Express Should be Stopt by the way . . . as there will now be more safety on *your* Borders'. 'I have,' he wrote hurriedly from Dumfries, 'so much to write and so many Expresses to send off.'[10] Bryce Bell, the (acting) provost of Annan, likewise passed the intelligence along to Carlisle, saying that Annan also had on Sunday sent two persons north for further intelligence, and that either Provost Johnstone or himself would keep Carlisle further informed.

On the same day precisely the same information—with no element of error or exaggeration—made its way the length of Carlisle from a variety of other sources. The duke of Buccleuch's steward at Langholm castle, J. Boston, also had received the express from Moffat, and he passed it on to John Goldie of Craigmere at Carlisle—'according to my promise'—with the conjecture that 'this Country [i.e. this neighbourhood] will certainly receive a visit'. Chancellor Waugh at Carlisle had engaged 'a Clergyman of the Church of Scotland . . . to send an Express to

Selkirk'. The Rev. Mr Douglas's wife wrote from Selkirk on the Sunday in almost exactly the same terms, but added the immensely significant piece of intelligence that 'the Duke of Perth asked the Magistrates whether the West or South Road was best for Carlisle'; to which they answered 'that the West Road was the best for Carriages'.[11]

Carlisle, then, it was to be.

When Waugh received this in Carlisle next day (Monday, 4th November) he sent it direct to the secretary of state in London, and that morning the reverend gentleman of the Church of Scotland himself went north 'to try what further Intelligence he can get'. On Monday also not only did John Goddie receive the express from the duke of Buccleuch's steward at Langholm, but he received another in almost exactly the same terms from James Gilcrist, the postmaster of Dumfries, and James Ferguson of Craigdarrock received one from a merchant in Dumfries. John Graham's express from Moffat of Sunday the 3rd had been passed on from Dumfries and Annan respectively and were all in Carlisle and passed on to London by Monday the 4th. Everything was working with great promptitude.

In Carlisle Colonel Durrand, Dr Waugh and Mr Pattinson, the governor of the castle, the chancellor of the diocese, and postmaster and (deputy) mayor of the city respectively, met together. Although in general there was no love lost between them, they joined together in a letter to Wade at Newcastle providing him with up-to-date intelligence and agreed that the postmaster should send similar intelligence to the lord lieutenant of Cumberland and Westmorland, Lord Lonsdale, then at his seat at Byram in Yorkshire. As regards forward rather than rearward affairs, it was thought significant that Waugh's agent to Selkirk had not returned. In the meanwhile George Bell, the postmaster of Dumfries, had sent two messengers to Berwick, who got as far as Jedburgh on Saturday night, 2nd November. Jedburgh passed them on to Berwick on Sunday morning and despatched another express 'where you directed'. Jedburgh, however, had intelligence of considerable significance:

The whole Highland Army have marchd, the last of them, from Dalkeith and Newbattle this Morning, by this Night at Lauder. Their main Body moves from Peebles to Selkirk to Morrow and so forward by Langholm for the West of England. Whether theyll visit you by the way and whether the Party at Lawder will pass thence for Selkirk or come this length before they turn West that they may the better cover and conceal the March of their main Body is more than I have learned. But as the Intelligence I can depend upon and thought it worth while to run you this Express with it.[12]

This express was sent down from Jedburgh, 'Nov. 3. 1745, Eleven at Night', and was relayed to Carlisle by the postmaster of Dumfries: 'Dumfries. 4th Nov at 5 in the Evening . . . Please forward copyes to Whitehaven Penrith &c'. The tempo of affairs was quickening.

It appeared that a jacobite party, passing through Peebles and Lauder apparently direct for the border, had turned 'backwards to Peebles'.[13] The story was 'that they were feared of the Advance of the King's Troops' [? from Berwick] but this may have been a mis-report or intended to conceal the insurgents' real intentions. An express came into Langholm from Drummelzier, eighteen miles north of Moffat, four miles southward of Peebles, close to where the more direct road from Dalkeith and Edinburgh comes into the main road southward to Carlisle. This express contained the information that at two o'clock on Monday afternoon 500 men were marching for Bield on the Moffat road. Furthermore, the intelligence was that the insurgents intended to march south-ward *not* by way of Kelso—that had been merely a feint—but to file off before Selkirk or Peebles and march by way of Tweedhead and Moffat, southwards by the western route, and this at the rate of one thousand men a day; the first column might be expected at Moffat on Tuesday the 5th. On the receipt at Moffat of the express from Drummelzier, Moffat relayed the intelligence at seven in the evening of Monday the 4th, to Buccleuch's steward at Langholm, who further relayed it to Francis Hewit, merchant and mayor of Carlisle, on Tuesday morning. On this Tuesday, at about one o'clock mid-day, insurgent quartermasters actually entered Moffat to secure quarters for 4,000 foot and 600 horse. An express thereupon left Moffat for Dumfries and said 'he saw them within half a Mile of the Town before he came away'. A despatch was sent from Dumfries at eight o'clock the same evening to Carlisle: 'I beg you will despatch Expresses to Penrith, Kendal, Lancaster and Whitehaven'. Chancellor Waugh covered it to the secretary of state with a letter of a single line, dated Wednesday the 6th. Bryce Blair, (acting) provost of Annan, wrote a little additional information and addressed his express '11 at Night—To the Mayor of Carlisle—Haist'.[14]

On Tuesday the 5th James Gilcrist, the postmaster of Dumfries, wrote to Carlisle, 'The Highlanders will be here tomorrow, so send me no Baggage or Letters 'till I write you',[15] and George Bell, the provost, wrote, 'I design to step out of the way to Morrow Morning but so as to be near at hand least any Event should happen that may require me'.[16] By Tuesday the 5th, therefore, the unofficial network of magistrates, the duke's steward, diocesan dignitaries, the clergyman and his wife, some merchants, traders, countrymen and other agents, had gathered together completely last-minute information and reliable intelligence throughout the counties of Peebles, Selkirk, Roxburgh and Dumfries; had laid it all on a quasi-official network of provosts and postmasters for relay to the professional military, namely, Handasyde in command at Berwick, Wade in command at Newcastle, and Durand in command at Carlisle; to the amateur military, namely, the militia of Cumberland and Westmorland at present mustered at Carlisle, the lord lieutenant, still at his country seat in Yorkshire and the lords lieutenants of the Yorkshire ridings, to the secretary of state in London, and to Penrith, Kendal and Lancaster, the interested towns in the anticipated route to the south.

On the evening of that day, Tuesday, 5th November, Handasyde, at Berwick, wrote to Wade at Newcastle,

My last without Date bore that youre to expect no more from me. . . . This is to advise you that the Highlanders, the last of them, marched from Dalkeith this morning at 4 OClock . . . and tis given out for certain that they are to go by Carlisle.[17]

Similar information (now from one professional military man to another) had been received by Wade, by way of the unofficial civilian network, some days before. Handasyde had advised Wade of the state of play: he now advised him of the state of the betting:

Great Betts are laid that they will get by your Army undiscovered; and tis for that Reason I send you this last Express that you may calculate their March so as to intercept them, for if they got once past to the Southward of our Army, It will occasion a great Fatigue to the Men.[18]

This was good enough information, although a bit belated.

Handasyde, however, wrote in somewhat different terms to the secretary of state in London next day. Of course it was all a feint.

For myself, I can never believe, tho' they may have set their faces Southwards, that it is intended to be carried into Execution. . . .

Then consider, the Highlanders were never fond of passing the Borders: and great Desertion—should they do it—will certainly be the Consequence. Wherefore, I think, this is only a Feint to amuse [i.e. to distract] His Majesty's Forces. But after all Should they proceed to Carlisle, the Army here will intercept their Retreat, and consequently they will be between two fires.[19]

This was bad intelligence. It is to be noted that the good information and the reliable intelligence had come from the amateur *ad hoc* get-together. The belated information and the bad intelligence had come from the professional army.

On Tuesday morning, 5th November, the provost of Annan and his colleague, Provost Johnstone and Bryce Blair, crossed the Solway to Bo'ness on the English side. They wrote Friday morning that they had left two persons on the Scottish side specifically detailed 'In Observation of the Rebells Motions', and they had 'Notice from them twice each 24 hours'.[20] At '40 Minutes past 5 at Night' the same day, Blair wrote to Carlisle—'in Haist'—to the effect that 'A Gentleman had been sent from Dumfries to Moffat for Intelligence'. This man had left Moffat on Thursday night 'and hired several Guides to take him By Roads [i.e. side roads], did with Difficulty get to Dumfries at 12 at Night'. In his view, 'That part of the Highland Army which came to Moffat was marching for Dumfries'. This was confirmed by 'another person sent from Dumfries this Morning to observe their Motions'. Yet another messenger sent on Thursday to Lockerbie returned on Friday with the information that 'a part of the Army would be there by ten o'clock, having got Orders to march as soon as the Moon rose'.[21]

One agent, the minister at Canonbie (across the border, twelve miles forward from Carlisle) reported that he had sent three messengers northward to Selkirk, Hawick and Kelso, but none apparently had got through. Nonetheless, the information coming into Canonbie (and relayed thence to Carlisle) conformed exactly to the anticipated pattern. The forward elements that had been at Kelso were filing back through Jedburgh, those at Selkirk through Hawick, and both for Langholm and thence for Carlisle; and it was known from Moffat that the rearward elements, baggage and artillery, were coming that way and taking 'the West road, [being] the best for carriages'. Intelligence from Canonbie even specified the address at which 'the Pretender's son is to ly . . . to Night', and the address at which 'they are there preparing for his reception', the number of nights 'they are to ly . . . here till all the Troops come up', and the grounds for supposing they would make for Longton and Brampton. Before going forward from Carlisle to Newcastle and London, the minister of Canonbie's letter was annotated: '[Mr Boston, where Charles Edward was to stay] is Steward to the Duke of Buckcleugh at Langholm Castle'. '[Rowanburn is] a place about a Mile into Scotland from our Border'. '[Brampton is] a little Market Town belonging to my Lord Carlisle about 7 Miles from hence'. '[Longtown is] a very poor Market Town about 7 miles from here belonging to the Preston Estate in the Borders'.[22]

The postmaster of Dumfries managed to get a hurried letter away on Friday the 8th to John Goldie of Craigmere to the effect that although 'it was not in [his] Power to learn where the main Body is', at nine o'clock that morning quartermasters arrived in Dumfries to demand quarters for that night for 5,000 foot and 1,000 horse. He doubted the numbers—but not the fact.[23] On the same day Carlisle received advice from Wade at Newcastle that advanced jacobite elements had crossed the border on the eastern side and had reached Wooler in Northumberland.[24] They were apparently on their way to Newcastle. The invaders were coming *east*.

On that very day some Cumberland militia light horse from Carlisle crossed the border into Dumfriesshire—query, with what authority?—and captured a jacobite quartermaster. It was England's first prisoner. The invasion had come to England—but the invaders had come *west*.

So far as concerns the sequence of information and intelligence on the English side of the border, the mayor and deputy mayor of Carlisle, on 9th November, put on to the intelligence network the fact that a jacobite quartermaster had been captured and that the insurgents were massing for Carlisle. Apart from the usual despatch to the general post office in London, a letter was sent to the postmaster at Lancaster and another to Sir Henry Hoghton of Hoghton Tower,[25] the most ardent whig justice in catholic Lancashire, deputy lieutenant and commander of a unit of the county militia. Hoghton undertook to muster his regiment at Preston and sent an express saying so on the 10th to Lord Derby, his lord lieutenant.[26] Yet another express was sent to Wade in Newcastle.[27] By the 10th the information had fanned out also to Barnard Castle[28] and to Byram[29] to the lord lieutenant there. As a direct result, Lord Cholmondeley, for example, lord lieutenant of Cheshire, lying before Chester (with special responsibility for the roads and bridges on the rivers crossing Lancashire), received orders as to measures 'which may render the Passage difficult to the Army of the Rebels',[30] and the council directed instructions to the lords lieutenants of Cumberland and Westmorland, Lancashire, Derby, Staffordshire, Shropshire[31] and the three ridings of Yorkshire.[32]

When it was reported in Carlisle that the town was about to be surrendered, the news likewise was fanned out to Wade in Newcastle, Cholmondeley in Chester, Lord Lonsdale at Byram in Yorkshire, the postmaster at Penrith on the route south, and Ligonier (curiously enough 'at Preston'). This information was at Penrith at 11 p.m. on Friday 15th, at Byram on the Saturday and in London on Sunday the 17th.[33] When at three o'clock on the afternoon of Monday the 18th a quartermaster arrived in Penrith to bespeak billets for 250 of the advance horse that day and for 8,000 foot for Tuesday, Thomas Richardson, the deputy postmaster, delayed his express to the general post office in London and Lord Lonsdale in order to check the real numbers, and said in a very brief despatch that 'the Horse, upon counting, were not half that Number'.[34] On Thursday the 21st, at six o'clock in the evening, the mayor of Kendal passed hurried information down to the corporation of Lancaster to the effect that three countrymen had just come in to say that the invaders were only about half a mile away ('Please pay the Messenger—they are upon me').

Robert Macmillan, the (acting) postmaster of Lancaster, passed it on, to arrive in London on the Saturday.[35] A later express left Kendal at eight o'clock that night[36] to arrive in Lancaster at three in the morning, when Robert Macmillan expressed it to Sarah Blackburn, the postmistress at Warrington,[37] for it to arrive in London on the 24th.[38] Further information was expressed by John Nocks, postmaster at Preston, on the 22nd[39] at one o'clock in the morning and arrived in London next day.[40] A later express left Warrington post office at 8 p.m. on Friday night and was in London on Sunday the 24th.[41] The story continues by way of the postmasters of Stone, Coventry and so on.

In the meantime Wade managed to get his army back to Newcastle on the 22nd[42] after its abortive march for Carlisle. He called a council of war of his general officers on the 23rd[43] and laid before them an 'Extract of Intelligence'[44] that had been communicated to him from time to time. From all this the general officers concluded: 'The Field Marshal having communicated to us the intelligence he hath received in relation to the March of the Rebels, it appears that they are undoubtedly going to the South by way of Lancashire'.[45]

There is no need to continue in detail the later stages of the exercise. Obviously the situation in England did not exactly resemble the earlier situation in Scotland. There was later little or nothing of the man who happened to be travelling, the merchant, the clergyman's wife, or the steward at the estate office. Such mayors, deputy lieutenants, and even lords lieutenants, who now come into the process at all come into it 'for information only'. All has the appearance of having now become fully professionalized.

I am commanded by the Post Master General to send Your Grace. . . .

Agreeable to the Commands I received from the General Postmasters. . . .

Enclosed . . . I send to your Lordship in obedience to an Order from the post Masters General. . . .

Events might be thought to have been one great relay race. They were, however, unlike any relay race in this respect, that those who had earlier been smartly passing on the baton from one relay stage to another, successively shifted up to the *start*: events caught them up and in turn they were then put out of the race—off the track. It is not necessary to detail here how very much the same practice—in reverse—operated during the jacobite withdrawal. Some of the postmasters who during the occupation had not arranged 'to step out of the way' were badgered to furnish horses or posts, but in the main they seem to have 'stepped back *into* the way' again in order to carry on during the retreat.

All this should be compared against the rate at which intelligence travelled by the more formal official channels at about this period—particularly urgent diplomatic or military intelligence. For example, Culloden was fought on 16th April. The despatch from Inverness, dated on the 18th, did not arrive in London until late on the 26th—'too late to be inserted' in that day's issue of the *London Gazette*.

So far as concerns the machinery of central government in the provinces at this period, it consisted effectively of the customs, the excise and the post office. The machinery of the customs was then confined to the ports and the coastline. Certain aspects of its importance have been dealt with elsewhere[46] and need not be enlarged upon here. The particular significance of the excise in both the Fifteen and the Forty-five has also been dealt with elsewhere[47] and again need not be enlarged upon here. Both the officers of customs and the officers of excise had to enter into bonds and give security, the latter varying according to the rank and responsibility of the person concerned. The officers of both services were commissioned and were required to take the usual oaths of office; this might seem to imply an absolute loyalty to the established government, but the oaths of office were mainly religious in form and an element of religious toleration had long entered both services. Already by 1688 there is evidence that a notion was coming into being that the service should be loyal to 'the crown' rather than to the king: kings may come and kings may go, but 'the service' goes on for ever.[48] It is sheer lack of historical understanding to sneer at this and to mumble something about the vicar of Bray. Such political sympathy with the jacobite cause as there might have been in both the customs and the excise services was later inquired into, and less was disclosed than might have been expected.[49] Although it is difficult to believe that the public moneys could have been collected as easily as they were without some active collusion by the local excisemen, there is no doubt that if any information or intelligence from any source whatsoever, for transmission to an official destination, had been laid on either the customs or the excise network, such information or intelligence would have made its way to the respective boards of commissioners in London and thus to the secretary of state—without any siphoning off *en route* for the benefit of mayors, corporations or justices on the civil side, or deputy lieutenants, lords lieutenants or the regular army on the military side.

With the post office, however, the position was entirely different. At each post town the 'deputy' of the postmaster general had a 'deputation' and was required to take the oaths of office and give bond for his own security. The fees of office, however, fixed for the carriage of the mail and other duties (riding work, etc.), unlike the salaries in the customs and the excise, were not fixed on a career scale. Officers of the customs, or of the excise, were mostly *forbidden* to follow any other calling; the postal deputies were *expected* to. The latter were often innkeepers or otherwise keepers of post-houses, that is, keepers of livery stables, suppliers of horses, post-boys, guides, and so forth. Such an innkeeper would enter the postal service not primarily on account of the fees of office, but in order to attract as customers to his house all those travelling post, awaiting the London newspapers, or calling for letters. Incidentally, it was convenient in this combination of occupations that the local postmaster, in that capacity, was exempt from serving local office[50] and from billeting—both of them important to an innkeeper.[51] It was statutorily provided that 'none should carry letters or *provide horses for riding post*' except the postmaster general or his local postmasters.[52] These, however, had an obligation so to do, and travellers could 'provide themselves with horses from other Houses' only if the postmasters 'neglect it for half an hour after demand made'.[53] Thus, the local postmaster became the local nerve centre of news, nearby and afar.

It had long been clear to the central government the special part the post office could play in the matter of the transmission of information and intelligence. From the earliest days of the post office the government had assumed the power to open letters in transit from one private person to another, presuming to base its authority upon an unexpressed prerogative power. Immediately after the Restoration letters being lawfully conveyed were being opened 'by authority of the Secretary of State'. Later, to acquire a statutory title, the forms of words then being officially used were written into the act of Anne by which a new general post office was erected, incidentally with a power to delay, detain and open letters passing through. The exercise of this power, however, required a specific warrant, in writing, under the hand of the principal secretary of state, in every case. In the Atterbury case, for example, the principal evidence against the accused was that of the post office clerks and others who, in obedience to the warrants of the secretary of state, not only 'detained and opened' but also 'copied and deciphered' letters to and from the accused. In the committee on the bill against Atterbury in the house of lords, although counsel did not question the authority of the secretary of state to detain and open, they did question the authority to copy and decipher.[54] Furthermore, some of the warrants of September and October 1745 were questioned as being 'of a very general and unlimited character'.

However, with a rising on its hands, the ministry in London, having already issued directions about the availability of horses, considered introducing, through the local postmasters, a scheme of personal passes. The statute of Anne precluded anyone from providing 'horses for riding post' except through the postmaster, and the proposal was that the postmaster should refuse to provide a horse to anyone not already furnished with an official pass.[55] Furthermore, intercourse and correspondence between Edinburgh and England was to be stopped 'and the letters that were to have gone by that, be sent to the Post Office [in London]'.[56] The lord chancellor, however, said that he could find in the statute nothing 'relating to Passes, but there are strict Clauses inflicting Penalties on the Post Masters for *not* furnishing Horses'. However, another clause in the act required 'the Post Master General and his Deputies [to] observe all such Orders Rules and Directions as shall be made and ordered' by the crown; there might be something in these rules already made relating to passes, but he (the lord chancellor) did not know of it; perhaps 'some new Instructions may be given under the Sign Manual'.[57]

Already in September Lord Malton[58] and the other lords lieutenants in the Yorkshire ridings had been discussing with George Shelvocke, the secretary to the post office, a scheme for gathering up information and intelligence through the mediumship of the local postmasters, for transmission to the lords lieutenants. Shelvocke, in the absence of the joint postmasters-general, wrote on 13th October that 'the several postmasters north of Boroughbridge and the Post Master of York' would receive from London 'full and necessary Orders thereupon'. Expresses as necessary were authorized, to and fro, the postmasters to receive proper allowances. By the end of September printed instructions were issued to postmasters,[59] and later the posts were regularly opened on the main and the cross roads.[60]

In any case, the cabinet council saw fit on 4th October to direct the postmaster-general 'to stop not only all treasonable or seditious printed Papers, but also all written Letters that contain any seditious Matters or that may tend to the Disservice of His Majesty's Government'.[61] As to what exactly constituted 'seditious matters', and what might 'tend to disservice', is not easy to determine, but it is unlikely that it could be determined *from the outside* of the letter. In the matter of directing the postmaster-general, it seems not to have been noticed hitherto that the postmaster-general at the time was none other than General Sir Everard Fawkener,[62] Cumberland's military secretary. However, that this fact has generally escaped notice is of no significance, for Fawkener seems to have taken no particular interest in the post except, of course, to draw the salary—in the manner characteristic of the mid-eighteenth century. He had been awarded the post early in 1745 in recognition of his military services in Flanders, and it may very well never have occurred to the Turkey merchant turned ambassador turned soldier that in his other capacity he held in his own hands the reins of communication in England.

To come to the people who mattered more—the local postmasters—they seemed to have been more concerned about Mr Shelvocke and Mr Robinson in the office than about General Fawkener in the field. Doubtless the various postmasters each knew by name their colleagues along the line and were a fairly closely knit network. It is not surprising, therefore, that this postmaster network quickly became the received mode of intelligence communication, civil and military.

There were, however, other intelligence antennae, other lines of communication than that of the post office, of purely private (or civic) origin, in which the players seem to have been on the ball even earlier than the postmasters.[63] By the time, however, the ministry had, through the secretary of the post office, alerted all provincial postmasters to the necessity to secure and transmit intelligence to head post office in London, the private (*ad hoc*) arrangements came more and more to have to rely upon the postmasters for prompt and regular transmission. Doubtless there were certain jealousies as to the character, importance and transmission of the intelligence and information procured, but in the nature of the case the postmasters were bound to win in the end.

The most interesting, closely integrated, keen and effective private network was that operating across the border on the Carlisle side. It had got itself informally into being before the actual rising—in anticipation. In origin it was essentially civil and civic in character. Early in 1745 a question arose about the proposal to turnpike a particular road from the border through part of the county of Cumberland. The normal practice in such cases[64] would be for a number of justices and other interested gentlemen (or potential trustees) to meet informally to discuss among themselves the conditions under which they would take the road off the county, and the terms of the necessary parliamentary bill. To this end a number of gentlemen from both sides of the border met in Carlisle in the early part of 1745 and, naturally enough, the conversation got round later to the subject of the possibility—or probability—of a rising this coming summer. The opportunity was taken therefore to enter into a friendly agreement to exchange intelligence across the border if such occasion arose. Out of this informal agreement there grew up—when the emergency came— quite a system of communication in the Scottish south-western counties whereby information and intelligence were consistently forwarded, through links fanning out from Dumfries across Moffat, Peebles and Selkirk to Kelso and Jedburgh, to be channelled back through Annan, Ecclefechan and Longtown to Carlisle. The nerve centre was John Waugh, chancellor of Carlisle,

who sought to maintain churchly channels, through his friend
Dr Bettesworth, dean of the arches in London, and the secretary of state. Certainly Chancellor Waugh desired most particularly to stand well with the ministry in London. As one of
the ardent whig justices, he lined up (in the local factions) with
the county gentry, the justices and deputy lieutenants against the
urban elements, the mayor and corporation and the civic side. It
irked him, therefore, that he should have to be beholden to the
(later notorious) Thomas Pattinson, sometimes signing himself
'deputy mayor' and sometimes signing himself 'mayor', a mere
innkeeper of 'The Bush' public house—*the local postmaster*. When
the lords lieutenants of the northern counties, including the great
lord lieutenant of Cumberland and Westmorland himself, had
failed to hold mustered the county militia because of some defect
in the militia laws,[65] the ministry had authorized certain civic
dignitaries to raise forces locally by virtue of a royal warrant,
altogether independently of the lieutenancy. The secretary of
state himself, his grace the duke of Newcastle, had addressed such
a royal warrant to the mayor of Carlisle, this innkeeper, this
postmaster, and had even given directions and orders to the Tower
of London to deliver out small arms and ammunition and convey
them to Carlisle, the critical fortress on the border, but to convey
them not to the lord lieutenant, not to the governor of the castle,
but to the *innkeeper*—by name.

In the matter of intelligence, therefore, the critical place in
critical Carlisle later settled itself down to be not Carlisle castle
and Governor Durand, not the cathedral close and Chancellor
Waugh, but the 'Bush' inn and Postmaster Pattinson. It seems of
particular significance (in view of the then current factions in
Carlisle) that when certain details of the light horse crossed the
border and seized the jacobite quartermaster (already referred to)
the prisoner was carried not to the castle, and not to the courts,
but to the 'Bush' inn, Pattinson's place, before being conveyed
across to Wade at Newcastle. Occasionally one can sense something of the friction between the prelate and the postmaster. On
23rd September—immediately after Prestonpans—the chancellor
told the secretary of state that it was with great pleasure he could
assure his grace 'that all private Interests seem to be laid a Sleep
by the common Danger'; that the two factions, 'the Magistrates

for the Town and County that are in it, with the Gentlemen of the Place, meet every Hour that they think they can be of use'.[66] Within a few weeks, however, when the common danger had become more dangerous, the old frictions returned—if they had ever gone. It seems clear enough that not only were the pair of them *not* working exactly hand-in-glove, but that furthermore Pattinson was not offering Waugh even such facilities as he could.

I hope Your Grace will have received that Letter in due Time. I thought to have sent it by a flying packet the Post Master talked of sending off; but he not sending one, or not taking my Letter, I sent it by an Express going into Yorkshire to be forwarded to Your Grace sooner than the Post if any Opportunity offered.[67]

The chancellor implies that his own arrangements were more reliable than those of the official post: 'I send this off into Yorkshire by a Messenger I am sending, least it should be stopped.'[68] In his letter of exculpation after the fall of Carlisle (writing from Barnard Castle on 1st December) he snatches the opportunity to take a side swipe at the postmaster; 'I have hardly had an opportunity to write a Letter to your Grace, for during the time the Rebels were before us Mr Pattinson denyed to me that he could send any Express to London'.[69] The likelihood is that the chancellor felt that he, for his own part, had in some measure organized, if indeed he had not initially instituted, a whole system of intelligence in the border country, and had expected in consequence (through the dean of the arches) to 'get his name on the file' in the matter of the later preferments. The postmaster-innkeeper, on the other hand, was sitting contented with confidential—if not secret—authority from the ministry permitting him, by the interception of the post (and even by the physical breaking open of letters), to come into possession of intelligence and pass it on that the chancellor in his innocence had no hint of.

To be of any value at all, intelligence—and also, indeed, the merest of information—requires to be both timely and accurate. If either not prompt or not correct, it could be not only (negatively) of no value, but could indeed be (positively) dangerous.

Certainly, all precautions seem to have been taken on this score by all those in the *ad hoc* network. So far as timeliness is concerned, it might be considered, firstly, in the getting of the information at the forward point, and secondly, in the transmission of it down the line. As regards the gathering of it one is conscious, in reading some of the hurried scraps, that in many if not most instances the forward agents delayed sending back until the last practicable moment. 'I have an Express waiting their Motions', says Buccleuch's steward, 'whose report shall be directly communicated to you'.[70] 'The Man we have waiting . . . for Observation', said Bryce Blair at Annan, 'Returned this Night, Seven a Clock', and he got a report southerly by 11.[71] The provost of Annan reports that a 'Messenger We had sent last Night . . . returned this Day and brings Advice that Early this Morning a Highland Officer, attended by one Servant, came there and gave out That a part of the Army would be there by ten o'Clock having got orders to march as soon as the Moon rose'.[72] Francis Hewitt wrote from Carlisle on the 10th November to the postmaster at Lancaster to the effect that the besiegers had 'taken up their Quarters at Grinsdale (2 Miles from hence)' and 'we expect every hour they will attack Us and how it will turn out, God knows'. However, 'If we have an Engagement this Night, shall acquaint you tomorrow'.[73] The postmistress of Warrington provides precise and timely information to Ligonier about the retreating insurgents: 'the Foot and Baggage pass'd by a Place called Pendleton Pole (which is one mile from Manchester) this morning and took the Road which leads to Legh Wigan and Preston'. She had been told that 'the Horse design'd to stay in Manchester all Night' but added, 'as that was only a Report, can't tell what to say to it'. A postscript, however, says, 'Since the above We are assured that the whole of the Rebels have left Manchester and taken the above Road'.[74] John Bateman, writing to Lancaster from Kendal, late on 10th November, said he was unable to go down to Lancaster as he had to return to Carlisle; 'after I had left that town, in a Short Space of time, I think before 11 oClock, [I heard] the Cannon from the Town begin to play and continu'd so till I came to penrith'.[75] One can often sense something of the urgency and excitement of the occasion: 'There is a Gentleman just now alighted at my House who came last Night from Moffat'.[76] The keenness to get the latest can occasionally bring the agent into personal danger:

> I was going to say more . . . but am forced to fly from Mr Baty's whither I was come just now at full gallop from my house, 1,000 Highlanders being within 2 Gunshot of me.[77]

The postmaster of Dumfries said: 'This I am certain of, for I lay last Night surrounded by them'.[78] A townsman of Lancaster arrived there from the north on 14th November; he had 'left the Rebels camp yesterday afternoon' and had 'viewed their Camp from a Hill and was pursued and narrowly escaped being taken'.[79]

For the agents deliberately sent forward from the advanced listening posts there was naturally a considerable element of danger. On 4th November, 'the Messenger I sent [from Carlisle] to Selkirk is not yet returned'.[80] On the 7th, 'Near 3 a Clock' in the afternoon: 'as there is nothing in the way to have stopped the Messenger, I doubt the poor Man is taken';[81] but a little later the same day: 'As I was sealing My Letter a Messenger is come . . . with a Letter to say that he has a Messenger just come from Selkirk'.[82] Or again: 'I have since sent three Messengers North with promises of good reward if they wou'd deliver some Letters at Selkirk Hawick and Kelso &c. They all said they had Courage and would execute my Orders, but they have all disappointed me'[83]—they had not come back.

With regard to timely transmission, there are two factors here: one, to get the subject matter funnelled to the point (mostly to a postmaster) where it can be laid on a regular network for immediate transmission to London; and two, the task of siphoning it off, as necessary, to other interested parties on the route. For example, when the latest occupation details were got out of Penrith by the postmaster they were communicated to the postmaster of Brough. The latter found the time, as the postmaster of Penrith could not, to make sufficient copies to relay it to Lord Lonsdale (the lord lieutenant of Cumberland and Westmorland, who in his turn relayed it to Wade, to the commanding officer at Chester and the secretary of state), and by special arrangement to Lord Malton in Yorkshire, who in his turn also relayed it to London.[84] The necessity was early realized to siphon off this timely accurate information at as early a stage as possible, bearing in mind, however, that this had two repercussions: one, the possibility of advance parties of the insurgents intercepting the expresses; and two, of placing a heavy burden of copying on the forward agents, who were already hard pressed in other respects and also in physical danger.

For example, George Bell, the provost of Dumfries, closed a brief and hurried note to Carlisle, excusing himself: in case 'one Express should be Stopt by the way, pray do you despatch another Messenger', as 'I have so much to write and so many Expresses to send off'.[85] Or again: 'I have been up most part of the night settling Despatches and doing other Duty. [You] may be sure we have Bussiness enough now, so hope you will excuse my hasty Letter'.[86] The (acting) mayor of Carlisle reported on 9th November that England had been invaded—'within 3 Miles of us'—'With sitting up and fatigue am now more sleepy than afraid'.[87] The following day the mayor himself wrote, 'Ive been all Night upon Guard with Captain Wilson[88] and other Gentlemen, when we went about the Walls every 2 hours'.[89]

It seems very likely that when, at a particular post office, two or three further copies of a piece of incoming information were wanted, the quickest way to make the required copies was for one person to read the original and two (or three) others to write— perhaps hurriedly—from this dictation. Such copies as the following, with their variant spellings and other minor differences, arriving at the same destination by different routes, are quite consistent with such a practice:

Kendal. 21st Nov[r] 6 oClock, Evening.
Here is three Countrey men, just come to informe me they left about 100 of the Scotch behind them at a place called Host about Seven Miles off. they came on Foot, and by a due Calculation they are about half a mile off us. I am determined to stay. If I can I'll inform you in what Manner they behave. If I cannot I doubt not but some other may

John Shaw Mayor[90]

And another version:

Kendal. 21st Nov[r] 6 Clock Night.
Here is 3 Cuntrimen chust come to Informe me they left abought one hundred of the Scoch behind them at a place cald Host about

Seven miles off. they came on Foot and by a Due Calculation they are abought half a mile of us. I am determined to stay, if I can I'll informe you in what manner they behave if I cannot I doubt not but some other may.   Jno Shaw.[91]

This copying and wider distribution became a normal part of the process, at least where it was possible. Occasionally, however, it was not completely practicable. For example, the postmistress at Warrington, Susan Blackbourne, undertook to pass on 'any intelligence that I think may be depended on' to the surveyor at Chester (Richard Lloyd), but she, for her part, had to rely largely upon Robert Macmillan, the acting postmaster at Lancaster. She expected a post from there next day—'but the Chastre Paquet being so soon despatched after that comes here I am afraid I cant have time to copy them for you'.[92]

As the invaders get farther south, time becomes more pressing —and consequently, the letters briefer. For example, the hurried note from the postmaster at Stone (R. Saxby) 'to Mr Ald^r Kilsby, Post Master In Coventry'. 'Mr Kilsby—Copy this and Send the original directed to the Postmaster-Genl at London—put in cover. Sr. Your Ser. R. Saxby'.[93]

The speed with which some of these letters got up to London or cross-country is truly amazing.

Part of the Scotch amounting to about six score are just now entering this Town.   Walter Chambers
Kendal. Nov 21st 8 OClock at Night
This is about 120 Horse came into Town and only about 2000 foot is to come to night, commanded by Ld Geo Murray
                                                 Thos Willson
Lancaster Nov 21st [? 22nd] 1745
3 o clock in the morning
The Post Mrs
Warrington
Madam.
    The inclose is the Copy of a note which the Express brought here, they are in vary great Confusion at Kendall. He adds nothing more, only that they are very civil and intend to be at Lan[caster] on Satter-day
                                                 Robert Macmillan

These papers were in the secretary of state's office on the 24th.

Or again, John Nocks, the postmaster at Preston, sent a very brief note direct to the secretary of state:

May it please Your Grace,
Enclosed are Copies of some Accounts which I just now reced from Kendale and which I send Your Lordship in Obedience of An Order from the Post Master Genl.

The letter is subscribed, 'John Nocks, Post Mas^r at Preston, 22 Nov 1745. 1 in the Morning', and is endorsed (by the secretary of state's office) 'Preston, Novr 22nd 1745. Mr Nocks, Post-Master. R[eceived] 23rd (by Express)'.[95] A very similar letter in very similar terms was despatched by '. . . Warrington Post Office, 22 Nov 1745. half hour past 7 oclock in the morning' and received in London next day. Another leaving Kendal on the 21st, and Warrington on the 22nd at 8 p.m. was in London on the 24th.[96] The (acting) postmaster at Lancaster sends a despatch at 7 p.m. on 23rd November and it is in London on the 25th.[97] Intelligence despatched on Wednesday 20th November, 'Penrith, 12 at Night' was relayed from Brough and received at Byram in Lancashire on the 22nd, and in London on Sunday 24th.[98]
In the nature of the case, some of the letters could not be addressed very exactly. As the postmistress of Warrington reported to the surveyor at Chester: 'Saturday morning 16th Nov near 9 oclock. An Express is just gone through here for London, and a Paquet directed for Legonier where ever he is'.[99] 'Where ever he is' is not very precise for purposes of delivery. An earlier letter had been addressed to Ligonier 'at Preston'.[100] They all seem to have got through. A letter from Lancaster post office of Friday 22nd November (at '3 of Clock in the Morn') addressed to the postmaster by his son (acting in the absence of the father who was out with the militia) and directed to 'Mr John Macmillan, Preston, Blackburn, Ormskirk or Elsewhere', reached him and, furthermore, was in the office of the secretary of state in London by Sunday the 24th.[101]
This son, Robert Macmillan (perhaps not quite certain of the exact mode of address) wrote to 'The Right Hble & Hble Post Mr General' in London on 18th November to enclose 'the Coppy of an Express Rec^d this Morning at 4 oClock', which he thought it his duty to transmit, and would continue so to do

'as if my Father was at home'.[102] The letter intercepted was going between Kendal and Liverpool. The express had journeyed from Colonel Graham, in command at Liverpool,[103] to Wade at Newcastle. Wade, however, sent the express word 'that he had nothing to send back to the Colo[nel] but his Honble Service', so the express was returning empty-handed. Wade, for his part, round about Newcastle, 'had employed so many Horses to draw and carry his Baggage [to Carlisle] as I could not get one . . . but was forced to ride most of last night to get here [to Kendal]', but as Kendal was stategic in relation to Carlisle and Liverpool 'I think to stay a few days longer here and shall continue to give you as good Acct as possible'.[104]

One might reasonably conclude, therefore, with regard to timeliness, that both in the collection of the material and in its transmission the scheme of communication was working very reasonably well—indeed, surprisingly well. There remains the factor of accuracy. It is a noteworthy fact that very little rumour as such seems ever to have been transmitted. Considerable care seems to have been taken to get the material accurate in the first instance, and to keep it accurate in the course of transmission. For example,

After writing the enclosed I have hover'd about within a Mile . . . and sent in several Messengers, least I should have sent you something false or uncertain.[105]

In the significant matter of the strength of the invaders the liability to error in making any actual count was in the likelihood of missing odd straggling parties or counting any particular detachment twice. The most effective place to make any count, therefore, would be at some particular place that must be passed once but could not be passed twice. This point was, apparently, firmly taken by those primarily concerned. Intelligence provided a count at the bridge over the Eamont, near Penrith. The account from Penrith, dated 22nd November, via the postmaster of Brough, said

By the best Reckoning I could make by persons at Eamont Bridge and at Fallowfields Bridge in the Town, the Highlanders Might be about 3000. They have od Straglin Parties wch makes an Acct Difficult. The Cariages for Baggage wch came here yesterday I counted this

pans he admitted that he owed his life to one of the jacobite officers, the duke of Perth; Henderson thereupon filled his glass, drank a toast to the duke and called upon the soldier to do the same—which the soldier refused. The two men of Lascelles', 'suspecting him to be a Spy', severally left him and then denounced him, but denounced him *to the civil arm*.[15]

On 31st October (the day the jacobite force marched south from Dalkeith) Richard Gilpin the recorder and four other justices examined Henderson pretty closely in Carlisle. According to his story, he had come to Carlisle on 25th October 'to take a Lodging there for his wife till the People now in Arms for the Pretender were gone from Edinburgh'. This, of itself, was an unlikely story, for that was just about the time when it was coming to be known in Edinburgh, as firm information, that the army would be marching south at the end of the month. It seems likely also that the recorder—of particular significance below—pressed Henderson into certain inconsistencies or contradictions, minor in themselves, but significant to establish that Henderson's story could be shaken. He 'does not deny that he ever declared that . . . the Person who came with him was his Servant'—which he was not. He 'does not deny that he ever declared that he came to Carlisle to sell 12 Cattle'—which he did not. He now 'saith he brought 2 Horses to Sell there to raise Money for his Wife's Support during her Stay at Carlisle'—which was another story. He now

Confesses to the best of his Memory he made some Enquiries of his Landlord and Some Others then in Company of the Strength of the Garrison and also desired them to Show him the Ramparts.

Saith he made the said Enquiries and desired to see the Ramparts[16]

but this was 'only for his own Curiosity'. He denied, however, that he had as much as been in Edinburgh since the end of July, 'or ever mentioned to any person that he had been there Since that Time'. The examining magistrates, however, had no doubt. They wrote to the secretary of state on the 3rd November, by which time Carlisle knew the insurgent force was on the move.

My Lord,

Last week one John Henderson, a Scottsman, was taken up as a Spy in this Town.

2—G

After examining Him we committed him to Gaol, there to ly till he should be discharg'd by due course of law.[17]

But what the justices feared in the case of Campbell and Jackson did in fact happen in the case of Henderson. Committed to gaol 'there to ly till . . . discharg'd by due course of Law', he did not, in the outcome, lie there until discharged *by law*. Instead, he lay there, charged with being a jacobite spy, until Carlisle was captured by the jacobites. Thus it was the Scottish jacobites, not the English law, that discharged him. Now were the tables neatly turned. Now, 'with broad sword and white Cockade [Henderson] came and threatened the Turnkey, because he had told lies to the Governor'. However, Henderson did not move off with the insurgents when they moved south from Carlisle.

White cockade or no, he had no intention of marching south with them—even under duress—and, presumably because he knew his way about between Carlisle and Lochmaben, he remained in Carlisle in charge of the Scotch gate. It may very well be, having regard to the circumstances of his earlier arrest, that during the occupation of Carlisle and his brief spell of authority, Henderson made some 'difficulties' for the turnkey, the city bailiff, the recorder, and such like. For example, when news came, in the second week of December, that the jacobites were *northward*-bound, some of the more substantial of the inhabitants of the city—who could not this time take their effects up to the castle—sought to remove them beyond the city. But when Richard Gilpin, the recorder (he who had taken the espionage depositions against him), was moving his stuff out, who was on the gate but John Henderson, 'who prevented the Recorder's Goods from being carried out . . . He said at the gate the Recorder's Goods should not go out', much to the annoyance, one imagines, of the recorder.

If, however, Mr Henderson of Lochmaben had, like many since, gone to Carlisle about horses, he had backed the wrong horse this time. On the Sunday after he had mounted the guard on the Scotch gate, he was seen by a later witness 'going over Eden Bridge with his wife—and there was a serv[an]t before with Horses which I thought to be his—he pull'd off his cockade on the Causeway between the Bridges'.

'He pulled off his cockade': was this the end of another 'auld song'? Scarcely: because, to use the words of another later witness, 'he had left some accounts in Carlisle unsettled' (this witness does not specify whether they were accounts about horses, or accounts with the recorder, bailiff and turnkey). He returned to Carlisle 'and didn't come home till two or three days after the Rebels return'd Northwards with the Duke in their Rear'.

He had now got himself out of England—but not out of danger. The old charge of espionage was still outstanding against him, unanswered. He was therefore rooted out and taken to Carlisle to stand his trial, but not for espionage. He was charged now with treasonable practices in Carlisle during the occupation, a charge easier to prove than espionage. His defence was the favourite one—he had been 'forced'. According to the notes of the trial judge,[18] one witness testified,

Henderson they forced to take a cockade and cursed him they would stick him if not let it remain—above twenty of them about him, and held on his hat with their drawn swords.

The evidence of his conduct at the gate, however, was against him. Doubtless the recorder saw to that. They brought it out that he had not been a mere sentinel at the gate, but *in charge* of the guard there. For a plea of 'forcing' to succeed, a prisoner had to show that he had initially been forced to the fear of his life— which the prisoner had shown; that he remained under duress— which the prisoner contended; and that he took the first opportunity to attempt to escape—where the prisoner failed completely, if he were in charge of the guard on the Scotch gate, and lived at Lochmaben. Certainly, last November and December the prisoner had neatly turned the tables on the turnkey, gaoler, bailiff and recorder; but now the tables were turned on him.

It is interesting to note that Richard Gilpin, the recorder, John Waugh, the chancellor, and other justices who had originally examined Henderson on the espionage charge were present when the commission of *oyer* and *terminer* was opened at the Carlisle trials.[19] They were interested that he should not slip through the net again.

Richard Jackson, whom we know from other sources[20] to

be one of the bailiffs of Carlisle, now came forward and gave evidence against him.

> Saw him among the other Rebels often, as one of them—with a cockade and a broadsword under his arm—he was open and frequent with them.[21]

One piece of evidence might have turned the scale in the prisoner's favour, when another prisoner—of the jacobites this time—testified that he himself

> was taken prisoner at Penrith by the Rebels who brought me to Carlisle Gaol where Henderson was to see me, and in Morning before the Rebels left the town he opened the Gaol and favoured my Escape at five o'clock in the morn[ing].[22]

But the jury were not impressed. Baron Clarke noted:

> N.B. This man a better sort of them—Jury did not Stay a Minute to debate—never went from the Bar and he appeared throughout the whole Trial to have been a very active busy man.[23]

Doubtless the recorder and the chancellor looked with some satisfaction on 21st October 1746 when they saw Henderson's head spiked over the gate at Carlisle.

The third case history may be opened with a brief enough document. In the Cumberland quarter-sessions minute book there is an order, made in the Epiphany session of 1746, ordering ten shillings to be paid 'for conveying Anthony Sim, a Rebel, to the prison at Whitehaven'.[24] Who was this solitary prisoner, then, conveyed from Wigton, not to the castle at Carlisle but to the prison at Whitehaven—that is to say, not as a military prisoner, but as a civil?

The order was made 'upon petition', and therefore it should be possible to find the relative petition. If one turns to this on the appropriate roll it is to find the entry:

> The Humble Petition of Robert Grave [in company with two others] who Apprehended Anthony Sims, a Servant of Mr Sacald, as a Spy of the Pretender, from Wigton to Whitehaven.[25]

Anthony Sim (or Sims) was suspected, then, of being 'A Spy of the Pretender'. The 'Mr Sacald' referred to in the petition may be taken to be the Henry Salkeld who was the last male representative of an old Cumberland catholic family, formerly of Corby Castle. The seat had been sold in the reign of James I to Lord William Howard of Naworth, when the Salkelds settled at Whitehall, about fourteen miles west of Carlisle. It was here that Henry Salkeld and his wife were residing in 1745.

Henry Salkeld, on account of his estate, would (catholic or protestant or neither) have his statutory liabilities to the militia. If, therefore, we look at the lieutenancy papers it would be to see that he was in fact required to 'find' a rider in the militia light horse—and that the man he nominated was none other than Anthony Sim (or Sims),[26] he who had been apprehended as a spy. A little further searching discloses the fact that among those who joined Towneley's so-called Manchester regiment was a John Sanderson, formerly steward to this Henry Salkeld; but whatever his late steward did, Salkeld himself, so it was said, intended to remain quietly at home. Mounsey says that in November among the rumours going the rounds locally was one to the effect that a letter had been intercepted, addressed to Salkeld, containing treasonable matter in which he was implicated. The writer was taken up and thrown into Newcastle gaol, and a person named Roger Gibson went off to arrest Salkeld to send him off to Newcastle also. Another reference to the muster roll among the lieutenancy papers will show Roger Gibson as 'riding' for Sir Gilfrid Lawson, who was an ardent whig justice and one of the deputy lieutenants who, incidentally, in October gave the order to the militia captains to require the high constables throughout Cumberland and Westmorland to summon the men of the respective wards (or hundreds) in order to complete the militia strength.

But Salkeld appears to have been warned in time. According to Mounsey, entirely 'conscious of his own innocence', he set out for Carlisle, there to surrender arms he had carried merely for his own safety on the journey, and to apply to the magistrates to take his affidavit. Therein he declared his intention to remain quiet, and denied any association with the treasonable letter referred to. But this affidavit, although clearing him with the civic authorities, incriminated him with the Scottish governor when the city fell to the jacobites. He would have been thrown into prison, but for the intervention of Francis Strickland, one of the 'seven men of Moidart', and the only Englishman amongst them. Strickland came of an old Westmorland family and was a distant cousin of Salkeld. When Strickland fell ill—he later died at Carlisle—Salkeld, who had earlier practised as a physician, was asked to attend him, and actually did so, thus reciprocating his kindness. Salkeld is said to have sought the advice of the magistrates first, and was given their permission, but when the duke of Cumberland arrived Salkeld was committed to gaol on a mere parole order, and without any charge or information being laid against him. The only persons, so it was said, who could have laid any information, passed on to Scotland with the army without doing so. The lawyers in London thought of attempting to extract some incriminating information from his servant, then in custody, but apparently not successfully.[27] He could not apply for bail, for the Habeas Corpus Act stood suspended, and he had therefore to remain in gaol at Carlisle for no less than seven months.

Thus far Mounsey.[28] The next clue cannot be picked up on the whig side: James Ray, the Whitehaven gipsy, Andrew Henderson, the Edinburgh schoolmaster, Michael Hughes, the City of London volunteer; for these, being whigs, would have little opportunity to gather up confidential information implicating any of the English catholic families. If on the jacobite side, then, not among the almost purely military details of Lord George Murray or Maxwell of Kirkconnel, for example. We should look among the accounts of the catholic faction, and preferably among Charles Edward's confidants. The highly idiomatic narrative of Sullivan yields nothing; but when the Taylers edited this account they included a manuscript of old Sir John Macdonald, a French citizen in the Spanish service, found among the Windsor papers and until then unknown. 'Old Spanish John' said, in a passage that must refer to Salkeld:

As soon as we arrived at Brampton a Catholic gentleman named Sawel, who had property in the neighbourhood, went to Strickland, who was a relative of his wife, to know whether his services would be agreeable, as in that case he would join the Prince. Strickland considered that as the gentleman was alone and infirm, he had better remain at home, especially as the weather was then very cold.[29]

So Salkeld 'stayed at home'—stayed at home, that is, until Carlisle was retaken. He was then, as we have said, committed on 'military verbal orders' alone, with no actual evidence of any sort being produced against him of his being concerned in any way with espionage or in treasonable intercourse with the jacobite leaders. The earlier event would have taken place between Monday 11th and Wednesday 13th November. The story now shifts from the Scottish border to the Welsh.

On the following Saturday night, the 16th, two horsemen came to a nobleman's house on the Shropshire–Cheshire sector of the Welsh border. On being informed that My Lord was in London, they—or rather, one of them—handed My Lord's son a letter. It was the letter from Charles Edward at Brampton.

My Lord,   Brampton, Nov. 11, 1745
    This is to acquaint you with the success we have had since our arrival in Scotland, and how far we are advanced without repulse. We are now a numerous army, and are laying siege to Carlisle this day, which we are sure cannot hold out long. After that we intend to take our route straight for London, and if things answer our expectations we design to be in Cheshire before the 24th inst. Then I hope you and all my friends in that county will be ready to join us. For now is the time or never. Adieu.

                              Charles, Prince Regent.

My Lord was the earl of Barrymore who (after the defection of the earl of Gower) was now the acknowledged head of the English jacobites. A peer by prescription in the Irish peerage, he was the premier baron of Ireland and senior lieutenant-general in the British army. Although he had taken his seat in the house of lords in 1702, he had sat in the commons in the tory interest in every parliament since before the Fifteen, except that of 1727–32. Although one of William of Orange's colonels, he had something of a jacobite background. He was, for example, arrested on suspicion of treason in 1715. More importantly, Barrymore (who had been intriguing in Paris in 1740) had been in trouble only a few years before the Forty-five, about a letter delivered by him to the duke of Argyll, presumably from (or in the interest of) the jacobite court in exile. Argyll immediately communicated it to the secretary of state, but what could not be traced was how exactly it got into the hands of Lord Barrymore. In any case, on

27th February 1744 Barrymore was taken into custody and a guard, consisting of a file of musketeers, placed on his house. A letter from Castle Lyon, his seat in Ireland, said, 'sure he is too wise a man to forget his life and fortune for any foreign power'.[30] Notwithstanding this, when the invasion fleet assembled at Dunkirk in 1744 Barrymore is said to have sent a son to join the French on their landing. Warrants were issued to secure him (and his papers) on suspicion of treason,[31] and he was put into the Tower, although later released on bail.[32] His situation now, in 1745, with a jacobite army actually in England, was highly critical. In July Charles Edward had landed in Moidart and the clans, against all discretion, had not failed him. What would the accepted leader of the English jacobites do now that Charles Edward had 'come home' to England too?

The earl of Barrymore's son, Lord Buttevant, when in his father's absence he was handed the critical letter by the jacobite spy in Marbury, was 'in a Great Rage' and asked, 'What Business have you to deliver this Paper to me' (he taking the said Letter in his hand)'. It was 'a small piece of paper sealed up with a wafer, but it looked as if it had been opened'—but, it is particularly to be noted, although not specifically addressed either to the earl or to his seat at Marbury, it was there that it was delivered. Asked why he had brought it here, the night horseman replied, 'He had a Letter to any Man of Honour in Cheshire who co'd be trusted, and he hoped he was not deceived by his Lordship'. The horseman's 'Conversation with My Lord and the Servants was Chiefly to Magnify the great Numbers and Strength of the Rebells'. Lord Buttevant permitted two of his servants to see the letter and then 'being in an Hurry[33] and surprised at the Contents of the sd paper, Immediately burnt the same';[34] he 'threw it into the Fire and Kept no Copy'.[35] This, as it transpired, was about the worst he could have done with it. He would have shown himself more reliable to 'the Present Happy Establishment' if he had saved it *and produced it*. At about 10.30 that night Lord Buttevant ordered the two horsemen out of the house, but he consented to allow one of his servants to show the strangers 'thro the Fields into the Public Road leading to . . . the Fox & Hounds in Northwich', but asked them to say nothing at the 'Fox and Hounds' about having been at the earl of Barrymore's house that night. After about an hour's reflection Lord Buttevant realized he had certainly acted foolishly. There were already, in the circumstances, those locally who might very well inform against the family,[36] and Buttevant was now left with no paper and no person to testify. He therefore now armed himself and his servants and set out for the 'Fox and Hounds', Northwich. There he 'took them in Bedd together' at about two o'clock in the morning.

The two horsemen were later that day examined before the Northwich justices, and so also was Lord Buttevant. It was established that the two strangers were Peter Pattinson, grocer, of Cockbridge, near Cockermouth in Cumberland, and Thomas Newby, builder, of Kendal in Westmorland. Pattinson had travelled from 'a House in Brampton where . . . the Pretender's son had lodged', where he had received 'a Passport or an Authority to proceed on his journey through the camp, if he would promise to deliver a Paper to any Gentleman in Cheshire'. Pattinson and Newby were committed to Chester castle on a charge of treasonable practices and the lord lieutenant, the earl of Cholmondeley, was informed. At Chester the two men were further examined before justices and the lord lieutenant but, from an even longer statement, little of any real significance could be discovered. One of the Northwich justices reported that one of the men in Barrymore's house at Marbury heard 'Newby' call 'Pattinson' 'My Lord', and the earl of Cholmondeley said that 'the Person who calls himself a Grocer [Pattinson] seems to me to be one of higher Rank and by his Carriage I am convinced has bin in foreign Service'.[37] Copies of all examinations were made and forwarded to the secretary of state.

What it was now desired to establish was the real relationship between the earl of Barrymore and Charles Edward's small circle of jacobite leaders who had now come out of exile. This spy (or these spies) might provide the means. No connection was yet seen, nor even remotely suspected, between this Pattinson on the one hand, and on the other Anthony Sim (or Sims), 'A Spy of the Pretender', and Salkeld, his master, who so far had managed not to be taken up. Obviously, the principal of the two riders into Cheshire was Pattinson, and Pattinson seems to have been able to stand any amount of examination. He played a good straight bat in a perfect defensive innings. He gave nothing away in respect of those who sent him, he made a special point of protecting his travelling companion, and allowed no accusation to emerge in respect of the Barrymores; and if he disclosed anything to the authorities at all (e.g. that Sir Thomas Sheridan and Francis Strickland were working in England in Charles Edward's household) he told them only what they almost certainly already knew. However, the story Pattinson told, although unlikely in itself, was so replete with every circumstantial detail, every incident meshing in so perfectly with every other, that it seemed completely convincing, if only because only the truth could fit so neatly.

Pattinson was a grocer of Cockbridge. He wanted to go to the 'Phoenix' at Hexham in connection with his business but had to return because his debtor had removed to Morpeth. By the time he was on his way back, 'with an intent to return to Cockbridge', he ran into stray parties of the jacobite invaders and had to 'leave the public Road for a few Fields'. Near Brampton, however, early in the morning, he 'was seized by three Highlanders who were armed' and was 'Carryed to a Gentlemans House in Brampton . . . where the Pretender or his son was'. Pattinson said that when he was questioned by Sheridan and the other jacobite leaders—by Sheridan in particular—he said that if he had collected the business debt due to him in Hexham he would have gone to London on further business. According to Pattinson's story, Sheridan then offered to release him if he would carry a message for them on his way to London. Because Pattinson 'had a wife and children and would Go about his Business', he promised 'he would deliver It, Please God he lived, as he went to London if they would set him free'. Eventually Sheridan gave him a 'pass' through the lines and 'a small piece of paper, sealed up with a Wafer, without any Direction or Superscription Upon it'. No particular conversation passed between him and the jacobite leaders but later he met the duke of Perth, who gave him ten shillings to drink his health. He was duly released from Brampton and went straight to his home at Cockbridge. He thereupon set out for London as he had originally intended, but 'did not acquaint his Wife or Any person at Cockbridge with the said Letter' because 'it would have Given her Great uneasiness'. It was as casual as all that.

He resolutely denied that he had been specifically directed 'to Deliver the said Letter or Scrap of Paper to *any particular person in Cheshire*', and when asked why therefore he had gone direct from Cockbridge to Barrymore's house, he said—unconvincingly enough—that he had left Warrington on his way to London, had missed the way and in the dark, late at night, had chanced on this particular place. This did not—and does not—carry conviction. No questioning, however, could shake this unlikely part of the story. He gave nothing away about the English faction drawn towards the jacobite leaders now in Cumberland. Furthermore, this left the earl of Barrymore and Lord Buttevant apparently entirely blameless, unless they gave themselves away, which they need not. And he entirely exculpated his fellow horseman. He said that Thomas Newby was a relative of his, and when in Kendal he 'told him that If he would Go Along with [him] into Cheshire [he] wd bear his Expenses Backwards and forwards'. Questioned as to why he should take him and pay his expenses, Pattinson replied, 'because he apprehended that he should be less Taken notice of If he had some person Along with him'. It nevertheless is not clear why a man going from Kendal to London should require company to Cheshire rather than to Lancashire or Derbyshire or anywhere else on the road.

Pattinson seems to have succeeded in keeping his examiners interested in his *journey* and his intention to go to London, rather than in the beginning of it and its end—Brampton and Marbury. He named (or otherwise identified) every inn on the road from Cockbridge to Northwich, and accounted for every hour.

Thursday 14th November
Keswick. The 'Royal Oak': 'Stay'd about a Quarter of an Hour'.
Kendal. The 'King's Arms': arrived 'between 4 and 5 oclock in the afternoon'.
Friday 15th
Left Kendal 'before it was light'.
Lancaster. 'a publick House in the Middle of the Town': arrived 'about 12 o'clock of the same day'. 'Stay'd but About a Hour'.
Preston. 'Public House near Market House' ('Forgot whether there was a sign thereat'). Arrived 'Just as it began to dark'.
Saturday 16th
Preston. 'Left Preston as soon as It was light'.

Wigan. Arrived 'about 11 oClock same day'. 'Stayed very short Time'.
Warrington. Arrived 'About four of the Clock'. 'Staid only to Bait
their Horses, but at what House . . . doth not know, but it was in
the Middle of the Town'.

Pattinson said 'he ask'd the Landlord of the said House which
was the first Town in the London Road that was 6 or 7 Mile
off that [they] could lye at, Upon which the said Landlord Informed [him] that Northwich was about 7 or 8 Miles Off the
London Road, where [they] might meet with Good Entertainment'. The examining magistrates seem not to have questioned
the difference between 'the first Town *in the London Road* that was
6 or 7 *Mile off*' and '[Northwich] that was about 7 or 8 Miles
Off the London Road'. They 'stay'd about a Quarter of an Hour in
Warrington' and it was now that 'they set out with a Intent to
Go to Northwich, but it being Dark they mist their Road and
came to the House of Lord Barrymore'.

After his first examination at Grange, Pattinson said that every
detail of his 'statement' was true, but he refused to sign it as a
formal examination unless the justices 'would grant him a Pass
to go to London'. Instead of that he was removed to Chester
castle. At Chester again a second 'Examination was read over to
[him] who sayd It was True as Far as he could recollect, but
refused to sign It unless he could have a Pass to London'. On
consideration of these and Lord Buttevant's examinations, the
cabinet council directed that the 'two Persons should be brought
to London, in the Custody of a Mesenger,[38] in order to their
being further examined and proceeded against'. 'It seems probable, from the Circumstances . . . that he may be able to make
material Discoveries'. Also, as it would be necessary to receive
Lord Buttevant's 'more particular Account than can possibly be
given at this Distance', his lordship was required to accompany the
messenger for that purpose[39] (a messenger in this context being
a functionary of the secretary of state to apprehend state prisoners).

So far as Pattinson was concerned he felt, perhaps like Viola,
that what he had to say had been excellently well penned, and he
had taken great pains to con it; he took good care, therefore, to
say little more than he had studied and would not accept any
question that was out of his part. So long, therefore, as he stuck
to his story neither Salkeld nor Barrymore had much to fear, and

Newby nothing at all. There was a story that John Newby had originally left Kendal alone, on a 'journey to see his wife's relations near Preston' and 'was overtaken by a person who was a stranger to him', and was only then 'hired to conduct him to Cheshire'.[40] In any case, it was later officially accepted that 'Thos Newby seems to be entirely ignorant of the Business that carried Pattinson to Lord Buttevant'. Newby was ultimately discharged from custody on 12th November 1746.

Pattinson, Newby and Buttevant were all re-examined in Westminster, Newby on 22nd December[41] and Pattinson again on the 24th.[42] Pattinson found that his Whitehall interrogators, unlike the country justices, were not so ready to follow the leads he himself had so carefully prepared for them. Under more skilled and more intensive interrogation he had to make a series of admissions, unimportant at first, but building up later. It was not *he* who was the grocer at Cockbridge, but his wife. He had to retract, therefore, the circumstantial story about his going to Hexham in the capacity of a grocer and his creditor having gone thence to Morpeth; he had never been beyond Brampton—and it was this story alone that accounted for him being at Brampton at the time Charles Edward was there.

Why, then, had he gone to Brampton at all?

He had gone, in the first place, merely to Wigton market. It was there that he heard, in a casual way, 'that the Highlanders were a fine sight' and that they were at Brampton. He went, therefore, to Brampton only as an idle sightseer, leaving Wigton in the evening and arriving at Brampton at about four in the morning. There he was taken prisoner, by armed highlanders—and the rest of the story was true. His later disclosures, however, were of more significance.

Of what religion was he?

His parents had brought him up as a presbyterian—but he had turned catholic about two years ago.

If he was not a grocer, what exactly *was* his calling?

A personal servant.

Whose personal servant?

Since the age of eighteen he had been servant to Thomas Salkeld, of Whitehall, near Wigton, and, since his master's death, to his late master's brother, Henry Salkeld.

Pattinson appears to have disclosed no more, and resolutely adhered to the rest of his story. They did not succeed in extracting from him the fact that his master was the catholic gentleman who had himself narrowly escaped being taken up upon suspicion and whose servant, Anthony Sim(s), had already been taken as 'a Spy for the Pretender'. Although the ministry's men in London could not extract very much more from Pattinson, they continued to look upon it all as quite an important affair. So much so that the ministry specially provided that among the prisoners specifically 'excepted' from 'lotting' (to accept transportation instead of a formal trial) were the men 'who carried the Letter to Lord Buttevant which was destroyed'. Nothing much further came to light.

Reverting now to the reference in the account of Sir John Macdonald, already quoted, 'old Spanish John' continued:

The man who brought the message to Strickland at Brampton seeming to me to be zealous and intelligent, I asked him if he thought he could penetrate further into England.[43]

Salkeld's servant said he could, so Sheridan sent him forward to get the message through.

It seems somewhat unlikely that Salkeld would have selected Anthony Sim(s) to go with the vital message, if only because Sim(s) was already duty bound to appear at the muster of the county militia light horse. It is altogether more likely whatever Sims' part was, that he succeeded in passing the message to Pattinson before he himself was taken up and carried to Newcastle. Certain of the Cumberland justices must have had their suspicions, for recorder Gilpin had Sim(s) taken up—too late— and Sir Gilfrid Lawson went for Salkeld—but not quite in time. It seems that over a century ago there was a local tradition in Cumberland about the interception of a treasonable message between Wigton and Brampton in which Salkeld was involved. This story may very well refer to the Jackson–Campbell letter, the subject of the first case history, above, and that the details have become crossed in the passage of time. In any case, it seems clear that it was Pattinson who made off with the vital message, and in fact fetched up at Marbury, his goal.

Thus, there is not one definite end to this case history. There are three ends. The charges against the earl and his son were eventually not proceeded with. The old earl died shortly afterwards (in his eightieth year) to be duly succeeded by Lord Buttevant. As regards Pattinson, although he was specifically excepted from the procedure of 'lotting' (the ten-to-one chance for a formal trial), yet the ministry did not quite know what exactly to do with him. A note among the secretary of state's papers—presumably a rough memorandum or reminder for the cabinet council—queries: 'What orders about . . . Persons in the custody of Messengers and particularly the person that went to Lord Barrymore's with the Note from the Pretender'. The Habeas Corpus Act stood suspended until 20th November and parliament had been prorogued. If therefore Pattinson could hold out until that date, the authorities would have then either to formulate a specific charge against him or else release him. A further note in the secretary of state's papers says of him: 'Discharged Nov 12th'. In point of fact, parliament met on 18th November and its first act was to suspend the Habeas Corpus Act once more (this time until 20th February)—but before 18th November Pattinson was gone.

As to Salkeld, it was recorder Gilpin who had informed against him, and had kept in touch with Cumberland about him even before the duke arrived in Carlisle with the army. Cumberland, in his turn, had 'mentioned' Salkeld in 'some of his late despatches' to the secretary of state, and when he did arrive in Carlisle he ordered brigadier Bligh to arrest him. Cumberland then returned to London and later went to take command in Scotland after the battle of Falkirk, but without preferring any actual charge against Salkeld, thus leaving him to the care of the recorder—who had nothing by way of tangible evidence. During the suspension of the Habeas Corpus Act Salkeld had no redress in law. From actual imprisonment he was, however, later released on bail.

In London the 'solicitor for carrying on criminal prosecutions' said as late as the end of July 1746 that

There is one, Henry Salkeld, a Prisoner at Carlisle who seems to be a person of Consequence if we could get evidence to convict him, which I have been endeavouring at for some time.[44]

He had found that this man Pattinson, his servant, was in custody in London and could provide sufficient evidence to convict his master—*if he would*. He asked, therefore, for Pattinson to be re-examined.[45] Five or six weeks later, however, nothing further had come to light.

Philip Cartaret Webb, the crown solicitor conducting the trials at Carlisle, said that by the time of the expiration of the suspension of the habeas corpus procedure, the various prisoners who had been confined without any supporting evidence would be able to sue for release. 'Should they bring their Habeas Corpus and obtain their Discharge that way, it would not be so honourable for the Government and might make bad Impression.' It would be more creditable to the ministry to release them forthwith, with or without bail. And among these was Henry Salkeld, one of three 'that had Centinels at the Doors of their own Houses'.[46] In any case, at the beginning of September 1746, Salkeld petitioned the judge of assize.[47] Such a judge would in his *oyer* and *terminer* capacity 'hear and determine' the cases brought before him; in his further capacity of 'gaol delivery' he could (if no specific act prevented him) discharge from custody any prisoner, in any gaol he was 'delivering', who was *not* brought before him, if the evidence against him was not *then* sufficient to indict him. At this point of time neither the military, nor the recorder who had 'informed' to them, could offer any evidence and, notwithstanding that the Habeas Corpus Act stood suspended, Salkeld was released—to die shortly after in exile.

The fourth and last of our brief case histories will be that of Dudley Bradstreet, or 'captain' Bradstreet as he called himself and preferred to be called. Whilst on his one and only agent/double agent assignment he hinted to the Hanoverians that the Stuarts had hinted to him that in recognition of his having saved their army from destruction at Derby they might appoint him their ambassador to France (non-French speaking), in which case he could expect to be addressed as 'Excellency'. In the meantime, however, he would settle for 'captain'.

His highly idiomatic autobiography, *The Life and Uncommon Adventures of Captain Dudley Bradstreet*, was published in Dublin in 1755,[48] 'for the Author', and between the highly picaresque *full Account of his and Others Amours* and his very discursive narrative as a lottery pusher, bottle-conjurer, magician and fortune teller, he wedged a characteristic account of 'His being employ'd in Secret Services by the M---stry of G---t B-----n in the late Rebellion'. This *Life* claimed to be 'The most Genuine & Extraordinary, perhaps, ever published'. This was partly true: it was the 'Most . . . Extraordinary perhaps'. He tells us that his early background was in Templemore in the county of Tipperary, but does not specifically lay claim to any direct association with Blarney in the county of Cork. Many will see in his story—given the demands of the contemporary genre of each period respectively—many of the characteristics of, and a number of parallels with, the accounts still produced in response to the current vogue in 'security memoirs' and spy fiction.

After a series of what he calls 'amours', direct and vicarious, Bradstreet turns from an ingenious but illicit mode of selling gin in London, to being ponce to a doctor of 'about sixty-five Years old, that had commonly about twenty-five women in Keeping'. Because Bradstreet managed to double-cross one of this twenty-five (who was contriving to swear a rape against the doctor with intent to blackmail) 'Dr M-------d' rewarded him handsomely and also made him 'Governor and Judge of the first Seraglio in England'. In the year before the rising, however, Bradstreet perceived the doctor's friendship to cool somewhat, and the doctor, wanting to be rid of him, recommended him 'to get into the Government's Service as an Agent or Spy', telling him that he 'might call on him for a Character if required'. Bradstreet had earlier thought of a number of ways of making easy money, but never of that one. After treating the readers of his *Life* to a discourse upon the practice and the philosophy of espionage,[49] Bradstreet says,

In the midst of [Britain's] foreign and domestic Troubles, by Advice of my Friends, I offered my Services to the Duke of Newcastle at the Cockpit; his Grace ordered me to call at his House next Day, which I did and sent my name to him.[50]

Andrew Stone, joint private secretary to the secretary of state, 'asked me many Questions about my Station in Life, and if any Persons of Consequence knew me'. Bradstreet thereupon gave him a couple of names, including that of the doctor 'that had commonly about twenty-five women in Keeping'. Much after the fashion of current days, apparently, the would-be spy was altogether insufficiently screened; even his references were, presumably, not taken up—and thereby hangs a tale—and within a week Bradstreet was on his first espionage assignment. His first taxiing along the runway was in the area of Hackney, Highgate and Hampstead, gleaning unconsidered trifles from the harvest of migratory Irish (catholic) workers who used to come to England at that time of the year for the other harvest. This pleased the joint private secretary to the secretary of state 'greatly', and in his next run he was fully airborne—a conspiracy to capture the Tower of London. The discovery of this plot, of which the authorities had known nothing, understandably carried Bradstreet, the spy, direct to the secretary of state himself.[51]

Already by 11th November Bradstreet was able to write to his principals: 'what I am informed greatly concerns all that are well affected to King George'. He went on: 'I am told the Rebels are in England'—a piece of information the ministers almost certainly, by this time, had picked up from yesterday's papers. News released from Whitehall on the 5th, and published in the *Gazette* on the 9th said they were marching for the border and 'their intention was to proceed directly into England'. A news release of the 9th said they 'were believed to be by that time near Carlisle'. Bradstreet followed this scoop with some advance information on the intended strategy the coming campaign would take. 'They will avoid fighting the King's troops as much as possible and will very soon march as fast as they can to London and for that purpose will draw as much of the King's force from London as near as they can to the North of England and then give them the slip.'[52] The ministry's attention was specifically drawn by this astute agent to 'a book published very lately called *Killing No Murder*, addressed to Oliver Cromwell. I hear the Intent of it is against our King and Government.' The agent apparently only *heard* 'the Intent of it', although it was openly available at the London booksellers. The ministry 'I know, will form a good Judgment of these hints I give'. A last word on his sources: Bradstreet said he had for the last couple of years received advance intelligence from the same channels and 'always saw it come to pass what I was told'. Naturally enough, the joint private secretary to the secretary of state said to Bradstreet, the spy, that 'those persons ought to be taken up who were in the secrets of the Rebels'. And naturally enough, Bradstreet the spy said to the joint private secretary to the secretary of state that it was precisely those who 'were the channels of my Intelligence, and that I could no longer be useful if any Notice was taken of them'. Bradstreet then tells us in his *Life* rather too tall a story about a collusive frame-up, in which he offered to be charged, was in fact convicted and actually committed to prison for no other reason than to appear to give credulity to his being 'agin the government'[53]—and thereby hangs another tale.

According to Bradstreet's *Life*, 'the Rebels [had now] advanced as far as Manchester, which put most degrees of People in London in the Greatest of confusion and Consternation'—all, of course, except the lords of the ministry, whose courage in the universal panic remained unshaken. It was in their quiet confidence amidst the general consternation that, again naturally enough, the ministry sent for Dudley Bradstreet. 'They desired I might write a Scheme of my own to them, to know how I could serve the Public.' He says he wrote and suggested two schemes: one, that he 'would go among the Rebels, and endeavour to make a Mutiny that would ruin the Pretender's affairs'—'the Danger to be mine, the Success theirs' (that is, the *ministry's*)—and the other, he says, 'that I would take one of the finest Women in London with me and, as the Young Chevalier was reported to be a Man of Gallantry, she might perhaps get into his Confidence'.[54] The version, however, contained in the state papers is not quite in agreement with that in his *Life & Adventures*. Bradstreet's letter is dated 29th November, and opens: 'You ordered me yesterday [that was the 28th, and the insurgents were not yet in fact in Manchester] to write in what manner I wo'd serve the King and Government wch I now do.' What he proposed here was that he could

be soe recommended to the pretended Regent, now at the head of the Rebels as to know a good deal of their intentions and strength and perhaps may be commissioned by him to go to France or Ireland wch shall all be made known to your Grace to make what use you please.[55]

In the suggestion, however, of his going to France as a double agent, it apparently slipped his memory, although he admitted it later, that he knew no French; the suggestion about 'the finest Woman in London' must have slipped his memory altogether at the time—for him to remember only about ten years later. As an alternative to going to the jacobite camp and procuring a commission to France or Ireland, Bradstreet had another suggestion —not 'the finest Woman in London'—'but there is another way much more essential wch is to have a Watchful Eye on the Citty of London and out parts'. For the last two years he had made it his business to resort to 'Coffee houses, Taverns, Ale houses and other assembleys and by a Correspondence with the Romish Clergy and gentlemen who have French Denisions'.[56] [This remark was to come home to him later]. He added, with his own characteristic modesty, that there was not a private man in London who could equal his intelligence in these matters and he was 'of oppinion' that 'no Conspiracy of any Consequence' would be possible but that he could give the ministry 'timely notice of it if Employed'. A last word: 'Intelligence of this kind has often saved Empires from ruin'.[57]

This fustian certainly impressed the secretary of state—which might be read as indicating that the top secretariat and their ministers were no less gullible, over two centuries ago, than some of their counterparts appear to be today. Bradstreet said they gave him a pass, a hundred pounds, a watch-word ('Oliver Williams') and an assurance that they would take care of his family 'if any thing happened'. He said,

I saw Mr St[on]e write a Letter to his Royal Highness the Duke of C[umber]land, which was signed by the Duke of N[ew]castle, importing that he had sent a Man amongst the Rebells upon whose Courage and Integrity he must rely; that Oliver Williams was the Word.[58]

A copy of the letter Bradstreet refers to is among the state papers. It is dated 1st December, from Newcastle to Cumberland, marked 'private'. It was to say that there was 'a Person whose real name is Broadstreet' [sic] who 'is conversant with the jacobites'. (Incidentally, it might perhaps be noted that Bradstreet had never at any time produced anything to anybody, except his own word, to prove that he was in any way 'conversant with the jacobites'.) Newcastle went on: he 'has often given me Intelligence relating to them'. We have already seen what must pass, then, for 'intelligence'. Newcastle went on further that Bradstreet sets out tomorrow for the jacobite camp, and if Cumberland would send any person there he could rely upon, 'in a countryman's Coat', inquire for Bradstreet, and then speak to him in private by the name of 'Oliver Williams', Bradstreet would acquaint the commander-in-chief 'with all the Discoveries he shall have been able make of the Motions and Designs of the Rebels'. And then, somewhat lamely perhaps, although he was 'far from being sure that this will be of any Service' to the commander-in-chief, yet 'at a Time like this nothing ought to be omitted'.[59]

Bradstreet received a pass as a private gentleman going to Ireland by way of Chester ('where the Rebels were supposed to be going'), and a warrant for post-horses. He thereupon made his will, 'buried an hundred Pounds I had to spare in a Cellar', gave a party in a local tavern to various of his cronies, and set off at 10 p.m. on Monday, 2nd December, from the 'Swan' in Holborn. He was at Dunstable by four next morning and stayed there until nine. From there he left for Northampton in a stage, in company with two others, one of whom professed to be an officer in Cumberland's army. From Northampton they set out that afternoon with a guide ('I believe not nine Years old') who led them astray that night, 'which was very dark, for near five Hours, upon a Moor and Heath', but the following morning they set out for Coventry.[60] By this time the government spy suspected that his travelling companion was a jacobite spy. The latter professed to be a captain in Ligonier's horse, had been in the French service, but refused to show his papers. 'If he is an Enemy he is a very great one, and if not Employed by our Government, is a quarter Master General for the Rebels'. At Coventry, therefore, Bradstreet slipped away from him and denounced him to the mayor and magistrates, who arrested him accordingly. He was working, he said, on the principle that it is better to get twenty friendly persons thus arrested 'than lett one enemy go to the Rebels'.[61]

That day (Wednesday, 4th December) Bradstreet got a post-horse for Lichfield but failed to reach the town that night. He was, however, so he said, able to wait upon the duke of Richmond, commanding the cavalry, at Lichfield before 11 a.m. on Thursday the 5th. Cumberland himself arrived at Lichfield at 3 p.m. that day, and when Bradstreet presented himself Cumberland said 'that he had heard a great character of me, and that now was my Time to fulfill it'. According to Bradstreet, Cumberland said that he 'dreaded the consequences' of the jacobite army getting to Derby 'without his being able to force them to Battle'. Bradstreet thereupon gave the commander-in-chief (according to his own version) some very good strategic and tactical advice about the disposition of the army, horse and foot, and about troop movements and commissariat. Cumberland, however, begged Bradstreet more importantly to proceed direct to the rebel camp, 'to delay them but twelve Hours'—and name his own conditions.[62]

On Thursday, 5th December, therefore, 'past four o'Clock in the Afternoon', Bradstreet set out from Lichfield to Derby,[63] with 'the Litchfield Post-boy with me for a Guide'. On 'the darkest Night I ever remember' the post-boy dared not approach nearer to Derby than two miles. Bradstreet then threw away his warrant for the post-horses and his pass to Ireland and entered the town, displaying 'as much of my Lace as I conveniently could' and fretted his charger to create respect. In a short while one of the rebels seized his rein.

I told the Fellow that I was a Man of Quality come to serve the Prince Regent, and would be followed by all my Friends, if my Usage was good, and desired to be brought to the Prince's Quarters directly.[64]

Naturally, the Scotsman took the Englishman for a lord. They showed him, without any more ado, into the company of the jacobite leaders, the duke of Perth, Lord Kilmarnock, Sullivan, Colonel Roy Stuart and the others. As is, of course, very well known, the insurgent army at this point of time was nearer to London than the government army sent out to defend it. Posing now as a jacobite English nobleman, Bradstreet professed to be able to provide really reliable military intelligence not otherwise available to the insurgents. He had come through Northampton, Colehill and Lichfield. He knew for a fact, so he said he said, that as soon as the jacobite force moved south from Derby towards London, Cumberland with eight or nine thousand foot at Lichfield planned to cut off any retreat north; the duke of Richmond with his cavalry planned to attack their western flank as it lay exposed; and another army of no less than eight or nine thousand men, commanded by Hawley or Ligonier lay still between them and London. It was annihilation or retreat. ('Observe that there was not 9 men at Northampton to oppose them', much less nine thousand.) 'For this Report to them, I am as certain as of my Existence, was the only Reason and Motive for that fortunate and dreaded Army (until then) to retreat, from which Period date their inevitable Ruin.'[65]

The chiefs withdrew with Charles Edward to council. Bradstreet was later called into the council 'and there asked the same Questions' and gave the same answers. Charles Edward said, 'That Fellow will do me more Harm than all the Elector's Army', and then to the council: 'You ruin, abandon and betray me if you don't march on', and then 'shut the door in a Passion'. However, 'I had them all on my side of the Question, except Cameron of Locheil and Colonel Sullivan, both which were for marching to London'. Bradstreet, alias Williams (and now also alias Macdonald) spent the evening drinking with the jacobite lords and chiefs, until he heard that his plot had been successful —they were to retreat from Derby.

He had saved his country.

Say rather that he, an Irishman, had saved England from the Scots.

Incidentally, on the first day of their retreat from Derby, because of his influence with their council, he saved the life of Captain Vere, another government spy.[66] When the retreating force reached Standish in Lancashire, he chanced to quarter at a house where the curate lodged, and 'felt his Pulse as to our Cause'. He prevailed upon him to send, secretly, expresses to both Newcastle and Cumberland, 'to inform them that Oliver Williams told him the Rebels were marching to Carlisle and that the Army would soon after divide'.[67] It is certainly difficult to conceive what a Scottish army might be doing marching northwards through Standish if it were not bound for Carlisle. But Edward Smally, curate of Standish, had more to communicate than that. He was to inform His Grace that on their arrival at Derby the rebels had been 'for marching within three Hours, directly for London; with a full Purpose to throw into Confusion and sack the City'. But, as fortune would have it, Oliver Williams arrived in Derby just in the nick of time and 'threw himself into the Hands of the Rebels'. 'Their Prince was very urgent [i.e. pressing] for advancing', but Oliver Williams '[observed] to them that there actually was an Army of 10,000 Men at Northampton' [a recent increase of one or two thousand] and therefore a council was called and 'it was at last resolved on to retreat'. Oliver Williams had saved England. Furthermore, Oliver Williams was 'dertermin'd to carry them back to Carlisle, and in the meanwhile to foment amongst them such Discontents and Divisions as may be happily Instrumental towards rescuing the Nation from any further Fear . . .' He passed on through the curate, again with his characteristic modesty, that 'nothing is resolved on amongst them w'out his Privity'. The curate knew all this for the truth—for Oliver Williams himself had told him.[68]

From Standish they moved northwards to Preston and there Lord Kilmarnock informed him that Secretary Murray wanted him immediately. He was now told that it had been decided to send him out as a spy, to spy against the English—his dream of double agent come true—'to learn where the Duke of Cumberland's and Wade's Armies were, likewise those of Hawley and Ligonier, or if they had joined the Duke'. Bradstreet thereupon made south, met the curate again at Standish, and Cumberland at Wigan. From Wigan he wrote to the secretary of state, giving the letter itself to Fawkener, Cumberland's military secretary, and travelled post to London.[69] On his arrival in London, he naturally expected, if not a hero's welcome, at least some recognition of the fact that he and he alone (he, an Irishman) had saved England from the Scots. On 17th December, according to his own story, he was shown into the presence of the premier himself and other lords of the council, to report direct about his adventures, how he saved England, and so on. A great shock, however, awaited him. According to his *Life*, the duke of Newcastle 'called me aside, and took a Letter out of his Pocket, which signified to his Grace that I was a Papist; I assured him the Contrary, and that I believed it was wrote out of Malice or Envy and hoped that his Grace would not regard it'.[70]

All this, however, is not quite what he admitted in correspondence with Andrew Stone next day, which for some reason he does not mention in his *Life*, and which is apparently unknown to his more recent editor. Bradstreet said that the last fortnight had given him greater pleasure than any part of his earlier life—and for the great pleasures of his earlier life, see his *Life*, including a 'full Account of his and others Amours'. He was, however, yesterday 'much shocked' when Newcastle produced a paper stating that he had a criminal record—perhaps his reference had now been taken up from the doctor 'that had commonly about twenty-five Women in Keeping'—had served two months' imprisonment for keeping a disorderly house, and was in any case a papist convict. It is particularly to be noticed that he did not say in his defence what he said in his *Life*, namely, that he himself had been a consenting party to a frame-up to get himself imprisoned *for the good of the cause*. The charge had not been suspicion of treasonable practices but keeping a disorderly house. He did not speak of a collusive action, but of a certain 'Malicious insinuation' and an 'incensed Bench and Jury'. In any case, he denies he got two months: it was '14 days and fined 40 shillings'.[71]

All this, however, put an entirely different complexion upon affairs, and he speaks now, not of the hero's welcome he had so confidently expected, but of being kept 'from sight of a beloved wife and family after soe dangerous an Expedition'. He was now under some official restraint. According to his *Life* he says,

The Ministry were greatly embarrassed at the Time to know a young Gentleman that was a Prisoner in the Tower, whom they suspected to be the second Son to the Pretender; in order to come at a Knowledge of him, it was agreed to keep me from the Sight of all my Acquaintances for some time, and send me a Prisoner to the Tower, to discover who he was.[72]

A week later he certainly wrote to Andrew Stone, with regard to 'being here so long', although he admitted he was being 'very well used',

The thought of seeing My wife and family, which I always banished from me when among Rebels as base and un manly, is even now troublesome to me while it is your pleasure I should stay here or go elsewhere, but having nothing to do was always the greatest pain to my Mind.[73]

He tried to bid for another trick in the spy game. He now remembered—but could not recall whether he had told Stone or not—that

The Rebels intended to send 20 or 30 men only to Connaught, a province in Ireland, and most of them papists, to raise a Rebellion there. One Gordon [in the Rebel Army when I was there[74]] who was in King George's Army in Ireland, was to be the most active man in this affair.[75]

Also he wanted to report that

it was agreed between the Rebells and their friends in London when the Rebels were to be near to London to raise all the reports of the French army being Landed near London and report every other thing that wo'd Occasion tumults.[76]

But all that now was stale kale: the insurgents had left England last week.

He wrote to Andrew Stone on the day before Christmas day and the day after. On the day after, he complained about 'being kept here 10 days instead of 2 or 3'—although 'under no Manner of restraint'. He would be willing to confine himself 'in one of the cells of Newgate [or some other place like it[77]] for ever' unless he regained the ministry's goodwill. 'I do not want to know what I am destined for': he wanted only to see Andrew Stone or the duke.[78] According to his own story, when the young gentleman in the Tower was identified as Derwentwater, Bradstreet was sent to 'Lodgings in Pall Mall about a fortnight' and then released, to find himself 'almost ruined'.[79] This, however, is not borne out by the state papers. Again and again he wrote pleading, threatening and intriguing letters: pleading with them for release or at least to be informed more specifically as to his offence; threatening them with the rebels' return; intriguing with them for a new assignment or some further naive or ingenious piece of espionage. His grace could send him

to Dover, or anywhere else most likely for the French to land, among whom I believe there is some of my acquaintances, w'ch I wo'd renew and do them what harm I co'd.[80]

Or, a more ingenious one, this:

If his Grace pleases to send me on to Edinburgh, no nearer the Rebels, there I could get proper persons to carry letters to those Lords [and chiefs[81]] I was most intimate with, but I shall only write to 2 or 3, but will insinuate to them two or three that I held a Correspondence with most of the Chief Officers and privy counsel. the Messenger I send shall know from me that I only send one letter by one Messenger, but I will take care that this Messenger shall see several letters upon my table wch I never intend to send, some directed to the Duke of Perth, some to Lord Elcho, Ogilvie, Coll. Sullivan and others. if the letters I do send are revealed and what the Messenger saw it will occasion shocking Mistrust wch is the certain forerunner of the ruin of the Army.[82]

His espionage may or may not have been very impressive, but even the highest in the ministry must have realized that his understanding of military strategy was really not very profound.

The Rebels when they have increased their numbers Sufficiently, if they can, will return with fire and sword and attack either Carlisle or Newcastle, wch ever is the weaker.[83]

Five and a half weeks after Newcastle had faced him with the charges of having served time for keeping a disorderly house and with being a papist convict, Bradstreet wrote plaintively to Andrew Stone:

If it be thought convenient to confine me for any long time, or till the war is over, I beg it might be in this man^r. that is, to be sent aboard one of his Majesty's Ships of War, for never more will see home wth out your Goodwill. I wo'd not be so restless if I had but any answer from you.[84]

Although, in due course, Bradstreet was released from this restraint, he failed to extract from either Andrew Stone or the secretary of state any payment for his late services as a spy. He pleaded that if he could not receive any pay as such, at least he deserved his expenses actually incurred. The official response was completely unsympathetic. Being Bradstreet, he tired of dealing with such small fry as the secretary of state; he petitioned the king direct. Towards the end of February he made it plain to the king that he had been 'among the Rebels in Derby and in their Councels for nine days after . . . while I was with them I did yr Majesty what service I co'd. That in this time I spent £204 in yr Majesty's Service and am not yet paid that Expence.'[85] The £204 expenses seems somewhat extravagant; the £120 he admits later receiving[86] seems somewhat generous.

In any case, there was the £100 that he buried.

Or was there?

One cannot forbear to compare the informational yield of official espionage with that of the amateur get-together-cum-postmaster service, originated by some chaps concerned about turnpiking a piece of road in Cumberland.

This paper opened with an example of espionage provided by Michael Hughes, the London volunteer with Cumberland's army. It might, perhaps, appropriately close with another. On the day when the army halted at Nairn (nearby Culloden) 'a lad of seventeen Years of Age was [taken] for being a Rebel Spy'. He was thereupon condemned to be 'hanged in the Camp'. However,

A Scots Kirk Minister, by good Fortune hearing of this Affair, acquanted His Royal Highness that he [the spy] had only lately been with the Rebels, and was naturally but a simple Youth whom they deluded away. Whereupon the Duke, according to his usual Goodness, sent immediately to have his Life spared.

The reprieve, however, had come late—the poor lad had already been hanged. He had, in fact, 'hung about ten Minutes when the Reprieve came'. They decided nonetheless to cut the lad down.

The Executioner in cutting him down carefully let him fall to the Ground, the Gallows being very high; but he was young and strong; he was let Blood and came to Life, though much disordered in his Senses when the Army went away.[87]

Notes

[1] P. 32.

[2] Intercalated.

[3] SP Dom. 69/47 enc.

[4] Not in Cumberland a division of the city, but a hundred of the county.

[5] Cumb. QSR, Easter 1746, petitions, 90 (of John Barnes, high constable of Cumberland ward; Jarvis, *Jac. Risings*, 262).

6 SP Dom. 69/47 enc.

7 *Ibid.*

8 *Ibid.* 69/47.

9 As to whom, see Paper 22, p. 266.

10 SP Dom. 69/47 enc. and Cumb. QSMB, 1740–7, pp. 325 and 364, and Cumb. QSR, Epiphany 1746 (Cockermouth), recognizances. (I am indebted for part of this information to Mr B. C. Jones, Joint Record Office, Carlisle Castle.)

11 Examination: SP Dom. 73/17 enc. (or 35); Hudson's information, 73/17 enc. (or 37).

12 Leroid's information: 73/17 enc. (or 35).

13 Hudson's information: SP Dom. 73/17 enc. (or 37).

14 *Ibid.*

15 It is of note that the letter reporting the facts to the secretary of state, signed by four of the examining magistrates, is endorsed: 'Deputy Lieutenants'. SP Dom. 73/17 (or 33).

16 SP Dom. 73/17 enc. (or 34).

17 *Ibid.* 73/17 (or 33).

18 Clarke nb.

19 *Scots Magazine* (September 1746), viii, p. 437.

20 Cumb. QSMB (Easter, 1746), 328.

21 Clarke nb.

22 *Ibid.*

23 *Ibid.*

24 Cumb. QSMB, 1746, 309.

25 Cumb. QSR, Epiphany, 1745–6, 14.

26 List of Light Horse, 1 (dorse).

27 SP Dom. 85/310.

28 *Carlisle in 1745* (1846), 259–63.

29 H. and A. Tayler, *1745 and After* (1938), 96.

30 H.MSS.C. XL, Rvii, p. 328.

31 Newcastle MSS (cab. minutes), ff. 71–2.

32 He desired to be admitted to bail, but this was initially refused (Newcastle MSS (cab. minutes), f. 77); he was later called, further examined and admitted to bail, in the sum of £15,000 (£5,000 for himself, and £2,500 each for four other sureties. *Ibid.* f. 82).

33 In the eighteenth century sense, not in haste, but in confusion.

34 Buttevant's examination, SP Dom. 74/32 (or 100).

35 Examining justices, *ibid.* 74/32 (or 92–3).

36 E.g. Add. MSS 23707, f. 439.

37 SP Dom. 74/11 (or 89 or 256).

38 *Ibid.* 85b (or 247).

39 *Ibid.* 91 (or 264).

40 *Ibid.* 91/216 (or 235).

41 *Ibid.* 78/1 (or 3).

42 *Ibid.* 39.

43 H. and A. Tayler, *op. cit.*, 96.

44 SP Dom. 89/133 (or 145).

45 *Ibid.* 85/310.

46 *Ibid.* 87/109.

47 *Ibid.* 87/65.

48 Reprinted, London, N.D. [1929], ed. G. S. Taylor. The page references that follow are to this latter edition, as being obviously the more accessible.

49 *Life*, 111–12.

50 *Ibid.* 112.

51 *Ibid.* 113–14.

52 SP Dom. 73/94 (or 278 or 273).

53 *Life*, 114–15.

54 *Ibid.* 116–17.

55 SP Dom. 75/70 (or 168 or 214).

56 *Ibid.* 75/70 (or 168 or 214).

57 *Ibid.*

58 *Life*, 117.

59 SP Dom. 75/3 (or 137), and Stowe MSS, 158, f. 203.

60 *Life*, 119–20.

61 SP Dom. 76/132 (or 124).

62 *Life*, 122.

63 In the 1929 edition the editor says, 'one or two trifling errors have been corrected', but says nothing about any errors being introduced. In this passage (p. 123, p. 139 in the 1755 edition) Bradstreet is made to say that 'the computed Miles from London to Derby are sixteen'. (Thus for Lichfield to Derby.)

64 *Life*, 124–5.

65 *Ibid.* 126–7.

66 Vere also had been despatched with £100. For this and earlier payments, from February 1744 to September 1745, of £150, see SP Dom. 76/32.

67 *Life*, 120–39.

68 SP Dom. 73/87 (or 261).

69 There was some dispute later as to whether he privately travelled post or as the secretary of state's prisoner.

70 *Life*, 138–40.

71 SP Dom. 77/84 (or 208).

72 *Life*, 140.

73 SP Dom. 78/36 (or 80 or 78).

74 Intercalated.

75 SP Dom. 78/36 (or 80 or 78).

76 *Ibid.*

77 Intercalated.

78 *Life*, 140.

79 *Ibid.* 140.

80 SP Dom. 80/72 (or 67).

81 Intercalated.

[82] SP Dom. 80/72 (or 67).
[83] *Ibid.* 80/1 (or 59).
[84] *Ibid.*
[85] Newcastle MSS, 32706, f. 209.
[86] *Life*, 118.
[87] *Narrative*, 36.

16 *Propaganda*

The political overtones of the *Beggar's Opera* are, of course, well known. The extent to which the theatre became a field for political propaganda during the decade between the *Beggar's Opera* and the Licensing Act—between 1728 and 1737—is a commonplace. It may very well be that with the franchise very restricted, parliament as yet unreformed, a fair number at least of the seats filled by 'arrangement' without any election, and some at least of such elections as *were* held, 'managed' in any case, the freer theatre could genuinely claim to be a truer barometer of political feeling than parliament itself or any parliamentary election. The theatre became, then, a place of political propaganda. One of the principal propagandists in the theatre, against both the king and the government, during the whole of that period and in the press for some time after, namely Henry Fielding, later withdrew entirely from the field of politics altogether, and stated and published his complete disgust with the government and the opposition alike. Yet, notwithstanding that he gave a solemn promise never again to publish a single word save over his own name, at the outbreak of the Forty-five he did in fact not only publish a number of anonymous propaganda pieces against the jacobite interest; he jumped to the defence of the ministry—whom almost no one else would defend—the selfsame government against which he had a year or two earlier turned with such utter moral disgust. He even entered the fray to defend the king whom earlier he had lampooned and ridiculed, some would say with cruel raillery. The story of this propaganda effort is, perhaps, worth following through, if only because it quite certainly provided at least the temporal background for

The notes and references are on pages 138–9

Tom Jones and almost certainly produced the circumstances for his appointment to the Bow Street magistracy.

Henry Fielding turned from the social comedy of *Love in Several Masques* (1728) and *The Temple Beau* (1730), to the burlesque of *The Author's Farce* and *Tom Thumb* (both 1730), and to the social satire of the *Coffee House Politician* (1730). It was at about this time that Walpole, impatient of all criticism, was alienating the goodwill of some of his fellow whigs in office, when the 'whigs out' (of office) were craftily intriguing against the 'whigs in' (office), and when in any case the prestige of the crown and the royal family had fallen to a fairly low level. According to one member of the ministry, John, Lord Hervey— Pope's Sporus ('that thing of silk, that thin white curd of Asse's Milk')—the attacks upon Walpole had come to be not only ungentlemanly, they were positively inhuman. 'For these attacks were frequently joined to all the Ribaldry that could cast odium, all the coarsest satire that could give Ridicule, and all the strongest Invective that could raise the Indignation of the People.' To all this the opposition spokesman could only reply, when at last they had encompassed his downfall, that the opposition had nothing to apologize for: public policy required that the king's first minister should be discredited. 'It was prudent necessary and wise to distress him in every respect.' Some of this prudent necessary wisdom makes rather poor reading now. Certainly it would be of no interest here, but for the fact that Fielding thrust himself into the midst.

It was in 1731 that Fielding entered the propaganda battle against 'the Great Man'. His attack took the form of a play depicting Walpole in his relationships with his ministerial colleagues, his mistress, the king and royal family. It was in addition a biting satire on the court and a broad burlesque of royalty. To account for the Hanoverians' pidgin English, the king was depicted as a little upstart Welsh squire trying to lord it over his English tenants; the scene was laid in 'Wales; North or South' and the piece was called *The Welsh Opera*. He later wrote a somewhat enlarged version of it—which may or may not have got the length of the stage—under the title *The Grub Street Opera*. The action in the squire's household consists entirely of two sets of intrigues, one within the (royal) family circle, and the other between the (ministerial) upper servants. It was essentially in contrast to the pidgin English of the un-English upstart squire that a scene in this ballad-opera would finish with the most English of all English songs—'The Roast Beef of Old England'. Not only the royal family but the ministry also had to withstand the slings and arrows of the outrageous Fielding. The various characters are only thinly disguised, and can in any case be directly identified by their christian names. Thomas, the gardener, looked after the fruits of the household. He was Thomas, duke of Newcastle, who in the ministry, by common knowledge, looked after the royal and other political patronage and in general 'managed' the elections for Walpole. In the play he had his eyes for ever on 'the fruits on the wall'. John the groom was John, Lord Hervey, Walpole's and the queen's go-between when something was being done behind the king's back. In the play he leaves the horses unattended to whet Robin the butler's knives; he neglects to muck-out his own stables in order to put some polish on the family plate which the butler has been fiddling. William the coachman is Pulteney, lately Walpole's colleague, now his rival. In the play he would drive so hard for his goal that the butler feared at times that he would turn the whole coach over and break master's neck and madam's into the bargain. Robin the butler was of course Robert Walpole, for to say 'Robin' is but to say 'robbin'.

As if all this were not sufficiently daring, the downfall of Walpole was directly predicted. When rumour had it that the family are about to discharge him, he consoles himself by saying that by petty theft of the family plate and glass and so on 'I have made a shift to get together a little comfortable subsistence', to last the rest of his days and 'if this storm blows over'. But 'I don't care to be *turn'd* away'—he would give notice himself and 'leave the family' and buy a little estate. This was a straight tip to Walpole to clear out whilst the going was good, and so long as audiences turned up at the Haymarket to applaud such palpable hits as these, the inference seemed clear. The ministry was stung into doing something. Some sort of action was taken against the New Theatre in the Haymarket and the company was dispersed in the summer of that year. Fielding had threatened in the prologue of the *Coffee House Politician* that 'the Great Man's title would not serve 'to save the great right honourable fool'. But he spoke truer than he knew when he said that vice had 'grown too great to be abused'. He had challenged 'the great man'—and found himself knocked out in the first round.

The spring of 1734—and the forthcoming general election— brought political propaganda back again into the news-sheets and the coffee-houses of the town. Already all sorts of political propaganda, broadsides ballads and prints, were being bandied round the town. The bribery corruption peculation jerryman- dering jobbery and place-hunting seemed to beckon Fielding back once more into political farce and satire. Back he came there- fore with a highly provocative ballad-opera entitled *Don Quixote in England*, first performed in the April of 1734. The play was almost certainly a re-worked early piece with election scenes, otherwise unconnected with the plot, worked in for the topical occasion. In the course of some adventures in England, Don Quixote is prevailed upon to stand for parliament, lest another candidate should be returned (by 'arrangement') unopposed. The borough would obviously lose the money that would otherwise be spent in corrupting its voters. As the mayor saw, with his high regard for the borough, the one thing the borough wanted above all things was to be 'corrupted'. It was entitled to it. 'The Roast Beef of Old England' returns; no wonder, as Boswell relates in his London Journal, that 'The Roast Beef of Old England' remained the rallying call of the popular element in the London theatre for the whole of the generation.

From the *Beggar's Opera* to *Don Quixote* the theatre was paying more and more attention to parliament. So likewise parliament was coming to pay more and more regard to the theatre. Efforts had already been made the year before *Don Quixote* to test the legality of producing plays without a licence at a non-patent theatre. A City quaker-vintner introduced a bill to clear the air, and al- though the bill was withdrawn it received wide attention. A print of the day, 'The Players' Last Refuge: or The Strollers in Distress', predicts the downfall of the theatre and the downfall of Fielding with it. It depicts a large open space where stood a theatre, and sitting in front of a half-ruined booth a number of well-known figures: Cibber the younger, attended by Despair and Poverty, supported to his grave by Harlequin, Orpheus

Falstaff and Hamlet. The chief mourners are Hippesley and Fielding. The quaker-vintner rides in triumph over the ruins of Troy, Punch's Opera, sausage-stalls and what not, and points to a black cloud overhanging the play-house. Below is engraved the doggerel:

> Mourn Smith-Field Muses, Mourn!
> Your Fall's decreed.
> Forth from the Fair the Hero stalks Dismay'd
> Doubtful to take ye Board or Learn a Trade
> F . . . . . . g whom once did Gods with nectar cheer
> Pawns his full Bottom wig for a pot of Beer.

In the British Museum copy, the word 'F . . . . . . g' is filled out in manuscript to read 'Fielding'.

This was in March 1735. But Fielding had not the slightest intention to pawn his full-bottom wig to buy a pot of beer. As a matter of fact, by the recent death of his mother-in-law, he had conveniently come into some money. Hitherto he had been merely a playwright of varying fortune. Now, he would go into management. He would take over the theatre in the Haymarket, the scene of some of his earlier successes, *Tom Thumb* and the *Welsh Opera*; he would form his own company of players and—here is the point—devote the whole organization to social satire and political propaganda in the service of the opposition. In his new capacity of opposition playwright Fielding chose the title of 'Pasquin'—Pasquin, the caustic wit. The first piece he brought out in his new role was entitled *Pasquin: a Dramatic Satire on the Times*, and certainly it took the town. Its structure, if it can be said to have had any structure, was a burlesque, satirizing the corrupt fashionable life of the time, the corrupt lawyer, the corrupt churchman and, most of all of course, the corrupt politician. Its success was immediate; so great in fact as to rival even the *Beggar's Opera*. Where in *The Author's Farce* Fielding had provided a stage author to point the drama during its rehearsal, in *Pasquin* he goes one better; he provides two plays within the play, one a comedy and the other a tragedy, the comedy of 'The Election', and the tragedy of 'The Life and Death of Common Sense'.

All this 'Comedy called the Election' and 'the Life and Death of Common Sense' hit off the public temper to a nicety. Pasquin and *Pasquin* were roaring successes. The piece played before numerous and enthusiastic audiences from all the fashionable squares, who would go again and again, and still find the theatre 'extreamly crowded'.[1] It brought to Fielding more profit than any earlier piece. It was obvious, however, that the public's chief interest was in the political scenes, and it was not long before an unofficial sixpenny key to the characters and allusions, *A Key to Pasquin*, was on open sale on the streets. Although Fielding was not by any means the first to declare war on Walpole—very far from it—he was the first to wage the war at a good profit. Pasquin himself, therefore, determined to go on from success to success, from political propaganda to more political propaganda.

He decided to write another piece, still in the vein of burlesque, in which he had made such a mark. It was loosely—very loosely —based on the annual reviews of occurrences and personages, contained in the so-called *Historical Registers* of the time. He called the new play *The Historical Register*. Even so, there was the familiar rehearsal of a farce, for 'when my politics come to a farce they very naturally lead me to the playhouse'. The principal government newspaper said that Fielding had impudently compared Walpole's government 'to the playing of a farce and kept the allegory throughout'.[2] Walpole—Quidam, 'a poor impudent fellow'—was depicted for all the town's disgust, as not only openly engaged in unashamed bribery, jobbery, peculation and corruption, duping even those whom he was buying, but also cheating his political friends as well as his political foes. On second thoughts, perhaps not, for in fact he had no *friends*—only 'friends'.

The play, like *Pasquin*, is of additional interest to the discerning in that there are ironies within ironies, and most of the thrusts have double points, one directed towards the theatre and the other towards politics. Some of the political points, however, could scarcely be missed, even by the most undiscerning, for Fielding provided a stage author to explain them to a stage critic. This further piece of political propaganda, this even bolder attack on Walpole and the government, was extremely daring and outspoken. *The Historical Register*, written only to be played as an after-piece, was fetching all the applause in the theatre. Fielding decided, therefore, as if he had not tempted fate enough already, to promote it to the main item and round it off with a tail-piece which should predict—indeed, depict—the fall of Walpole, how when the crunch at last came, his corrupted friends deserted him at his fall and left him to his miserable fate. This new piece—'a Merry Tragedy'—was called *Eurydice Hiss'd* and, like the earlier, contained theatrical as well as political satire. Poor actors come looking for places in Pillage's farce, but the public, led by Mr Honestus, an honest man, damns the whole show. Pillage's pillaging at last was over and Honestus found Pillage—the honest man found Walpole—too drunk to say 'Drunk'.

Such was the state of political feeling in London at the time that the two pieces, *The Historical Register* and *Eurydice Hiss'd*, were 'acting every night at the Haymarket to the most splendid audiences'; there was 'universal applause'.[3] Such political propaganda in the theatre was so outspokenly daring that something had need be done about it. It had now become something more than an attack—it was a challenge, and a challenge the ministry scarcely dared overlook. At this point of time someone might very well have written on the wall the warning words of the great master of latin comedy, Terrence: *Nimia illaec licentia profecto evadet in alequod magnum malum*— 'assuredly this extreme licentiousness will end in some great disaster'. In what may have been an inspired article, the ministerial organ seemed to point to the possibility of censorship,[4] but Fielding must have felt very confident that the government *dared* not introduce any sort of censor, for he went on to publish the text of *The Historical Register*, and aggravated his offence by insolently holding up Walpole to further mockery.

This could not be tolerated. Walpole looked round for an excuse to legalize a censor. To this end he professed to have had handed to him the text of a further play, a play which the Walpole faction have not hesitated to attribute to Fielding. There is in fact no evidence whatsoever that Fielding had anything whatever to do with the play—indeed, there is no evidence that there even was such a play. It has been altogether more credibly suggested that the whole affair was a frame-up. The supposed play was said to be entitled *The Golden Rump* and was more after the style of the *Grub Street Opera* than *The Historical Register* or *Eurydice Hiss'd*. If the text of the play was anything like the theme going the rounds at the time, it was a coarse indecent thing. There is a print of the period in the British Museum collection entitled the 'Festival of the Golden Rump'. It has the legend: *Rumpatur quisquis Rumpitur invidia*', and has been described as a satire of high political and most suggestive significance hardly to be equalled in the whole unique collection. On the altar sits the idol—none other than the king—and what a mumbo-jumbo is there. The queen is his high priestess and Walpole his chief magician. It is the magician, of course, who looks after all the offertories brought to the altar. No wonder Walpole can outwit the king; for where the magician is served by a magic wand, the king has for a head no more than a block of wood. But where Walpole has a silver belly, the king has a golden rump—hence *The Golden Rump*—and all the toadies in the show queue up to lick the king's backside—to kiss the royal bum.

Walpole professed to be shocked, and presumably it took a lot to shock Walpole. With great parliamentary adroitness—and in that, at least, he had no master—he slipped a Licensing Act[5] through at the end of the session, and Fielding found himself legislated off the stage. Fielding's reaction was characteristic. He uttered not one syllable of complaint. In the November of 1737 he entered himself in the Middle Temple as a student of law, at the mature age of 30. He had a great ambition now to succeed as a lawyer; he applied himself most assiduously to his studies, and was in fact called to the bar as early as June of 1740.

Even so, he was doing a certain amount of journalistic work. In particular, he became editor and part-owner of a new opposition, tri-weekly newspaper, *The Champion*, in which he kept going, with all his old verve, his propaganda against Walpole and his corruption. At long last there came a time, in the autumn of 1741, when the Walpole stock was on the fall and when it looked that Fielding's propaganda had at last paid off. The goal that Fielding had worked for so hard and so long was actually in sight. Walpole was as good as out. Instead of clearing out, however, he offered to do a deal with the opposition; and immensely to Fielding's surprise—and disgust—his friends, 'the patriots', whose praises he had been singing in season and out of season, particularly lately in *The Champion*, whose fight he had been fighting, the men whom he had been championing, these men—instead of spurning Walpole's overtures—*did a deal with him*. Fielding was disgusted. Indignant and disillusioned—despondent, dispirited and depressed—he dipped his pen in vinegar and gall and, in *The Opposition: A Vision*, told the opposition what he thought of them. In this vision he saw himself as a long-sided long-eared ass, braying beyond all other asses, labouring through the mud and mire lugging to town the opposition waggon; and in the result, merely so that some of the idle passengers on the waggon might desert it for the Walpole stage-coach, the ministerial band-waggon—leaving as provender for such asses as he only the thistles that grew on the wayside. He severed all connection with *The Champion*—and those he had been championing.

It was in this mood of disenchantment that he wrote that great work of ironical genius, *Jonathan Wild the Great*. This ironical prose epic is a political satire the irony of which is remarkably accute and superbly sustained. The subtle Lucianic irony of the theme, the sardonic humour of the details, the caustic wit and corrosive sarcasm running through it all, and indeed the immense energy of the whole, is so devastating that those who have brought to it some knowledge of contemporary affairs have declared it to equal, if not to surpass, anything to be found in *Gulliver's Travels*, the *Modest Proposal* or the *Tale of a Tub*. In *Jonathan Wild*, the thief-taker and thief, the provocateur and double-crosser, runs his own Tammany. Tories and whigs, rory-tories, wags, wigs and prigs, they are all one. Poli-tics is poly-tricks; it is all poly-trickery by poly-tricksters. It is all one big racket. Even the rack-sters and the poly-tricksters themselves can distinguish each other only by their habit of wearing hats, and the hat in the behaviour of a gentleman is never worn at court, and in any case the best hat was the one with the most swag in it. The 'boss' kept order in his gang by the simple ex-pedient of dubbing this or that one of his under-racketeers to be 'captain', and giving another some bit of ribbon to wear. If the sceptic should ask where the *substance* lay behind all this shadow, the answer is that one is sufficiently rewarded by what procures honour and precedence *in the gang*, without enquiry into substance; 'Nay, if a Title or a Feather be equal to this Purpose, they *are* the Substance and not mere Shadows.'[6] When at last the great boss is brought to his fall—and it was this that reflected Fielding's current mood—an upstart boss within a couple of days is strutting round in all the late boss's trappings, vouchsafing no other apology than that they fit him better.

Fielding had done with political propaganda. Fundamentally shocked, profoundly disgusted, he left politicians to stew in their own hateful juice. In 1742 he got together anything he had of any literary value, published it by subscription in three volumes of *Miscellanies*, and determined to devote himself henceforth exclusively to the law. As a lawyer, he rode the western circuit and attended the courts at Westminster Hall and there is evidence[7] that he had early succeeded in winning the goodwill, and indeed the respect, of his fellow lawyers at bench and bar.

Then, there fell upon him the cruellest blow of all his chequered career. A certain scurrilous attack, an intensely bitter satire upon lawyers and their profession, an attack upon certain personally identifiable respected members of the bench and bar, was published in the form of an anonymous pamphlet, *The Causidicade*. Who was its author was a mystery—and still is; but published at precisely the time when Henry Fielding, late anonymous past-master in satire raillery and irony, now a briefless lawyer—said to be hard-pressed for money—the piece was fathered upon Fielding. Fielding protested, of course. But he had protested—ironically— before. It all made it appear that with incredible ingratitude, he had grossly and spitefully abused his position in order to lampoon and mock anonymously those very men to whom, over his own name, he had acknowledged his debt for their being among the first to help him into the profession of law. He complained, and complained most bitterly, that he had been accused, and falsely accused, of being the author of half the scurrility, bawdry, treason and blasphemy that these few years had produced. He now knew too well the reward that fame confers upon authors to endeavour any longer to obtain it; 'nor was the world ever more unwilling to bestow the glorious envied prize of the laurel or the bay' than he would be to receive it. The Muses, he found, were 'the most infamous harlots'. He would follow them no more.

He would follow the Muses no more.

Assiduously he had studied the law. Assiduously he had applied himself to the texts. He had commenced to gather himself together the nucleus of a valuable law library and was studying, copying, annotating the collections of statutes-at-large and the rare early texts.[8] Clearly he had his eyes on the bench. It was in the law that he would succeed. The year was 1744.

The next year was 1745. Early in the course of the rising it became perfectly clear to the ministry, if only from the apparently effortless capture of Edinburgh and the easy victory of Preston-pans, that there was no enthusiasm in Scotland for the house of Hanover. Scarcely a hand had been raised against the jacobites. No chief had raised his clan against them; no lord had raised his tenants; no county had raised its militia; no town its trained bands. Only Edinburgh had raised a corps of volunteers, and of that the less said the better. Fielding, writing in retrospect and looking back to the time of the fall of Carteret and to the formation of the Broadbottom Administration, said he saw a ministry struggling against every disadvantage and handicap it could be their lot to meet. Upon their first accession to power they found, so he said, the whole nation

immersed in an immense debt and torn and divided by faction; a mad man[9] pushing by every method to reinstate himself in power; many parties endeavouring to set their country in a blaze hoping from its ashes to produce each his own favourite pernicious scheme of government; all the heads of these parties satisfied with the highest probability of public ruin, provided they could but discover the lowest probability of converting it to their own private interest; and the whole body of the people debauched with luxury and licentiousness; their resentments fired with imaginery grievances, their hopes raised with vain expectations, surfeited with ease and desirous of *Change*.[10]

The state of public opinion at the time might perhaps be illustrated by any of the prints doing the rounds. One, for example, was entitled 'A Hint to the Wise' or 'The Surest Way with the Pretender'. The supporters of the parliamentary settlement are shown on one side opposed to the jacobite faction on the other. But even those who are opposed to jacobitism, who can see the 'Danger of Regency' and 'Liberty's only Friends', can still hold back and say, 'What a pass these men have brought us to', meaning the ministry, the ministry of Fielding's friends. The broad-bottom ministry, with drawn swords, appeal, 'Won't you fight for your Liberties?' only to receive such answers as, 'You told us we had none', and 'Have you made it worth fighting for?'

QUESTION: What, are your spirits sunk?
ANSWER: Yes, they are sunk.

The 'hint to the wise' is clearly enough expressed as good advice in bad verse—

> Be loyal, Britons, but be wise;
> And Stickle for your Liberties.
> Trust not the Men who oft have flinch'd;
> They'll ne'er compound but when they're pinch'd
> Deem equally your Foes those Birds of Prey,
> Who won't restore, and those who take away.

There can be little doubt that Henry Fielding, ardent controversialist that he was, a man who lived only for the struggle, must have itched to dash off, as he had dashed off in the old days, a reply to this, a rejoinder to that, a retort to the other. How 'Vinegar' of the old *Champion* days could have whetted and sharpened his tongue; how Hercules would have swung his mighty club. On exactly what account Fielding once more entered the fray cannot now be said. Perhaps a number of motives entered into a complex situation. One thing, however, is certain: from whatever motive, Fielding in the autumn of 1745 once more lunged into the field of political propaganda. The cause once taken up, absorbed a large part of his total energies for a period of about three years. He now undertook to defend against all comers not only the very politicians whom he had last viewed with despair and disgust, but also even the king, the little upstart un-English squire.

In the autumn of 1745, therefore, he quickly dashed off a number of pamphlets; one *A Dialogue between the Devil, the Pope and the Pretender*, an unblushing appeal to all that was worst in religious intolerance and hatred; another, *A Serious Address*, an altogether more dignified appeal to principles, reason and interest. A third was issued under the title, *A History of the Present Rebellion*, which was not a history at all in the modern sense, but a piece of intensive political propaganda. In addition he looked out an old anti-papistical play, *The Old Debauchees*, which had been written in the old days before the passing of the Licensing Act. Most critics can find little to say in its favour. It has been said of its unbridled licence that the strongest condemnation in our day is that it was condemned even in its own. According to the *Grub Street Journal* the piece met in 1732 with 'The universal detestation of the Town'. According to Fielding it played to 'great applause before a numerous audience in Continual good Humour and often in the highest Rapture of Approbation'. If the truth lies somewhere between these two extremes, doubtless it lies nearer the Grub Street end. It is, however, quite understandable how in the changed political circumstances of 1745 the public might be willing to listen to the stuff they could not tolerate in 1732.

A further instance, for example, of this sort of toleration could be found in one of Colley Cibber's rehashes of Shakespeare. During 1736 he had written and had actually rehearsed a piece which he entitled *Papal Tyranny in the Reign of King John*. He does not appear however to have brought it actually on the stage until February of 1745, when the threatened invasion might have been expected to create enough anti-papistical feeling to assure the play if not success, at least a hearing. The poet laureate however was only rebuked for having meddled with Shakespeare and the play had to be withdrawn. The actual landing, however, in 1745 completely changed the public's susceptibilities—and apparently its taste for Shakespeare—for on 8th February 1746 *Papal Tyranny* was revived and played at Covent Garden. Incidentally, the last part Colley Cibber the actor (poet laureate since 1730) played on the stage was that of Pandulph in *Papal Tyranny*, the papal legate who excommunicated John and persuaded the dauphin to invade England in the papal interest. Another anti-papistical play produced as a propaganda piece in London during the rising was Cibber's *Non-Juror*. Others with varying degrees of appositeness were, for example, Nat Lee's *Massacre of Paris*, which he wrote (query, for the Glorious Revolution?) between a couple of bouts of madness, and John Ford's *Perkin Warbeck*. The latter was a sympathetic study of that pretender, sometimes said to be the finest piece of historical drama outside that of William Shakespeare. Its supposed topicality was the welcome given in Scotland to an imposter from the continent who pretended to the crown of England. Stuart Scotland invaded England with the avowed intention of setting the upstart on the English throne, but later deserted him to his fate; the upstart was defeated, was captured, confessed his imposture—but was hanged. It was the practice in the London theatre during the rising to take up collections from the audiences after these propaganda pieces, for the benefit of various patriotic funds. For example, John Rich (of *Beggar's Opera* fame) paid £602 7s od from the Theatre Royal, Covent Garden, and the patentee of Drury Lane contributed £131 7s 6d 'to the fund for the Relief Support & Encouragement of such Soldiers . . . Employed . . . during this Winter season . . . towards the Suppression of this present Unnatural Rebellion'.[11]

But Fielding was in the field before his old enemy, the laureate. During the rising, *The Old Debauchees* was revived at the patent theatre at Drury Lane as early as 17th November. It played the rest of the month and on beyond the middle of December. It received enough public support for it to be played again at Drury Lane both before and after Christmas. In the meantime the theatre at Goodman's Fields put it on on 2nd December, where it ran until the middle of the month, and where it was played again a few times in January and again in February. Whatever success it had, however, the whole thing—lashing up religious hatreds—could not be thought to do Fielding much credit. Furthermore, the pamphlet, *The Devil, The Pope and the Pretender*, although written with some wit and much satire, is certainly not in Fielding's characteristic vein.

Of the two 'histories' of the Forty-five generally ascribed to Henry Fielding, it is not very difficult to demonstrate that the *Compleat And Authentick* is quite definitely *not* by him, and that the *History of the Present Rebellion* just as definitely *is*.[12] This *History of the Present Rebellion in Scotland* is a 'history' only in the sense of Fielding's characteristic usage of that particular word. It is a running account, a narrative, of a particular sequence of events, a series of incidents indifferently true or imaginary. Not that it was Fielding's conscious intention deliberately to make a short armistice with the truth. But if one would fully understand his title, one must consider his idiosyncratic use of certain words. One of his usages, highly individual, was the use of the word 'history' itself: *The History of Tom Jones*, not the 'story of Tom Jones'; *The History of the Adventures of Joseph Andrews*—not 'An Account of the Adventures of Joseph Andrews'; *The History of the Life of the Late Mr Jonathan Wild the Great*; *The History* . . . To Fielding the term 'poet' or 'historian' means no more than the narrator, in verse or prose. In his *True Patriot*, for example, he would refer to the *writers* in his rival journals who were responsible for stating the news of the week, as 'these modern *Historians*' or 'the *Historians* of last week'. We notice Shakespeare's use of the word 'history' in the older sense of 'narrative'.[13] Perhaps we see the word in the process of its growth when Caxton makes Aesop say, 'the carpenter told th' story to his fellows'. Perhaps, therefore, Fielding in his *History of the Present Rebellion in Scotland* was using the word in its older sense—as, in fact, he usually did, namely as a story currently told. He said in his last work, on the voyage to Lisbon (from which he was never to return), that he was far from supposing that Homer, Hesiod and other ancient poets and mythologists had any settled design to pervert and confuse the records of antiquity; but for his part he would have 'honoured and loved Homer more had he written a true history of his own times in humble prose than those noble poems . . .'. The *History of the Present Rebellion*, however, was not to be—as its title might imply to any bibliographer caught off his guard—a true history of his own stirring times, told in humble prose. Not in 1745, with an invading army marching victorious through the land—maybe to the very gates of the capital—could Fielding say with Martial, *Qui Musas colimus severiores*. To cultivate the severer Muse was not for him—but to call to arms—to man the walls: not the king only is challenged:

All is at stake in the Contest, and as every Englishman, we are confident, will exert his utmost Spirit and Force on this Occasion, so we trust in God that the Religion, Laws Liberties and Lives of this Country will never through the Indolence or Cowardice of its Inhabitants, be exposed to the Mercy and Disposition of the licentious Rabble and Cruel Banditti.

Appropriately enough, this 'history' is rounded off with another 'serious address'. 'I repeat it once more', he said, 'all is at Stake'.

This is not the Cause of a Party: I shall be excused if I say it is not the Cause in which the King only is concerned, Your Religion, my Countrymen, your Laws, your Liberties, Your Lives, the Safety of

your Wives and Children: the Whole is in Danger, and for God Almighty's Sake! lose not a Moment in Arming Yourselves for their
Preservation.[14]

For Mars, then, this 'history'; not for Clio.

The *History of the Present Rebellion,* therefore, was to be a
stirring narrative, told by a great storyteller, a fascinating tale
unfolded by a great character delineator; it was not to be a calm
unhurried unvarnished recording of the facts. The tragic urgency
of the occasion—as Fielding saw it—required not a dispassionate
examination of the truth, but rather a cry from the heart. The
present was not exactly the time to stake one's life for mere
literal truth. In any case the wider truth was, if only people
could be brought to see it, that to meet the invader with arms in
one's hands was not to defend George II merely: it was to defend
our way of life. The *History* itself opened:

The present Rebellion is a matter of such Consequence to this Country,
and must so seriously engage the Attention of every *Briton* who hath
the least Regard either to his own real Good, or the Welfare of his
Prosperity, that I shall make no Apology for the present Undertaking;
in which my Reader may be assured that as the utmost Pains have
been taken to procure the best Intelligence, so he may safely rely on
the Truth of the Facts related.[15]

As regards 'the utmost Pains . . . to procure the best Intelligence',
Fielding had spent long enough in Grub Street to know just when
to pose as 'our *own* correspondent'. As one might expect in the
circumstances, he knew just the fellow to put him (exclusively)
in the way of a scoop: a certain James Macpherson who was said
to have held a captain's commission in the jacobite force and had
(according to the title-page) taken 'the first opportunity of leaving
the Rebels into whose Service he was forced'. Certainly Fielding
succeeds in introducing this Macpherson into the narrative with
much skill and casualness. This need not in any way surprise us,
for Fielding the lawyer might be expected to have just the right
witness handy; Fielding the journalist would see that the witness
would say just the right thing at just the right time; Fielding the
novelist would see that the story would hang together all right;
and Fielding the dramatist could be relied upon to see in general
that the entrances and exits were all properly stage managed.

It is not absolutely clear that Fielding intended Macpherson the informer to be the same Macpherson whom he introduces as living down near the shore at Moidart, and in any case a good clan enthusiast might very well ask what a Macpherson would be doing down in this most exclusive preserve of the ClanRanald MacDonalds; but that would be mere quibbling. Let Fielding tell the tale: it *is* one of his:

Charles presently came up to him, and giving him a French Pistol [a neat touch that! Not 'a guinea piece', 'not a golden sovereign', not merely 'a piece of gold'—but 'a French Pistole'. Just like the French, seducing honest men with their damned foreign gold!] asked him if he would not bear Arms for his King and Country, to which Mac-Pherson readily answered he would, and then Charles very graciously held forth his Hand for him to Kiss, which he accordingly did.[16]

Incidentally, on the title-page Fielding claimed that Macpherson had been 'forced'. But that, again, is quibbling.

At the raising of the standard at Glenfinnan, when Charles Edward had finished with his 'several hundred Paternosters and Ave Marias', he inquired of one of the clansmen 'how far they were from a House' and was told 'that he was full seven Miles from any Town or indeed from any House, unless some Huts such as his own, which were scattered here and there and were inhabited by Highlanders'.[17] Although the syntax is confused the sense is perhaps clear—and the clansman changed once more to be captain Macpherson. Or again, one night while the army lay at Perth a person came into the camp and was by his desire conducted directly to the presence of Charles Edward himself. There was a close conference for several hours to which only the duke of Perth and Tullibardine were admitted. Soon after the departure of the secret and mysterious person from the camp, 'it was rumoured through the whole Army that the City of Edinburgh was to be betrayed to them and that they were to march in a Day or two to take Possession'.[18] If anyone should ask how Fielding came by this most valuable piece of 'exclusive' intelligence—since the probability was that neither Perth nor Tullibardine would have betrayed it to him—the answer is that that very night 'Macpherson happened to do Duty as one of the Young Pretender's Guards'.

In the matter of the celebration of the mass in the principal kirk in Edinburgh, it was not without the utmost persuasion, Fielding says, backed by some strong remonstrances from the cooler and more polite of the party, that Charles Edward was prevailed upon not to insist on an action that would have incensed the whole kirk of Scotland:

the Reluctance with which this Design was laid aside, and indeed the whole Temper of these Men, may well be gathered by the Language of one Callaghan, an Irish Priest, who had newly joined them, and who declared . . . that no further Success was to be expected by those who durst not publickly celebrate the true Religion in Defiance of a Sett of Protestant Dogs; nor could they hope the Lord would fight their Cause, who suffered his Temples to be polluted by Heretics.[19]

If one should ask the source of this story, once again the ubiquitous clansman, captain Macpherson was standing by.

There is not much need, then, to insist upon the authenticity of captain Macpherson, the highland spy. Notwithstanding all this 'inside intelligence', there is nothing in the *History* that Fielding did not make up that Fielding could not have obtained from already published material. It is not difficult to trace that material. His casualty list of Prestonpans, like others, was neither complete nor correct in the names it did give. There is much that would lead us to suppose that he threw his 'facts' together somewhat hurriedly without much effort to impose any sort of check, or to base them on much evidence outside the *London Gazette*. To give an example taken almost at random, he gives the date of the landing as the 10th August. The particular passage is interesting as showing also the manner in which Fielding worked on the text of the *London Gazette*. The official version in the *Gazette* reads:

Letters from Edinburgh, of the 11th instant, bring an account that a French vessel of 16 or 18 guns had appeared on the West Coast of Scotland; which after having cruised for some days off the Islands of Bara and Ust, stood in for the coast Lochabar; and had there landed betwixt the islands of Mull and Sky, seven persons. . . .[20]

Fielding in his version firstly deals briefly with the action with the *Lion* man-of-war. He then goes on to tell us the *Du Teillay* escaped and made immediately for the coast of Scotland.

No English Man of War being at that time in those Seas, they cruised for some Days off the Islands of Bara and Ust, and at last stood in for the Coast of Scotland, and on the 10th of August in the Evening landed between the Islands of Mull and Skie.[21]

The *Gazette* mentions that the *Du Teillay* 'cruised for some days off the Islands of Bara and Ust'. It was the good whig journalist in Fielding who inserted on his own account, the words 'no English Man of War being at that Time in those Seas'. It was (you will take it) sheer luck—not the inefficiency of the government or the command. He was already slipping into the practice of putting the best face on things for the ministry. There is, furthermore, an air of exactitude about 'on the 10th of August in the Evening', but for all that, it was of course inaccurate. Fielding may have taken his date from any one of nearly a dozen contemporary versions appearing in the various news-sheets and other suchlike current material; or he may have taken it from the main source, the *Gazette*. The *Gazette* spoke of 'Letters from Edinburgh on the 11th instant'. Fielding sub-edited the fact reported on the 11th into 'On the 10th in the Evening' as, at the same time, having all the air of accuracy and being near enough anyway. It was a reasonable guess—but in fact over a fortnight wide of the mark.

It would indeed be churlish to complain too much at the distance by which Fielding occasionally missed his mark when he made up some of his 'facts'. It must be admitted, however, that none of them was such as would seem at all unreasonable or unlikely to a good English whig at the time. Now and again, he made a good guess—but his luck was out on the guess. For example, it had been realized that Charles Edward had landed at a very remote spot in the west and had later mustered in a quite remote glen. When at long last the sheriff-depute of the county was able to pass along some information to Edinburgh, he had to add an additional note to let even the ministry in Edinburgh know where exactly Arisaig might be. In some such obscure glen the clans thus mustered might be expected to give rise to an acute shortage of food locally, since provisions thereabouts had been short for years, even for the ordinary population of the area. The clansmen would naturally have to send foraging parties out

over the hills, whose arrival would very naturally be very unwelcome in the glens but very welcome back in camp:

The chief Care of the Rebels began now to be procuring Provisions,
as their Mouths grew very numerous; in order to procure which they
sent out a Party, who, on the 22nd in the Evening, drove a Herd of
black Cattle into the Camp, which were received with great joy.[22]

With the now familiar touch, 'on the 22nd in the Evening',
Fielding contrived to give this incident all the appearance of
first-hand information, although it is a pity that captain Macpherson had not led the foraging party. However, a completely
unexpected incident put an entirely unforeseen complexion upon
the whole food situation in the glens.

In order, possibly, to burn his boats behind him, Charles
Edward dismissed *Du Teillay*, and captain Walsh sailed back
from Moidart. It happened by mere chance that in her passage
the vessel ran into three ships between the Isle of Skye and the
mainland, the *Princess Mary* and 'two West Country Ships'. *Du
Teillay* took them as prize and then ransomed them 'upon
condition', as Sullivan says, 'that they wou'd come to Kenlock
Moudiogh and sel their meal there, wch they performed'. This
account goes on to the effect

The Prince bought the meal and got it distributed proportionally to
the numbre it was in each family; people came from all parts to get
their proportion. . . . It was a Vast Succor in that jouncture, for the
poor people had not a Scrap of meal for above six months before.[23]

Thus, it came about that by such unforeseen—and indeed un-
foreseeable—occurrence that the muster of the clans was able
not only to provide food for themselves, but also to issue it to
the local inhabitants. Fielding's guess, then, was quite rational—
but quite incorrect.

Fielding's method of working his sources (such 'sources' as
he had)—even his very turns of phrase—are of interest, if not
to the historian, at least to the literary critic. Indeed, it would be
an interesting exercise in the examination of literary method to
study how exactly he manipulated his available sources, in the
haste and hurry of those stirring days, when the invasion of his
country was daily expected. It would be interesting and informative to find out which particular sources he did in fact tap, not

only for matter but also for treatment and hints as to manipulation. It would be interesting and informative also to know which sources were available to him that for one reason or another he rejected out of hand for reasons of political principle, intellectual bias or literary method. This, however, is a topic which it is not possible to pursue here in detail. We might take, however, if only by way of example, that curious little item of whig propaganda, a modest little threepenny pamphlet, *A Genuine Intercepted Letter* with which Fielding's various propaganda items of the Forty-five show some interesting parallels. In fact, it was not a letter, of course; it had not been intercepted; and it certainly was not genuine. But after all, there was a war on, and in war the first casualty must need be truth. The *Genuine Intercepted Letter* need not now attract any particular interest, perhaps, except for its (possible) relation to Fielding's pamphlets. One might even wonder whether Fielding himself—first class propagandist that he was—had not worked upon it in order to work it up into something else. Its full title was: *A Genuine Intercepted Letter from Father Patrick Graham, Almoner and Confessor to the Pretender's Son in Scotland to Father Benedict Yorke, Titular Bishop of St David's at Bath.* It is a clever propaganda title in every word: it is genuine —you really may rely on it; it was intercepted—not really for your unprivileged eyes, but mere chance brings it that you may see it; the pamphlet is not really a pamphlet at all—it is a letter, quite private, of course, very confidential; it is from 'Father Patrick Graham'; 'Father'—shades of the papacy; 'Patrick'—shades of the Irish; 'Graham'—shades of the Scots; it is from the pretender's almoner—the dispenser of royal (that is, Stuart) gifts. And what of our property will he not, upon some pretext or other, be giving away to some of his favourites (Irish, Scottish or Roman!); it is from the pretender's confessor—shades of the papacy, the inquisition and the fires of Smithfield. To the titular bishop of Bath; shades of the crypto, the fellow-traveller, the collaborator, the fifth-columnist, the enemy in the midst. Every single word of the title is heavily charged with feeling, emotion, bias, prejudice—everything but reason. It is, in other words, first-class propaganda.

It is not to be wondered at, therefore, that this 'Father Graham' was a jacobite figure very popular with the whig faction at the time, and a veritable thorn in the flesh of the jacobites. The whigs took care that he made his way from the pamphlets into the prints, and in all this pushing up the bogey man, Fielding took a good part. One of the engraved broadsides, for example: *The Procession, of the Pope's Nurselings riding in Triumph* (1745) published by J. Collier 'Father Graham, Confessor to His Highness' was depicted—in obvious contrast to the 'brave archbishop' of York—rejoicing, 'now shall our Smithfield Fires Blaze Again', while a monk, attending the banner of a catholic order, says, 'Soft Pennance for English Women'. Yet another engraving of the period, *A Hint to the Wise, and the surest way with the Pretender*, contrasts archbishop Herring with 'Father Graham'; it makes the jacobite almoner's confessor attribute all their success hitherto to the English clergy's neglect. 'Father Graham's' followers pretend to claim for him no less than three thousand converts in a couple of years. How busy they intend to be, rooting out the heretics!

It is perfectly clear that on the propaganda front, in the main the whig dogs did in fact not have the best of it. But 'Father Graham' was something of an exception. Perhaps it was that the whigs in their propaganda were too inclined to 'admit no force but argument', but on this occasion their best propaganda piece was not an argument, but a bogey, and against this bogey all the jacobite faction could do was to argue—to argue that it was a lie, that there was no such person as Father Graham, that there never had been any such person. Indeed, a note was published in the Edinburgh papers, 'by order', stating that

the whole of this letter is one continued lie; that it is so notoriously known that there never was such a person as Father Graham in the Army or retinue of the Chevalier, and that the Chevalier's conduct had been strictly conformable to the declaration and manifesto published by himself[24]

But all to no purpose. Father Graham continued to thrive. Mere truth could not kill such a lie. A number of hints from this Father Graham will be found plentifully scattered among the whig ephemera of the day. Certainly in the *Serious Address*, in the *Dialogue between the Devil, the Pope and the Pretender* and in the *History of the Present Rebellion in Scotland* one can see the influence of the *Genuine Intercepted Letter*. Fielding borrowed, and worked up, a number of hints; about the hocus-pocus and the mumbo-jumbo, for example, about the relics and medals, more seriously about the resumption of the abbey lands and the extinction of the national debt, and about the papal release of Charles Edward from the terms of his published proclamation. All these were, of course, fine propaganda points, and Fielding, ardent whig that he was, worked them well.

It is, however, quite noteworthy that Fielding, frankly ministry propagandist that he was, could occasionally be factually more accurate than any of his contemporaries. There are two incidents, for example, that relate to Cope. His version of Cope's march north is of particular interest: it is so explicit and precise that one wonders whether he did in fact get his information from some 'inspired' source, the more so that nothing so accurate had as yet appeared in the *London Gazette*.[25] He picks up the thread from 13th August, the day on which the somewhat belated order was issued by the secretary-at-war for all officers to repair immediately to their respective posts:

General Cope had now assembled a pretty considerable Body of ¡the King's Forces near Sterling; but the Ways towards the Rebels were such that it would have been impracticable to come at them without the utmost Hazard of losing the Whole Army in the Attempt: Nor had he indeed any other Way of attacking them, than by taking a vast Scope round which he declined, as he chose rather to keep himself posted between them and the City of Edinburgh; well knowing, that could the Capital of Scotland be preserved, any Success they might have of assembling a Body in the Highlands, where they must soon be starved, would be in the end fruitless and ineffectual.[26]

Fielding goes on:

However, the Alarm of their success daily increasing in England and the Numbers which from time to time joined them giving a very just Cause of Uneasiless to our Ministry here, the General received peremptory Orders to march forwards, which he did.[27]

Fielding continues: 'and in the meantime the Rebels gave him the slip and on the 29th march'd towards Perth'. The facts were perfectly plain and simple. No other contemporary account gets it so.

On another point, minor in itself perhaps, but significant in the misrepresentation it later acquired, Fielding was fair to Cope where all contemporary historians—and balladists—were definitely unjust, namely, the matter of his arrival at Berwick. It has now, beyond all possibility of recall, been enshrined in the ballads for all time that Cope was the first to arrive at Berwick after Prestonpans with the news of his own defeat:

> Now Johnnie troth, ye wasna blate
> To come wi' th' news o' your own defeat
> And leave your men in sic a strait,
>   Sae early in the morning.

Fielding has it:

General Cope, finding it impossible to rally the Army, escaped after the Dragoons to Lauder: some of these as well as the Foot, got safe to Berwick, where General Cope is since arrived with the rest, who we hope will take a future occasion to regain the Honour, at the Expense of these Rebels, which they lost in the Action.[28]

Although the hopes were not well founded, the facts were. On the day of the action Cope withdrew to Lauder where he wrote a despatch saying he had prevailed upon about 450 of the men to keep together and that he 'thought it most advisable to march this body towards Barwick'. The *following day* he wrote from Berwick saying, 'the principal officers *I found here* are Brigad^r Fowke and Colonel Lassalls, some few others of lower rank, foot soldiers not above 30'. Thus, Cope firstly withdrew to Lauder and later marched to Berwick, *where he found* brigadier Fowkes and other details. One of the earliest accounts we have of these circumstances as they were early talked about across the Border —but not published until 1846—is to be found in that nerve centre of intelligence, the correspondence of chancellor Waugh of Carlisle. He said, writing to London,

I cannot help telling you a story . . . of old Lord Mark Kerr, who was in Berwick when Brigadier Fowlks and Coll. Lassells come there; he saies the night of the battle, this old General asked them very gravely where the army was,—they looked confounded, and said, totally routed;—he held up his hands, 'Good God! I have seen some Battles, heard of many, but never of the first news of a defeat being brought by the General Officers before'.[29]

It did not take the balladists long to touch up the facts a bit, to transport Cope from Lauder to Berwick, to substitute Cope for Fowkes—and the ballad is complete. That is the job of balladists, and they did their job well, for it is a good ballad. Where the mistake lies is not with the balladists, but with those historians who have been content to accept the jingles of the rhymsters as the very stuff of history—and with all the texts—and Fielding— against them.

However, facts or no facts, there was one point that even the most solid and stolid Hanoverian would have to admit, namely, that the Stuarts could at least touch the imagination of their adherents, arouse their ardour, fire their spirit, in a manner in which the Hanoverians never could—and maybe never would. The utter romance of this present venture could not fail in its appeal to the romantic spirit. This boy—this Charles Edward— born, and like his father before him, lived his whole life in exile— lands in a remote corner of the Western Isles, with half-a-score of men, mostly middle-aged to decrepit, to win back his father's crown. He struck a sure note—in great contrast to much of the whigs' ranting, anti-papistical, unreasoning and unreasonable appeals to religious prejudice bias bigotry and hatred—when with a complete absence of rhetoric or hyperbole he told in straight-forward language the simple story of his own success:

But listen only to the naked Truth. I with my own Money hired a small vessel; ill provided with Money, Arms or Friends, I arrived in Scot-land, attended by seven Persons; I publish the King my Father's Declaration, and proclaim his Title. . . . I have I confess, the greatest Reason to adore the Goodness of Almighty God, who has in so re-markable a Manner, protected me and my small Army through the many Dangers to which we were at first exposed, and Who has led me in the way of Victory, and to the Capital of this ancient Kingdom, amidst the Acclamations of the King my Father's Subjects.[30]

With seven men only to win back his father's crown. . . . Here is a human story! The difference, then, between jacobite and whig is the difference between bubbling champagne and Norfolk dumpling.

Clearly, the main outline of Charles Edward's romantic picture was already drawn, and drawn beyond all Fielding's re-drawing. Very well. If Fielding could not re-draw it, he could at least colour it—stain it indelibly, maybe, with the colour of political and religious prejudice. Who said the Whig dogs should not have the best of it? Who said they knew no force but reason? Henry Fielding, author of *Tom Thumb*, *Don Quixote in England*, *The Welsh Opera*, *Pasquin*, *The Historical Register* and *Eurydice Hiss'd*, would give them an object lesson in propaganda.

Was the first landing on the mainland the scion of the ancient house of Stuart come home *to his own* again—or was it a pretender accepting Britain from a priest as a fief of Rome?

> The Young Pretender then threw himself on the Ground, and Kiss'd it, after which his Confessor cut a Turf and presented it to him, saying, In the Name of the most holy and infallible Pope I present thee this as Regent for thy Father, and do hereby, by virtue of the full Powers to me delegated, invest the most puissant James III with the Possession and Rule of the Kingdom of Great Britain; which he is to hold at the Will and Pleasure of the Holy See. Dost thou therefore, in his Name, accept the Government of these Realms, on the condition of fighting the Cause of our holy Mother the Church, to the utter Extirpation of the Persons of Hereticks; and wilt thou persevere manfully in the same till the Blood of the Hereticks shall be washed away from the Face of the Earth.[31]

All this Charles Edward solemnly promised in his father's name and thereupon received from the hands of 'Father Patrick Graham his confessor' the turf in token of his acceptance of Britain as a fief of the holy see. This is a second playing of *The Devil, the Pope and the Pretender*. It is easy at this length of time to smile at this sort of fustian now—but the *History of the Present Rebellion in Scotland* quickly ran out of print.

The raising of the standard at Glenfinnan received similar treatment. There was no 'high minded Moray, the exiled, the dear'. The whole affair was not so much a raising of the standard as the army takes the field: it was the observance of some superstitious rite—a lot of mumbo-jumbo.

> On the 22nd [actually the 19th] they erected their Standard with great Solemnity: The Priest first washed it all over with Holy Water, and blessed it, then a certain number of Ave Marys and Paternosters were said, besides Prayers to the Saints; in all which Acts of Devotion, Charles distinguished himself with greater Zeal (if possible) than the Priests themselves.[32]

As regards the brush at High Bridge, there was little in the facts that could be disputed. At the earliest stage certain troop movements were decided. Amongst others, Cope ordered a company of Sinclair's regiment under captain John Scott of Scotstarvet to march to Fort William to go into garrison there. On their march between Fort Augustine and Fort William they were attacked by some irregulars under MacDonald of Tiendrish. The regulars could not cut their way through to Fort William so tried to retreat to Fort Augustus. Keppoch came up to assist Tiendrish and later young Lochiel also, and the regulars were surrounded and compelled to surrender. The clans had drawn first blood. Although quite unimportant in itself, it gave an immense fillip to jacobite morale. They could actually take the redcoat prisoners to the raising of the standard. They could— *and did.*

By far the best line for any whig apologist was that taken by Duncan Forbes of Culloden:

Two companies of the Royals made prisoner sounds pretty well and will surely be passed for a notable achievement; but when it is considered that these companies were not half compleat; that they were lads picked up last season in the Low Country, without any thing Royal but the name, and that their officers were raw, the achievement is not by any means so important.[33]

The High Bridge incident is notable at least for this: that under the influence of 'the gentle Lochiel' the civil war broke out in the most gentlemanly manner possible. After the surrender of the whig companies, the jacobites found that captain Scott, the commanding officer, had been wounded. They thought, therefore, that he might get better treatment for his wound from the garrison surgeon of the beleaguered Fort William than they for their part would be able to give him outside. In the friendliest manner possible, therefore, they sent to old Alexander Campbell, the governor, asking him to send the garrison surgeon out under a safe conduct. This the governor refused to do. At this refusal, 'the gentle Lochiel', 'shocked at the old man's barbarity', gave up his prisoner and sent him into the fort 'to be cured'.

Fielding, plainly, would have none of 'the gentle Lochiel'

stuff. Best exchange the gentle and the barbarous. It is a good line in propaganda to be similar to the truth—but opposite:

On the 23rd a Party of 400 of the Rebels, chiefly belonging to the Royal Regiment of Highland Guards [there was, of course, no such regiment] attacked and defeated a small Party of the King's Forces, under the command of Capt. Scott. The Captain himself was wounded in the arm; and a Serjeant even after the Battle was cut all to Pieces; which Fate all the rest had shared, had it not been prevented by one Stewart, a Captain of the Highlanders. These Fellows had already so well profited under the popish Instructor, as to learn the Language of Heretick Dogs! and the true Arts of propagating Religion with Fire and Sword.[34]

Another picture which generous romance had drawn—which Fielding must now colour—was Charles Edward crossing the Forth, his Rubicon. The young Stuart, on foot, at the head of his beloved clansmen, sharing with them their hardships and winning with them their glories. When they came to the waters of the Forth, with the Hanoverian stronghold of Stirling Castle looming up sullen and threatening on their flank, the regular dragoons fled rather than stay to oppose by force of arms the legitimate heir of Scotland's ancient kings. It is Charles Edward who dashes forward to be himself first to plunge into the historic waters of the Forth. Fielding must produce something of good propaganda value here. Best agree again with the main outline of the narrative, but give it a new twist to remember it by:

On the 13th they again marched at Day break, and in the Morning passed the Firth at the Ford of Frews, five Miles above Sterling. Here Charles attempting to give an extraordinary Instance of his Bravery by passing the Water first, and mistaking the Ford, very narrowly escaped drowning, from which he was preserved by Lieutenant Duncan Madson, who at the Hazard of his own Life, rescued him from the Waves.[35]

The small points are not to be missed: Charles Edward was actuated by motives of petty conceit and vanity rather than personal courage—and he crossed his Rubicon on the 13th.

Fielding was too good a journalist to push all his points home. He had been to market too often as a chapman not to know just which trinket to leave on the front of the tray for each of his more discerning customers to pick up for himself. Ram something down his throat and as likely as not he will miss it; leave it lying casually—but carefully placed—and a whole lot of them will snatch it up, each thinking it an individual discovery. The showmanship of Drury Lane, plus the journalism of Grub Street equals the propaganda of Paternoster Row.

The name is Henry Fielding.

Notes

1 *Egmont Diary.*
2 *Daily Gazetteer*, 7th May 1737.
3 *London Evening Post*, 16th–19th April 1737.
4 *Daily Gazetteer*, 7th May 1737.
5 10 Geo. II, cap. 28.
6 *Jonathan Wild*, book III, chap. xiv.
7 E.g. the subscription lists to *The Miscellanies.*
8 See sale catalogue of the Fielding library in the BM.
9 Carteret.
10 *Jacobite's Journal*, no. 10, 6th February 1748.
11 Guildhall MSS, 186–7.
12 See next Paper.
13 And therefore will he wipe his tablet clean
   And keep no tell-tale to his memory
   That may repeat and history his loss
   To new remembrance
                              2 *Henry IV*, II, *act iv, sc. 1.*
14 Pp. 45, 46–7.
15 Pp. 1–2.
16 P. 4.
17 Pp. 5–6.
18 Pp. 25–6.
19 Pp. 33–4.
20 *London Gazette*, 13th–17th August 1745.
21 P. 3.
22 P. 11.
23 H. and A. Tayler, *1745 and After*, p. 58.
24 *Scots Magazine*, September 1745.
25 See Paper 1, volume I.
26 Pp. 12–13.
27 P. 13.
28 Pp. 44–5.
29 See also *Fitzherbert MSS*, p. 160.
30 Proclamation dated 10th October 1745 (*A Full Collection of all the Proclamations* (1745), p. 30).

[31] Pp. 4–5.
[32] P. 11.
[33] *Culloden Pp.* 376.
[34] Pp. 11–12.
[35] Pp. 26–7.

v Controversy

17 *Fugitive Histories of the Forty-five*

Various accounts of the last jacobite rising were written or edited —under slightly different but somewhat confusing titles—by Henry Fielding, Robert Dodsley, John Marchant, Michael Hughes, Andrew Henderson and James Ray, or else have been ascribed to them, thus giving rise to some curious controversial little issues. The purpose of this present paper is not so much to study the historical or literary content of these pieces, but rather to consider the somewhat curious relationships between them, and to clarify their bibliographical distinctions and thereby to remove them—it is hoped finally—from the field of controversy.

The works in question are, firstly, Fielding's slight pamphlet, a *History of the Present Rebellion in Scotland* (already referred to in the previous paper), put out by Cooper[1] in September of 1745.[2] Secondly, the 'Succinct History of the Rebellion' originally published by Dodsley in serial form in his new fortnightly *The Museum*,[3] and afterwards reprinted among the collection of pieces compiled from that periodical.[4] This latter history, slightly adapted and somewhat supplemented, was later reissued by Cooper in 1745[5]—without acknowledgement—under the title *A Compleat And Authentick History of the Rise, Progress, and Extinction of the Late Rebellion.*[6] It has, however, quite erroneously been ascribed to Fielding.[7] It was later further adapted, and embodied in 1748 into the fourth edition of Defoe's *Tour of the Whole Island*[8] under Richardson's editorship, and continued to appear in that work until the ninth edition (1779). Thirdly, the collection of odds and ends, extracts from the official bulletins in the *London Gazette*, and snippets from news-sheets and pamphlets, got together by John Marchant under the title *The History*

The notes and references are on pages 164–8

2—L

of the Present Rebellion, and published—so it was claimed—'by His Majesty's Authority' in London in 1747.[9] Fourthly, two other histories, of less importance, however, for this present purpose, namely, Andrew Henderson's *History of the Rebellion*[10] which has some similarity to John Marchant's above, and Michael Hughes' *Plain Narrative*[11] which, in its turn, has some similarity to James Ray's *Compleat History* below. And lastly, the various editions of the history credited to James Ray. *A Compleat History of the Rebellion*, by the north-country gipsy, 'Mr James Ray, of White-haven, Volunteer under His Royal Highness the Duke of Cumberland'.[12]

With regard to the first and second of the pieces, the *History of the Present Rebellion in Scotland* and the *Compleat And Authentick History*, the questions have been confusedly posed as to whether either, neither or both were written by Henry Fielding. It is fortunate, in this connection, that the literary critic, in order to enable him to identify what is and what is not Fielding's work, is possessed of a handy touchstone of style that can easily be applied as a reasonably reliable test of his authorship.[13] A marked verbal idiosyncrasy of Fielding's has long been recognized, namely the habit, consistent throughout his whole life, of making use of the older forms *hath* and *doth* where most of his contemporaries would undoubtedly have used the current forms *has* and *does*.[14] Professor Cross accepts this as 'an almost infallible test' of his authorship.[15] It is interesting to note that so consistent in general is Fielding's habit in this respect that even when he quotes, presumably from memory, he often converts the auxiliary *has* into *hath*. For instance, even in such a well-known passage as 'who steals my purse steals trash', he slightly misquotes it by continuing—

> —'tis something
> 'Twas mine, 'tis his, and *hath* been slave to thousands.[16]

His memory was rather more at fault in a misquotation which I do not think has been noticed before. In quoting[17] from Addison's *Cato*, he makes Sempronius say to Portius

> Thy father's greatness
> *Hath* set thee in the fairest Point of Light.[18]

On another occasion he was quoting from *Hudibras*:

> He that *has* but Impudence
> To all things *has* a fair Pretence.[19]

But apparently all unconsciously he misquotes it as

> He who *hath* but Impudence
> To all things *hath* a fair Pretence.[20]

This apparently ineradicable 'hath and doth' habit of Fielding's comes to our aid to remove any lingering doubt there may perchance be as to the actual authorship of these pieces. It is particularly significant that the *History of the Present Rebellion in Scotland* is written entirely in the *hath/doth* idiom, while in contrast the *Compleat And Authentick* is in the *has/does* form throughout. Even before the discovery of the genuine text in the *History of the Present Rebellion* Professor Cross recognized the difficulty, for the merest glance at the *Compleat And Authentick* will disclose that it is not in the slightest degree in Fielding's characteristic style. Cross therefore felt it necessary to postulate that Fielding must have been writing in disguise—although it is difficult to understand why.[21] The discovery of the genuine work, however, written throughout in Fielding's own *hath/doth* form, entirely disposes of the point. We may safely conclude, therefore, that the *History of the Present Rebellion in Scotland* is Fielding's work, and that the *Compleat And Authentick* is not.

The piece, although obviously hurried—or perhaps, precisely because it is hurried—displays all the technical idiosyncrasies and verbal mannerisms of Fielding's work. It is technically anonymous; but if the author did not put his name on the title-page, he left his mark plainly enough over all the text.

However, Professor Cross, having missed the clue, noted the title quite finally, 'No copy known',[22] and thus found himself with a vacancy in the Fielding bibliography. In the course of his search for the correct title, he had found another—not Fielding's at all, as a matter of fact—but he decided to propose this as a candidate for the vacancy: *A Compleat And Authentick History of the Rise, Progress and Extinction of the Late Rebellion*. This, however was dated in 1747, not in 1745, but was 'for M. Cooper, price a shilling'. If there were some doubt in Cross's mind about the exact title of Fielding's *History of the Present Rebellion,* so also there might be doubt—although Professor Cross did not apparently know it—about the anonymous *Compleat And Authentick.* Notwithstanding that its title-page reads *A Compleat And Authentick History of the . . . Rebellion,* its 'running title' is 'A Succinct History of the Rebellion', a title that appears at the commencement of the text, that is to say, immediately below the printer's head-piece. It is now clear that this latter title was the original wording, that is to say, its title in its earliest—periodical—form, and the title by which it was earliest cited, for example, by that odd Dublin eccentric, Samuel Boyse, in the first year of its publication.[23] There are, upon closer examination, bibliographical and other reasons for supposing that the elaborately-worded title-page, which alone bears the words 'Compleat And Authentick', was only an afterthought. Almost certainly it was printed last.[24]

For one reason or another, Professor Cross jumped to the conclusion that the two titles were two variant references to the same work, that the work was in fact the *Compleat And Authentick History,* and that Fielding must be the author. He therefore admitted the *Compleat And Authentick,* not to the 'Uncertain or Doubtful' category of his bibliography, but quite unjustifiably to the full canon. This was scarcely scholarly, for it was already known to Cross[25] that Colonel W. F. Prideaux, who was recognized as 'an assiduous collector of Fielding', had implied that he himself had seen copies of the *History of the Present Rebellion in Scotland, under that title,* although not 'good uncut copies'.[26] This fact alone ought to have led Cross to make further investigation before he intruded into the Fielding canon, in substitution for it, a title that had never before been associated with Fielding.

However, we have it that the serial 'Succinct History' first appeared in Dodsley's *Museum* in the spring of 1746, a date that is of considerable significance to Fielding biography. The history was collected and republished in book form in 1747 and given the title *A Compleat And Authentick History,* and from here it was borrowed in part by James Ray's printer or publisher, and in whole by Defoe's.

Having pieced it together so far, I naturally sought to check the current state of knowledge as to Fielding's more fugitive political pieces. I found that some part of the above had already been independently discovered by an American scholar, Miss Mabel Seymour,[27] except that the American research had not led as far as the various editions of Ray's History.[28] As already stated, the date of Robert Dodsley's commencement of the serial history in his *Museum* is of crucial significance. In the spring and early summer of 1746, partly perhaps owing to waning interest in affairs after the retreat of the jacobites to the far north, but partly at least owing to the pressure of his legal pursuits, Fielding could not find the time to continue his *True Patriot*. It may be accepted that Fielding could not edit a busy London newspaper, and at the same time attend the courts in Westminster or the assizes in the western circuit. He could not cultivate both the press *and* the law. It was at this time—so he felt—absolutely necessary for him to succeed at the law. It is not surprising, therefore, that he gave up the press.[29]

It was doubtless with some regret that he closed down his *True Patriot*[30]—for which, in the circumstances, he doubtless had some fondness—and devoted himself exclusively to the law. There seems no evidence of any sort that he had any association with Robert Dodsley and the *Museum*, and only the strongest positive evidence that he did in fact contribute to some other completely dissociated periodical at the very stage when he could find no time to keep his own alive, would lead us to accept it that he deliberately killed his own paper in order to have time to hack for a stranger. In other words, Fielding could not have written the serial history for Dodsley—that is to say, did not write the *Compleat And Authentick History*—and there is, in fact, no reason why he should have done so, and no tittle of evidence that he did.

The *Museum* 'Succinct History', then, and its various derivatives are anonymous works not to be confused with Fielding's polemical tract, *The Present Rebellion*, nor with anything else that Fielding wrote.

For some reason or other, however, those who have advanced the claims of the *Compleat And Authentick* seem latterly to have changed their ground somewhat, without, apparently, fully realizing it. The two books were first thought of—erroneously—as variant references to a single work; it has now become the practice to regard them—just as erroneously—as two separate works, both by Fielding, one known, and the other lost. For example, Dr Homes Dudden admits both the *Compleat And Authentick*[31] and the *History of the Present Rebellion*,[32] but says of the latter that 'no copy seems now to be extant',[33] or more confidently, 'this pamphlet is now lost'.[34] Not only had the little work, on the contrary, already been found, but further *editions* as well as further copies are now well authenticated. Apart from those in private hands—such as the one in my own collection of jacobite material—there are also a couple of copies where one would most of all hope for a rare history of a rebellion in Scotland to be, namely in the National Library of Scotland.[35] There was also an edition printed in Dublin (and probably pirated), and copies of both this and the first are in the British Museum[36] and the Bodleian, and a number of copies have been elsewhere recorded.[37] Furthermore, although it could not have been known in 1918, it ought to have been in 1952, the piece was again reprinted as recently as 1934 in a line-for-line, page-for-page reprint.[38]

This reprint, however, which ought to have simplified the situation, only complicated it. Mr Ifan Kyrle Fletcher, when he put out this 1934 reprint, might very well have said—indeed *ought* to have said—that because Fielding's *History of the Present Rebellion* had now been found, the *Compleat And Authentick* could no longer be a candidate for the vacancy the *Present Rebellion* now filled. It had all been a mistake. But instead of this, the editor of the 1934 reprint of the genuine pamphlet, not realizing, apparently, the real effect upon Fielding bibliography of the discovery of the *History of the Present Rebellion*, said in his introduction, 'Fielding issued through Cooper in 1747 a booklet entitled *A Compleat And Authentick History*',[39] which was, of course, just the thing the editor was then in a position to demonstrate he had *not* done. Fletcher failed to grasp that Cross had ascribed the *Compleat And Authentick History* to Fielding, only because he had failed to trace the genuine title. The discovery of the genuine work made Cross's false assumption no longer tenable. In the result, however, Fielding was now saddled with two titles instead of one.

Although clearly we need only one title to fill the gap, and notwithstanding there is no evidence or suggestion anywhere that Fielding wrote two, the *Cambridge Bibliography of English Literature* in 1940 followed by admitting *both* to the canon. *The*

Cambridge Bibliography even went one step farther to state categorically without any caveat or query, what is manifestly false, namely that 'his *History of the Present Rebellion* was expanded by Fielding from 48 to 156[40] pages as *A Compleat And Authentick History*'.[41] One has only to read the two works to realize that the second is certainly not an expansion of the first.

Close bibliographical examination of contemporary copies of various other histories of the Forty-five discloses some unexpected relationships. For example, the *Compleat History of the Rebellion* ascribed to James Ray, described on the title-page of an earlier little work as a Whitehaven gipsy, has—curiously enough—a number of long passages in common with the *Compleat And Authentick*, which as we have seen above has commonly been ascribed to Fielding. The historical passages of Ray's *Compleat History of the Rebellion* are liberally interspersed with topographical information, a search for which might lead, naturally enough, to the current edition of Defoe's *Tour of the Whole Island*—the fourth (1748) (? Richardson's) edition—a standard book of topographical reference at the time. In the last volume of that edition—the Scottish volume—one will find a repetition, practically word-for-word, of the history of the rising as found in the *Compleat And Authentick*. Owing to the ill-feeling (at least on Richardson's part) between Richardson and Fielding, it is highly improbable that we would find in 1748 the two rival novelists sharing the publication of the same historical text. I set myself therefore to seek for a source elsewhere. After a search I found it in a new periodical which had recently been started neither by Fielding nor by Richardson, but by Robert Dodsley, footman turned poet, entitled *The Museum, or the Literary and Historical Register*.[42] This discovery required me to stop now to consider whether the ascription of the *Compleat And Authentick* to Fielding could possibly be well-founded, for where it is merely very unlikely that Richardson would be using Fielding's 'copy' in 1748, acquaintance with Fielding biography would suggest that it would be almost impossible that Fielding would be supplying 'copy' to Dodsley's new periodical in 1746. This, it will be recollected, was just at the time when Fielding was having to let his own journal, *The True Patriot*, die merely because he was too hard-pressed for the time to keep it alive.

It is uncritical therefore to conjecture on such flimsy evidence—
or rather on none at all—that at a period when he could not find
the time to keep even his own *True Patriot* alive, he could find the
leisure to contribute to Dodsley's *Museum*. Professor Cross was
of course entitled to conjecture that during the course of 1746
and during the spring of 1747, between say *The True Patriot* and
The Jacobite's Journal, Fielding, together with the other odds and
ends which he did, helped his own publisher out with a piece of
hack work by way of a history of the rising. But the conjecture is,
I believe, altogether less likely, that in the spring of 1746, when
he was working against time on his own *True Patriot*, he found
the opportunity to contribute to another journal with which he
had never before been associated. The only feature in its favour
is the gap between the contributions of 26th April and 13th
September. The main point is that the whole thing is conjecture,
not only not supported by any real evidence, but not supported
either by any reasonable likelihood.

Miss Mabel Seymour whilst engaged on some work on the
fugitive pieces of the period[43] noticed for the first time that the
Compleat And Authentick was based on *The Museum*[44] which was
also the basis of the additional matter included in the 1748
edition of Defoe's *Tour of The Whole Island*.[45] She was, however,
led, I think, to the wrong conclusion. She might reasonably have
argued:

(1) Defoe's editor borrowed from the *Compleat And Authentick*;
but

(2) it can now be shown that the *Compleat And Authentick* was
republished from the *Museum*;

(3) Fielding could not have been writing for the *Museum*;
therefore

(4) Fielding was not the author of the *Compleat And Authentick*.

Instead however she chose to argue, somewhat uncritically I
think,[46] that

(1) Defoe's editor borrowed from the *Compleat And Authentick*.

(2) It is now known that the *Compleat And Authentick* was republished from the *Museum*.

(3) The *Compleat And Authentick* is ascribed to Fielding; therefore

(4) Fielding was a contributor to the *Museum*.

This seems to overlook entirely that there is no real evidence—
and to do Professor Cross justice, he did not pretend that there
was—that Fielding wrote a single line of the *Compleat And Authentick*. The false ascription in the first instance depended upon the
slightest of coincidences that can now be satisfactorily explained
away: it depended solely upon the assumption that the two titles
were variant references to a single work.

The *Compleat And Authentick* was originally brought forward by
Cross to fill an apparent gap. The gap has now been filled by the
genuine title; therefore the spurious one must naturally now be
dismissed. There is no longer a gap to fill, and hence no longer any
place in Fielding's bibliography for the *Compleat And Authentick*.
Biographers, however, finding the item still in the old bibliographies, feel themselves compelled to work it in somewhere. So
Dr Dudden continued to tell us, as his more immediate predecessors told us, that such evidence 'as there is, fairly warrants
the attribution of the work to Fielding's pen'.[47] Such evidence as
there is does not. There is no reason whatsoever, and no evidence
internal or external, why the *Compleat And Authentick* should be
any longer credited—or debited—to Henry Fielding.

Nor is the book commonly described correctly in its physical
features. Professor Cross, who incidentally transcribed the title
inaccurately, described the book as one of 155 pages,[48] which the
Cambridge Bibliography of English Literature 'corrects' to 156.[49]
In point of fact it contains 163 pages of text.[50] Furthermore,
Cross described the volume as containing a folding chart: 'A
plan of the action at Seatonne'.[51] That this plate is no part of the
actual book, but an intruded separate publication, may be adduced by its legend: 'Published according to Act of Parliament,
Oct. 17, 1745. By G. Hawkins at Milton Head in Fleet Street,
Price 1s. plain and 2s. coloured.'[52] Professor Cross, although he
does not say so, was presumably describing the British Museum
copy.[53] The plate is not in my own copy, nor is it known in any
other. I think it may be taken that it is a mere insertion in a
single copy.

There are other points about the British Museum copy. Like
my own, it lacks a half-title, but unlike any other copy known to
me it has what purports to be a leaf of advertisements at the
back. Thus the title-page (without the half-title) seems conjugate

with the two leaves of text and leaf of advertisements, which appear to constitute the last gathering. But when I learned of a copy with a half-title (which gives one more leaf than is required for a simple gathering) it led me to examine the British Museum copy more closely and I found that the leaf of 'advertisements' is, like the 'plate', also an intrusion, and no part of the actual book. The volume 'advertised' is the *State of the Nation for 1748*, whereas the *Compleat And Authentick* was noticed in the *Gentleman's Magazine* for April, 1747.[54] Furthermore, the rest of the leaf refers to the *Reasons for Giving up Gibraltar*. The leaf is in fact a half-title which has got separated from the volume to which it refers. The first leaf of the British Museum copy of the *Reasons for Giving up Gibraltar* corresponds exactly with the last leaf bound up with the *Compleat And Authentick*.[55]

To pass now to the third limb of this paper, to Marchant's *History of the Present Rebellion*, it is to be noted that its somewhat elaborate title-page contains no reference to any event later than the battle of Falkirk.[56] It has until now been thought to be a history of the *present* rebellion because its last page leaves Charles Edward still at large in the highlands. It can however be shown by reference to advertisements in the provincial press[57] that the work was originally put out in parts and commenced in April of 1746, hence 'of the *present* Rebellion'. It is a hotch-potch of snippings from the *London Gazette*, the morning and evening papers and the pamphlets and broadsides, and even the doggerel of the day. In addition to all this we find footnotes containing topographical information and the natural and local history of the various places concerned in the rising. Of these notes, more presently.

To pass now fourthly—and briefly—to the two accounts of Andrew Henderson in Edinburgh and Michael Hughes in London: Henderson aroused the contempt of John Murray of Broughton, Charles Edward's secretary—the 'ignorant little scholmaster'—but that of itself is no valid condemnation. Already in 1746 he published in Edinburgh an eight-page little poem *Expeditio Militaris, sive Britannia liberata, carmen in honorem Cumbriae Ducis*. After 20 years he moved from poetry to prose and published in London in 1766 a *Life of William Augustus, Duke of Cumberland* in nearly 400 pages. He followed his poem to

Cumberland with *A Letter to . . . the Duke of Newcastle on the Dangers arising from Popery and Disaffection* in 1747. *The History of the Rebellion, 1745 and 1746* appears to have been produced in the first instance in parts and the volume dated 1748 did not bear the author's name. It was 'By an Impartial Hand who was an Eye-Witness to most of the Facts', but he was not, of course, an eye-witness to any of the 'facts' he relates in England. He wrote with a marked whig bias, of course—hence Murray's affected contempt —but like Marchant in England he collected together some very readable accounts from one source and another.

Michael Hughes was a Londoner who had been 'Educated in the Blue coat Hospital'. He had, as he said, had his education 'about twenty Years ago' and had 'enlisted as a Volunteer in Brigadier General Bligh's Regement [the 20th Foot] where I had the Opportunity as well as the Inclination to see and hear and collect the following Account'. Bligh's Regiment was certainly in London in October of 1745. It went north on the 9th and later shipped from Leith to Aberdeen. The regiment (and Hughes) was present at Culloden and after Culloden helped to harry the highlands. Hughes wrote his *Narrative*[58] in circumstances, there-fore, that may well have been very similar in the first instance to James Ray, the Whitehaven gipsy (dealt with below). The London blue-coat boy and the Whitehaven gipsy had this in common: that each wrote in his own characteristic idiom; that each apparently thought that the fact that he himself had actually engaged in the campaign was as good a qualification as any— and better than most—to write his own account of it; and that (notwithstanding certain blatant errors) each contains certain circumstantial points of detail of a quite characteristic nature. They were, however, very unlike in this: where Michael Hughes dedicated his narrative 'to the Lord-Mayor, Aldermen and Citizens of London' and published it in London without (ap-parently) any editorial intervention, Ray suffered severely from his editors. In the result James Ray seems to have been altogether insufficiently appreciated for what is authentically *his* work, and— by way of compensation—to have been much praised for what can quite easily be shown to be spurious.

We pass therefore finally in this paper to Ray's *Compleat History of the Rebellion*, which has long been thought of as a genuine and original 'source'. He was an eye-witness of the events he describes. He speaks from 'occular Demonstration'.[59] His testimony, he says, 'will be more acceptable to my Countrymen from me (being an Eye-Witness) than from Strangers who must write on Hearsay'.[60] Hence his *History* has been regarded 'in many ways the best and most trustworthy account extant of the campaign and of the state of feeling in England'.[61] Because, as his title-page says, the history contains 'the natural History and Antiquities of the several Towns thro' which I pass'd with his Majesty's Army', even historical scholars have accepted him as 'an antiquarian as well as a soldier'[62]—a veritable scholar gipsy. It is not surprising therefore that Ray has come to be cited with such satisfaction by historians of the Forty-five. A detailed examination of his *History* will however be found to furnish some interesting results.

The Manchester edition, 'printed for the Author by Robert Whitworth' is commonly dated 1746.[63] Fishwick and others however have dated it 1760.[64] It was reprinted in 1749 by John Jackson of Petergate, York, the printer of the *York Gazette*, and in 1750 by S[amuel] & F[elix] Farley of Castle Green, Bristol, the family concern who printed *Farley's Bristol Journal* and other earlier and later newspapers of Bristol and Bath. There were further editions 'for the Author' in 1754 and 1755 (the former commonly described as Whitehaven[65]), and a London edition by Robert Brown in 1758. I have found references to other editions in 1748 and London editions in 1757 and 1760.[66]

It was during the course of a somewhat detailed study of the ornaments and type used by the early Manchester printers that I was drawn to doubt the ascription of Whitworth's Manchester edition of Ray to either the year 1746 or the year 1760. It was certainly not Whitworth's invariable practice to include a date on his title-pages.[67] His work can nevertheless be sorted into reasonable chronological order, firstly by reference to occasional announcements in *Whitworth's Manchester Magazine*, a weekly newspaper from the same printing house, and secondly by observing the wear and tear suffered by certain of his ornaments, particularly, in this instance, the crack developing on the top left hand corner of the head-piece used on page 11 of Ray's *History*, and the changes effected in the tail-piece used on pages x and 102. As regards *Whitworth's Manchester Magazine*, as is the case

of most early and mid-eighteenth century news-sheets, unfortunately no complete 'run' of the paper has survived. Among
the collections of the Central Library at Manchester, however,
there are a fair number of issues contained in a number of broken
'runs'. In none of these have I been able to find any advertisement
or announcement bearing on the publication of Ray's *History*.
As regards Whitworth's ornaments, the head-piece already referred to shows a crack in a particular state, and having regard
to certain other impressions, it could not possibly have been in
that particular condition in 1760. On the other hand the tail-
piece points to about 1746–7. This latter ornament is a shield
with three motifs inescutcheoned, 'one over two', with two
eagles (?) as supporters, surrounded and surmounted by the
characteristic decoration of the period. This piece appears to have
suffered some damage in about 1740, which became rather worse
some three years later. In time the three inner decorative devices
had to be removed from the shield altogether and it is in this
'doctored' state that the tail-piece is used in Ray's *History*.
Geoffrey R. Axon in his valuable handlist, *The Manchester Press
Before 1801*, places Ray under the date 1746, and Henry Brook's
Essays Against Popery under 1747. But this particular tail-piece, as
it frequently appears in Brook, has the centre pieces still intact,
but in Ray they have already been removed. The relative position
of the two works in the scheme of chronology must therefore of
course be reversed.[68] On looking through Ray for some internal
evidence in confirmation of this later date one is surprised to find
an account[69] of the execution of the last of the rebel lords, which
took place on Tower Hill in April of 1747—surprised, that is
to say, that a work containing an account of incidents which
took place in 1747 should have remained so long dated as
'1746'.

Although it is not possible, by reason of space, to report here
in detail the results of a close collation of the various editions, it
can be said that Ray's *History* does not appear to have been set up
again from the original 'copy' after Whitworth's Manchester
edition. The York 1749 edition was set up direct from Whitworth, the Bristol 1750 from the York of 1749, the York 1754
from the Bristol 1750, and the York of 1755 from the 1754, and
Robert Brown's London edition of 1758 from one or other of the

York editions of 1754 or 1755. All this can be shown by the study of certain literals and other misprints. The force of the evidence is cumulative, but the following are examples of the method. Among the casualties at Prestonpans Whitworth misprints the name of lieutenant Grafton (of Gardiner's dragoons) as 'Graston',[70] and the error persists through all editions. In the York edition of 1749 there is an odd misprint, which Jackson cannot correct even with an erratum note:

> Miss was obliged to keep at home for some Days, not having quite courage enough to get home, conceal'd his being of the Party, and remain'd in his Place.[71]

The error in all probability arises from the printer, in 'setting up' from Whitworth's edition, allowing his eyes to wander from the words 'enough to face' in one line to the words 'enough to get' in the next line but one.[72] Whitworth, in his copying, 'The Drapier's Letter',[73] misprints '*On* the contrary' as '*No* the contrary'.[74] The York edition of 1749 repeats '*No* the contrary'.[75] In the Farleys' Bristol reprinting of 1750 the error must have been noticed, for in order to 'correct' it a comma was inserted— 'No, the contrary',[76] and his comma was reproduced by Jackson in 1754 and 1755,[77] and again in Brown's London edition in 1758.[78] Whitworth in referring to the *seizures* lying in Leith custom house misprints the word as 'scissars'.[79] Jackson of York follows him in 1749.[80] Again it is corrected by Farley of Bristol in 1750.[81] Whitworth in referring to the raising of Lord Loudoun's Highland Regiment says, 'There is no cause to *value* the expence of raising the Troops' in error for 'no cause to censure'.[82] The 1749 edition repeats '*value*'.[83] But in 1750 the whole phrase is recast in order to make sense,[84] and again in 1754 and 1755 editions follow the 1750,[85] and Brown again adopts the form of words which is to be found in the 1750 edition but not in Whitworth.[86] As regards these editions of 1754 and 1755 (both 'Printed for the Author', the 1754 usually referred to as 'Whitehaven'[87] and the 1755 as 'London'), both can be shown by reference to the printer's ornaments used, to have been the work of John Jackson of Petergate, York, who had been responsible for the earlier edition of 1749. But all editions subsequent to Whitworth contain additional matter not found in the Manchester edition. It is quite possible to identify the actual source of all this additional matter and we shall have occasion to return to some of it later.

The most uncritical reader of Ray cannot but be conscious of a sudden break here and there both in form and in content. Part of the book—the greater part—is written in the ordinary journalistic English of the period. The other and lesser portion is couched in a highly characteristic idiom.

> Their Hussars were most of them young Men dressed in close plaid Waistcoats, and large Fur Caps, but having very bad Horses it occasion'd them to exert all their Vigour in bringing them to a Gallop, tho' very often (in Spite of them) the poor Beasts would immediately drop that Speed and take to one more suitable to their Age and Infirmities. If the common Men got a belly full of Victuals (they were not very curious about the Goodness of it) and a little Straw to lie upon they were intirely easy. The Excise they collected here for six Weeks.
>
> Kendal, called also Kirkby Candale, i.e., a church in the Valley . . . is the largest Town in the Country of Westmorland, and is enriched by the Industry of the Townsmen and the Wollen Manufacture, with which they have drove a trade throughout England ever since the Reigns of Edward III. As early as Richard II and Henry IV special Laws were enacted on Purpose for regulating Kendal Cloths: Queen Elizabeth . . .[88]

In the middle of the passage there is a distinct break noticeable, both in the subject matter and the manner of expression. On this and on various other accounts one is led to suspect that some fair portion of 'Ray's' *History* may not be the work of Ray at all. For instance, of the action at Prestonpans Ray writes throughout in the first person. '*We* lay on our Arms. . . *Our* Patroles could scarce perceive any Motion. . . .'[89] But Ray of course was never at Prestonpans. He did not join up with the army, as he himself records,[90] until he had reached Stafford, and that was some ten weeks later.

As a matter of fact, one can identify 'Ray's' account of Prestonpans as being substantially that written by one of the officers who marched with Cope in the expedition to the north and was later taken prisoner at Prestonpans. This 'Compleat Journal'[91] was originally printed in the *London Evening Post*[92] and has been frequently reprinted.[93]

Thus anyone at all well acquainted with the news-sheets, pamphlets and periodical literature of the time can easily recognize whole blocks, even of ostensibly original reminiscence, that must have been lifted bodily—of course without acknowledgement—from already printed sources. If then we proceed to a closer examination of this 'History' of 'Ray's' it will be only to find that the greater part of it was written with no more literary equipment than a pair of scissors and a paste-pot. Its very opening words:

In the Summer of the Year 1745, it was known that some Preparations were privately making for an Expedition in favour of the Pretender.[94]

we recognize as coming, word for word, from Dodsley 'History', either as it appeared in the *Museum* periodical,[95] the *Museum* collection,[96] in Mary Cooper's *Compleat And Authentick*,[97] or Richardson's 1748 (fourth) edition of Defoe's *Tour of the Whole Island*.[98] A couple of pages of almost *verbatim* agreement with Dodsley lands Charles Edward in the west and brings out the Camerons to his standard. Now Ray, or Robert Whitworth, or whoever it was who was responsible for compiling the 'copy'—shall we in order to remain non-committal say the Manchester editor?—on the somewhat flimsy pretence of the mere mention of the name of Cameron, thinks fit to introduce about thirty pages of the life of Jennie Cameron, that somewhat mythical person, Charles Edward's mistress. This is an apochryphal and somewhat scurrilous piece of fiction taken from the pamphlets of the day.[99] Having at last returned to the matter of the rising, the Manchester editor now lets Dodsley take him as far as the Firth of Forth, when it seems only fair to lay in turn someone else under tribute. A phrase about Edinburgh—Charles Edward 'being not only invited but solicited thereto, by the Jacobites in and about the City'[100]—reminds one of an account in a contemporary news-sheet, which version was reproduced in turn in Marchant's *History*.[101] The Manchester editor is now snipping from Marchant, who himself 'wrote' so much with the scissors at one elbow and the paste-pot at the other. The Manchester editor's next fifty pages, which take us as far as Carlisle are a garble, passage by passage, of Dodsley and Marchant. Another eleven pages of the eloquent, but entirely imaginary speech of the duke of Perth—although not imagined by either Ray or his editor —gives us a total of over one hundred pages of entirely borrowed matter, before we come to a single word of James Ray, the elusive Whitehaven gipsy. But at last we have the pleasure of meeting him—exactly where we would most of all have expected to meet him, namely, hard by Whitehaven. But before we enjoy two full pages of his enjoyable company we are again whisked off, firstly by Marchant and then by Dodsley. The editing is fairly bold, for it includes all sorts of incidents, the details of which Ray could not possibly have witnessed.

Ray's account is often interwoven with some other version, but even then in such a way as to leave no student of the sources in any doubt as to where it came from. The following, for instance, are taken from two accounts of Culloden:

On the 16th, we marched from Nairn betwixt Four and Five in the Morning, with our Foot divided into three Columns of five Battalions each; the Artillery and Baggage followed the first Column on the Right, our Cavalry covered the Left Wing and composed the Fourth Column.

After we had marched about eight Miles, our Advanced Guard perceived the Rebels at some Distance making a Motion towards us on the Left; (which was the Point we imagined the Rebels would strive to gain, as we had the Sea on our Right and the Hills on our Left, therefore the Rule was observed in all our March, that the Horse covered the Left Wing) on which we immediately formed, but finding the Rebels were a good way off, and that their whole Body did not move forwards, we put ourselves into marching Orders as before, and continued in it till within a Mile of them where we made a stand to reconnoitre their Situation.

We gave our Men a Day's Halt at Nairn, and on the 16th, marched thence, betwixt four and five, in Four Columns. The three Lines of Foot (reckoning the Reserve for one) were broken into three from the Right, which made the three Columns equal, and each of five Battalions. The Artillery and Baggage followed the first Column upon the Right and the Cavalry made a fourth Column on the Left.

After we had marched about eight Miles, our Advanced Guard, composed of about 40 of Kingston's and the Highlanders led by the Quartermaster-General, perceived the Rebels at some distance making a Motion towards the Left upon which we immediately formed: but finding the Rebells were still a good way from us, we put ourselves again upon our March in our former Posture, and continued it to within a Mile of them when we again formed in the same Order as before.

The first is 'Ray's' account.[102] The second is Cumberland's, communicated in a despatch written from Inverness on 18th April and published in the *London Gazette Extraordinary* of the 26th. The latter was republished in the *Gentleman's Magazine* in the April issue,[103] and again in Marchant's *History*,[104] from which doubtless Ray paraphrased it. Cumberland for his part continues his despatch:

> After reconnoitring their Situation we found them posted behind some old Walls and Huts, in a Line with Culloden House.

Ray continues his version by saying he volunteered to go forward to reconnoitre, and one is not in the circumstances very surprised to learn that he found the rebels extended to a park wall and 'formed into a Line with Culloden House'.[105] In other words the greater part of 'Ray's' *History* is not Ray's at all, and can in any case no longer be regarded as original matter. It seems then that someone—most probably other than Ray himself—set himself the task of transforming the manuscript, a piece of purely personal reminiscence, into a full-dress *Compleat History*. Something similar of course happened to the account of Michael Hughes. In the case of Ray this was done apparently by reference to Dodsley and Marchant.

Only one edition of Marchant is known, but it remains to determine which of the various available versions of Dodsley's *History* was used for this purpose. It will be recalled that *The Rise and Progress of The Rebellion* began to appear in Dodsley's *Museum* in the issue dated 29th March 1746, and was included in the volume of collected excerpts which appeared in 1747. Mary Cooper issued the anonymous *Compleat And Authentick History of the Rise, Progress and Extinction of the Late Rebellion* in 1747. (Dodsley could not refer to the *Extinction* nor to the *late rebellion* in March of 1746.) Richardson's fourth edition of Defoe's *Tours* appeared in 1748. After collating these texts it is found correct to say, briefly, that where in any minor verbal variation the *Compleat And Authentick* varies from *The Museum*, both 'Ray' and 'Defoe' agree with the *Compleat And Authentick*, and that where the latter version omits any words from *The Museum* version neither 'Ray' nor 'Defoe' picks them up. It seems reasonable then to suppose that the *Compleat And Authentick* was 'set up' from *The Museum*, and that both 'Ray' and 'Defoe' were independently 'set up' from the *Compleat And Authentick*. The later versions are in certain passages, simpler than the earlier. Here again the force of the evidence is cumulative, but an example or two will serve to illustrate the method. The reference in the first extracts is to the arrival of *Du Teillay* at Loch nan Uamh. *The Museum* reports:

> As for the Frigate beforementioned, she cruised for some days between the Islands of Bara and Uist, and at last stood in for the coast of Lochaber.[106]

The *Compleat And Authentick* agrees. That is to say, it was set up from *The Museum* (or from another version in agreement therewith). 'Ray' has it:

> As for the Frigate beforementioned, she stood in for the Coast of Lochaber.[107]

and 'Defoe's' *Tour* reads

> The Frigate cruized for some days between the Islands of Bara and Uist, and at last stood in for the Coast of Lochaber.[108]

Thus although both 'Ray' and 'Defoe' *could* have been 'set up' from either *The Museum* or the *Compleat And Authentick*, none of the others could have been 'set up' from either 'Ray' or 'Defoe'. The next reference is to Cope concentrating his troops at about Stirling in August 1745. *The Museum* had it,

> he drew together his troops then *in that part of the Kingdom*, and took *such* other Precautions as he thought *requisite*.[109]

The *Compleat And Authentick* took it:

> he drew together the troops *in that Kingdom, armed* the Militia, and took such Precutions as he thought *requisite*.[110]

'Ray' reads:

> he drew together the Troops then *in that Kingdom, armed the militia*, and took *what other* Precautions he thought *necessary*.[111]

'Defoe's' *Tour* is in agreement with the *Compleat And Authentick*. It is parallel passages such as these that raise the presumption that the *Compleat And Authentick* was 'set up' from *The Museum*, and that both 'Ray's' *History* and 'Defoe's' *Tour* were 'set up', but independently, from the *Compleat And Authentick*. A collation of the texts and a detailed study of the literals and other misprints confirm this presumption.

A detailed collation of the various editions of 'Ray' also provides some interesting results. Generally speaking Whitworth's Manchester edition is the simplest and can be shown to be the earliest known edition. Fishwick's date (1760) can therefore be dismissed.[112] Most of the topographical detail, which Whitworth had printed up in the actual text, Jackson of York pushed down in 1749 into footnotes, and by 1754 none of it was up in the text. Incidentally, the characteristic envoy which Sir C. Sanford Terry quoted with such evident pleasure in his happy collection on the Forty-five,

> The Reader is desir'd to excuse any Errors that may have escap'd the Corrector, or Press; the Author's principal Aim, throughout the whole, being to set forth Matters of Fact, tho' not flourish'd with that Illustration and emebllishment of Stile as might be expected from a more able Pen.[113]

is not to be found in the earlier editions. It was born apparently in Bristol in 1750. The Manchester editor commenced his story with the summer of 1745, but Jackson of York in 1749 went back to the earlier intrigues in Madrid, Rome and Paris, borrowing therefore six additional pages from the *Compleat And Authentick*, indicating thereby that he was fully aware that a good deal of 'Ray' was to be found in the earlier *Compleat And Authentick*. In 1750 Farley of Bristol added some topographical detail about the Island of Mull, and as he appears to have gone direct to Marchant for this and direct to the *Compleat And Authentick* for certain other detail it seems fairly likely that he too knew how much of 'Ray's' *History* had been written by Ray. Although Jackson's earliest edition from York repeated all the absurd detail about Jennie Cameron, Farley of Bristol dropped a good deal of it,[114] and in 1754 Jackson dropped the rest, and after that date it does not seem to have reappeared. In the earliest York edition (1749) Jackson inserted a paragraph about the steps taken by Scarborough to defend itself,[115] and inserted it apparently for no better reason than that he was a good Yorkshireman. In the next year Farley, in his Bristol edition, left in the paragraph about

Scarborough[116] (for all the interest that would have been in Bristol) but inserted an additional one about Bristol's mayor and corporation.[117] The later York reprints included both the Scarborough and the Bristol details,[118] and Robert Brown left them both in his London edition,[119] presumably for no better reason than they were in the place he had copied them from. Jackson added also the story about the quaker brewer of Edinburgh, and other matter regarding Fort William, Fort Augustus, Loch Ness, including a deal of post-Culloden detail about Tullibardine, Cumberland and parliamentary proceedings, and further details about the rebel lords. The 1754 and subsequent editions were yet further supplemented by details of the van Hoey correspondence, the bill of attainder, and so forth.

There is little left of Ray then as a 'source', the 'best and most trustworthy account extant', the account of an 'antiquarian as well as a soldier'. A good deal of the 'history' historians have been happy to quote from Ray was not only borrowed without acknowledgement, but—what is more to the point—was already at least second-hand before it was borrowed. And the claim to be anything of an antiquary—which, to do him credit, he appears not to have made himself—is founded solely on some footnotes which his editors have stolen from someone who had already borrowed them from somewhere else. But if Ray the historian disappears in a paste-pot, and Ray the antiquary drops clean away through a footnote, we are still left with James Ray the Whitehaven gipsy—and an entertaining enough character he is. Like a true gipsy, he is keenly interested in the weird highlanders, not as an historian nor as an antiquary, but as a Whitehaven gipsy. He observes their highland plaids, their food and drink, their habits—sanitary and insanitary—and, being a gipsy, he has a keen eye for colour, the game laws, women and horse-flesh. He writes a unique and obviously genuine story of his own adventures in the rising, and then perhaps like so many before him— and since—he seems to have suffered at the hands of his editors. Very likely it is they who pad it up and spin it out, and will not let him say a word of his own. A genuine story—first hand and first class—has been overlaid and interlarded with a whole lot of second rate, second-hand stuff. But when James Ray is let speak at all—a snatch here and a snatch there—we get the gipsy's story. When he is narrowly pursued he dismounts his horse, hides the harness in a hayloft, takes off his boots, and obviously he belongs to the place.[120] But when he is on the road on the king's business, he, *a gipsy*, can put up at proper inns (he gives the names of them to prove it[121]) and sometimes he actually hob-nobs with parsons, gentlemen and even magistrates.[122] He is a gipsy and well content 'with some good old Beer and a couple of stewed Rabbits'.[123] But being a gipsy, his contempt for the jaco-bites is almost unspeakable: they are insanitary—they are light-fingered—*they are vagrants!*

Notes

[1] Mary Cooper, widow and successor to Thomas Cooper, a prolific publisher of pamphlets at the time. Fielding had gone over to Cooper in 1742 with his 'Opposition. A Vision'. (Cooper printed some at least of the numbers of *The Champion*.)

[2] *GM* (September 1745), xv, 560; *Scots Magazine* (September 1745), vii, 495; *London Magazine*, xiv, 571.

[3] *The Museum, or The Literary and Historical Register*. 29th March 1746–12th September 1747.

[4] *The Museum*, vol. i, 25–40 (29th March), 75–80 (12 April), 109–20 (26th April), and 507–21 (13th September) (with a separate index, 531–3).

[5] *GM* (April 1747), xvii, 204, and *Scots Magazine* (April 1747), ix, 200.

[6] Thus the title-page. The 'running title' throughout however is 'A Succinct History of the Rebellion', and it was early cited under that title, cf. S. Boyse, *The History of the Rebellion* (1747), pp. 64, 71, *et statim*.

[7] W. L. Cross, *History of Henry Fielding* (Yale and Oxford, 1918), ii, 56–7; iii, 314–15. M. Seymour, 'Fielding's History of the Forty Five' *Philological Quarterly*, Univ. of Iowa (April 1935), xiv, 119, 113–14, 'Cam. Bibl. Eng. Lit.', ii, 519.

[8] Vol. iv, Letter VI. 'Containing a Brief Account of the Rise Progress and Extinction of the Rebellion . . .', pp. 322–68.

[9] 'Printed for the Author, and sold by R. Walker, in Fleet Lane, and at his Printing Office at Cambridge'. For Marchant's petition for the 'Royal Lycence for the sole printing publishing and vending' for the term of fourteen years, see SP Dom. 92/328 (or 268).

[10] *The History of the Rebellion, 1745 and 1746 . . . By an Impartial Hand . . .* Edinburgh, 1748.

[11] *A Plain Narrative or Journal of the Late Rebellion*. London, 1746.

[12] See below.

[13] On this habit and its use for identifying items of Fielding's anonymous and fugitive work, see my note in *Modern Language Review*, xli, No. 2 (April 1946), 126.

[14] This fact was first noticed by Thomas Keightley, who, however, somewhat overstated the case. *Fraser's Magazine* (February 1855), lvii, 217; and cf. also G. E. Jensen, *The Covent Garden Journal by Sir Alexander Drawcansir, Knt. Censor of Great Britain* (Henry Fielding), Yale (1915), ii, 187, 201–2, *et statim*; Cross, i, 135, 256, 286; ii, 55; H. K. Banerji, *Henry Fielding* (Oxford), p. 107.

[15] I, 135.

[16] *Othello*, act III, sc. iii, 157–8.

[17] *Champion*, 6th March 1739.

[18] The actual quotation is:

> Thy father's merit sets thee up to view
> And shews thee in the fairest point of light.
>
> (*Cato*, act I, sc. ii, 33–4)

Fielding was quoting—apparently from memory—in the issue of *The Champion* which appeared on 17th November 1739. On the 15th *Cato* had been revived at Drury Lane (Nicoll, *Hist. of Eng. Eighteenth Century Drama, 1700–1750*, p. 295).

[19] Butler, *Hudibras*, ii, 109–10.

[20] *Covent Garden Journal*, No. 48 (16th June 1752).

[21] Professor Banerji at least found this unconvincing.

[22] iii, 310.

[23] *An Impartial History of the Late Rebellion*, 94n.

[24] The title-page and the half-title are apparently conjugate with the last two leaves constituting the last gathering.

[25] ii, 57n.

[26] *Notes and Queries*, seventh ser.—7th January 1888—v, 1.

[27] *Philological Quarterly* (University of Iowa), xiv, April 1935.

[28] *Notes and Queries*, clxxxix (1945), 90–2, 117–20 and 138–41.

[29] *Miscellanies* (1743) Preface, xxvii (*sic*) (error in pagination, sig. D.3).

[30] See Paper 19, below.

[31] i, 538.

[32] i, 538 and ii, 1130.

[33] ii, 1130.

[34] i, 538.

[35] One lacking half-title and page 47 (text) with verso blank.

[36] Of the two first editions in the British Museum, one lacks the half-title.

[37] See *Book Auction Records*, xxviii, 231 and 374, and xlv, 203.

[38] Edited I. K. Fletcher, Newport (1934).

[39] Fielding, *History of the Present Rebellion*, Newport (1934), Intro.

[40] See below.

[41] ii, 59.

[42] As to the preliminary announcements of which, see the advertisements in (for example) the *London Evening Post*, between 8th and 22nd March, 1746.

[43] Cf. *London Mercury*, 1931, and *Philological Quarterly*, xiv, 105.

[44] *Philological Quarterly*, xiv, 119.

45 *Ibid.* 121.

46 In other respects also her judgement is, I suggest, a little bit hasty. E.g. in referring to the diary of events within the besieged Fort William (March 1746), she says this is 'transcribed from the *Gazette* where it had been represented as "drawn up at the Time by an Officer of the Garrison" (the conventional introduction used to validate news from the front)' (*Phil. Qtly.*, xiv, 116). But the diary is well known to historical scholars to be perfectly genuine, and the original is in the Public Record Office. (SP Scot. 30/2 and 17.)

47 i, 538.

48 iii, 314.

49 ii, 519.

50 This mistake derives from an error in pagination, where both signatures B and C are numbered '9–16'.

51 iii, 314, and ii, 5.

52 It was advertised right away in the news-sheets; see for example, the *London Evening Post*, between 19th October and 19th November.

53 Although the set-up of the title as he gives it is not in exact agreement with it—nor, incidentally, with my own copy.

54 xvii, 204.

55 The work might therefore be described as an octavo in fours: Half-title (verso blank), title-page (verso blank), text, pp. 1–8, 9–16 twice, 17–155 (verso of 155 blank) = $[X^2]$ A–U^4, X^2.

56 17th January 1746.

57 *Manchester Magazine*, 15th April 1746.

58 *A Plain Narrative or Journal of the Late Rebellion* . . . 1746.

59 Ray, Preface, v (Manchester ed. Unless otherwise stated all quotations in this paper from Ray are from the Manchester (N.D.) edition).

60 *Ibid.* p. 187.

61 *D.N.B.*

62 H. Broxap, *A biography of Thomas Deacon* (1911), p. 99.

63 G. R. Axon, *op. cit.*, 3 and 6 ('Better here' he says, quite correctly, 'than 1760'). A. J. Hawkes, *Lancashire Printed Books*, 72 ('1746?') and *D.N.B.* I do not think it has been noticed before that although this date is incorrect it is supported by an early and rare catalogue, *A Catalogue of Several Libraries and Parcels of Books* . . . [1766], p. 36.

64 H. Fishwick, *Lancashire Library* (1875), p. 312. *Lon. Lib. Cat. Supp.*, 1920–8, 772.

65 *Brit. Mus. Cat.* ('Whitehaven'), *Lon. Lib. Cat.* (1914), ii, 660 ('Whitehaven?').

66 These dates are, I think, suspect.

67 Geoffrey A. Axon, *op. cit.*, pp. 1–9.

68 As a matter of fact the *Essays Against Popery, Slavery and Arbitrary Power* was advertised in *Whitworth's Manchester Magazine* for 23rd September 1746.

69 Pp. 395–408.

[70] P. 61.

[71] P. 28.

[72] P. 27.

[73] A contemporary broadside, reproduced in *GM*, xv (October 1745), 531-2, and in the provincial presses. See also Marchant, pp. 134-8.

[74] P. 93.

[75] P. 87.

[76] P. 82.

[77] P. 74 in both editions.

[78] P. 74.

[79] P. 65.

[80] P. 59.

[81] P. 53.

[82] P. 80.

[83] P. 74.

[84] Pp. 69-70.

[85] P. 61 in both editions.

[86] P. 61.

[87] *Brit. Mus. Cat.* ('Whitehaven'), *Lon. Lib. Cat.* (1914), ii, 660 ('Whitehaven?'). W. T. Lownes (H. G. Bohn), *Bibliographers' Manual*, etc. If Thomas Cotton printed *The Whitehaven Weekly Courant* 1736 and 1737, there has not, I believe, been any copy traced.

[88] Pp. 139-40.

[89] Pp. 54-5.

[90] Pp. 187-8.

[91] *Compleat Journal of Sir John Cope's Expedition In a Letter from an Officer.*

[92] 17th October 1745.

[93] *Scots Magazine*, vii (October 1745), 477-81. *GM*, xv (October 1745), 518-21. Marchant, 81-4 and 99-103. George Charles, *History of the Transactions*, ii, 17-19.

[94] P. 11. Thus the Manchester edition. Others commence, 'As soon as the War broke out on the Continent the Irish and Scots Partizans of the Chevalier at the Court of Madrid judged it a fit Opportunity . . .,' which is an earlier passage from the same source.

[95] 29th March 1746.

[96] i, 26.

[97] P. 10 (sig. B v°.)—there is an error in pagination, both gatherings B and C being paged 9-16.

[98] iv, 322.

[99] Whitworth's printing some of the unsavoury details of the alleged adventures occasioned some comment, not to say controversy, in Manchester at the time (see *MM*, 22nd April and 9th September 1746), and this may have suggested to Whitworth their inclusion into 'Ray's' *History*. See also end of Paper 13, above.

[100] Ray, 49.

101 Marchant, 96.

102 P. 361.

103 xv, 210–12.

104 Pp. 383–91.

105 Pp. 363–4.

106 29th March 1746, i, 26. The account is based of course on *The London Gazette*, 13th–17th August 1745.

107 P. 13.

108 iv, 323.

109 29th March 1746, i, 27. The italics are not in the original.

110 P. 12 (sig. B2 v°.)

111 Pp. 46–7.

112 See note 33.

113 *The Rising of 1745: a Narrative of the Last Jacobite Rising by Several Contemporary Hands* (Camb. 1922), p. 188. (Ray: Bristol ed., p. 440).

114 Probably because he could make nothing out of Jackson's odd misprint referred to at n. 40. If this were the case, the presumption would be that the Farleys reprinted by reference to Jackson, Marchant, and the *Compleat And Authentick*, but were without a copy of Whitworth.

115 Pp. 155–6.

116 Pp. 146–7.

117 Pp. 66–7.

118 Pp. 58–9 and 159–60.

119 Pp. 58–9 and 139–40.

120 Pp. 157–8.

121 Pp. 146, 150, 163 and 187.

122 Pp. 152, 159, and 165.

123 P. 187.

18 *Fielding and the Forty-five*

For the whole of this present century students of the Fielding text have had to rely upon W. E. Henley's 'complete and unabridged' edition of 1902. A new edition, which promises high, is now commencing to issue from the Wesleyan University in Connecticut. Mostly, however, the fugitive pieces referred to in these present papers do not find any place in the various 'complete and unabridged works'—the 'complete' works being not in fact complete. The two standard Fielding biographies are a two-volume work from Oxford by the late Master of Pembroke, Dr F. Holmes Dudden, *Henry Fielding: his Life and Work*;[1] and a work from Yale in three volumes, but of about the same length, *The History of Henry Fielding*[2] by Dr Wilbur Cross.

The biography by Dr Dudden is a critical yet sympathetic work, tending in its literary judgements to endorse and confirm those of Professor Cross. Fielding studies owe a great deal, of course, to Cross, who did so much to recover his character from the calumny under which it lay so long buried. Professor Cross's work, however, was published over half a century ago, and the results of a good deal of detailed research that has gone on in the meantime have, for some reason or other, failed to get taken up into more recent works. Hence some of Professor Cross's assumptions have unfortunately been given a new currency, notwithstanding that in the light of recent research certain of them are no longer tenable.

It is a commonplace in Fielding biography that some time before the outbreak of the Forty-five Fielding had gone into a period of literary silence. Legislated off the stage in 1737[3] and disgusted by the common horsedealing of his 'Young Patriots'

The notes and references are on pages 186–8

in 1742,[4] he bade farewell to the Muses, forsook 'the ragged nine', and determined thereafter to follow exclusively the law.[5] Whether it were Charles Edward's landing in 1745 that beckoned him back into active journalism and the rough horseplay of English politics, or the defeat of the government forces at Prestonpans and the then imminent invasion of England, or whether it were some other cause, the energy he threw into the anti-jacobite cause is truly amazing. In the October of 1745[6] alone he put his old anti-catholic play *The Debauchees*[7] through another edition; he wrote a clever (if not very creditable) anti-papistical pamphlet, *A Dialogue Between the Devil, the Pope and the Pretender*;[8] he wrote a stern pro-ministerial tract, a stirring call to arms, *A Serious Address to the People of Great Britain*;[9] and in order to counter the over-romanticized over-glamorized jacobite versions of jacobite success so far, he wrote another pro-ministerial tract, *The History of the Present Rebellion in Scotland*.[10] All this was in the month of October 1745; and already by the first days of November he had the first number of his new pro-ministerial newspaper, *The True Patriot*,[11] on sale on the streets of London. After he had wound up his *True Patriot* at the close of the rising in the spring of 1746, and when the political issues were sharpened again by the impending general election of 1747, he produced another defence of the ministry, *A Dialogue Between a Gentleman of London . . .*[12] and yet another, *A Proper Answer to A Late Scurrilous Libel*.[13] He also launched in 1747 and edited until the end of 1748, another pro-ministerial newspaper, *The Jacobite's Journal*,[14] in which—with characteristic Fielding ironies and double ironies—he argued the jacobites' case for them, and drove it to its logical conclusion of untenable absurdity. For three and a half years, therefore, Fielding lived in this atmosphere of whig-tory-jacobite controversy, and drove himself—and there is evidence that he drove himself to the very limit—to write and write and write, ever on the jacobite theme. When therefore in 1749 his great masterpiece appeared, it is not to be wondered at that Tom Jones had his being in a background of the Forty-five. Indeed, it is not going too far to say that the rising was something of a water-shed in Fielding's life. Yet his work in connection with it has been sadly mishandled, by biographers and bibliographers alike.

This paper, therefore, will attempt, firstly, to show that certain of Fielding's titles (in his political writings of this particular period) continue to be declared 'lost' when in fact they have been found, and that a number of various copies of them have come to light since the publication of Professor Cross's painstaking bibliography, and these clearly disclose hitherto unknown editions which nevertheless have not got noted either in the standard works or in the subsequent biographies or studies; secondly, to show that certain other writings are universally admitted to the biographies and bibliographies as unquestionably Fielding's work whereas, in point of fact, there is no evidence to show that Fielding wrote them, and both the internal and the external evidence is against his authorship; and thirdly, to compare and contrast (in their literary content rather than the bibliographical facts) two little works on the same topic, namely, *A Serious Address* and *A Calm Address*, both of which have been admitted to the canon, but one of which only is unquestionably by Fielding and the other is just as unquestionably not.

The first of the works declared to be lost is the *Charge to the Jury* (1745), not to be confused with the much better known *Charge to the Grand Jury* (1749). It is in general acknowledged that Fielding's political pamphleteering fell mainly into two periods; the first was that between the passing of the licensing act of 1737,[15] when Walpole legislated him off the stage, and the fall of Walpole in 1742 when the principal butt of his wit was removed; the second period was that between the outbreak of the rising in 1745, when he threw himself whole-heartedly into the political fray, and 1748 when he accepted his Bow Street magistracy, which removed him from such active political controversy. During the first period he was the ministry's most bitter opponent; during the second he was the ministry's most ardent supporter. It has, without exception, been held that the latter period was immediately preceded by a year of complete literary inactivity, owing—so it has been said—to the paralysing grief occasioned by his wife's death. It was only the insurrection and invasion, it was held—and is still held[16]—that could rouse him out of his lethargy.

Professor Cross,[17] leaning on the not altogether reliable authority of Arthur Murphy,[18] followed Miss Godden[19] in supposing that it was perfectly in accordance with all we knew of Fielding's passionate devotion to his wife, that her loss should have shattered his energies for the whole of the ensuing year. More recently Dr Dudden[20] brings Lady Mary Wortley Montagu to confirm this. As long ago as 1758, however, there appeared in a publisher's posthumous list[21] of Fielding's works the title of a fugitive piece, *Charge to the Jury*, which alone is sufficient to disprove this theory. This title of 1745 was assigned by Cross—without any particular reason being adduced, but presumably in association with his Bow Street magistracy—to the year 1748. He commented: 'No copy known, nor does the title (probably a subtitle) appear in the lists of books given in the magazines of the period.'[22] The title is not noted in the *Cambridge Bibliography of English Literature*, and is unknown alike to Miss Godden, Professor Banerji[23] and Dr Dudden. Yet notwithstanding Professor Cross's note, the title was in fact listed in the contemporary magazines.[24] To settle all doubts a copy appeared at Sotheby's as long ago as 1926,[25] and since then other copies have come to light.[26] The exact effect of this pamphlet on Fielding's biography has already been examined in detail.[27]

Briefly one could say that the pamphlet was Fielding's charge to a jury imagined to be sitting at the inquest on the death of his old enemy, Robert Walpole. Walpole's death—like his life—was the subject of bitter controversy. The first announcement said that he had died of 'an Inflamation in the Lungs',[28] and a later said he died of a stone.[29] In consequence the physicians on the one hand and the surgeons on the other were soon at loggerheads.[30] Then Fielding in his own typical manner, charged into the midst, held his own inquest, and found on the evidence, in his characteristic legalistic and ironical way, that poor Walpole had died, not from an inflammation nor from a stone; he had died from the incompetence of his doctors. This pamphlet is the *Charge to the Jury on the Sum of the Evidence*.

Apart from adding to the Fielding bibliography a highly characteristic piece in his richest ironic vein, this title adds something to Fielding's biography also for, written as it was, *after* his own wife's death, and *before* the outbreak of the rising, it shows Fielding hacking for Cooper, his old publisher, during the very period which has hitherto been universally accepted as his period of silence. Whatever it was, then, that roused him from his lethargy or his grief, it was *not* the Forty-five.

Whether Fielding had been initially roused from his late political inactivity by the jacobite rising or not, one fact cannot be disputed, namely, that on one account or another, jacobitism—or rather the whig ministry's struggle against the jacobites (bearing in mind his practice at the law)—came to absorb practically the whole of his available time during the next three and a half years; led, at least indirectly, to his appointment to his Bow Street magistracy; and opened, therefore, the last great phase in his life, in which, as it turned out, he was to work himself to death. One would have thought that these factors alone, or the mere fact that Fielding himself had been credited with a *History of the . . . Rebellion* would have led his biographers and bibliographers to chase this fugitive title until they had solved its curious little mysteries.

The story of the bibliographical confusion of the *History of the Present Rebellion in Scotland* starts with Fielding's sister, Sarah, and their publisher, Andrew Millar. A few years after Fielding's death, Millar issued a second edition of Sarah's *Lives of Cleopatra and Octavia*, a work that had originally appeared anonymously. On the fly-leaf of the 1758 edition (the fly-leaf does not appear in the British Museum 1757 copy), Millar listed among the work of Henry, an item: *The History of the Rebellion in Scotland*. It is now clear that the title ought correctly to have read, *The History of the Present Rebellion in Scotland*. If Millar was doing violence to Fielding's title,[31] it was under the impression that he was merely bringing it up to date, for he dropped the word 'present' on the ground, apparently, that by 1757 the rebellion was in fact no longer present. It was this slight misquotation that seems to have raised in Professor Cross's mind some doubt as to the exact title of Fielding's *History*, particularly in the absence not only of any *copies* of the book itself—and Cross admits he had never seen a copy—but in the absence also of any reliable *record* of one.

There is, however, a reference in the magazines of the period, a title that fits as near as may be: '*History of the Present Rebellion in Scotland*. 1s. Cooper.'[32] Fielding's *History* is a piece of skilled

counter-propaganda, which, if it is a 'history' at all, is one dedicated to Mars rather than to Clio.[33]

Another work of Fielding of about this period that continues to
be recorded as 'lost' notwithstanding that it has been found is
Ovid's Art of Love Paraphrased and Adapted to the Present Time.

It is anonymous but was advertised in the *Jacobite's Journal*[34]
and listed by Millar among Fielding's works.[35] Professor Cross
said 'no copy known'.[36] Professor Banerji did not include the
title in his bibliography, but mentioned the Rice-Oxey copy[37] in
his text.[38] Dr Dudden, notwithstanding four references[39] in the
interim, follows Cross as usual, and says, 'no copy of the original
booklet is known'.[40] The item is touched upon here as relating to
the Forty-five because it testifies to Fielding's preoccupation with
the rising. He professes, for example, to have found in *De Arte
Amandi* some curious references to the duke of Cumberland, not
only 'his wound at Dettingen, his Danger and Intrepidity at
Fontenoy', but also 'his Toils at Home, in defiance of Cold and
Fatigue, his Pursuit to Carlisle and his Victory at Culloden'.
Fielding then goes on to give advice—ironically presumably—on
how to write royal biographies. 'If thy Memory fails, go on
nevertheless; for Invention cannot here outdo the Reality, and thy
Fictions shall recommend thee equal with the Truth.'[41]

Ovid's Art of Love Paraphrased was anonymous, but was advertised in Fielding's *Jacobite's Journal*,[42] and listed by Millar in the
revised but posthumous (1754) edition of *Jonathan Wild*,[43] and in
Sarah Fielding's *Lives of Cleopatra and Octavia*,[44] referred to above
in connection with the *Charge to the Jury* and the *History of the
Present Rebellion*. Professor Cross, although he says 'no copy
known', refers to this edition, but gives a wrong set-up for the
title-page and an inaccurate imprint;[45] he admits, however, as his
only authority, the advertisement in the *Jacobite's Journal*.

The little work is now traced,[46] 'Printed by M. Cooper . . .
A. Dodd . . . and G. Woodfull . . . M.DCC. XLVII'.[47] There is
a copy in Yale.[48]

With regard to the second limb of this present paper, works
erroneously ascribed to Fielding, the first of them is the *Calm
Address to All Parties*, appended to the so-called 'second' edition
of the *Serious Address*. Although its ascription to Fielding has

never before been questioned, I suggest it had been admitted to the canon in an altogether unscholarly way.

Fielding's pamphlet *A Serious Address to the People of Great Britain* was a call to arms in 1745 in the face of a threatened invasion, a challenge to arouse the people of this country out of their apathy, an appeal to them to join the Home Guard and repel the invader. As such it has frequently been described in Fielding biography and bibliography. What seems to have been hitherto entirely overlooked is the fact that the *Serious Address* went through another printing.[49] This latter printing may very well have been a pirated edition—the pirates did not usually pirate the failures—and perhaps it was the appearance of this unauthorized issue that prompted Fielding or his publisher or bookseller, to put out a second authorized edition.

It is not quite clear what exactly happened, nor does reference to the surviving printer's account books solve the mystery. Certainly, like the first edition and unlike the title-page, it was not in fact 'printed for M. Cooper'; it was printed by Strahan for Andrew Millar. As J. Paul de Castro has pointed out,[50] something as yet unaccounted for seems to have happened, possibly in the setting up or the running off of the 'second' edition. However, we do at least know that for one reason or another it was decided to re-issue two anonymous pamphlets together. One of these was Fielding's *Serious Address*; the other was a piece, never until then associated with Fielding, entitled, *A Calm Address to All Parties*. The latter title had, as a matter of fact, already appeared from the house of John Oliver in Bartholomew Close, a printer who had not long started up. This *Calm Address*, like the *Serious Address*, had been issued in the October, shortly after the battle of Prestonpans, and was doing the rounds in the booksellers' shops and the coffee-houses at the same time as the *Serious Address*. This can be seen from the news-sheets of the period, where it is announced as 'printed and sold by J. Oliver'.

John Oliver, printer and bookseller, appears to have been a whig of less violent persuasion than Fielding, a moderate whig of the solid nonconformist wing. The author of the *Calm Address* seems to have been, like his bookseller, also of less violent opinions. To him, if not to Fielding, the jacobites were not necessarily rascals, bandits, vandals or huns. Indeed, they might conceivably be actuated by some sort of motive or ideal—entirely mistaken of course—but nevertheless, an ideal of sorts. What is needed therefore, at the present juncture, is not the violent denunciation and immoderate accusations we find in the *Serious Address* and *the Devil, the Pope and the Pretender*. On the contrary, we need a dispassionate inquiry as to whethe rthe restoration of the family of Stuart would or would not be averse to the civic interest of the commoners generally of Great Britain, supposing, that is, that the pretender were to succeed in his present attempt, and allowing—merely for argument's sake of course—that he afterwards conducted himself according to the principles of honesty and honour.

This point of view—this moderation—was in considerable contrast to anything that Fielding for his part had yet written about the rising. *His* was an altogether more whole-hearted denunciation. Nevertheless, the two pamphlets now appeared together, as a kind of double-bill, ostensibly from the house of Cooper. One might very well think, unless Cooper or Millar had come to some arrangement with Oliver, that this was doing violence to the doctrine which today has become either more refined or more defined, in the law of copyright. But certainly the two pamphlets appeared under the single imprint.

When Professor Cross found this 'second' edition of the *Serious Address*, he did not apparently consider whether or not the *Calm Address* were in fact entirely new material. He forthwith ascribed it unequivocally to Henry Fielding. A closer acquaintance with the fugitive political pamphleteering of the time would have saved him from this error, for he would then have known not only that that particular tract had appeared earlier with a different imprint, and that it had been earlier announced in one of the familiar 'this-day-is-published' advertisements, but furthermore that the text of the piece had already been reproduced in the October number of the *Gentleman's Magazine*.[51] He almost certainly did not know that the *Calm Address* was no more than a reprint of some other piece, completely unconnected with Fielding, added—quite possibly in total disregard of what we should now call copyright—to one of Fielding's pamphlets. In other words, no evidence of any character has ever been brought forward that Fielding actually wrote a word of the *Calm Address*.

Since such external evidence as is at present known is rather against Fielding's authorship, we might turn to the internal evidence. In the *Serious Address* the *hath* usage already referred to is very marked throughout. There are over a score of *haths* to one single *has* (and that one might very well be a printer's slip). One finds on some pages two or three *haths* on the page, and on one as many as four. There are occasionally two *haths* in a single sentence and in one passage as many as three:

> In this Branch she *hath* lately felt the Force of British Opposition, and is at present thoroughly sensible how dearly she *hath* bought her success on the Continent, by a War which *hath* totally ruin'd her Trade.[52]

This is in great contrast to the *Calm Address*. In the latter there is not a single *hath*; in every case the auxiliary is used in the form of *has*. The internal evidence therefore, like the external evidence, points away from Fielding's authorship. There is in fact no evidence that he wrote a word of it. Yet such is the state of Fielding scholarship that this bare ascription of a new title to Fielding has been commonly accepted, not only on no evidence, but indeed *against* the evidence, and has never since been subject to any critical examination.

Until we know in greater detail precisely the parts played by Mary Cooper and Andrew Millar in the production of the 'second' (joint) edition of the *Serious Address* and the *Calm Address* it would perhaps be as well not to attach too much importance to Cooper's somewhat unsavoury reputation. Mary Cooper as a bookseller is known to have been not above backing certain genuine work with spurious 'additions'. In the Dodsley case,[53] for example, she was selling a genuine first part and a spurious second, notwithstanding Dodsley's protests. Even after the author publicly advertised his repudiation of the spurious 'second' part, Coopers in 1751 put it through a second edition, and bound it up with the genuine first part, and sold them together. Both Fielding[54] and Andrew Millar[55] referred to the *Serious Address* as Fielding's work. Neither, however, at any time made any reference to the *Calm Address*. There has in fact been no evidence brought forward to connect the *Calm Address* with Henry Fielding.

The other work inaccurately ascribed to Fielding, the *Compleat*

And Authentick History, has been sufficiently disposed of in dealing above with the *History of the Present Rebellion*. As the genuine work is admitted to the canon, the spurious is necessarily dismissed.

There remains the various editions of Fielding's works dealing with the Forty-five, yet usually omitted from the bibliographies and the biographies.

The *Charge to the Jury* has already been mentioned. The title is misquoted by Cross, it is erroneously attributed to 1748, and assigned to his 'Uncertain or Doubtful' category. The title was unknown to Godden and is not noted in the *Cambridge Bibliography of English Literature*. Professor Banerji and Dr Dudden have not gone behind Cross who said 'no copy known'. There are however copies in the British Museum, the Bodleian, John Rylands and Yale.[56]

The *Serious Address* is usually stated to have gone through two editions.[57] In fact it went through four. The first is well known. It is without the *Calm Address* of course and was 'printed for M. Cooper at the Globe in *Paternoster Row*. MDCCCLV'.[58]

There is another issue, dated '1745', not recorded for example in Cross or Dudden. It is done in somewhat smaller type, runs into 26 pages only, and bears no price on the title-page.[59] It is not referred to by de Castro in his examination of Strahan (the printer's) books,[60] and is probably a pirated edition. If so, this might account for the issue of the so-called 'second' edition.

In the edition claiming as its title-page to be the 'second edition', Fielding's *Serious Address* appeared for the first time together with the anonymous *Calm Address*.[61] The piece was 'printed for M. Cooper . . . MDCCLV'.[62] There are copies in the British Museum, the Manchester Central Library, Yale and elsewhere.[63] There is also a fourth edition, namely, 'The Third Edition Corrected, with Additions'. London, M. Cooper, 1745, of which there is a copy in Yale.[64] I do not know of this being noticed before.

The first edition of the *History of the Present Rebellion in Scotland* has already been referred to.[65] A further edition has been overlooked, which carries the imprint: 'London: printed. Dublin: Re-printed for the Booksellers, 1745'.[66] There are copies in the British Museum and the Bodleian.[67]

The conclusions, therefore, of the first two parts of this paper are as follows:

1. The following 'lost' works have been found, locations of copies and other references stated, and the effects on Fielding biography noted:
   (*a*) *Charge to the Jury* (1745).
   (*b*) *History of the Present Rebellion* (1745).
   (*c*) *Ovid's Art of Love Paraphrased* (1747).
2. The following works are upon detailed examination found to be spurious and should be dismissed from the canon:
   (*d*) *A Compleat And Authentick History of the . . . Rebellion* (1747).
   (*e*) *A Calm Address to All Parties* (1745).
3. The following editions, not recorded in the standard bibliographies and biographies, should be noted:
   (*f*) *A Serious Address to the People of Great Britain* (1745), being a reprint of the first edition, which did not include the *Calm Address* (which latter was added to the 'second' authorized edition).
   (*g*) *A Serious Address . . .* the third edition corrected . . . 1745, which may in fact be the fourth.
   (*h*) *History of the Present Rebellion in Scotland* (1745). In addition to (2) above, there was a Dublin reprint, also dated 1745.

It remains to compare and contrast *A Serious Address to the People of Great Britain* with *A Calm Address to All Parties*. The *Serious Address* was an anonymous shilling pamphlet which appeared in London just after the battle of Prestonpans. It is a stirring call to arms. The rebellion should no longer be the object of your derision; the progress the rebels have made is such as should awake at least your apprehension, and should no longer suffer you to neglect proper methods for your own defence. He goes on—being Fielding—to pour scorn on the fact that it is not really the pretender to the crowns of Britain who has landed in these Islands—not the real pretender, that is to say, for the real pretender has already been once driven from our shores. The present visitor is only the pretender's son, a deputy pretender, a sort of pretender's pretender, a pretender once removed.

'Shall we be cheated by so gross an Imposition?' he asks.[68]

For what is this son but the tool of his father, the tool of a fool who has already been sent packing? Does this deputy pretender act merely by his father's commission? Has he taken himself the title of regent only in his father's name, that is to say, in the name of, and in the absence of, one whom the country has already not only rejected but also ejected? After some preliminary skirmishing Fielding proceeds to develop his argument. In this he takes the strictly ministerial line. His appeal is partly to political principle and partly to religious prejudice. In political affairs he went back to the parliamentary settlement of 1688 and beyond, to the period of rule, or rather misrule, of Charles Edward's reputed grandfather, James II—'reputed' because, as a good whig, he cast doubts upon the legitimacy of both pretenders, old and young. In religious affairs he appeals to the religious (and national) prejudice against France and Spain. One gathers, at least for this present purpose, Fielding's history was all blacks and whites—there were no greys. However, in form, certainly, his appeal is for religious national and political *toleration*, and he speaks of the present king 'who, during a Reign of eighteen Years hath not stained a Scaffold with a single drop of English Blood, an Instance not to be paralleled in any one Reign since the Conquest'.[69] He speaks of the political liberties the English have come to take for granted:

Can the greatest Man among us, even the King himself, take one of these from the poorest? Can any Man be imprisoned wrongfully, without present Redress and future Satisfaction? Can he be punish'd without a Trial, without an unanimous Conviction by twelve Men of his Equals, having been first accused on the Oaths of a Grand Jury of the like Number? Is he then liable to any Sentence than that which the express Letter of the Law adjudges him, a Sentence which the King can neither aggravate nor alter? Is his Property less safe than his Life. May he not enjoy it how he will and give it to whom he pleases? Can any Man take from him an Acre, or a Shilling, but by due Course of Law in which his Cause is to be determined by the same Jury of his Equals?[70]

It is Fielding the lawyer speaking. And this he compares with political liberty and religious liberty in catholic France.

No Man in the Kingdom (of what Quality whatsoever) dares cut his Corn, when ripe, till the King's Officers have chosen what Part they will receive for his, and this at his own Price.[71]

Can the nation of Britain

hope for better legal Securities for the Toleration of its Religion under a Catholick Prince than the French Protestants had for the Toleration of theirs by the Edict of Nantz? And yet did not Lewis XIV revoke that Edict though it was the Act of his Grandfather, a Prince whom he always affected to make the Model and Example in Government.[72]

If France, if Spain, would make their choice of a monarch to rule over us, 'Common Sense cries aloud to us, reject him'. The pretender comes to our shores, if not under the arms of catholic France and Spain, at least with their support. If it be in their interest to support him, it must be in ours to reject him. Basically, the argument adopted by Fielding was that of the orthodox whig constitutionalist. By what right can a pretender presume to land uninvited in this country contrary to the pronouncements of parliament, and pretend to claim the crown? Only by some doctrine of indefeasible hereditary right. This doctrine has been long exploded.

The Legislature of the Kingdom have unanimously declared against such Principal: The Reverse of it is Law, a Law as firmly established as any other in the Kingdom; nay, it is the Foundation, the Corner-Stone of all our Laws and of the Constitution itself. . . . Whatever, therefore, tends to the Shaking of this Fundamental Right, doth of itself introduce an opposite System of Government, and *changes not only the King, but the Constitution*.[73]

Therefore, Fielding goes on

Let us look back to the History of that Prince from whom this Pretender claims. It was not only the Difference of his Religion from that of this Country which made him unfit to be King of it; he was unfit to govern even a Catholick Country which had Liberties to defend, because his Mind was strongly tainted with all the Notions of Absolute Power. Passive Obedience and Non-Resistance on the Part of his Subjects, and a dispensing Power in the Crown, with an indefeasible Hereditary Right, *Jure Divino*, were . . . Articles of his political Creed. . . .[74]

Fielding then went on to argue the absolute necessity to defend the present constitution. He laid it down, for those who might still be in doubt, that even so long ago as the time of Henry VII it was statutorily declared that any man may support the king *de facto* without incurring those penalties which certain wicked persons had put about might affect such law-abiding citizens in arms. It was fundamental in English law not only that a subject *may* legally support his sovereign *de facto*, but that legally a subject *must* do so. Fielding was obviously relying upon the act of 1495 which declared that no person serving 'the King and Sovereign Lord of this Land for the time being' shall be attainted for treason. The statute went on to declare that 'if any Act or Acts or other Process of Law hereafter thereupon for the same happen to be made, contrary to this Ordinance, that then that Act or Acts, or other Processes of the Law, whatsoever they shall be, stand, and be utterly void'.[75]

After denouncing the highlanders in thoroughly intemperate terms—a banditti . . . from a barren country . . . with as barbarous manners . . . who would 'by their swords cut their way into the Wealths of richer climates'—he makes his serious address:

Let us therefore unite in Associations:[76] let us call forth the old English Spirit in this truly English Cause: let neither Fear nor Indolence prevail in one Man to refuse doing his Duty in the Defence of his Country against an Invader by whom his Property, his Family, his Liberty, his Life and his Religion are threatened with immediate Destruction.[77]

So much for Fielding's *Serious Address*. This was in so great a contrast to Oliver's *Calm Address* that it cannot be thought that anyone who had read them both would have thought of ascribing them to the same author. The *Calm Address* had appeared earlier than Fielding's piece, from the house of John Oliver in Bartholomew Close, a printer who had not long started up. The two pieces were however both doing the rounds of the booksellers' shops and the coffee-houses at the same time, a fact that can be seen from the news-sheets of the period.[78] John Oliver, printer and bookseller, appears to have been a whig of less violent persuasion than Fielding, a moderate whig of the solid nonconformist wing. The author of the *Calm Address* seems to have been, like his bookseller, also of less violent opinion. For Fielding in his *Serious Address*, the highlanders were no more than a banditti, 'a Rabble of Thieves and Outlaws' who had already exercised 'the most barbarous Methods on those who have yielded to their Force'; they were savages from a barren country having 'the barbarous Manners of Huns and Vandals'; a gang of wretches with a desire for plunder and an innate love of rebellion. The *Calm Address to all Parties, whether Protestant or Catholick, on the score of the Present Rebellion* was altogether a different piece. It had none of this rant. It proposed no more than 'a brief and dispassionate Enquiry, whether the Reign of the Pretender would be advantageous to the Civil Interest and Commerce of Great Britain, supposing that he was to succeed in his present Attempt, and allowing that he afterwards would conduct himself according to the Principles of Honour and Honesty'.

The tone is calm throughout,

It is not to be doubted but that the Friends and Partizans of this Gentleman believe and give out, That it would be greatly for the Welfare of this Nation, that he should prevail: That his Reign and that the Restoration of his Family would take away the Cause of Party Factions and Divisions; That the Liberties and Properties of the Subject would be secured upon as good, or rather a better Footing than they are at present; That Trade would encrease and flourish; The People be eased of a great Part of their Taxes; and lastly, That he himself is a good, sincere and honest Man, and will give clear Proofs of it during the Course of his future Government.

Surely, therefore, it behoves all thinking persons to consider now the certain—or at least, the probable—results of another Stuart restoration. The subject, then, is reviewed under eight topics:

1 The hereditary principle
2 Spain's influence as to the future of Gibraltar and Port Mahon
3 France's influence as to the future of Cape Breton
4 The Import duties upon French goods, particularly wines
5 The national debt
6 The pressure of France upon British foreign relations
7 The pretender's (i.e. the restored king's) obligations of honour to France, and
8 His obligations of honour to his own subjects.

On the hereditary principle, the author of the *Calm Address* opens by taking—like Fielding, only more calmly—the orthodox whig point of view. It is a fact that parliament has settled the crown upon the present reigning family; to claim it from them now, therefore, a pretender must necessarily base his claim upon grounds of indefeasible hereditary right. He must therefore come 'to assert and regain his property which has been so long detained from him'. He can have no other pretence but this. Either the crown of Britain is a piece of property or it is an office in trust. If it is a piece of property, hereditable and inalienable, it cannot be transferred by the people according as they shall see it most convenient for the security of their liberties. Such inalienable property is not to be diminished, and any mere statute made to the contrary must be null and void. Hence it must follow that the subject is born the property of the prince and has not any right to terms and conditions. 'His only Duty is patiently to submit to the Will and Command of the Proprietor'. Indefeasible hereditary right for the prince; passive obedience and non-resistance for the subject. Or—the crown of Britain is an office in trust.

It would be tedious to rehearse here the arguments under the remaining topics. If the pretender succeeds to the throne he can do no less, consistently with the principles of gratitude, than to restore to his benefactor, the king of Spain, the important ports and fortresses of Gibraltar and Port Mahon, and to deliver up Cape Breton to France. The French interests would require the reduction, if not the repeal, of the various (heavy) customs duties on specific French goods, particularly wines, and this would have important repercussions upon not only the Portuguese trade but also upon British commerce. With regard to the national debt, the argument was particularly astute—although it was much the same argument used, or hinted at, in the *Serious Address*. It was at about this period that some at least of the public were coming round to the view that the national debt was perhaps not so much a debt owed to the public by the crown, as an interest-bearing form of wealth which the public owned. To extinguish it, therefore, would be not so much to cancel a debt as to destroy wealth. It may very well be that the electors of Hanover relied more for their British crown upon 'the funds' than upon the Act of Settlement. The act could be put on one side, as a number had before

—and many since. But the Bank of England had been opened to lend money to the Dutchman who drove the native Stuarts into exile. If the Stuart exiles ever returned it was unlikely, to say the least, that they would repay the bank with hard cash and soft words. Hence the point: how will the funds stand? The author of the *Calm Address* had no doubts: there are a number of reasons to suppose that the taxes would increase; but even if they did not

either the Government would have the same load of Debt upon it, that it has at present, or not.—If not, the National Debts must be wiped out with a Sponge, (for in such Circumstances there could be no other Method of paying them) and then all public creditors would be defrauded, many thousands totally ruined.

The author of the *Calm Address* then passes on to consider relations with France more specifically, and finally responsibilities at home.

These Considerations should weigh with People of all Persuasions in Religious Matters, who have any regard to the Welfare of their Country, and have Property to lose.

Even those who are catholic cannot reasonably hope for any solid and substantial advantage by a change.

They now do, and always have enjoyed under his present Majesty, and his Royal Father, as free and undisturbed an Exercise of their Religion as if they had obtained a legal Toleration. And all true Friends of Liberty of Conscience wish them the Continuance of it, as long as they behave like good and dutiful Subjects in their civil Capacity.

There is nothing they can reasonably expect from the success of the pretender that can compensate for the evils that will inevitable ensue, 'since they are already permitted to serve God according to the Dictates of their Conscience'.

One need, perhaps, say no more about the *Serious Address* and the *Calm Address*, except to say that the *Serious Address* was priced at one shilling; the *Calm Address* was copied by the London and provincial press and off-printed 'at 1 Halfpenny a-piece, or 25 for 6*d*'. Many would think the *Calm Address the better value.*

Notes

1 Oxford University Press, 1952.

2 Cambridge (Mass.), 1918.

3 See Paper 16, above.

4 Cf. *The Opposition: A Vision* (1742).

5 Sarah Fielding, *David Simple* (1744), preface.

6 *London Evening Post*, 22nd–24th October 1745; and *GM*, (October 1745), xv, 560.

7 The first edition (of 1732) was entitled *The Old Debauchees*.

8 *London Evening Post*, 15th–17th October 1745; and *GM* (October 1745), xv, 560.

9 *London Evening Post*, 13th–15th October 1745; and *GM* (October 1745), xv, 560.

10 *London Evening Post*, 13th–15th October and 2nd–7th November 1745; and *GM* (October 1745), xv, 560. See also Paper 16, above.

11 No. 1, Tuesday, 5th November–No. 33, 17th June 1746. See next Paper.

12 *GM* (June 1747), xvii, 300; and *Jacobite's Journal*, 19th December 1747.

13 *GM* (December 1747), xvii, 596; and *Jacobite's Journal*, 19th December 1747.

14 No. 1, 5th December 1747–No. 49, 5th November 1748.

15 Statute, 10 Geo. II, cap. 28.

16 See, e.g., M. A. Locke, *True Patriot* (1965), p. 39.

17 *Op. cit.*, ii, 11.

18 'Essay on the life and genius of Henry Fielding.'

19 *Henry Fielding: A Memoir* (1910), 136.

20 *Op. cit.*, i, 508.

21 Sarah Fielding, *Cleopatra and Octavia* (second edition, 1758) advertisement.

22 ii, 15–17, iii, 312, 338–9.

23 *Henry Fielding*, Oxford, 1929.

24 *GM* (August 1745), xv, 445; *London Magazine* (August 1745), xiv, 416; and *Scots Magazine* (August 1745), vii, 400 (in slightly varying terms).

25 *Times Literary Supplement* (Notes on Sales), 4th March 1926; and *Book Prices Current*, xi, 337.

26 See John Rylands Library and British Museum catalogues.

27 R. C. Jarvis, 'The death of Walpole; Henry Fielding and a forgotten *cause célèbre*', *Modern Language Review*, xli (1946), 115–30.

28 *London Evening Post*, 16th–19th March 1745.

29 J. Ranby, *A Narrative of the last Illness . . .* (1745).

30 Anon.: *An Epistle to J. Ranby* (1745).

31 Millar was, for instance, inaccurate as to the exact wording of another title in the same announcement, namely, 'The Charge to the Jury on the Trial of ABC', which must refer to 'The Charge to the Jury on the Sum of the Evidence on the Trial of A.B. C.D. and E.F. . . .'

[32] *GM* (October 1745), xv, 560; *London Magazine* (November 1745), xiv, 571; and *Scots Magazine* (October 1745), vii, 495. The *London Evening Post*, 13th–15th October and 2nd–7th November, gives the title in all its elaborate detail which, including the words '. . . from the Relation of Mr James Macpherson . . .' gave the catch-word under which alone the title used to be noted in the British Museum General catalogue.

[33] See next Paper.

[34] No. 15, 12th March 1748.

[35] *Jonathan Wild*, 1754, revised edition (leaf wanting in the British Museum copy), and in Sarah Fielding's *Lives of Cleopatra and Octavia*, second (1758) edition.

[36] iii, 313.

[37] This is the same as that at *Book Auction Records*, xxiv, 60.

[38] P. 175.

[39] Banerji, 60; and *Book Auction Records*, xxiv, 60; xxiv, 175; and xxxiv, 407.

[40] ii, 1130.

[41] Pp. 25–7.

[42] No. 15, 12th March 1748.

[43] Leaf wanting in the British Museum copy.

[44] Second edition 1758.

[45] iii, 313

[46] For a brief reference to the interesting story of Douglas Cleverdon's copy, see *Radio Times*, 8th October 1954, p. 9.

[47] It collates: octavo in eights: A^4, $B-F^8$, G^4.

[48] Pressmark 747 ab.

[49] See below, p. 178.

[50] *Library*, IV, L, iv (1921), 259–60.

[51] xv, pp. 541–4, October 1745.

[52] *Serious Address*, 'second' edition, p. 36.

[53] *The Oeconeomy of Human Life*, 1750.

[54] Millar referred to 'The Certain Consequences of the Rebellion in 1745'; in fact the sub-title reads: . . . *The Certain Consequences of the Present Rebellion* . . . a misquotation which is significant in view of the very similar misquotation of . . . *the Present Rebellion in Scotland.* . . .

[55] Fielding acknowledged it in a note in his later pamphlet, *A Proper Answer to A Late Scurrilous Libel*, where he said 'see the Serious Address, published in the time of the late Rebellion . . . by the Author of this Pamphlet'. The *Proper Answer* in its turn was acknowledged by Fielding as 'By the Author of the *Jacobite's Journal*'.

[56] See also *Book Auction Records*, xxv, 589, and xxvi, 175; and *Book Prices Current*, xlii, 365, and liii, 256 (title in earlier entries misquoted).

[57] C B E L says '*bis*'.

[58] Examined copies, one in the British Museum, two in the Bodleian and one in the National Library in Scotland, collated: octavo in fours: title-page [i], verso blank [ii], text, pp. 1–45, [46] blank; = [A], $B-F^4$, G 1–3. Perhaps there was also a half-title, and a blank leaf after pp. 45–[46], this making

[A]², B–G⁴. On the other hand the title-page may be conjugate with G1 (but the position of the watermark is against it).

59 See *Book Auction Records*, xxxiv (1936–7), 407.

60 *Library*, IV, L, iv (1921), 259–60.

61 Dr Dudden says the *Calm Address* occupies ten pages. It is correctly eleven.

62 This collates: octavo in fours: title-page [1], verso blank [2], text, pp. 3–51, page [52] blank; = A–F⁴, G².

63 A perusal of *Book Auction Records*, *Book Prices Current* and *American Book Prices Current* will show that a number of copies have come to light.

64 This collates: octavo in fours: title-page [1], verso blank [2], text, pages 3–47. [48] blank = A–F⁴.

65 It collates: octavo in fours: half-title [i], verso blank [ii], title-page [iii], verso blank [iv], text, pages 1–47 [48] blank; = [A]², B–G⁴.

66 It collates: octavo in fours: title-page [1], verso blank [2], text, pages 3–32; = A–D⁴.

67 I should like to say that, as a result of my researches in the British Museum, certain amendments and cross-references have now been made in the General Catalogue.

68 P. 10.

69 P. 12.

70 P. 13.

71 Pp. 17–18.

72 P. 35.

73 Pp. 3–4.

74 Pp. 4–5.

75 11 Hen. VII, cap. 1.

76 If 'association' is here meant in its technical sense, see Paper 5, volume I.

77 P. 45.

78 *GM* (October 1745), xv, 560.

19 *The 'True Patriot'*

Physically the *True Patriot* was a double-leaf production, that is to say, a newspaper of four pages. Ordinarily it opened with a leading article from the editor, upon a political or other topical issue; there followed various items of foreign or domestic news, and paragraphs dealing with the different aspects of the rising and more general topics. There was also a weekly précis of home and foreign news; the foreign was included under the title 'The Present History[1] of Europe'; the home news, which was really a more or less weekly account of the progress of the rising, he commenced under the title, 'Observations on the Present Rebellion', but later amended to 'The Present History[1] of Great Britain'.

There is much in the *True Patriot* that reminds one of other of Fielding's work. For example, if a letter from 'Heliogabalus' anticipated *Tom Jones*, a sermon from Parson Adams looked back to *Joseph Andrews*. Clearly Fielding enjoyed explaining not only his policy but also his technique. His technique was, as he said, to cook up with propriety the entertainment he was serving up to the public. He would serve first of all his leading article—'a Dish of substantial Food'—for his customers when their 'Appetites are brisk and keen'. After that he would serve up 'several *petit Plats* from the News Papers'. In these twice-told tales from his contemporaries he had 'a most excellent was of ragooing' and serving up a dish which, as one of his correspondents said, gave as much satisfaction to those who 'have some taste besides that which is seated in the Palate and are capable of relishing Wit as well as any Dainty'. What he dished up 'with Italic Sauce', he added by way of remark, 'gives a *delicious Flavour* to what was at first *flat* and *insipid*'. And lastly he would send his patrons away with a *Bon*

The notes and references are on pages 210–11

Bouche of his own. As well as being something of a hand-out from the ministry and a piece of persuasive propaganda from a clever journalist, the *True Patriot* was to be a veritable feast for epicures.

The various items that have been selected by later editors from amongst the different leading articles of the *True Patriot* to have place among Fielding's collected *Works* do not by any manner of means provide adequate material either to appraise his skill as a wit or to get his measure as a working journalist. Still less do they enable us to assess the value he must have been to the ministry in the influence and formation of contemporary opinion. Not even the old files of the *True Patriot* itself (nor Miriam Austin Locke's photographic reproduction of numbers 1–32, together with notes and commentary[2]) can do that for us. To see Fielding as he was, in London in the exciting days of the rising and invasion, one must read not only the *True Patriot* in the sheets of the *True Patriot*, as distinct from the edited extracts from the pages in the collected editions of the works, or the whole text in a photo-copied volume, but also the pages of the current *Daily Advertiser*, the *Daily Gazetteer*, *St James's Evening Post*, the *London Gazette* and so on, and all the run of the daily and weekly news-sheets of the time. In the by-play and the thrust and parry, week by week, Fielding is seen as the stern protestant, the real patriot, the super journalist and the great wit that he was.

Apart from the leading article, the first number opens casually enough: to a countess a daughter is born; the death of dean Swift is announced; today is 5th November, the anniversary of the Gunpowder Treason Plot. These and similar items worked off the current news. There was also an 'Apocrypha'—a characteristically Fielding stroke, this—which contained the uncanonical news as he said, that is to say, the items of more than doubtful authenticity, 'a curious collection of certain true and important WE HEARS from the newspapers'. These were the items of his 'most excellent was of ragooing'. Under this heading he ridiculed his contemporaries, either on account of the false news they published or else on account of their inconsistencies, or sometimes positive contradictions. Being a weekly he had, of course, in that respect a considerable advantage over the morning and evening press. In order to lighten his pages in those serious days he would seek out and publish occasionally a funny story, make a humorous comment on the news, or present some item in a comical setting.

The first words in the first column of the first issue of the new journal were: *Ille ego, qui quondam*, associated with the opening of the *Aeneid*. He might have continued—but did not—*'gracili modulatus avena carmen . . . ac nunc horrentia Martis'*. 'I am he who once tuned my song on a slender reed—but, leaving the woodlands, now sing in Mars' rough bristling key'. *Ille ego, qui quondam.* . . . Was Fielding, one wonders, worried about his past?

The first leading article—under that rubric—was a clever little piece of writing. It struck the seemingly unpromising note of 'Fashion'. Some interesting little variations were introduced, however, after the opening bars, and then he proceeded to enlarge and develop the theme. Incidentally, one is reminded of one of his earlier leaders in his old *Champion*³ which also was an essay on fashion. Again, he spoke of fashion as being the 'great governor of this World'; of fashions in Shakespeare in poetry, of Handel in music and Coke in law. Of all those who should conform to fashion there are none who should take greater care than authors. So far as the editor of the *True Patriot* was concerned, he had been informed by his bookseller (publisher), a man of great sagacity in his business, *'that nobody at present reads anything but newspapers'*. In strict obedience therefore to the sovereign power of fashion the editor was determined to conform to the reigning taste. Yet not apparently conform too closely, for upon perusal of contemporary journals, he fancied he 'had discovered two or three little imperfections in them all'. Thus, although he would confessedly imitate his contemporaries he would, in imitating them, improve them.

For example, the first little imperfection he had perceived in them, he said, with characteristic Fielding irony, 'was that there was scarcely a syllable of *Truth* in any of them'. The second 'little imperfection' was that besides there being no truth in them, there was no sense in them either. And thirdly—well, in point of fact there was nothing in them at all. It was in consequence of this remarkable discovery, therefore, that he proposed to offer the public the option of a higher alternative standard of reading. Gentlemen would now be able to read, besides the journals of the Grub Street hacks, a news-sheet written by a gentleman. He did not say so exactly, but he clearly implied that, judged by the quality of its English and of its politics, the *True Patriot* might be written by Bolingbroke; judged by the quality of its wit and humour, by no other than the earl of Chesterfield; judged by its zeal for the protestant cause, by the well-known Dr Hoadly of Winchester; it might in fact be edited by such political and literary notables as Lyttelton, Winnington, Dodington, or by Mr Fielding, or by Thompson the poet; in fact, by anyone else 'who hath ever distinguished himself in the republic of letters'. But, whoever he be, the reader may rest assured he is a gentleman and a 'True Patriot'.[4] It was Fielding's declared intention, then, to aim at a standard in journalism definitely higher than had ever been attained—or, indeed, attempted—before. Although however this was so, that particular aim could be taken as secondary. The primary object was to support the whig administration, to discredit the jacobite cause, and to instil into his lethargic fellow-citizens a sense of alarm as to the dangers by which, as he considered, the religious and civil liberty and the rights of private property were now threatened.

Fielding's scathing comments on his rival news-sheets naturally enough called forth the retort that he himself was only a paid hack, a pensioned scribbler. A reader now might wonder, after Fielding's experience on the *Champion*, and all the scurrilous abuse and libel he had brought down on his own head, and particularly after his unfortunate experience of the *Causidicade*, why it was that Fielding should have gone so deliberately out of his way to bait his rival editors, why he should so deliberately be so scathing about his rival journals. These attacks need not have been any essential part of the *True Patriot*'s wider policy, and would in any case inevitably call for the retort that he, for his part, was no more than a common hack, a political trimmer, a broken down playwright, and a broken down editor; now a broken down lawyer and shortly to be a broken down editor again. Although there are grounds for the assumption that his patronage by Lyttelton and Dodington may possibly have opened to him avenues of inside information presumably not available to his rivals, yet there is no evidence whatsoever that he was at any time in the actual pay of the whig administration. Yet the mere fact that he could get any inside information at all inevitably laid him open to the accusation of being a hireling scribbler. However, with whatever motive that may be, Fielding appears to have started off by deliberately trailing his coat. It was only to be expected that sooner or later, on one pretext or another, someone would step on it.

In the meantime, the standard of the *True Patriot* was to be high. Everything that Fielding wrote was realist; much was polished; much was witty and much was characterized by sound common sense; and never once in the whole run of the paper— at a time particularly licentious and particularly coarse and abusive—did Fielding stoop to the level of mere personal abuse. In his first issue he coupled a sturdy call to arms with a dignified appeal for moderation in temper and sentiment. He may of course have had one eye on the bitterly criticized administration when he denounced the 'indiscriminate censure of over hot men'. Certainly his appeal was one that moderns also may harken to with advantage particularly when, for example, he reminds his countrymen that they must preserve the spirit of tolerance even when they are preaching against their enemies; that they must throw themselves heart and soul into the defence of their country, their principles, their way of life and all that they hold dear—but without for one moment coupling with that total effort an irrational hatred of those whom the historical circumstances of the time have thrown against them. Fielding found himself with a difficult task, or rather a combination of difficult tasks; he had on the one side to arouse a people out of its lethargy, on the other to defend a ministry charged with supineness, and yet in the same situation to restrain some of the 'over hot men' from the intolerance into which their enthusiasm was leading them.

Cool and temperate Councils will be of singular use at this time, when the rashness of inconsiderate tho' well meaning Men may do Injury to the Cause they desire to support with their All, and on which their All depends.[5]

With regard to the enemy's amazing advance, he strikes a note reminiscent of the days of 1940. The enemy's initial successes have been astonishing—almost frightening, but

Let us however keep in our Remembrance that the odds are greatly on our side; so greatly that nothing but Contempt, Neglect, the most absurd Folly or most abject Pusillamity can destroy us.[6]

Although, however, he so frequently pleaded for religious and political toleration and moderation, yet it must nevertheless be admitted that he himself, in some of his more wordy tirades, was guilty of fanning intolerance and hatred.

In an early number, for example, published about the time of the fall of Carlisle, Fielding painted for his readers' benefit a picture of London in the occupation of the clans. It is a blood-curdling picture of loot and rapine, murder and massacre—happily in great contrast to the wise moderation and humanitarian consideration that everywhere characterized any actual occupation by the clans. Fielding held up for public contemplation a picture of religious persecution and wholesale massacre; protestants were roasting on the fires of Smithfield; even the instruments of torture, the rack and the wheel, indeed the gibbets themselves, ceased to bring horror; the streets were littered with the dead bodies of men, women and children; highland soldiery in the streets were openly fighting for the possession of such of the women as were still left alive.[7] Completely satisfied, at least for the time, one must suppose, with such a frightening vision, Fielding treated the reader of the *True Patriot* a little later to a more detailed diary of London in the occupation of the clans. In this diary there was something for everyone, from the restoration of the abbey lands to catch the interest of the reformation families, to the itch for the idle bystanders in the street who did no more than see the scabby highlanders pass.[8]

These passages have often been quoted, curiously enough, with evident satisfaction. The distinction between the understanding of literature and the understanding of history may perhaps be illustrated by the comments of two literary scholars upon these imaginary journals. 'The best numbers of the *True Patriot*,' says Professor Banerji, having just quoted from the two numbers concerned, 'are those in which Fielding tries to forecast the immediate consequences of the success of the Jacobite rising.'[9] 'This is what might have been,' says Professor Wilbur Cross.[10] Fielding himself, however, on reflection, seems not to have been so sure. Later, when he had had time to consider, he regretted them. They lay long on his conscience. Certainly, he offered his apology when he came to sing his swan song. At least he had the decency to recant.

However, not many of the pages of the *True Patriot* were filled, week by week, with this sort of stuff; nor did Fielding seem always altogether happy in his subject matter. He could dash off a lot better stuff than a good deal of this fustian. Some, even of the mere propaganda pieces, were altogether more polished; some of the leading articles were in their own way gems of literary composition; some of the 'We hears' were little jewels of irony. Although his humour was always healthy and his irony always keen, the more political of the moderate whigs liked him best in his closely reasoned arguments and his more dignified appeals to all and sundry. One such appeal was written in the middle of December.

Fielding had been nonplussed, as many another patriot must have been at the time, that a pretender could land on some obscure island that no one had ever as much as heard of, off the western seaboard; that he could muster a force of inexperienced mountainy men, and out-march, out-manoeuvre and out-fight a regular army; capture the northern capital; not only defeat, but rout, the government's only army in the field in Scotland; capture Carlisle, itself sited to hold the northern march; out-manoeuvre and out-march Wade, and then head southward through the counties towards London itself. There must surely, Fielding felt, be some deep-lying fundamental cause for so complete a collapse of all effective opposition in the face of the invader. In this dilemma Fielding turned his search inwards rather than outwards, as some may very well have done before him, but as many must surely have done in the dark days of 1940. The matter was one of high moral purpose. It was no topic for ranting. It was no subject for lecture. It was material for a sermon, rather.

Fielding summoned, therefore, into the columns of the *True Patriot* the character of Parson Adams from the pages of *Joseph Andrews* to preach to his readers a sermon on the text:

—Go upon the Work
Having first prayed to the Gods for Success.

It is impossible for any man, said Parson Adams, opening this sermon of his, to reflect seriously upon the progress which the rising had undoubtedly made, without imputing such unparalleled success to some cause other than had as yet been manifest, some strength other than that which any visible human means had placed in the hands of the rebels. So, therefore, will it be extremely difficult to assign any adequate cause whatsoever to the late occurrences, without turning to that grand cause, for the particular examples of which one must turn to sacred history— namely, the judgement of God against an offending people. From the following considerations, God's judgement upon the nation might be concluded:

First, from the rapidity of the rebels' progress, so unaccountable from all human means; for can history produce an instance parallel to this, of six or seven men landing in a great and powerful nation, in opposition to the inclination of the people, in defiance of a vast and mighty army (for though the greater part of the army was not then in the kingdom, it was so nearly within call that every man of them might, within the compass of a few days, or a week at farthest, have been brought home and landed in any part of it). If we consider, I say, this handful of men landing in the most desolate corner, among a set of poor naked hungry disarmed slaves, abiding there with impunity till they had as it were, in the face of a large body of his Majesty's troops, collected a kind of army, or rather rabble, together; if we view this army intimidating the King's forces from approaching them by their situation,[11] soon afterwards quitting that situation, marching directly up to the northern capital, and entering it without surprize or without a blow. If we again view this half-armed half-disciplined mob, without the assistance of a single piece of artillery, march up to attack, and smite a superior number of the King's regular troops, with cannon in their front to defend them. If we consider their returning from the complete victory to the capital, which they had before taken; there remaining for near two months in contempt of twelve millions of people, above a hundred thousand of whom have arms in their hands, and one half of these the best troops in Europe.[12]

He then passes from Scotland to England. When the jacobites moved from Edinburgh to invade the southern kingdom, Wade moves across an augmented second force from Newcastle to intercept them. But Wade cannot come at them, and a third army is hurriedly got together. Regiments are recalled from abroad, from Flanders and from Ireland; the king's own son is recalled from the continental campaign to take over command, and determines above all things to bring the invaders to action before they can reach London. This force the invaders neatly sidestep and now, having either out-fought some and out-marched the others, and then out-manoeuvred some of the best troops in Europe, they have nothing between them and London but—Barnet Common. Who can study, asks Fielding in the person of Parson Adams,

this almost unbelieveable progress of our enemies and not come to the conclusion that there is in their advance upon us some divine purpose. Not that God's blessing is upon our enemies. No. But His judgement is upon *us*. Who, I say, can consider such things as these and retain the least doubt whether he shall impute them to a judgement inflicted on this sinful nation; especially when, in the second place we must allow such judgement to be most undoubtedly our due.[13]

To run through every species of crime with which contemporary England was filled would have exhausted the whole paper; but although the (then) modern Sodom was as wicked as the Sodom of old, it was wiser than the old Sodom in its wickedness. If, therefore, England would avoid the final judgement which was denounced against it; if England would avoid that total destruction with which it was threatened—and not threatened remotely and at a distance, but immediately and at hand: if England would pacify that vengeance which had already begun to operate: if England would pacify that vengeance which seemed bent upon the country's destruction: what England had to do was to

—Go upon the Work
Having first prayed to the Gods for Success.

No sterner, no more dignified note than this, was ever addressed to England in those fateful days.

Not always, however, was Fielding so serious. His *True Patriot* had wit, merriment and irony—and irony (perhaps characteristically) often in passages where the undiscerning may easily fail to notice it. One of the later papers, for example, under the heading of 'Royal Virtues display'd', in praise of the royal family, has occasionally been quoted as though to show that Fielding had renounced his earlier opinions, disavowed his former attacks on the royal family, for example, in the *Grub Street Opera*. Speaking now of liberty, he says that besides liberty of conscience there is liberty of thought, that is, political liberty and the freedom of the press, freedom to criticize even those in high places—the king's ministers and even the king himself.

The impunity with which this liberty hath been of late years practised must be acknowledged by every man of the least candour. Indeed, to such a degree that power and government, instead of being objects of reverence and terror, have been set up as the butts of ridicule and buffoonery, as if they were only to be laughed at by the people.

Now this is a liberty which hath only flourished under this royal family. His present majesty, as he hath less deserved than his predecessors to be the object of it, so he hath supported it with more dignity and contempt than they have done.[14]

The vision of Henry Fielding, the creator of Squire Ap-Shinkin and his old grey mare, protesting that his present majesty hath not deserved to be set up as the butt of ridicule and buffoonery; the creator of Robin the butler, and Quidam the poor impudent fellow, protesting that the ministry hath been abused instead of being reverenced—all this is indeed a precious vision.

These passages, however, contain ironies within ironies which the hasty reader is liable to miss. It is often difficult to appreciate when Fielding expects to be taken seriously—as witness his establishing a later paper, *The Jacobites Journal*, to argue the jacobites' case for them. In this present passage, however, the discerning reader can see the bulge in his cheek where his tongue is. To make the point clearer, one must read on (realizing the danger of quoting *not* in full context). He passes on from those who love liberty to those who love money, and addresses himself to that 'large body of men whose whole trade would be ruined' if the present royal family were removed from the throne. He seems to expect that his reader may be left in some measure of doubt as to what that trade is, exactly, that is carried on by the men he now refers to, men indifferent alike to material, intellectual or spiritual freedom. What follows could not have been written by any other political journalist of the time but Henry Fielding. It is Fielding in his most characteristic ironic form, and we must take it—unless we suppose a quite sudden change of mood—that the earlier laudatory passage on the king and the royal family must have been written with his tongue in his cheek—and no recanting from the days immediately before the Licensing Act. He now addresses himself, therefore, to the men who will be ruined by any jacobite success:

How much more will he be surprised to hear that it is the principal trade which of late years hath been carried on in this kingdom. To keep him therefore no longer in suspense, I mean the honest method of selling ourselves, which hath flourished so notably for a long time amongst us, a business which I have ventured to call honest, notwithstanding the objections raised by weak and scrupulous people against it. . . . For if it be granted, as surely it will be, when we are free men we have certainly a right to ourselves, and whatever we have a right to, we have a right to sell. . . .

Now this trade, by which alone many thousands have got an honest livlihood for themselves and families, must be totally ruined; for, if this nation should be once enslaved, it would be impossible for an honest man to carry on this business any longer. A freeman (as hath been proved) may justly sell himself, but a slave cannot.[15]

By a variety of arguments, therefore, some sound logic, some compounded with a deal of prejudice, often with a leaven of his inimitable irony to lighten the whole, Fielding sought to show that there was none among those to whom he addressed himself, not even the already thoroughly corrupt, who did not stand to lose by the introduction of arbitrary power. One objection, however, he professed to see. Doubtless the estates of all the lords and commons of the kingdom would be forfeit to the conqueror. The personal fortunes of others will, in the confusion at least, be liable to plunder. Those therefore who are at present without any estate, real or personal, have (so it might seem) at least nothing to lose—and may therefore have something to gain.

I own there is something plausible in this argument, and it might perhaps have great force if the pretender's son had landed in England, as he did in Scotland, and had been pleased to place that confidence in an English rabble, with which he hath vouchsafed rather to honour these Highland banditti. In this case, I grant, no man could justly have been blamed who had fixed the eyes of his affection on his neighbour's estate, gardens, house, purse, wife, daughter, for joining the young man's cause, provided the success of it had been probable, such a behaviour would then have been highly consistent with all the rules taught in [the philosophical-political school], and none but a musty moralist, for whose doctrine great men have doubtless an adequate contempt, would have condemned it.

But the fact is otherwise. The *Highlanders* are those to whom he must owe any success he may attain: these are therefore to be served before you; and I easily refer to your own consideration, when Rome and France and Spain are repaid their demands, when a vast army of hungry highlanders and a larger army of hungry priests are satisfied, how miserable a pittance will remain to your share? Indeed, so small a one must this be, that the greatest adept in our philoso-political school would think it scarce worth while to sacrifice his conscience to the certainty of obtaining it.[16]

Fielding professed in his *True Patriot* to reason with everyone who could be reasoned with. He reasoned with those whose wealth was in land, with those whose wealth was in funds, with those in trade, with those who had no wealth at all. He reasoned with the tories as well as the discontented whigs; with non-jurors, freethinkers and republicans. He could reason even with the rabble who had nothing to lose and could not be much worse off anyway, and could show them that the rising would be of no good to them—because another rabble had got there first.

All this while, Fielding's wit never deserted him. The columns of the *True Patriot* were enlivened with many a humorous story and many an astute little dig at his contemporaries and rivals. In an early number he collected together one or two differing reports as to the exact whereabouts of Wade's army, which was to intercept the invaders before they could reach London. His comment was brief—but to the point:

Those several Letters give us the great Idea of Marshal Wade's army, which if they are all true, was in four different Places at Once.[17]

Or again: the *London Courant* reported, apparently with great satisfaction, that the duke of Cumberland had set out 'with a large Retinue to take upon him the Command of the Army now assembling in the Counties of Cheshire and Lancashire'. But, added the *True Patriot*, 'there is no such Army'.[18] The *General Advertiser* published some accounts of 'shocking villainies of the Highlanders during their Possession [of Carlisle]'. But Fielding, if not as a journalist, at least as a practising lawyer, knew what evidence rang true and what sounded false. After one man's account of himself being stripped and seeing his three daughters outraged, the *General Advertiser* asked, 'What does this wicked crew deserve!' Fielding answered, 'As much credit, I believe, as this [report].'[19] Rather more biting was his retort to the *London Courant* after the battle of Falkirk. That particular paper took the opportunity to correct a false report, but did so saying somewhat portentously that 'it is with great satisfaction we take this Opportunity of setting the world right in this particular'; to which the *True Patriot* added: 'As the Historian[20] had himself set the World wrong the Day before, it must be certainly a great satisfaction to him to set them right, and avoid begging Pardon a 4th Time for injuring Reputation.'[21] In the number published immediately after Falkirk, Fielding, quoting from the latest editions of the *General Advertiser*, *London Courant* and the *Daily Courant*, could show that among the casualties were Lord Elcho, who commanded the horse; Lord George Murray, lieutenant-general of the army, commanding the first line of foot; Lord John Drummond (who brought the contingent over from France), commanding the second line; Sullivan, quartermaster and adjutant-general; young Glengarry, commanding the Glengarry MacDonalds; and the (titular) duke of Perth, who had earlier shared with Lord George Murray command of the army under Charles Edward himself. At that rate, if Hawley and his regulars had not exactly won the battle, at least (said the *True Patriot*) 'the Rebels have lost all their Chiefs'.[22]

Another matter that earned Fielding's scorn was the practice some localities had that lay in the invaders' path or on the flank, to send up reports to the effect that the marauding banditti, although committing all sorts of outrages, were in fact but a despicable collection of poor vagrants. To describe them as though 'no eye had seen such scarecrows', to remind the reader of Falstaff's 'tattered prodigals, lately come from swine keeping', was to prove too much—that is to say, too much for their own good name. For if the second half of the story were true—that they were poor despicable vagrants—the first half ought not to be, namely, that they were terrorizing the countryside; and the stories did no credit to those who sent them along in either case. Thus, the *General Advertiser* was saying too much when it said that the invading force 'appear to be nothing but a ragged crew of Miscreants, who commit every Outrage without regard to law and Decency'. Too much, thought Fielding. 'If these are such a ragged Crew as here represented, the greater shame it is to the Militia of those Parts to suffer such Outrage to be committed by them with Impunity'.[23]

Although the time did not come in England that the invaders should be defeated in action, the time did come when they were to be defeated in their hopes. They were in retreat. Now, even the whigs had to admit to the tories that the jacobites had accomplished a march 'not to be paralleled in History', as the *True Patriot* said. Most amazing of all—and Fielding was frank and honest enough to admit it, Fielding, who with a good journalist's anticipation had manufactured out of his own fertile imagination a whole host of the most shocking cruel barbarities and atrocities —most amazing of all, the cruelties had fallen altogether short of what had been apprehended. Fielding may have been a keen whig propagandist, but he had also a keen sense of justice, the same sense of justice that all his life had drawn him to the study, and now to the practice, of law. He had in fact done his enemies an injustice. They were hardly out of the country before he tendered his reparation:

Thus are the Banditti arrived once more safe in their own Neighbourhood after an Expedition which is not to be parallel'd in History. In which as the loss they have suffered hath been much less than they could have reasonably promised themselves, so have the Cruelties they have committed fallen altogether short of what have been apprehended from such a Rabble especially when incensed with Disappointment.[24]

Fielding was willing to admit, furthermore, that those tales that were coming in about the depredations of the invaders would very often bear another interpretation; it was in fact the local populace as often as not preying upon the marchers—or attempting to—and if they for their part were sometimes over-reached it was probably only because they were trying to over-reach some poor clansman. Hence, some of the stories appealed often enough not only to Fielding's own sense of justice, but to his sense of humour also.

There are some which seem to have affected a kind of Humour. One of these fellows sold his Horse to a poor Countryman for 10s, which was not the tenth part of its value; but as soon as he had touched the Money, instead of delivering the Horse he told the Purchaser he was a damn'd Rogue to take Advantage of a poor Stranger's Ignorance of Horseflesh, and immediately rode off with both the Money and the Beast.[25]

Fair enough! And on whose side is the sympathy of the decent man, on the biter's or the bitten? When all the danger was past and the souvenir hunters were out, they would have the shirt off a retreating clansman's back, or his plaid off his shoulder by way of a souvenir to show, to say nothing about the kilt off his middle —and this notwithstanding all the talk about the itch and the scab. There was the case of a clansman who

having sold his Plaid for a Crown, told the Person who bought it he should have occasion to wear it on his Journey Home, but he would be sure to surrender it if he ever saw him in the Highlands.[26]

Fielding felt: good luck to him! May he get safely home—*and* his plaid.

What Fielding could not understand was the spirit of the jacobites in defeat—for surely they were in defeat. He tells a story —'from very great Authority'—of how an old acquaintance of Lord George Murray's told him he was surely in a 'desperate situation'. Lord George replied he 'knew very well the Danger' but he had already gone too far to withdraw 'with safety or Honour'. The rank and file must by now surely know that they too were in a 'desperate situation'. Why do they not throw down their arms, if only to escape complete annihilation? Why then do they still carry their arms? Why do they not surrender out of hand? Why *do* they keep together in the form of an army? Can they really even *hope* to see their Scotland again! However fast, however orderly, they retreat, a government force must sooner or later come up with them—and annihilate them. Indeed, he frankly admitted himself completely puzzled as to what it was that kept the retreating jacobites 'in the field' at all. The mere *name* of the duke, he thought, ought to be enough to scare them out of the land!

We own ourselves at a Loss to comprehend what can induce the Rebels in their Present distress'd condition, and without the least Prospect of

Success, to delay their Dispersing and shifting for themselves one Moment, especially since they can have no Hope of receiving any additional strength. . . . For the Troops in the King's Service in that Part of the United Kingdom are already double their Number, and must soon inevitable destroy them unless they can preserve themselves by Flight.[27]

In his very next number the *True Patriot* was able to report that 'the Troops in the King's Service . . . already double their Number' had in fact come up with the jacobite force in order to 'destroy them'. The result was—the battle of Falkirk. After the relief of Carlisle the duke of Cumberland had returned to London and general Hawley was given command, presumably of the mere mopping-up operation. From Edinburgh Hawley pushed through Linlithgow and came up to the jacobites at about Falkirk. The action was fought on 17th January. Hawley failed to take a knoll of tactical advantage, had his left and centre overcome by the clans, although his right repulsed their left. Neither side was left with the strength to push home its tactical advantage and both sides left the field; but Hawley had to surrender one of his guns, to burn his tents and abandon his baggage, retreat to Linlithgow and later to withdraw to Edinburgh.

This was indeed a surprise to the whigs—a sensation, in fact— for the whigs had already written off the jacobites, as the *True Patriot* had, as lost. Nothing had remained to do but to hang them. After Falkirk Cumberland was recalled. The campaign that followed is often reported as though the clans did nothing but withdraw to the fastnesses of the west and north, until Cumberland ferreted them out to destroy them at Culloden. This is very far from the facts, however. After the victory of Falkirk the jacobites set about the detailed reduction of 'the chain', that chain of forts across the Great Glen, strategically designed precisely to keep the western, jacobite, clans in awe. Fort George was reduced, Fort Augustus was reduced. The barracks at Ruthven were captured, as the posts at Bernara and Inversnaid had been. A whole network of government military posts in Atholl was, by a well planned series of actions, surprised and overcome, and the net round Fort William, the strongest fort of all, was drawn tightly and all land communication cut off.[28]

In the meantime, however, Cumberland moved leisurely

northward, and his crossing of the Spey was not opposed. On 16th April the government force and such jacobite body as could be drawn together met on Drummossie Muir, seven miles to the east of Inverness. The clans were not destroyed, but crushed they certainly were. For all practical purposes the rising was at an end.

With jacobitism crushed, the question would arise whether the *True Patriot* was to retain a place among London's normal news-sheets. It might be doubted whether, in its circulation, it was ever really a very great success. Certainly the first issue was not sold out, for in the colophon of No. 2 were included the words, '. . . where may be had No. 1'. The same form of words was used for No. 3; but apparently some copies of the second and third issues must have been left on the publisher's hands, for the colophon was amended with No. 4 to read, '. . . where may be had former numbers'. This formula continued to be used right up to the beginning of March, when there were other signs not only of a lagging interest on the part of the public, but also of a relaxing interest on the part of the editor. According to a statement made in the paper, there had been 'Many malicious and base endeavours' to hinder sales; but it may be thought likely that this was one way the editor had of accounting for a lessening circulation.

After the withdrawal from Stirling the war had seemed less urgent. Perhaps, after all, the highlanders had done what the *True Patriot* had suggested they should do—since they had 'no Hope of receiving any additional strength', since they were in a 'distress'd Condition and without the least prospect of success'—namely, decided to 'disperse and shift for themselves'. With dwindling sales, a relaxing editorial direction and less topicality, the *True Patriot* tended to fall away from the high standard it had set itself. Already in the new year Fielding included a two-column article on the militia and followed it, week by week, running later on to the mere reprinting of long extracts from a book on the subject. The jacobite rising 'certainly owes its Beginning and Increase to the Absence of our Troops and to the slender Force left in this Kingdom'. To revive now any of the old arguments formerly used against the maintenance of a standing army would be 'a Mark of Disaffection'. Fielding would therefore enter into an impartial examination of the arguments for and against the establishment of a militia. This series of articles has been referred to as a mere fill-gap, but it is often not sufficiently realized that the militia at the time was the subject of considerable interest and controversy.[29] In a series of three articles, Fielding, himself professionally a lawyer, examines constitutional warrant, citing not only the earlier statutes, but also *magna carta* and Coke's *Institutes*. In later issues he republished extracts from a new edition of colonel Martin's *Plan, A Scheme for establishing a more effective militia in Great Britain, Ireland and the American Plantations*, a work that had just been put on the market by Cooper and Millar (both of them Fielding's publishers).

All this, however, although interesting, was not topical in the sense of his earlier matter. By March and April of 1746 the tendency was even more marked. The leading articles were on such subjects as taste, the taste of the musician, artist, writer and politician; the execution of justice; domestic economy; virtuosity and the thermometer of wit, the latter tracing good sense downwards through the degrees of gravity and pertness to dullness and stupidity or folly, and upwards through the degrees of vivacity and true wit or fire, to wildness and madness.[30] All this could very well have been written some while earlier, and left in the office to be brought out as required. Indeed, on more than one occasion a leading article was produced that was in all probability not written by Fielding at all. The little story, for example, of a man who tried to force his daughter Fanny to marry a man with whom she was not in love, was certainly not written by Fielding and has all the marks of his sister's hand. It is commonly thought also that a leader a month later, Philander's on 'True and False Patriotism', was not Fielding's either.

The 'Apocrypha' also disappeared from the paper, probably because Fielding was no longer available in London to give anything like a topical comment on the current news. The whole point about so many of his quips was precisely their topicality. When the 'Apocrypha' was dropped—and it was never resumed —the *True Patriot* lost Fielding's most characteristic contribution. It can hardly be a mere coincidence that the Lent assizes opened on the western circuit on 4th March. It is probable that Fielding went on circuit after his usual custom, for it was still the law that was his profession; it was only incidentally that he was a newspaper man again. If this is so, if he left London—*and* the *True Patriot*—to go on circuit, he journeyed to Southampton in the first days in March and followed the circuit by way of Salisbury, Dorchester, Exeter and Taunton. This would account for his contributions to his paper in London being confined to topics of more general interest, and for the fact that he could no longer keep his 'Apocrypha' going with pithy comments on topical paragraphs. When he at last completed his tour of the assize towns of the west he would be due to attend the sittings of the King's Bench in London. Thus, once his grip on the *True Patriot* had loosened at the commencement of term he would have little opportunity—that is, of course, supposing he had the inclination—to tighten it again. By the time the *True Patriot* had ceased to interest the public, it had ceased also to interest its editor; for it was time now for Fielding to be off again to the western circuit on the summer assize.

It may therefore be taken that, viewed from the narrow personal angle, the *True Patriot* was a venture into journalism which Fielding was able to conduct during his own leisure between law terms; which, even during the rising itself when interest was high and excitement was tense, he could maintain only with some help from others; but which he found himself unable to sustain when public excitement subsided, his own interest lagged and the courts demanded almost his full time. In any case, when the military and political situation became less acute, there was no longer need for him to make the sacrifice. He had therefore, through sheer pressure of legal duties, to reconcile himself as best he could to the demise of his *True Patriot*—or rather, to stand afar off and watch it die by inches, owing to his lack of sufficient time to put any of the vitality of his genius into its pages. The point is stressed here because of its importance at least as regards the ascription to Fielding of the *Compleat And Authentick History of the Rebellion*, dealt with elsewhere in this volume.[31]

In the June of 1746, therefore, the editor of the *True Patriot* bade his farewell to his readers. The *True Patriot* had been born with the rising; it should properly die with it. It had come into being at a time of general panic, and its primary object had been none other than to alarm its public with the dangers that threatened. This the editor had striven to do with all his might

—but with a zeal tempered with tolerance. Now Culloden had removed the threat. The rising was crushed. The rebellion was dead. Let the *True Patriot* die with it.

As the Rebellion is now brought to a happy Conclusion by the victorious Arms of his Royal Highness the Duke of Cumberland, it is a proper Time for this Paper, which was entirely occasioned by that Rebellion, to cease with it. The intention with which the Patriot was undertaken was to alarm my Fellow Subjects with the Dangers which that Rebellion threatened to their Religion and Liberties, indeed to everything valuable which they possessed. These appeared to me to be immediately attacked by the Followers of that standard which a Popish Pretender had openly set up in these Kingdoms, and who was at the Time attended with an Appearance of success that struck the whole Nation with a general Pannic.[32]

It was not now his purpose, he went on to say, to claim for himself any extraordinary merit on account of that undertaking. To do all that lies in one's power at such a time is no more than one is strictly obliged to do. For his part he did no more than merely discharge his duty. The credit that he *could* claim was due to him not on account of his support of the constitution, but in respect of the manner of his rendering that support. It was not on account of his *zeal* that he laid any claim to credit, but on account of his *tolerance* towards his political enemies, his lenity towards his foes, and particularly towards his defeated foes.

Whoever hath taken the pains to read these writings must likewise own that I have done this with as little Bitterness and Invective against those very Parties whose mistaken Tenets had, I am afraid, too much encouraged this Undertaking, and had flattered the Invader with too great Hopes of final success. I did my utmost to disuade the well-meaning but rash Part of my Countrymen from general and violent Attacks on the whole Bodies of Men, even on Roman Catholicks themselves, while they retained the Duty of their Allegiance, and preserved that Peace which the Law requires. I endeavoured likewise to obviate, as far as I was able, the Disinclination which was arising among too many against the whole Scottish Nation, which I thought was at once unjust and dangerous to common Cause.[32]

It seems likely, after the retreat from Derby, when the immediate danger to the capital had been averted, or at least in the latter stages of the campaign, that some of his earlier stuff lay, perhaps, rather heavily upon Fielding's conscience. To some extent, possibly, he regretted it—regretted it, that is to say, in so far as it helped to promote and inflame hatred and unreasoning and illogical intolerance against all who were merely catholic in religion, altogether irrespective of whether they were jacobite tory or whig in politics; against all who were merely Scottish, whether Stuart or Hanoverian, rebel or loyal. The immediate danger now is mercifully past. But what disgusted Fielding was that those who a few short months ago, in the dark days, had been the most supine, were now the loudest in their cries for vengeance. It was blood they wanted—provided, of course, they had not the spilling of it. Was it in some measure that he, Henry Fielding, had lashed them up into this frenzy of fear and hatred? Certainly it was he, Henry Fielding, who had pictured for them the robbery and violence, murder and lust, stalking their own streets; the violation of their liberties, the extinction of their freedom; the destruction of their homes and property and the raping of their wives and daughters. The only defence Fielding could make for himself and the late violence of certain of his writings, was that that sort of stuff—and that one paper in particular—was written in the excitement when the invaders were advancing victorious through the land, *not* when they were being hounded out of the glens and brushed fugitive over the braes. The rising was now all but over: what was wanted now was not blood and vengeance, but kindliness and human understanding. Such vehemence as he himself once exerted against the enemy, he wrote 'only when he was arrayed against us'

For the Paper principally intended to inflame this Nation against the Rebel was writ whilst they were at Derby, and in that Day of Confusion which God will, I hope, never suffer to have its equal in this Kingdom.[33]

It was written, as he said,

When the Rebels having, as it was thought, slipt the Duke's Army, were feared to be approaching this City by hasty Marches; and when this Apprehension joined to that of an immediate Invasion from France had thrown all Men into the most dreadful Consternation.[33]

Now, the danger was happily past; but most of all he felt unhappy in the vengeance that might be wreaked upon the poor wretches who had been left in the hands of the government. Their lives were, of course, forfeit. All these things Fielding turned over in his legalistic mind. What was needed in this situation, therefore, was not *justice* in any form. It was ordinary human *understanding* and a spirit of *tolerance*. It may very well be true that if ever there were a time when 'Incentives to Acts of Severity would be reasonable, it is the Present'. But nevertheless it is another instance of his lenity and the lenity of his paper that, as he said, 'I have been totally silent with Regard to the Punishment of those Wretches whose Lives are become forfeited to justice upon the Occasion'. Whoever knows the editor at all, he went on to say, must know that cruelty was most foreign to his disposition. He would therefore leave these unhappy men to that mercy which he for his part hoped they would find.

Notes

[1] Note the use of the word 'history' (see Paper 16).
[2] *The True Patriot* (1965).
[3] *Champion*, 16th February 1739/40.
[4] No. 1, 5th November 1745.
[5] *Ibid.*
[6] *Ibid.*
[7] No. 3, 19th November 1745.
[8] No. 10, 7th January 1746.
[9] *Op. cit.*, 173.
[10] *Op. cit.*, ii, 31.
[11] A reference, presumably, to the Corrieyairack—see Paper 1, volume I.
[12] No. 7, 17th December 1745.
[13] *Ibid.* This, in some respects at least, resembles in mood the royal proclamation on 24th September 1857, proclaiming a day of solemn fast, humiliation and prayer, in connection with the British losses in India.
[14] No. 4, 26th November 1745.
[15] *Ibid.*
[16] *Ibid.*
[17] *Ibid.*
[18] No. 5, 3rd December 1745.
[19] *Ibid.*
[20] Note again the use of the word 'historian' (see Paper 16).
[21] No. 15, 11th February 1746.
[22] No. 14, 28th January 1746.

[23] No. 5, 3rd December 1745.

[24] No. 9, 31st December 1745.

[25] *Ibid.*

[26] *Ibid.*

[27] No. 12, 21st January 1746.

[28] See Paper 11, volume I.

[29] See Papers 5–8, volume I.

[30] March and April 1746.

[31] See Paper 16.

[32] No. 33, 17th June 1746. This last number is missing from the Burney collection in the British Museum (otherwise complete). It is quoted here from the *London Magazine*, June 1746, 298–9.

[33] No. 3, 19th November 1745.

20 *London*

In the spring of 1744 the French squadrons at Brest and Rochefort and the army under marshal de Saxe at Dunkirk looked poised for an invasion of England. The British fleet at Spithead was cruising the Channel along the Downs, and customs officers (afloat and ashore) were specifically instructed 'to transmit the earliest intelligence'.[1] Already by the middle of February it was realized that London now was under threat.

If the French should win through the British fleet, the Thames must be defended. All officers, therefore, of Tilbury and Sheerness were ordered to return immediately to their respective posts. Any marines left at Rochester were to be put into garrison at Tilbury or Sheerness. For fear the French might penetrate even farther, the cabinet council ordered the Admiralty to give immediate directions for taking up all the buoys in the river; in London itself the militia of the City and of Westminster and the Tower Hamlets was ordered to be drawn out,[2] and a complete battalion of the guards was to be constantly kept at the Tower. As to the landward defence of the capital, such regiments as were available at home were ordered to hasten their march direct to London. These, however, were feared to be insufficient. The lord lieutenant of Ireland, therefore, was ordered to ship certain of the regular units of foot quartered there to Bristol, 'or to the most convenient Place for Landing, when they can Make and March immediately for London'. Regiments of horse and dragoons should be shipped from Ireland to Chester, also with orders to march for London.[3] On 15th February the council wrote to the lord mayor and on the 17th the court of lieutenancy ordered a loyal address to be presented, the laws against the catholics to be put into execution (in

---

The notes and references are on pages 232–4

the sense that the statutory oaths were to be tendered, and restraint placed upon the arms, horses and movements of 'refusers'); the militia was to be placed 'in readiness fit for immediate service'; the justices of the peace of Middlesex, Westminster and the Tower Hamlets were to assemble daily, and provisions were made for the militia—the trained bands—'the Six Regiments of the City'—the Red, the Blue, Green, Yellow, Orange and White —to be mustered for the defence of the City.[4]

From certain entries in the lieutenancy minute book, however, one might wonder whether the commissioners of the court of lieutenancy themselves were altogether familiar with the details of lieutenancy procedure, and furthermore there is a note in the records about 'a Malicious desire of Confusion'.[5] None the less, those men liable to militia service were charged by the respective captains of the trained bands 'to find arms', to appear by summons and serve in person or else nominate a satisfactory substitute. The arms to be found were:

a Musket, with a Bayonet to fix to the Muzzle thereof, a cartouch Box or Pouch, a Belt of Buff,[6] four inches broad, and a two-Edged Sword.[7]

Each man was to appear by summons 'as often by Beat of Drum as otherwise', to come 'clean dressed' and 'to bring with him half a Pound of Powder and half a Pound of Bullets of a Size for the Musket'. Any personal substitute once listed was 'not to be Exchanged or desert the Service or be discharged thereof but by the Leave and Order of the Lieutenancy'.

Things, however, were not quite as brave as they might appear from some of the order sheets. The various companies were already 'much Indebted and in Arrear' for their incidental expenses and 'consequently less able to serve than they would otherwise be' (which is rather well expressed). Furthermore, the lieutenancy appeared to fear they lacked, of their own authority, adequate power in law to levy a 'Militia Tax for the City'. They therefore requested a royal warrant.[8] This they promptly received,[9] but still many refused to pay any levy for the militia. In any case there could be genuine grounds for controversy: was, for example the amount due payable by the tenant or by the landlord, and if by the tenant, was it properly recoverable from the rent?[10] Some citizens had 'tender consciences', and hence declined merely to *pay* for services which they themselves would have conscientious objections to provide. Some on the other hand had no particular conscience, but had no money. When defaulters were summoned, although it was thought fit in some cases to 'impose small fines', it was in others thought fit to excuse them 'by reason of Poverty', that is to say, the 'Meaness of their Circumstances'—or 'some other reasonable Motive'[11] (which again was nicely put).

Where, by the assessment, any citizen might fall short of a liability to 'find' a full man, the citizen could (as in the country) be *fractionally* assessed. 'Several Persons charged to find Half a Man' had defaulted, but they defaulted 'on the Pretext that they have not been able to find the Person charged [to find the other half]'.[12] There were indeed many little controversies, but most of these controversies were resolved by a storm in the Channel which dispersed Roquefeuil's fleet and the Dunkirk invasion was consequentially abandoned. When in April a court of lieutenancy was called in the City, no business could be transacted because they could not muster a quorum.[13] The excitement was over.

In 1745 the news of the fact of the landing took much longer to reach London than the news of the rumour the year before. In any case, Loch nan Uamh, or wherever, was a long way away. There might be news, therefore, but there need be no excitement. On Wednesday 14th August the six regiments of the militia of the City were ordered to be mustered and exercised in the Artillery Ground,[14] but this was pretty routine stuff. Clearly, there was nothing for the City to get excited about and, in any case, when the court of lieutenancy met on 6th August it adjourned itself until 10th October.[15] On 3rd September, however, certain individuals, 'apprehending it absolutely necessary that a Court of Lieutenancy be forthwith held', met together and 'it was *by them* ordered' on the 3rd that a court be called on the 5th.[16] Furthermore a prompting from the privy council of the 9th[17] called another court on the 12th and it was then ordered that the six regiments should take it in turn (in order of seniority) 'to be called and exercised' each alternate weekday, Saturdays excepted, commencing Wednesday 18th September.[18]

Certainly, the authorities in Westminster were very patient in explaining to the authorities in Edinburgh that 'the show only' of some regular troops, 'The show of some artillery' in the highlands, would suffice to disperse the insurgent rabble. The insurgent rabble occupied Edinburgh on 17th September, and then at Prestonpans the following Saturday completely defeated the only regular field force in Scotland before breakfast. This put a slightly different complexion on the matter and the City trained bands were therefore ordered to exercise *two* units each alternate weekday (Saturdays excepted).[19] Again, the catholics within the City, and other 'refusers' 'judged dangerous to the Peace of the Kingdom' were ordered to be disarmed and (in order to hold them immobile) they were for the time being relieved of any 'Horses of the Value of Five Pounds upwards'.[20]

At Westminster the ministry, upon the news of Cope's defeat, summoned a board of senior general officers 'to meet immediately', to take into consideration the total number of regular troops there were in the country, and to recommend the disposition of them, with particular reference to the number that should be sent north to attack the insurgents, and the number that should remain near London for the defence of the capital. This board consisted of field marshal the earl of Stair, an old Scottish officer, Marlborough's aide-de-camp, who had been appointed commander-in-chief in the south of England during the invasion scare the year before; Count Nassau, commander-in-chief of the Dutch forces and son of one of William of Orange's stalwarts; Marshal Wade, who certainly knew his Scotland; and General Ligonier, another who had fought under Marlborough.[21] They found that the total forces then in England were sixteen squadrons of horse and dragoons and 29 battalions of foot; the force recommended to 'remain about London' was sixteen battalions of foot (including guards), two troops of horse guards, one of horse grenadiers and two of dragoons. Detachments of three regiments of the guards were urgently moved in to reinforce the garrison at the Tower, and this with such despatch, 'without calling upon the justices and constables . . . to be assisting'.[22] As regards military affairs on the continent, at the battle of Fontenoy in the previous May the British naturally covered themselves with glory—but the French won, and in war winning counts more than glory. In the result, Tournai fell, and Ghent and Oudenarde, and then the British base at Ostende. In September and October the British troops in Flanders had to be recalled with all possible speed for service at home. On Friday 13th September three battalions of foot guards and seven regiments of foot

left camp at Vilevorde and made long marches without having any Quarters assign'd them, but pitch'd their Tents each Night to the 19th when they embark'd at Williamstadt, near Antwerp. On Sunday [the 22nd] about 4 o'Clock in the Afternoon the above Regiments arrived at Gravesend, after the quickest Passage hitherto known.[23]

They landed from 'the 22 sail of Transports' the same evening: they had left camp in Brabant and marched through the City of London, all within 11 days which, boasted the London press, was the fastest movement of troops so far recorded. The seven regiments of Foot were Major-General Thomas Howard's (3rd Foot), Colonel Robinson Sowles' (11th Foot), Major-General Harry Pulteney's (13th), Major-General Philip Braggs' (28th), Brigadier-General William Douglas's (32nd), Major-General John Johnstone's (33rd), and the hon. James Cholmondeley's (34th). They were given scattered quarters, mostly north of the river, for example, Pulteney's 13th at Bromley, Braggs' 28th at Stratford, Johnstone's 33rd at Highgate and Cholmondeley's 34th at Islington. On the following day the whole seven regiments of foot (London by now being thought quite secure) 'were ordered to march Northwards, which they accordingly did', some by way of Highgate and others by way of Enfield. According to the newspapers, by the 24th they were expected to be at St Albans, and by the 25th at Dunstable, where they should wait for further orders.[24] For the horse and foot guards and the horse grenadiers shipped from Flanders, grounds were marked out in Hyde Park for their encampment. Other troops from Holland had landed at Tilbury and had gone into quarters at Islington, Whitechapel and Wapping.[25]

Before the end of October further detachments of the foot guards, regiments of horse and battalions of foot arrived in the Thames from Ostende, namely, Major-General Bland's dragoons (3rd Hussars), four troops of Lieutenant-General Ligonier's 'black horse' (7th Dragoon Guards), Lieutenant-General James Sinclair's (St Clair's Foot—the 1st Foot), Lieutenant-General

Harrison's (15th Foot), Major-General John Husk's (23rd) and Lord Henry Beauclerk's (48th). It was reported at the time that there were about 3,000 British troops still remaining in the low countries,[26] but within a week Lieutenant-General Roger Handasyd's (16th Foot), Brigadier-General Thomas Bligh's (20th), General James Campbell's (21st), Lord Sempill's (42nd), Brigadier-General John Mordaunt's (47th) and Lord John Murray's regiments all had arrived in the Thames.

The citizens of London therefore were enjoying a whole series of military spectacles. There was, for example towards the end of September a 100-horse train, dragging 'a fine Train of Artillery', brought up from Woolwich and across London Bridge for despatch northwards to Preston in the first instance.[27] 'Six Waggons with muskets' were seen in the Minories, bound for the army in the midlands, and later a train of artillery bound from the Tower for Ligonier.[28] On 1st October an extraordinary guard of seventy foot guards was ordered to be under arms in their guardroom day and night, 'against any sudden emergency',[29] and on the 6th a detachment of the foot guards took possession of the playhouse in Lincoln's Inn Fields to be their guardroom at one at least of the entrances to the City.[30] The press appeared to delight in identifying the particular units by their facings: A squadron of Bland's dragoons 'march'd through the City'.[31]

So far as the wards of the City itself were concerned, the trained bands were continuing to do dutiful service throughout the crisis. As already stated, 'the Six Regiments of the Militia of the City' had been mustered and exercised in the Artillery Ground already in August.[32] On 9th September the privy council prodded the City lieutenancy, as it had earlier prodded the county lieutenancies, particularly in the north. As a result, the six regiments were ordered on the 12th 'to be called and exercised', one regiment a day, by summons—Red, Blue, Green, Yellow, Orange and White—to commence on Wednesday the 18th. Each company was to meet at its usual parade by 8 a.m. and march to the place appointed by the field officers and thence to the Artillery Ground. Officers were to take care that all men were properly armed and the names of any defaulters were to be recorded and returned.[33] Forms of notice, charging the individual to appear as commanded, known as 'charging tickets', were ordered to be printed.

At the beginning of October, when night duty was ordered as well as day, it was directed that each regiment doing duty should detach four companies, to meet at five in the evening at its usual parade place, but to march from there, one company to the Royal Exchange, one to Devonshire Square House, one to St Dunstan's in the West (to the guest house there), and the fourth to St Bartholomew's hospital, 'and there severally keep Guard until 7 a Clock in the Morning'. The other four companies of the regiment should take the same posts the next night, and on the following night the posts would be taken by the first four companies of the next senior regiment and thus in continuous rotation until further orders.[34] Furthermore, detachments from the respective companies should be sent to the gates and the avenues into the City, each soldier on such guard to bring a quarter of a pound of powder and half a pound of ball.[35]

Some minor adjustments were made—and some major discoveries. As regards the minor adjustments, on one occasion for example, the two senior regiments, the Reds and the Blues, were excused their Artillery Ground training and ordered instead to attend the public entry of the Venetian ambassador.[36] Or again, the company for duty at the Royal Exchange on the 29th October was ordered instead to 'march to Guildhall Yard that Day and keep Guard there' from 4 p.m. until seven next morning that day being lord mayor's day.[37] On another (minor) issue: 'keeping Guard at St Bartholomew's Hospital is attended with many Inconveniences, as well to the Officers as the Soldiers'. The Strand–Ludgate guard kept a guardroom in the guest house of the church of St Dunstan in the West; the 'Newgate guard' therefore took over 'the Guest Room belonging to St Sepulcher's Church'.[38] Somewhat later in the year the lower part of the Royal Exchange was found to be too cold for the guard and application was therefore made for liberty to do duty in the upper part.

There were, however, major discoveries also to be made, and some of the officers of 'the Six Regiments of the City' made them. Orders had been given regarding closing the gates of the City and there were the standing arrangements about the (civil) constables and watchmen there, apart altogether from the military guard. A captain Blackwell of the trained bands, was doing his night patrol and found the gate at Ludgate open at one o'clock in the morning. The captain demanded the meaning of this from the constable then on civil duty at the gate. The constable said that the gates

were open and should continue so open, for his [the constable's] Convenience, and that if he [the Captain] had a mind to have them shut, he might go and shut them for himself, for neither he, meaning the Constable, nor his Watchman should do it.[39]

Furthermore, captain Blackwell had later to report no improvement, for on a subsequent duty he came through again at two in the morning and the gates were still not closed. Colonel Martin, likewise on duty, reported that when he passed through at about one o'clock one morning, although there were two watchmen at the gate the gates were open, and there was no constable in the watch-house.[40] What was even worse was that the City bars, for example, the bar on Tower Hill, 'are at Night left open'.[41] It may very well have been—and it may not—that 'the Six Regiments of the City' could frighten the insurgents, but they appear not to have been able to frighten the City. The trained bands, or militia, appear to have lacked any clearly understood *civil* authority. The utmost the officers could do was to report the matter to the court of lieutenancy—who reported it to the lord mayor. Perhaps the constables, the nightwatchmen and the strayed revellers were not taking the Home Guard sufficiently seriously.

Naturally, the trained bands were not as yet fully disciplined, either in arms, drill or general conduct. Instances occurred of some of the part-time soldiers, accidentally (or otherwise) discharging their firearms *in the street* on their way either to or from a muster.[42] One man, wounded by accident, had to be taken to St Thomas's Hospital, and the lieutenancy felt obliged to grant £2 2s od to provide for his family—to be taken 'out of the Money arising by Fines received from Defaulters'.[43] Certain soldiers 'had misbehaved when on their Night Duties' and the threat here was that, for the future, offenders would be taken 'not to one of the Compters, but to Newgate'.[44] By the end of October, however, it was felt that 'the Six Regiments of the City' were now sufficiently drilled for a royal review; it was arranged, therefore, that they should pass in review before the king in St James's Park on Saturday 26th October at twelve noon.[45] Naturally the men were ordered to parade two hours early[46] and naturally this latter command was countermanded: the six regiments were to muster in the Artillery Ground at seven in the morning, 'Officers to take care that they be at St James's Park by 10 a.m.' in time for the review at twelve noon.[47] Assuredly they were becoming fully disciplined.

By the end of October the court of lieutenancy itself, in control of the six regiments, was coming to feel altogether more confident in its functions and the general management of militia business. For example, one Sarah Wilson had been supplying coffee and tea to the court at the Guildhall whenever it was in session. When she put in her bill the clerk of the court was ordered to 'Examine the bill now delivered' and report to the next court 'how he find the same'.[48] The clerk duly examined the bill and reported that he 'found it right'. Sarah Wilson had not been paid since last July twelvemonth. The court ordered the bill to be paid, but ordered also 'that no Coffee or Tea be hereafter brought to Guildhall for the Use of the Commissioners of Lieutenancy at the Expense of the Court'.[49]

It was not, however, until the month of November that affairs in London began to assume a more serious shape. On 30th October the insurgents had concentrated at about Dalkeith and then commenced to march south. They crossed into England on 8th November and captured Carlisle on the 17th. The main body left Carlisle on the 21st, was at Lancaster on the 25th, Preston on the 27th, Wigan on the 28th and Manchester on the 29th. Not only were they at Derby on 4th December, they out-manoeuvred Cumberland and the army sent north against them, and then stood with no force between them and London. 'The Alarm of the Rebels having given the Duke the Slip and being in full March' for London 'struck such a Terror into several Public-spirited Persons' that the first thing these 'Public-spirited Persons' did (as Fielding said, possibly somewhat facetiously) was to 'begin to pack up and secure' their 'Money Jewels and Plate' and flee from town. The ministry's own (self-appointed) apologist spoke of the 'Panick which ran through this Town'—of 'the extraordinary Pannic with which the City was struck'.[50]

From this point of time there was a *confusion* of confusions—altogether apart from this confusion in the City. In the midlands Cumberland, who thought he was southward of the invaders, suddenly found to his surprise that they were southward of him: he had been out-manoeuvred and had left the direct road to London wide open. He had now to turn all his attention south. The invaders, strategically so well positioned, decided quite suddenly—and to most, quite unexpectedly—on altogether other grounds, to retreat, so that instead of making south for London, they now made north for Carlisle once more. Cumberland's attention now turned north again. He was determined to bring them to action and hence made off north in hot pursuit. It was at about this time that news was received in London that the French were landing in the south—indeed, had already landed— and Cumberland and all forces were again recalled for the defence of London, with all possible speed—and all this within the compass of less than ten days.

When the invaders were at Derby on 4th and 5th December and Cumberland was ordered to march direct for London, part of his cavalry was expected to be at Northampton on Friday the 6th and the remainder on the Saturday. The foot also were to encamp on Saturday near Northampton; it was therefore not doubted that he would again be able to place himself between the invaders and London. The various troop movements now ordered indicate a twofold strategy: one, to provide for the defence of London; and two, to attempt to bring the invaders to action in the midlands. To this end various units, mostly recently withdrawn from the continent and lying in suburban places south of the Thames for fear of a French invasion, were ordered through London to take post northward of the City, and various units of horse, foot and artillery were ordered to march towards the midlands. In the meantime, certain orders already given had to be countermanded. On Tuesday 3rd December orders had been sent drafting out a train of artillery at Woolwich, including '130 Matrosses besides Gunners and Bombadies', and on the 6th four or five companies of guards belonging to the four battalions of foot guards doing duty in and around London were now ordered to march immediately for St Albans. (This, incidentally, may be the source of Hogarth's well-known painting, and better known print, 'The March of the Guards for Finchley'.) Also on the 3rd, seven companies of Lord John Murray's highlanders ('The Black Watch') from Flanders were ordered to march next day from

Maidstone via Dartford and London for Enfield and adjacent places; three other companies, earlier deployed in 'Kent, Sevenoake, Tunbridge Town, Wrotham and Malling' were ordered to the same places. On the 4th a squadron of Rich's dragoons was ordered to Barnet. On the 5th five companies of Brigadier Mordaunt's 47th Foot, were lying south of the river at Greenwich, three were at Woolwich and one at Erith and the remaining company at Charlton; five of these were ordered north of the Thames to Highgate and Hampstead. On Thursday the 5th also 'thirty Field Pieces were mounted an Carriages at the Tower, for the Army that is to rendezvous at Finchley Common'. General Hawley's Royal Dragoons at their disembarkation from Flanders on 12th December had originally been ordered to Canterbury but were now ordered to Southwark in the first instance, and from there to Barnet and thence to St Albans where four troops were to remain. Eight companies of Richbell's regiment (the 39th Foot) were moved from Deptford on the 7th to Finchley, Totteridge and Whetstone. Several companies of Sinclair's Royals (1st Foot) were to be drawn together from various quarters at Lee, Camberwell, Lewisham, Peckham, Eltham and Bromley and likewise to move north of the river to Barnet and Kick's End, eight companies to Hertford and places adjacent and two to Hatfield and places adjacent. On the 6th Hawley's dragoons, notwithstanding any former orders to the contrary, were directed to march to Barnet and Whetstone.[51] When, for example, Hawley's dragoons and Lord John Murray's highlanders 'pass'd through the City' they 'both made a fine Appearance, the men appearing to be in good Health and Spirits'.[52]

Apart altogether from all these troop movements on the part of the regulars for the defence of London, directions were given to the lord mayor on Friday the 6th, 'for the security of the City'. The attention of the lord mayor was particularly drawn to the possibility of civil disorder *within* the City. The City's own guard therefore was to be augmented, orders should be given to commanding officers of the trained bands.

to be very vigilant in preventing or supressing any Disorders or Tumults, and to seize any Persons that may be assembled together in a riotous Manner, and also that a Guard may be constantly posted in the Squares and open Places in the City, and that there may be daily

Meetings of the Magistrates appointed in proper places to see these Services are performed.

Furthermore, with the secretary of state's regard to the necessity to have control of transport and communication, an exact account was ordered to be taken 'of all the Horses (as well Coach Horses as Saddle Horses) in the several Stables within the City whose Horses are kept for Hire', and the account was to be sent to the office of the secretary of state.

Alarm posts were fixed within the City and the suburbs and alarm signals appointed. The master-general of ordnance was authorized to appoint forthwith a 'proper Person to inspect the several Entrances into the City and to consider in what Manner, in case of an Emergency, the same may be obstructed'. The lord mayor was requested to furnish

an Account of the Number of Men that are at present appointed for the several Guards in the City, and of the Places at which they are posted; as also of what Number of Men you would propose to add for that Service and in what parts of the City they may most effectually be posted.[53]

The secretary of state's letter was communicated to a special court of aldermen and to the court of lieutenancy. Precepts were issued to the several beadles to ascertain and make returns of the (*a*) coach horses and (*b*) the saddle horses, (i) belonging to private persons and (ii) kept for hire or sale, in the various wards of the City. Quite incidentally, these returns provide some interesting information about the City at this time.[54] The matters of the signals and alarm posts were considered and one regiment was ordered to do duty every day and two every night, with special directions to be very vigilant in preventing or suppressing any civil disorder and 'to take into custody all who oppose or resist'.[55] At a meeting of the court of lieutenancy on Saturday the 7th it was decided that the Red and Green regiments should appear for duty at 5 p.m. that very afternoon, the Yellow on Sunday morning at 6 a.m. The Yellow was to march to the relief of the Red and the Green and these latter should not go off duty until actually relieved by the Yellow. The Yellow, in their turn, should not leave their posts on Sunday evening until relieved by the White and the Blue at 5 p.m. for night duty—and so on until further orders.[56]

Apart from the posts as earlier decided, the Royal Exchange, Devonshire Square house, St Dunstan's in the West and St Sepulchre's, application was forthwith made for the use of certain halls and rooms in the City as guardrooms, namely, The Bakers' hall in Harp Lane, the meeting house in Poor Jury Lane (now Jewry Street), Sion College near Cripplegate (then standing on the site of the old foundation of Elsing Spital, near St Alphage church, London Wall), the guest room near Aldersgate church, a part of St Bartholomew's hospital in or near West Smithfield, the hall ('or some proper place') in Staple Inn, Scotts hall in Black-friars (or the hall of the corporation of the Scottish 'hospital'—site of Ludgate Hill station), and the Fishmongers' hall on London Bridge—all locations convenient to the gates and bars. When Devonshire Square house (in relation to Bishopsgate) was not available on a Sunday, the guard was to be based on the London workhouse[57] on the opposite side of the street (where Liverpool Street station now stands).

By Monday the 9th information had come through that the invaders were now in full retreat. In fact on the 10th they were at Wigan and the duke of Cumberland was at Macclesfield. In the City 'there had been much Hardship and Expense' in attending the frequent guards and other duties, and it was therefore ordered that the Green and Yellow regiments might stand down that afternoon, and although the Monday night guard should be maintained, the Tuesday morning guard could be suspended and guards generally reduced consistent with the safety of the City. The excitement in the City was over.

By the time all this flurry had properly subsided, news was received in the City that Admiral Vernon had reported from the Channel that a considerable number of vessels had assembled at Dunkirk and that there was the greatest reason to believe that an immediate attempt would be made to land a body of troops in the south of England.[58] Following news had it that the French had already landed at Pevensey Bay.[59] According to an account which one can only call a pro-ministerial account, the panic which now seized the City on Friday the thirteenth was 'little inferior to that which had seized us on the Friday before',[60] and 'a Council

[was] summoned to meet at Break of Day', and met thereafter 'almost every Night and some times twice in a Day'.[61]

A memorandum (which is presumably a note for the cabinet council) not only takes note that the French army may land in different places and therefore notices must be sent to the lieutenancies of the maritime counties; that therefore new dispositions of the regular forces must be made, and a train of artillery must be provided; it noted also, more specifically in relation to London, that the force in the midlands, now at Lichfield and Coventry, *must* be called south for the defence of London, the lords of the Admiralty must 'get all ships from Spithead up', the buoys in the Thames must be taken up, the bridges of London, Westminster and Putney looked to, and steps taken with regard to the militia of London and Westminster.[62] A special despatch was addressed to the lord mayor.[63]

So far as the army in the midlands was concerned, Ligonier was instructed to bring his whole force to London 'with the utmost Expedition'.[64] The messenger going north with these orders left instructions with all mayors and other principal local authorities on the route that—notwithstanding the constitutional niceties regarding military transport—they were to do their utmost to facilitate the army's march to London, and that all 'the Expense [they] should be at upon this occasion shall be answered to [them]'.[65] The alarm signal for invasion or insurrection was to be 'Seven Cannons, one to be fired every Half Minute at the Tower, to be answered by the same Signals from St James's Park and vice versa, and that the signal should not be made but by Order of the Field Officer or Gold Stick in Waiting, by the Commander or Commanding Officer at the Tower, or upon Notice to be given by [the lord mayor] or in [his] absence by the Senior Alderman of the City to the Commanding Officer at the Tower'.[66]

The alarm posts now appointed were: Tower Hill (Red), Guildhall Yard (Green), St Paul's Churchyard (Yellow), the Royal Exchange (White), Old Fish Street (Blue) and West Smithfield (Orange). To these alarm posts the six regiments of the City were 'to be in readiness to march upon the first Notice of any Tumult or Insurrection within the Cities of London or Westminster', upon hearing the alarm signal, and 'without waiting for Orders from their Officers', 'without waiting for beat of drum or other notice', and immediately 'repair to their arms and usual quantity of powder and ball'. The two regiments of the militia of the Tower Hamlets had also like orders, the first to meet on Tower Hill and the second in Sun Tavern Fields in Shadwell. Notices were hurriedly printed and distributed throughout the City.[67] In order not to confuse the alarm signals, the Admiralty gave directions to commanders of all vessels in the Thames that they were not on any account to fire any gun, lest the agreed alarm signals should not be plainly heard and distinguished in the case of actual invasion or insurrection.

As soon, however, as these various directions for the defence of the City, from within as well as from without, were brought to readiness, the information about the French invasion was found to be utterly groundless. The City of London could once again subside into semi-slumber and read the account of the retreat of the jacobite force, to Kendal by this time (Saturday 14th), Carlisle by the 19th, and fording the Esk out of England altogether by the 20th. The City had now only to pick up the pieces. The regular troops were now dispersed from their defensive quarters in the north of London, and one regiment for example, Edward Richbell's 39th Foot, was ordered to withdraw to London itself, 'to be quartered in Barns and Empty Houses' in Mile End, 'and lye on Straw', the local constables to provide the straw together with any necessary wood.[68] The excitement in the City was all over.

But not everything was quite as brave as it all sounded. Notwithstanding all the *True Patriots*, notwithstanding all the *Serious Addresses to the People* . . ., the *Calm Addresses to all Parties*, and all the other calls to arms, appeals to reason and so on, not everybody in the City had been eager, nor even merely willing, to defend the gates, to man the walls, or march out into Middlesex or beyond. There was controversy. There were controversies. When credit in the City was in danger, one would naturally expect 'the most eminent merchants and principal traders of the City' to jump to its defence. *That* was different. That was *monetary* credit, called '*public* credit'. There was, however, the other form of credit, one's own credit or reputation for public action in public affairs, the sort of reputation one might have that is not referred to—at least not in the City—as a 'credit'. It was about this sort of public action in public affairs that the most controversy was.

Already in September the merchants in the City were concerned about *public* credit. It was said that there had for some days been something of a 'hurry' at the Bank of England—a 'hurry' in the eighteenth-century sense of a confusion. There had—quite understandably—been a run on gold. Some citizens who held paper required the bank to hold to its 'promise to pay'—that is, to pay specie. It was said—and people *will* talk—that those who demanded gold, required it to transmit to their friends, the rebels in the north.[69] Perhaps the bank, to some extent at least, parried the thrust by paying out, certainly in specie, but not in gold—in sixpences. What was required now, in the current state of public uncertainty, in the present lack of any confidence in the ministry —what was required to restore (or establish) general confidence in 'the present happy establishment'—was some significant public gesture. This the merchants of the City provided. Several of the principal traders and most eminent merchants in the City, themselves proprietors of public funds, met at Garraway's coffee-house in Change Alley (incidentally, where tea was first sold in Europe) avowedly to support public credit. They publicly declared that they, for their part, would not in any transaction insist on specie; they would, in the ordinary course of business, accept bank notes to any amount. To this undertaking they signed their names and left their list of names at the coffee-house for public inspection. By five o'clock the next afternoon no fewer than 1,140 had similarly signed—and the 'hurry' at the bank was over. Furthermore, the East India Company, notwithstanding that their bonds were currently standing at a ten-shilling discount, announced that at their regular Company sales, they would accept, in payment of goods, any of their own bonds, and accept them at par to any amount. By these moves confidence in the City was completely restored.[70]

Even so, many of the more ardent whig merchants in the City felt that something should be done beyond their 'solemn cavalcade of 160 coaches', by which the merchants of London went to Kensington to present their loyal address to the king. Not surprisingly, a number of well-to-do merchants expressed their willingness to subscribe sums of money to sustain volunteers who should go north to meet the insurgents, but—as some of the cynics said—only as an alternative to going themselves. From a glance at the readily accessible printed sources in this regard one could easily be led into supposing that the various merchant bodies, parishes, wards and other organizations were falling over each other to join the different 'associations' for 'the defence of the present happy establishment'. But upon closer inspection, not everything was quite as simple as it seemed. Indeed, there was a variety of schemes on offer. Certain of the merchants, for example, met at the Merchant Taylors' hall and agreed to raise the money to form two regiments at their own expense. The finance of the scheme was no difficulty to City merchants: what proved to be an altogether more difficult matter was to decide 'the properest method for putting it into execution', and like any good business meeting they referred the difficulty to a committee of their own members—and went home. Others went direct to the War Office (at Scotland Yard) with another proposal, to raise a thousand men; but they too found they could not themselves decide how proper officers could be found to instruct the men raised.[71]

Many in London, as many in the provinces, favoured the idea of 'associating themselves together' into an armed body for the defence of the crown and 'the present happy establishment'. For example, when the new lord mayor this year was sworn in at Westminster, his coach was attended 'by the Honorable Artillery Company, the Hanover & Cripplegate Grenadiers, and a large body of *associated Gentlemen* out of Fleet Street'.[72] As has so frequently been the case—before and since—the thoughts of London and those of Westminster have not run exactly parallel. The parish of St Martin, for example, adopted a scheme of raising subscriptions and from that fund offering £5 to every man who should volunteer to join the foot guards. They raised 200 men.[73] *Old England*, however, bluntly declared that 'the Sword ought to be put into the Hands of the People, who are to be bred to the Exercise of Arms'.

It is indeed not surprising that there should be so much controversy—not to say dispute—about how best to raise a citizen body to defend the capital. It had earlier been realized in the counties, and it was now being realized in the City and Whitehall, that the laws with regard to the militia and the trained bands were deficient, and that the too hurried attempts to remedy this deficiency had rendered the confusion worse confounded. It was by now realized, by some at least in the City, that it was not legal for subjects to appear in a body under arms, *even in their own defence*, save under the lieutenancy procedure, and therefore that the raising of 'associations' outside the scope of the lieutenancy (it could be argued) had no support in law. Even by specific royal warrant (it could be argued) it could be only doubtfully legal.[74]

In the December scare in the City—not to say panic—on Friday the 13th, at the supposed French invasion, the secretary of state (in the name of the king) professed to have been informed

that a considerable Number of His good Subjects, Inhabitants of the City, out of Zeal for His Majesty's Service and for the Preservation of Our Excellent Constitution, are Desirous of appearing in Arms on the present Occasion[75]

It is not hinted why, if they had all that zeal to appear in arms in defence of the excellent constitution, they had not already appeared in arms; but the secretary of state informed the lord mayor that in order 'to give all possible Encouragement to such a laudable Design', if the lord mayor would transmit 'the Names of any Persons that shall be willing to engage' the secretary of state would 'immediately procure a proper Authority from His Majesty for the Purpose'.[76] This seems to hint at raising men in the City by royal warrant and seems to suggest that the ministry at least were doubtful whether any of the other current methods were in fact fully legal as distinct from under the authority of the lieutenancy.

Although, as even the newspapers were beginning to see, one might be 'glad to see such a general spirit of association . . . on behalf of the Government' [no mention of the king], yet one might 'not wholly approve the method that is so much in fashion of raising men'. In the circumstances some of the citizens produced their own schemes and in these the citizens seemed keen to lay down for themselves the terms upon which they would 'associate', and these terms usually embraced (at the end) the terms on which they would *not*. The terms of one such 'association' were at the beginning of October left 'at the Thach'd House in St James's Street to be there signed by all well-wishers to the present happy establishment'. By it 'associators' agreed to be ready at all times to defend the king's royal person; to continue the 'association' until the rebellion was suppressed; to furnish themselves, at their own expense, with arms and accoutrements 'such as we are bound by law to provide for the Militia, together with uniform Cloathing, viz a Blue Coat with Brown Buttons'; but 'provided always [and here was the essential point] That During the Time our Service shall be accepted in this Form' they would not be charged to the service of the militia and they should not be subject to martial law, 'but in lieu thereof to such Penalties as are prescribed by Law to the Militia of the Kingdom'.[77] All this seems to add nothing to a statutory liability to serve in the militia—and to deduct something from it.

Another scheme, 'A Plan for a Military Association' for 'Merchants Householders and substantial Inhabitants of the City', received much publicity in the beginning of October.[78] The proposal was that proper persons should be appointed to the several districts of the City to enrol the names of such householders and others that would 'associate', and so that those who live near each other could (they and their personal servants) be formed into battalions of foot and squadrons of horse. They should apply to the king to appoint 'a General Officer of Dignity and Military Experience' to be their commander-in-chief, together with other 'inferior Generals', and to provide a train of artillery. Every horseman should provide himself with a good hunter or road horse, and a case of pistols and a broad-sword, and each foot soldier with a good musket, bayonet and cartridge box. The standards, colours, drums and trumpets required should be provided at the common expense. The foot should first attend in company formation three hours every morning for ten days to learn drill and the use of firearms, and thereafter in battalion formation once a week. This does indeed look very businesslike, but the terms of the 'association' go on to stipulate that the manual exercises and evolutions shall not be more than are necessary, and that although the customary oath should be taken '*in such manner* as His Majesty shall be pleased to appoint', yet the oath itself was stipulated to be to the *government*. Furthermore, although the associators undertook to 'pay all due Military Obedience to their respective Officers *while under arms*' they did not undertake to 'march at Command to any Place which the Service may require' if any such place was 'exceeding Twenty Miles from London' without their own consent. Again, the extent of their patriotic regard for either the king or the government fell short of what the ordinary militia law demanded.

Also, there were more general objections to these various schemes, certain social objections, for example, and constitutional objections—and others—all giving rise to a variety of controversy. On the social side, were certain of the contributors, it might be asked, paying into the fund no more than conscience money for neglecting their social responsibilities? Would they not do better to fulfil their social obligations rather than pay their guineas and feel good? Instead of raising the money and paying a man £5, for example, for enlisting, and considering their social duty well done, said the *Westminster Journal*, 'it would be much better for all the justices of the peace, Ministers, church wardens, constables and principal inhabitants to be diligent in their several stations to find out', with regard to such men in their respective parishes as 'go for soldiers', and take 'care of their wives and families in their absence'. As regards the constitutional issue, the volunteers ought *not* to be paid from voluntary funds. They should be paid 'by equal taxes, laid on regularly by Parliament'. Maybe 'the friends of the government . . . pay these "subscriptions" chearfully'—but by so doing they relieve from payment the enemies of the government, and thus 'the burden lies upon his majesty's most forward friends'. Thus, the more successful the 'loyal associations' and other similar schemes are, the more the country's enemies are being relieved of the charges that ought more justly to fall upon them.[79] When a somewhat similar controversy arose in the northern counties, it was authoritatively reported that some men would 'alledge one reason' against a particular scheme 'and some another', but at least where 'it was not possible but Gentlemen must differ in themselves, they all meant the same end'. In London and Westminster, however, although one man might allege one reason against a particular scheme and another man another, it did not by any means follow that they all aimed at the same end. However, although the retreat of the invaders did not end the controversy, it ended the need for any practical outcome.

And after all this, so it has been said, London did not, during the whole course of the rising, hear a single shot fired in anger. This latter, however, is scarcely true. Whether or not France had already laid aside any real intention of an invasion, she despatched to the east coast of Scotland early in 1746 a little expedition under FitzJames, with some troops, including his own regiment of horse and a few deserters from the British forces on the continent, and some military stores. These were intercepted at sea and FitzJames and the others taken prisoner.

On Wednesday 23rd April 'five deserters from the foot guards in Flanders, taken with FitzJames's regiments going to Scotland, were shot in Hyde Park'.

There is a footnote: 'Two of them appeared to be papists'.[80]

There is a comment: presumably three were not.

Notes

[1] Cab. minutes, ff. 60–3.
[2] Repertories, vol. 148, f. 165.
[3] Cab. minutes, f. 63.
[4] L. Lon. MB, 1714–44, p. 319.
[5] *Ibid.* 321–2 and 309.
[6] I.e. not buff in *colour* but buff in *material*.
[7] L. Lon. MB, 1714–44, pp. 313–14.
[8] *Ibid.* 326.
[9] *Ibid.* 330–1.
[10] *Ibid.* 333.
[11] *Ibid.*, 336–7 and 340.
[12] *Ibid.* 344.
[13] *Ibid.* 324.
[14] *Ibid.* 1744–9, p. 11.
[15] *Ibid.* 18.
[16] *Ibid.* 19.
[17] *Ibid.* 23–4.
[18] *Ibid.* 26.
[19] *Ibid.* 33–7.
[20] *Ibid.* 38–9.
[21] Cab. minutes, f. 85.
[22] *Ibid.* f. 88.
[23] *General Advertiser*, 24th September 1745.
[24] *Ibid.* 25th September 1745.
[25] *Ibid.* 23rd September 1745.
[26] SP Dom. 87/16–18; and *GM*, xv (October 1745), 557.

[27] *General Advertiser*, 23rd September 1745.
[28] *Ibid.* 27th September 1745.
[29] *GM*, xv (October 1745), 554.
[30] *Ibid.* 554.
[31] *General Advertiser*, 18th November 1745.
[32] L. Lon. MB, 1744–49.
[33] *Ibid.* 27–8.
[34] *Ibid.* 43.
[35] *Ibid.* 43.
[36] *Ibid.* 41.
[37] *Ibid.* 48.
[38] *Ibid.* 46.
[39] *Ibid.* 55.
[40] *Ibid.* 55–6.
[41] *Ibid.* 57.
[42] *Ibid.* 29.
[43] *Ibid.* 83.
[44] *Ibid.* 88–9.
[45] *Ibid.* 53–4.
[46] *Ibid.* 54.
[47] *Ibid.* 61.
[48] *Ibid.* 70.
[49] *Ibid.* 71.
[50] *True Patriot*, no. 6 (10th December 1745), no. 7 (13th December 1745) and no. 11 (14th January 1746). See also *GM*, xv (December 1745), 666.
[51] Army route books: 57.
[52] *General Evening Post*, 7th–12th December 1745.
[53] Astle MSS, 38–9; and SP Dom. 41/37, 9–10.
[54] SP Dom. 77/82 (or 290), or L. Lon. MB, 102.
[55] L. Lon. MB, 106.
[56] *Ibid.* 104–5, and SP Dom. 77/30 (or 64).
[57] *Ibid.* 107–9.
[58] SP Dom. 76/127 (or 316).
[59] *Ibid.* 142 (or 426).
[60] *True Patriot*, no. 7, 13th December 1745.
[61] SP Dom. 77/1.
[62] *Ibid.* 76/135 (or 397).
[63] *Ibid.* 77/5–6.
[64] *Ibid.* 47 (or 121) and 48 (or 123).
[65] *Ibid.* 48 (or 123) and SP Dom. 77/12 (or 26). See also Paper 3, volume I.
[66] Astle MSS, f. 40.
[67] L. Lon. MB, 125–6.
[68] Army route books: 57.
[69] *GM*, xv (September 1745), 499.
[70] *Ibid.* 497.
[71] *Ibid.* 499 and 497.

72 *Ibid.* (October 1745), 557.
73 *Ibid.* 557.
74 *Old England*, 23rd November 1745.
75 Astle MSS, 38–9.
76 *Ibid.*
77 *Daily Advertiser*, 2nd and 3rd October, 1745.
78 *General Advertiser*, 3rd, 5th, 7th, 8th and 9th October 1745.
79 *Westminster Journal*, 9th December 1745.
80 *GM*, xvi, 218.

VI *Courts*

21 *The Manchester Constables, 1745*

When Charles Edward approached Manchester on Friday 29th November 1745, his advance party—already in Manchester—did not contrive, as had been managed in Carlisle for example, to send out the mayor or civic officers to greet him. This may, or may *not* have surprised him; what almost certainly did surprise him, however, when he got there, was that Manchester had no mayor to send out. For Manchester had not, of course, in 1745 achieved the dignity of a mayor and corporation. Manchester was still only 'the greatest meer village in England',[1] governed not by a mayor and corporation, but by a court leet or view of frankpledge, sitting under a steward appointed by the lord of the manor.

At Michaelmas each year the lord's court leet appointed, or elected from among the Manchester householders, the whole range of manorial office-bearers. The scavengers, 'market-lookers', the 'Officer for Muzzling Dogs and Bitches', the 'Officer for Tasting Wholesome Ale and Beer', and others such. At the head of the imposing annual list was the borough-reeve, chief annual officer of the manor, and two constables whose function was to see to the good order of the place. Then came the miselayers who levied the local rates, and the misegatherers who collected them—terms of peculiar interest to the north-west and the Welsh marches. At the foot of the list came the beadle, last of all the named officers in the view of frankpledge, but who had (perhaps by way of compensation) the dignity of a beadle's staff and livery, and a stipend of £7 a year. It was, however, through the constables that general civic authority was exercised and each constable therefore had a 'truncheon', painted and mounted with silver, as a symbol of his office. Although themselves honorary, the two constables

---

The notes and references are on pages 253–4

had a (single) paid deputy constable who enjoyed, like his principals, a 'truncheon' of office and, unlike his principals, a stipend of £20 a year.

By Michaelmas of 1745 it had already become clear that the office of constable might very well be a critical one in the coming year. On 16th October the court leet appointed (Robert?) Fielding to be borough-reeve, and William Fowden, merchant and chapman, and Thomas Walley (or Whalley), gentleman, to be constables. Fowden, at least, although a protestant and one who 'never was suspected of having any disaffection to the Government', had no wish to be constable. When he heard it was likely to be his turn for office he tried to influence the court leet jury to pass him over; indeed he is said to have offered 'a considerable sum of money' to 'fine off'; but he was compelled to serve as constable 'much against his inclination'.[2] Benjamin Bowker continued to serve as paid deputy. It was they—William Fowden, Thomas Walley and Benjamin Bowker—who were the principal civic officers during the occupations.[3]

The point will not be lost, presumably, that at Carlisle for example, after all proper use right up to the last moment of bell, book and candle, the clergy most tactfully arranged to disappear just at the right time—just before the enemy arrived; that the military (regular and militia) after much sabre rattling, likewise dispersed, stood down or otherwise marched off, at a very convenient juncture, even if it were only 'to prevent their arms falling into the hands of the enemy'; that the justices, after all the fire and brimstone breathed, managed to shuffle off the scene just before the entrance of the other party. The common civic functionaries, in contrast, had no such escape route. And when it was all over and 'the others' could come back—and accuse those who had stayed of collaboration—it did at least relieve 'the others' of accounting for where they themselves had been in the interim.

For example, on 14th and 15th November the militia of Manchester and neighbouring places concentrated on Manchester, and more companies came in on 19th November. On Saturday the 23rd—the invaders' horse and van were at Lancaster—the lord lieutenant (Lord Derby) was in Manchester[4] because he 'expected expresses', being 'still uncertain' where exactly the invaders were, and hence what he ought to do. He thought to 'discharge the

militia on Monday the 25th or Tuesday the 26th'—and he himself
go off to London on Sunday the 24th. There is surely intended to
be a little ice—if not a little acid—in the entry in the 'diary'[5] of
the Manchester constable who was of necessity staying: 'Saturday
23rd: waited on Earl Derby at Bull's Head, being informed his
Lordship was for London next morning—to wish his Lordship
a good journey'.

The main sources for the constables' version of the story of the
occupations of 1745 are, firstly, the constables' cash accounts
which were presented to the court leet the following Michaelmas;
and secondly, certain memoranda of events (usually called a
'diary') which had been kept by one of the constables at the time.
Apart, altogether, from the story these records disclose, these
documents *as documents* have themselves an interesting story.
Because the matter was somewhat glossed over in the city's
commemorative centenary volume in 1937,[6] it might not be
thought inappropriate to relate the strange vagaries of these two
sets of records.

When the corporation purchased in 1846 the manorial rights
from Sir Oswald Mosley, the then lord of the manor, the manorial
records then handed over included those of the court leet or view
of frankpledge, but not the constables' detailed accounts that
were by custom declared to the court leet each Michaelmas. These
latter had apparently become unfortunately separated, and got
sold as waste paper. In any case they (or part of them) came into
the possession of a second-hand bookseller in Shudehill. Here,
about 1850, a batch of the constables' accounts, covering the
period 1612 to 1647, were recognized and bought by a private
person. It is fortunate that this person, being in fact a local
official, left them to the city upon his death in 1888. Shortly
after this batch had come to light, a second batch was found,
covering the period 1743 to 1776. These also were recognized and
bought privately in 1851. Upon the sale of James Crossley's
library they were bought by the corporation, so that both batches
were again associated with the court leet records which had remained in the corporation muniment room since the purchase of
the manor in 1845. In the meantime, the city of Manchester—for
these were enlightened times—had embarked on an ambitious
programme of publishing the early records, so that between 1884

and 1890 the seven folio volumes of court leet records were put into print, and in 1891 and 1892 these were followed by the three volumes of constables' accounts. As if not enough had happened about Manchester records in the 1880s, a further fugitive item now came to light. One of the constables of 1745, Thomas Walley, had kept some memoranda of the day-to-day happenings during the jacobite occupations, together with a copy of some of the correspondence of his office. The originals of these were impounded by officers of the crown in 1746[7] as incriminating him, possibly in treason, but a copy of them had apparently been hurriedly made at the time, and this latter copy came to the hands of J. P. Earwaker in 1889 who unfortunately does not favour us with any provenance.[8]

These then are the primary sources, sources which can, of course, be supplemented in some small measure by such accounts as Beppy Byrom's diary,[9] and by the texts of the assize indictment of 1747, and the prisoner's case to be found among the Kenyon family papers.[10] It is, however, not so much the conduct of the constables during the occupations that has given rise to doubts, but the sequel. When once the rising had collapsed, it is perhaps, understandable that—in accordance with time-honoured practice—there was a keen search for scapegoats. Indeed, already, on 10th December 1745, the duke of Cumberland had addressed (from Macclesfield) a directive 'to the Magistrates and inhabitants of the Town of Manchester', strictly commanding them in the king's name 'to cause to be seized immediately all persons who have been part of or who have aided and abetted the Scots Rebels', adding, 'and herein you are in no wise to fail as you will answer at your own great peril'. His somewhat free interpretation of his own directive is indicated by a later letter to the secretary of state from his headquarters outside Carlisle: he thought it would be 'greatly for His Majesty's present and future service and for the Repose of the Kingdom, if some examples were made'. Thereupon the game of scapegoat-hunting went into full cry, and the (deputy) mayor of Carlisle and, in the absence of any mayor and corporation, the constables of Manchester had all the scent—and hence later all the hounds at their heels.

In the event, however, it was found that Benjamin Bowker, the deputy constable, could not be indicted for treason for lack of corroborative evidence, but Walley and Fowden, the two constables, were arrested and duly charged. No true bill could be found against Walley. Fowden, however, had to stand his trial at the Lancaster[11] assizes—but was acquitted. The occasion, understandably, aroused considerable feeling locally—not to say ultimately riot. Yet, even so, not a great deal is now known about it. For example, the particular issue of Whitworth's *Manchester Magazine*—the only newspaper then established in Manchester—that would have reported the trial if the trial had been reported, is missing from the only known file in the Manchester Central Library.[12] In editing the constables' accounts in 1891-2 (already referred to) Earwaker reprinted an interesting contemporary broadside[13] and commented that there is 'little or no other record' of the event.[14] There are, however, certain other documents which have not hitherto been considered in this connection, namely certain letters and reports relating to the trial, and now to be found among the state papers and other records. These may shed a little light into a hitherto obscure corner of Manchester history.

In general, the doings of the Manchester constables have the characteristic mid-eighteenth century flavour. Paid 'to John Cummins, a disabled soldier', the sum of one shilling—that high sum being justified by the additional note: 'very lame'. The item might be compared with one for 30th October—the king's birthday—'paid Mrs Bartholomew', she being the landlady at The Bull's Head in Greengate, 'for wine this day to drink the health. p Bill, £05 = 09 = 08'. John Cummins had need be 'very lame'. Two shillings paid for 'a mittimus for a whore, cau't this Sunday morn in the Exchange'—leaving the social historian quite uncertain whether it is the more heinous crime to be caught at it 'in the Exchange', or on a 'Sunday morn'. 15th August 1745 —they had their traffic problems even then—one shilling and four pence, paid to the 'jurors at Broughton. Geo: Holland's child, kill'd by a cart wheel'.[15]

However, with regard more narrowly to the rising, the conduct of the constables seems to have been exemplary by any standard. They set a special town watch, and put a new fire-grate into the watch-house (complete with fire-irons), and kept it furnished with coal. Upon the raising of the militia they attended the deputy lieutenants as necessary, furnished messengers, issued warrants upon the various townships and hamlets for men and pay, supplied cockades, and assisted generally in mustering and quartering. They also admitted charges upon the common stock in respect of horsehire and expenses with the lord lieutenant to and fro, and to various places up and down and across country on account of intelligence. With regard to the regular forces, they rang them into the town, admitted various entertainment expenses whilst in town, and issued press-warrants for horses and carts to transport their baggage out.[16] In the unprecedented situation, however, there were bound to be margins for quite genuine disagreement. For example, when occupation looked very likely, Sir Henry Hoghton of Hoghton Tower came into the town, he being one of the most ardent whigs and most active justices in the country, a deputy lieutenant and one of the senior officers of the militia.[17] He was shortly followed and supported by the lord lieutenant himself, Lord Derby. Their principal concern was what the constables proposed to do about the quantity of gunpowder known to be in the town—in private hands. Edward Cheetham of Smedley, 'an eminent lawyer in Manchester', Robert Dukinfield (eldest son of Sir Robert Dukinfield), an ardent whig and active magistrate, Horton of Chadderton and other justices took it upon themselves to call the three constables together. The justices—and apparently the officers of the lieutenancy—tried to persuade the constables to buy the powder out of the hands of the traders, *at the expense of the town*, and then take care of it at their own risk. The constables withdrew from the justices and lieutenancy to the Old Coffee House, in order to consult with 'the gentlemen of the town'. Not surprisingly, 'the gentlemen of the town' thought that the lord lieutenant himself had 'the power to seize the said powder if he pleased', and if his lordship thought proper he himself 'might give an order upon the Treasurer of *the County* to pay for the said powder' and thereby take it into his own—or militia—custody. His lordship (also not surprisingly) was 'not pleased with the answer'. As a compromise, it was proposed that various inhabitants of the town should offer to buy (say) 20 or 40 lb each; but the constables said if it were wanted to get the stuff out of the town they themselves would undertake to remove it, and remove it at the town's cost, for example, to Chester castle or Cumberland's army—but they could not agree to buy it outright, *at the town's cost*. In the result, the lieutenancy, the justices, the constables and 'the gentlemen of the town' 'came to no resolution upon the affair'. The whig justices could profess to look upon this as a piece of mere jacobite obstruction—'your lordship now sees what a town it is!' —but the plain truth is that the constables had no real authority to incur such a charge against the *town*, while the lieutenancy had upon the *county*.

When the occupation appeared imminent the constables and certain of the county justices met 'to consider what was best to be done' and how the constables should 'act and behave if the rebels should send for them'. They met at the 'House of John Rawsthorne, the sign of the Griffin at Dangerous Corner, being the house that the justices met at'. It seems to have been decided there that 'whatever they forced the constables to do [the constables] must be obliged to observe'. With regard to quartering the invaders, the leading justices then pressed the constables to use their best endeavours 'that none shall be quartered' upon the justices or their relations 'but such as are likely to behave well', and having fixed this with those who were having to stay, themselves arranged to 'go from home'.

When, in due course, the constables were summoned to appear before the invading jacobite officers, Fowden, bearing in mind doubtless the late consultation with the justices, asked 'the Colonel' 'by what authority he sent and commanded him'; 'the Colonel' 'lay'd his hand upon the hilt of his sword and drew part of it out and said, "By that!" ' so the constables were 'forced'— and 'must be obliged to observe'. Even so, the local constables seem to have given the invading military a short weekend elementary course on English local government. For example, when the military instructed the constables—presumably in the absence of a mayor and aldermen—to go (taking their staves of office with them) out of the town to meet Charles Edward and conduct him in, as 'in all other places he had been received', the constables replied that Manchester extended only to Salford Bridge and they themselves 'had no power beyond it'. They were therefore commanded at least to ring the bells; one can imagine the local constables patiently explaining to the invading military that although the constables had full authority over the bellman —with one bell—they had no authority whatsoever over bell-ringers with lots of bells: *that* was a matter for the respective churchwardens. No; they did not know where the churchwardens were likely to be found this morning!

The most notorious occasion was, of course, the reading of the jacobite proclamation at the Market Cross. According to the constables' own stories they were taken—with their staves of office—under a military guard to the Cross, and ordered there to read publicly the proclamation. Fowden pleaded he could not read it, having left his spectacles at home, and Walley pleaded he could not read it either as he had an impediment in his speech—one could say it but could not see it, the other could see it but could not say it. Eventually the invaders decided that Fowden—short-sighted, but with no other impediment—could say it without seeing it, for he was compelled to repeat the phrases after they had been read out to him. Other incidents, occasioning much notoriety later, were the quartering of the troops and horses; requisitioning or pressing horses, carriages, and forage for transport, and the casting of leaden bullets in the town.

It must not be thought that after the December of 1745 when the jacobite force left Manchester for the north, Manchester then lapsed into its original state of quietude. Various accounts give different versions of the rejoicings. One account has it:

The Pretender was carry'd about the streets in effigy (dressed in plad and armed with sword and Target) by the populace. A person on horseback went before it beating a warming pan, and crying out, King George for ever; no warming pan brood; no warming pan Pretender; and at proper places the mob made a stand and cryed aloud, No Jacobite Parson, no Jacobite doctors, No Jacobite constables, Hanover for ever.[18]

Presumably the parson, doctor and constables were in ascending order of heinous guilt.

There was, however, the other point of view. We know, if only by the inhabitants' petition to the members of parliament for the county, that from the spring of 1746 Manchester and Salford suffered grievously from the general arrogance, often flagrant plundering, and indeed, occasional studied cruelty of the units of government horse and foot, which had in a quite illegal manner been quartered upon the inhabitants.[19]

In the meantime, since it had now become quite safe for the justices and deputy lieutenants to return, the justices and deputy lieutenants returned. These, prompted by the duke of Newcastle in London who had been prompted by the duke of Cumberland in Carlisle, soon got busy taking informations. In particular, Robert Dukinfield, Justice Bradshaw and Sir Henry Hoghton joined in taking a number against the constables and deputy constable and other persons in Manchester and neighbourhood, all pointing to the crime of treason.[20] The various informations were forwarded to the secretary of state[21] and in consequence two messengers[22] were ordered to come from London to take the offenders into charge at Manchester and to impound there such documents as might enforce the charges—or otherwise be needed at the trial.

By this time, feeling was running high in Manchester and Salford—on account of the conduct of the illegally quartered government troops. According to the petition to parliament the shameful behaviour of both officers and men had led so many inhabitants to leave the town that 'the returns by the trade in the town, by computation, are already found to have sunk a thousand pounds a week'. Dragoons' horses were being stabled in the living rooms of respectable inhabitants, not only were there 'very flagrant instances of plundering', but if the parliamentary petition is to be relied upon there were other incidents that might very well be called atrocities.[23] In this flagrantly illegal quartering only the constables could stand between the military and the townsfolk.

In April of 1746 during this period of ill will, 'two of His Majesty's Messengers . . . were sent down to Manchester to take four or five people up for High Treason', including the constables and the deputy constable, A 'messenger' was an official of the secretary of state's office employed to apprehend state prisoners, and it is particularly to be noted that escape from the custody of any such a 'messenger' of a person *charged* with treason itself constituted *treason*.[24] Nevertheless, the local justices advised that 'it would be dangerous to offer to take them up without having troops, for then the mob would rise and rescue them'. The officials from London applied to Lord Malpas at Chester—son of the lord lieutenant of Chester—who marched half a regiment to Northwich next morning, and into Manchester the following day. It was, however, understood that 'one, Fowden, the Chief Person that they were sent for', had left Manchester for London; but Lord Malpas 'happened by chance to see the man in Chester'. According to a letter from Malpas to the earl of Cholmondeley,

knowing that he was an acquaintance of Lieutenant Cleggs of our Regiment I ordered him to inquire whether he returned to Manchester, and if he did to pertend to have some business there and to go with him and not to quit him, which he did, and yesterday [25th April] in Northwich the Messengers took him, and Captain Wright with fifty men marched him prisoner to Manchester.

Lord Malpas added:

I believe our soldiers frightened them into a rejoicing, for they had just received the news of the Dukes having beat the Rebels [at Culloden] which I hope will prove true, upon which they made the greatest Rejoicing that ever was known.[25]

Matters now passed into the hands of Sir Dudley Ryder (later Lord Ryder) the attorney-general, who, after his examination of the case, considered in respect of Bowker, the deputy constable, that as 'there is but one witness of any Fact ag't him', there was therefore 'no Sufficient Evidence . . . to ground a prosecution for Treason Upon'.[26] In respect of both Walley and Fowden, however, there appeared sufficient evidence to sustain a charge of treason. The constables were therefore relieved of their office and committed to Lancaster to await trial.[27]

Because of the physical difficulty of bringing all the prisoners to trial, arrangements were made that certain of them who were willing to plead guilty should be permitted to cast lots; that only every tenth man (on whom the lot fell) should actually stand his trial, and that the remaining nine should receive the king's mercy and be transported to the plantations for life. The prisoners at Lancaster were 'lotted' accordingly, and those for trial despatched under guard for Carlisle.[28] The prisoners 'of the peace', including Walley and Fowden were however excepted from this arrangement, as the ministry was particularly concerned to secure in these cases the full rigour of the law. Therefore, before the judges set out on the northern circuit warrants of detainer were sent out against 'all prisoners confined for High Treason in any of the gaols in that circuit'[29] in order to prevent any prisoner from getting an easy discharge.

In the assize proceedings, however, at Lancaster in the summer of 1746 the indictments were laid before the grand jury, and although the grand jury found a true bill against William Fowden, they returned that of Thomas Walley, his fellow constable, *ignoramus*. John Sharpe, the solicitor in London who was managing the trials for the ministry, reported to the secretary of state that 'all Bills preferred at the Assizes for the County of Lancaster for Treason and Treasonable Practices have been found, the single one against Walley only excepted'.[30] Now two out of three had escaped the ministry. Only William Fowden remained. For prestige reasons alone, therefore, if for no other, there was a great political need to secure a conviction in this remaining case.

In Manchester, therefore, the justices looked to their credit and good name. An indictment had been prepared in London from the local affidavits, under nine counts, alleging particular overt acts upon which they relied principally to secure Fowden's conviction. They related to (1), reading the proclamation; (2), issuing directions for work in the artillery ground; (3), pressing whitesmiths to make bullets; (4), ordering other persons to cast bullets; (5), demanding horses; (6) demanding militia arms; (7), causing a drummer to beat up for recruits; (8), issuing warrants for forage, and transports; and (9), consorting with the rebels.[31] The various witnesses relied upon by the crown to support these charges had been 'very strong and particular in their Informations before the Justices' in Manchester, but in order to be certain of bringing the charges home, the examining justice 'examined and cross-examined them several times afterwards and before the Day of Tryal' in the hopes that the witnesses would 'stick up to the Points' at the trial itself. He found, however, upon finally rehearsing his witnesses

such a variation amongst some of them in favour of Fowden in regard to some material charges against him that [he] was obliged to draw the proofs of those over again, and made copys thereof for the Councel to prevent them being deceived.[32]

When the final briefs had been prepared and had been read over and considered by the counsel, a consultation was arranged between the counsel and the justices who had taken the original informations, 'in order to advise and determine what matters to go upon and how to introduce our Proofs Comfortable thereto'. Towards the end of March—the trial would come on in early April—John Sharpe, who in London was managing the trials for the ministry, received an 'earnest Request' from his 'agent in the Country'. The 'agent' would not be able, himself, to produce the Manchester witnesses in Lancaster. His 'earnest Request' was for two of the king's messengers to be sent down to Manchester to meet him there, and 'collect them together there and conduct them to Lancaster', as otherwise 'there will be no such thing as managing 'em'. This seems to have been done, but although the conducting of the witnesses to Lancaster could be managed, their conduct in court could not. On the whole they made a pretty lamentable show, notwithstanding all the examination, cross-examination and rehearsing of the prosecution witnesses. The prosecution found during the proceedings that they had been 'in some measure deceived in proving the charges in the 4th, 7th, and 8th Articles'—casting bullets, recruiting and issuing warrants —and that the crown witnesses generally deviated from what they had before declared—and that in favour of the criminals.[33] With regard to the broad decision of the constables to stay in Manchester during the occupation, in the effort to assure some sort of civic order, the defence made much point that this occasion had been made in close consultation, and indeed, with the actual agreement of the very justices concerned in this case. The constables and deputy constable concurred in their evidence that:

before the Rebels came to Manchester [the constables] were so cautious as to apply to and take the Advice of their Justices of the Peace in respect of their staying or going out of Town, that their stay was thought proper as it might be a means to prevent Damage to the Town.[34]

It was even stated on oath during proceedings that Robert Dukinfield, who had taken such a noted part in initiating these proceedings, had actually since thanked the prisoner 'for continuing in Town during the stay of the Rebels'. The justice later protested to the secretary of state that this 'was absolutely false', but he had not been able to deny it in court because he had been 'unfortunately necessitated during Fowden's Trial to go out of court for a short space of time', and that opportunity was then taken to swear it during his brief absence, and he 'was not informed of it till it was too late to rectify it'.[35] Certainly the point was not lost on the jury that by 'going out of Town' the justices had left the constables alone to maintain civic order. For example, when the incident was referred to when Fowden put one of the jacobites, on their return, into the house of correction—the incident that may possibly have provoked the situation which resulted in the demand for £2,500 from the town—Fowden said, firstly, he committed the man to the house of correction only for the man's own safety, to get him out of the hands of the mob, and secondly, it was *he* who committed the man only because there were at the time 'no Justices of the Peace in the town or neighbourhood of Manchester'.[36]

In general, Fowden did not deny the various overt acts alleged—and indeed, proved—against him. He pleaded military compulsion. He brought forward what one of the examining justices admitted as 'strong and Positive proof' of a 'continued force upon him', proof which was 'backt' with a crowd of witnesses—for he had no less than 32 examined'.[37] The witnesses for the defence apparently showed none of the 'general deviations' displayed by those for the prosecution. Walley and Bowker for example, first to be examined, 'distinguished their zeal for him by swearing every thing that was asked them—in his favour'.

The pretender had been proclaimed, the army quartered, the warrants issued, the horses and arms searched for, the forage requisitioned, the carts impressed, the bullets cast, not only 'with the greatest regret and reluctance', but also under an absolute military compulsion.

He had parties of armed rebels almost with a continuance at his house, threatening to kill him and burn his house for not executing their commands so expeditious as they said he ought to do; that Bowker Walley and Fowden were several times taken prisoners and kept confined several hours at a time by the Rebels, in order to enforce them the better to obey their commands in sending out warrants and issuing directions agreeable to the Rebels Demands.[38]

This evidence was followed by 'a chain of 16 other willing witnesses to corroborate their testimony' and although these sixteen witnesses 'did not speak so generally and circumstantially to every thing as Walley and Bowker did, yet their evidence put altogether accounted for almost every moment of time the Rebels were in Manchester and showed that Fowden's Transactions and behaviour began, continued and ended, with force'.[39] Not satisfied to rest their case there, the defence called John Clowes, the high constable for Salford hundred, John Smith, his clerk, John Wilkinson from Preston, Robert Bowker from Stockport, and others 'who were Magistrates of Towns when the Rebels went southwards'. These magistrates and officials declared that they also had been compelled 'to proclaim the pretender and to provide him with forage, carriages and what else they thought proper'—but had not yet been proceeded against for treason on that account. Further evidence was sworn that Fowden had made certain refusals to the jacobites when he was not in fact under military duress, but had 'chearfully furnished' horses and other facilities to government agents when he need not have done so. The case for the defence was closed when 'Sir Ralph Ashton and two other gentlemen . . . said Fowden had always been a Man of General good character, and reputed and esteemed to be well affected to the present Government'.

As the whig version had it: 'Our counsel upon the Reply made several learned and good observations and did and said all that he could do for the Government upon the occasion.'[40] The judge summed up, and the jury withdrew—to return in half an hour with a verdict of—'Not Guilty'.

The crown had now lost all its three Manchester cases. As if this were not enough, Walley, the other constable, although no true bill had been found against him, still remained bound by his recognizances, and now sought to be freed. 'We strongly oppos'd the discharging of Walley from his Recognizance' said the Manchester justices, 'but the Court would not continue him bound'[41] and released him accordingly.

Nor was this all. The crown then went on to lose a number of similar cases, mostly because the crown—too keen, perhaps, to draw indictments—had occasionally based them on the rather unreliable witness of easily discredited persons. For example, a man named Thomas Dix, one of the jacobite army, was known to have been 'in the van that came into Manchester'. When this Dix was later captured it transpired that he had been one of Cope's army defeated at Prestonpans and had taken on with the jacobites. His was a crime greater than the rest, for he was not only in rebellion—he had deserted to the enemy. In an effort to save his own neck he had turned king's evidence and again re-enlisted. Because he had himself occupied Manchester and had later marched with the Manchester men, the crown lawyers decided to make use of him and his evidence, at least to make certain of identification. As the Manchester justice said after the trial:

He told us several times that he well rembred and knew [the prisoner], and we had given him a great opportunity of seeing him before the Trial came on.

When, however, he went into court for the one purpose of identifying the prisoner, 'he was so impudent'—as well as so imprudent—to ask, within the hearing of others which one was in fact the prisoner he had come to identify. Then,

he denying on cross examination he had asked such a question, and the same being proved upon him, and a good deal of reflections being thrown upon him in respect of his being with and marching among the Rebels, the Jury would give no credit to his evidence.[42]

The obvious question to ask such a witness was what a soldier of Lee's Regiment was doing marching with the rebels. The one answer (in the circumstances) the witness could make was that he had been 'forced'—which was precisely the *prisoner's* defence. As the broadside expressed it: it happened

unfortunately that Thomas Dix the cheef of them, an honest drummer both for his magistie and the Pretender, and so a proper witness what was done by the ribbles Behavier, for want of better Instructions, perjured him self most shamfully in Court;

The other witness also did not come 'up to what was hoped for, being but mean Persons of no capacity'; so the jury found that what they had been guilty of was by 'meer force and compultion', largely because 'nobody of any carricter would appear against him'.

Some of the prosecution witnesses in the trials generally, 'who gave information before Sir Henry Hoghton . . . [proved] most egregarious villains, tho' they never discovered it before they came to be sworn; our Council threw up their briefs . . . These people are arrantly forsworn'.[43] According to the whig version, circumstances in Manchester and Lancaster were not very conducive to impartial trial. In Manchester 'the disaffected in Town are such a United determined people that no expense or any other method can be wanted to bring off their friends'. In Lancaster 'the town was as crowded with their friends to a party that it appeared more like an Election for a Member than to hear the trial of an Offender', said Robert Dukinfield, J.P., after the trial:

I do not apprehend it to be practicable to convict a rebel at Lancaster for what is deficient in the evidence is frequently supplyed by the jury; were the most notorious Rebels who were convicted at Carlisle to have been tried at the Assizes, not excepting Coppach himself, they would all have been acquitted.[44]

On the whole perhaps it is not very surprising that on the return of the three Manchester constables to Manchester on the night of the Lancaster assizes there should have been something in the nature of a demonstration—even a riot—in the town.

If we are looking for the right note on which to close this paper, there is one at least in the right key, in the rare broadside already referred to. In the mêlée in Manchester on the night of the trial—13th April 1747—

An officer of His Magisties army being in the street lane leading to the Constables House and heering a riotous shouting for joy among the townspeople,

drew his sword and said that 'he would kill the first man that should stir any further'. Someone thereupon assaulted him 'and laid him on one side upon his back'.

Did this develop into an earlier Peterloo?

The sequel: 'All was Quiet. Only the officer lost his las't [laced] hat and the silver hilt of his sword.'

'Whether it was found again or not,' we are solemnly informed, will appear when 'this horrid Insult' comes 'to be inquired into'!

Perhaps therefore, so far as Manchester is concerned, the Forty-five ended not at Culloden with a bang, but in Market Street Lane, in a whimper.

Notes

[1] D. Defoe, *Tour thro' the Whole Island* (1927 ed.), ii. 670.

[2] *Kenyon MSS*, 480.

[3] They are, however, occasionally referred to as 'the chief magistrates' (cf. A. G. Goyder, *Charles, Prince Regent* (1954), p. 68).

[4] LCAS, lxii (1950–1), 127 ff.

[5] As to which, see below.

[6] 'When purchasing the manorial rights, the Corporation obtained possession of the Court Leet Records relating to the manor. These records . . . cover the period from the year 1552 down to 1846. These records, together with the Constables' Accounts for the Manor from 1612 until 1776, have been printed . . .', *The City of Manchester*, 1937, 17.

[7] Taken, apparently, from 'Mr Walley's Scutore by Mr Nathan Carrington, one of the King's Messengers in Manchester upon Friday April 25th, 1746'.

[8] LCAS, vii (1889), 146–58.

[9] *In Private Journals and Literary Remains of John Byrom* (Chetham Society, 1854–7); or H. Talon, *John Byrom: Selections from his Journals and Papers* (1950), 224–42.

[10] *Kenyon MSS*, 478–87.

[11] *VCH Lancs* (iv, 180n.) is in error in saying he was tried at Carlisle.

[12] LCAS, lvii (1943–4), 47n.–48n.

[13] His transcription of it however, was not absolutely accurate. See LCAS, lxxi (1961), 88.

[14] *Constables' Accounts*, iii, Appendix, 354.

[15] *Ibid.* iii, 15–19.

[16] *Ibid.* iii, 17–22.

[17] As to whose activities, see the Hoghton MSS.

[18] *Fitzherbert MSS*, p. 166.

[19] *Kenyon MSS*, 487–90.

[20] SP Dom. 90/184.

[21] *Ibid.* 91/24.

[22] As to 'messenger', see below.

[23] *Kenyon MSS*, 487–90.

[24] Giles Jacob, *New Law Dictionary* (1762) (quoting Skinner's *King's Bench Reports (1681–98)*, 599).

[25] SP Dom. 83/171–3.

[26] *Ibid.* 85/239.

[27] *Ibid.* 108. (As to the lotting procedure, see next Paper.)

[28] SP Dom. 395.

[29] *Ibid.* 40/88.

30 *Ibid.* 86/73.
31 *Ibid.* 97/143.
32 *Ibid.*
33 *Ibid.* 96/107.
34 *Ibid.* 97/143.
35 *Ibid.* 96/107.
36 Beppy Byrom said, 'Mr Walley [the other constable] went to Smedley, but Mr Chetham [the magistrate] was gone.'
37 SP Dom. 97/143.
38 *Ibid.* 144.
39 *Ibid.*
40 *Ibid.*
41 *Ibid.* 146.
42 *Ibid.* 145.
43 *Ibid.*
44 *Ibid.* 96/107.

22 The Carlisle Trials, 1746

Although a great deal has been written about the trials of the jacobites at Carlisle in 1746 as a chapter in jacobite history, little has been written about them as a chapter in the history of Carlisle. It is proposed, therefore, to deal with them in this Paper from the latter point of view, relying mainly upon such unpublished records as the correspondence of the mayor, corporation and governor of Carlisle, the sheriff of Cumberland, and the crown solicitor for the trials in Carlisle at the time.

The surrender of Hamilton's jacobite garrison in Carlisle on 30th December 1745 left Carlisle, of course, with more prisoners than any other place in England. In the following August and September many more were sent in from Whitehaven, Penrith, Newcastle, Morpeth, Lancaster, Chester and other places, to face their trials; altogether a total of 315[1] were due to appear in Carlisle on charges of treason. Of those, 180 drew blank lots[2] and were excused trial; eight others were sick or otherwise not indicted or if indicted not tried; one pleaded his peerage, and one was returned by the grand jury *ignoramus*. This left 125 to be tried; of these, thirty-four were acquitted and ninety-one were convicted, some of these being in due course reprieved.

Ordinarily, one would expect an accused to be indicted in the county where the imputed offence was alleged to have been committed. But after the rising of 1715, the crown advisers appear to have doubted whether, in the current state of public opinion, they could empanel juries who could be relied upon to convict. Statutory power had therefore to be taken, ostensibly in order 'that Justice may more speedily and securely be administered', but more specifically 'that the offenders may not conceive any Hope of Impunity . . . from any Power or Interest they may have [in the counties]'. This act provided power, therefore, to try any person in custody 'in such shire as his Majesty shall direct, and no challenge for the shire shall be allowed'.[3] This was no more than a roundabout way of saying that the prisoners should be tried at those places, otherwise convenient for the trials, where good sound whig juries could be hand-picked; hence the trials in Carlisle in 1716. After the Forty-five also, prisoners were indicted in counties other than those where the alleged treason had been committed.[4] In any case, the Habeas Corpus Act had been suspended[5] and the suspension had been renewed.[6] Whenever possible only such charges would be framed as could conveniently be proved by witnesses from among the inhabitants of those centres, and only in respect of the remaining prisoners would witnesses have to be brought in from elsewhere to secure their conviction on other charges. It is clear from other papers[7] that the venues originally selected were Carlisle and Newcastle—obviously because of their convenience to Scotland. No trials, however, were in fact held at Newcastle, and prisoners already forwarded thither from Carlisle were later returned.[8]

It was clear at an early stage that there would be two main difficulties in the trials: (1) to produce in court credible witnesses in each case who could reliably identify each of the accused in some overt act of treason; and (2) to empanel responsible juries who could be relied upon to return verdicts for the crown. There were particular difficulties about prisoners taken in other parts of England or in Scotland, and even within the county of Cumberland, for instance, the situation was not simple. For example, with regard to those taken at Penrith, they could not remain in Penrith as there was no place of strength of sufficient size locally; nor could they be removed to Carlisle which was already full. They had, therefore, to be transferred to York. The solicitor preparing the prosecutions, however, writing from Carlisle in early August (that is to say, before the trials had commenced but after a close scrutiny of the briefs) reported to an official in London known as 'the solicitor for carrying on criminal prosecutions', that he could find no evidence in his briefs against the Penrith prisoners, and feared that he would be unable to procure any. 'The sending the witnesses from Penrith to York [to identify the prisoners and give evidence there] will be endless there being perhaps a hundred different persons engaged in taking the Rebells.' Nor could the indictments as yet be drawn in Carlisle, Penrith or York, 'the people who took [the prisoners] not knowing their names, and we not knowing the men's names who took them'. The solicitor could not see 'how it can be fixed' he said, 'unless these prisoners be removed from York to be tryed here [in Carlisle]. In that case we could summons in the Penrith people and should easily find witnesses to affect them.'[9]

Before the assize judges set out on the ordinary business of their English circuits therefore, warrants of declaimer were sent out against all prisoners detained for treason in any of the gaols of the circuit, to prevent the judges discharging them in the ordinary course of gaol delivery,[10] and the trials under special commission at Carlisle and Newcastle were pushed forward. At an early stage, however, difficulties began to mount. Within seven weeks of Culloden the duke of Newcastle, the secretary of state in London, was writing to the duke of Cumberland in Scotland about 'such a considerable number of prisoners' then being sent from Scotland into England. There was, for example, 'no strong place at Newcastle sufficient for keeping safely such a large number'; there were insufficient troops in garrison there, and the only regiment—one of the newly raised units—was about to be reduced anyway. Orders were given about the prisoners already in Newcastle 'for keeping them on board the Transports [with what effect, much jacobite literature is eloquent] 'till it can be considered whether they should be . . . sent to some other convenient place where they may be safely kept till they can be brought to tryal'.[11]

Later, all idea of staging trials at Newcastle had to be abandoned, and where the secretary of state had spoken in May and June of 'the trials in Carlisle *and Newcastle*', by the beginning of July he spoke of 'the trials *at Carlisle*'.[12] On 3rd July the commander-in-chief in Scotland was directed to prepare 'a particular account of all the prisoners now confined in any of the prisons in Scotland who were taken in arms . . . that the proper care may be taken and directions given for removing them to Carlisle, or to such other places as their trials shall be appointed'.[13] This referred to military prisoners; a letter in somewhat similar terms was sent a week later to the lord justice-clerk with regard to the 'prisoners of the peace'. The secretary of state decided that 'all such persons in any of the prisons in Scotland on account of their having taken up arms or of having personally joined those that were in arms against his Majesty should be sent under a sufficient guard to Carlisle' in order to take their trials.[14] It was at Carlisle, then, that the major trials were to be staged.

This course—of removing the prisoners out of Scotland into England—might prove difficult enough with regard to *prisoners*, but the lord justice-clerk (being a lawyer) inquired how any witnesses that 'are unwilling to go to Carlisle, and are not themselves with any accession to the rebellion can be compelled to go thither'.[15] Even an English lawyer, the attorney-general, who had earlier doubted whether witnesses would come voluntarily out of Scotland to Carlisle to give evidence for the crown,[16] now advised that there was no way to compel them to do so, save by a summons *sub poena*; as the witnesses, however, 'cannot be served with sub-pena till after the indictments', he thought they might perhaps be otherwise persuaded.[17]

Apart, however, from these legal niceties, it soon became apparent on altogether other grounds that even if prisoners, witnesses and juries could be produced in Carlisle, the prisoners were too many to be tried. As Sir Dudley Ryder, the attorney-general, said, the prisoners are 'so numerous that by trying of all will be impossible'. He inquired urgently, therefore, of the secretary of state by what means the number of trials could be reduced to more manageable proportions, or in other words, what prisoners or what categories of prisoner might 'hope for Royal Mercy', and so be excused trial. 'If speedy resolution is not taken concerning this point, they must all be removed to the place of tryal, which will create infinite confusion.'[18] As a matter of fact, there were already in Carlisle more prisoners than could be tried, and if more were brought in there would be confusion indeed.

It is clear from the lord chancellor's minutes of the cabinet council of 9th July that the cabinet based their decision on the precedent of the Fifteen. After calling for the minutes for 13th December 1715, it was decided that prisoners who were of no particular note, who had not distinguished themselves either in the rising or in subsequent custody, might be permitted (provided they would plead guilty and petition for royal mercy) to cast lots among themselves, and only one in ten or twenty (on whom the lot fell) would be reserved for trial.[19] The prisoners, therefore, who were already in Carlisle would be classified, divided and lotted in due course; but those who were due to arrive from other places could be lotted before despatch, and thus some, at least, of the otherwise inevitable congestion in the city would be avoided.

Already by the middle of June the congestion was very bad and it was destined to become very considerably worse. Even for the troops in garrison—to say nothing about the prisoners—service in Carlisle was a 'worse than Egyptian bondage'. They were not in quarters in the Castle, but in licensed houses or private billets in the town; there was a shortage of food and forage, and little or no possibility of getting a bed to lie on. 'Our quarters are very bad [and] our men have no small drink for five or six weeks together', a man in the duke of Montague's regiment[20] wrote, and if a soldier complained to his officer or landlord 'instead of having his grievance redrest, he is punished'.[21] To alleviate some of the congestion, and because there were prisoners in widely separated places in England as well as in Scotland—in Whitehaven, Penrith, Berwick, Morpeth, Newcastle, York, Lancaster, Hull, Chester, Lincoln, Derby, Coventry and so on—it was decided to stage trials not only at Carlisle but also at York and Lincoln.

Philip Carteret Webb, attorney and antiquary (and an early student and collector of record sources) who had already supported the whig government with a couple of anti-jacobite pamphlets,[22] was appointed for the crown to prosecute at Carlisle.[23] As he said (briefly enough) in his 'expenses account', he 'set out from London for the North the 18th Day of July 1746, and returned from thence the 14th Day of October 1746 being in all 89 days'.[24] Incidentally the expense of his journey from London to Carlisle via London and York, from Carlisle to York and return, and from Carlisle back to London, during twenty-nine days for himself, clerks and servants, amounted to no less than £134 4*s*, but this was in addition to the £243 (=£2 14*s* per day for ninety days) on account of his chariot and seven horses and four saddle horses.

Before his arrival in the north, however, Carlisle was already full. Richard Gilpin, justice of the peace and deputy lieutenant for Cumberland and recorder of Carlisle, had written to London at the end of July to the effect that there would be nowhere in the city to accommodate the considerable numbers of rebel prisoners that were expected. He suggested that the sheriff might have directions 'to erect in the gaol yard, deal hutts or boothes', or that the governor should have 'Orders to furnish the Sheriff with tents out of the stores in the Castle to pitch in the gaol yard, which is dry ground and pretty large'.[25] The mayor reported that a survey of the city's licensed houses and their beds showed only two hundred and forty-two beds over above what were required by the inhabitants themselves, a number far too few to billet soldiers, lodge juries and accommodate witnesses.[26] The principal trouble was that the garrison and the French prisoners were all billeted in the town—'especially as both English and French officers have each a bed'. Doubtless, in the circumstances of 1746, little love was lost between the civil and military elements in Carlisle; but it seemed to be the cause of some additional friction between them that in the castle were neither soldiers nor prisoners. What galled the mayor and corporation was not so much that the town was full and daily getting fuller, but the castle was all but empty, and apparently likely so to remain.

When, therefore, Philip Carteret Webb arrived in Carlisle in the first days of August, to make or superintend all the preliminary legal and other arrangements for the trials, there was, as might be expected, no accommodation to be had. He and his equipage of sixteen horses were kept waiting two hours in the street before stabling of any sort, public or private, could be found. Worse still, as he complained, there was 'an absolute refusal of furnishing any of us or our servants with beds'. Carlisle with its population of 359 (plus children under six) had 'but seventy-four public houses in town and in the suburbs', and the garrison and the 348 French prisoners in billets were 'in possession of almost every lodging that was to be had in the town'. In these circumstances it seemed impossible to carry out the business of the ordinary assize, still less the business of the special commission that Webb had come to arrange. For example, Sir Charles Dalston, nominated as foreman of the grand jury at the special trials, sent into town for

a lodging six weeks before the trials were due to commence—
'but could get none'.

Webb arrived at two o'clock on 1st August, and tired of his
chariot and his sixteen horses standing in the street, he applied
himself to Thomas Pattinson. It may have irked the ardent whig
pamphleteer to have to apply to the notorious Mr Pattinson, but
he applied to him not in the latter's capacity of deputy mayor, but
in his capacity as master of the posts. 'I informed him of the
service I came on and showed him my credentials,' says Webb
proudly. The credentials may or may not have produced the right
impression—but what they did not produce was a bed.

'He told me there was no lodging to be had.'

Pattinson probably realized that circumstances had placed him
and certain other Carlisle civic dignitaries in an unenviable pre-
dicament in relation to the trials. Pattinson told the crown solicitor that there was not a bed to be had in the city but, if he chose,
he would let him have lodging in his own house. This Webb
proceeded to inspect. The place happened to be undergoing
whitewashing at the time, and 'consisted (except his own) only
of two upper or garret beds', which the attorney thoroughly dis-
dained, leaving Pattinson

with telling him I expected he would make use of his interest and
authority and see that we were lodged. I saw by his remarks my
business was not grateful to him and that nothing would be done.[27]

The crown solicitor—so he said—'soon began to experience what
it was to be in a rebel town', and blessed his good fortune that if he
must come into Carlisle, he had come into it so early in the day.
As to Pattinson, who had offered him his own roof, this 'ruler of
the Corporation' was only 'a cunning designing fellow, and as
truly disaffected as if he had been born and bred in the Highlands'.

The solicitor then repaired to Brigadier Fleming, the officer
commanding the garrison, who agreed with him 'in opinion as to
Pattinson', offered his utmost services, and went with him again
to the deputy mayor and postmaster. The deputy mayor and
postmaster, however, who had offered two beds in his own house
to the crown solicitor, was apparently in no mood to be hectored
by a brigadier sitting in an all but empty castle, with all his men

and prisoners billeted in the town. The brigadier's efforts with the postmaster were, as might be expected, 'to no effect' and upon this, said Webb, 'the Governor gave me a billett for my servants and horses for one night', but the solicitor himself was still left as yet without a bed. Late in the evening he had the good luck, firstly to find Colonel Stanwix's house, and secondly *not* to find Colonel Stanwix—for he and his family were out of town. He was able to prevail upon the servants to admit him—'just as it was dark'—and contrived to stay (if we are to believe his expense account) for sixty days. Perhaps even Colonel Stanwix's house was not absolutely satisfactory in all respects, however, for there is an item for a payment on account of 'sundry repairs to Mr Stanwix's kitchen'.[28]

The very next day Webb addressed a strong letter to 'the solicitor for carrying on criminal prosecutions' in London.[29] There were many more people yet to arrive in Carlisle: four hundred prisoners were understood to be on their way from Scotland; then there were the witnesses from various parts of England and Scotland, and as soon as the trials commenced there would be the judges and their servants, the writers (attorneys and law-agents) from Scotland and their servants, and, of course, the jurymen from the county—for of the grand jury of thirty, only one came from Carlisle itself, and of the petty jury of 112, only four.[30] In any case something would have to be done urgently to secure that proper lodging be found at least for the crown witnesses, otherwise 'I foresee they will have none, and will be reduced to lye on straw'. A conference was called between the civic and military authorities, and was attended by the mayor, Joseph Backhouse, Richard Gilpin (recorder), Alderman Tate and Brigadier Fleming.

The argument from the civic side was quite simple: the city is overcrowded, the castle is vacant. The governor ought to be ordered to take the troops out of the city into the castle or the castle barrack, where 200 beds could be fitted up to take 400 men. The prisoners were in the main military prisoners and not 'prisoners of the peace'; they should therefore be in military charge, and not a charge upon the peace. As to the French prisoners, if they could not be taken into the castle, they should be taken out of the town, to Brampton or Penrith or somewhere. The argument from the military side was just as simple: 'I did not expect the worthless magistrates or corporation of this place, who I never found had his Majesty's service much at heart, to show much of their loyalty.'[31]

The matter of the French prisoners was an especially sore point. Mostly, they were French only in a technical sense; although they may have assumed French nationality, they were Scots or Irish or of Scottish or Irish extraction, and in any case spoke English. The trial judges and the crown solicitor all complained that these enjoyed complete liberty of the city within the walls, and were living in a very expensive manner. They even 'give balls or plays to the towns people almost every night'. Although this made 'the whole run of the Town incline to favour the rebels', certainly nothing was done to confine them.[32] In any case, 'the influence they have by means of the expense they live at prevents many persons giving their testimony'. 'It is scarce possible to describe to your Grace', wrote Webb to the secretary of state, 'how much this service suffers' in consequence.[33]

Jacobite pamphlets were openly bandied about the town and, indeed, placed in the hands of jurymen and witnesses, presumably in an attempt to suborn them. In particular, there were pamphlets which had been written during the reaction after the suppression of the Fifteen and the affair of 1722, now re-issued in London and appearing in Carlisle. There was, for example, a 20-page pamphlet, reprinted in 1746, doing the rounds in Carlisle, entitled *An Argument to prove the Affection of the People of England to be the best Security of the Government*. One passage,[34] characteristic of many, was very apposite in Carlisle in the later summer of 1746. 'I believe I speak the sense of every Dispassionate Man of the Kingdom, that the Rebels shall and ought to be pardoned.' One who was concerned in the circulation of this pamphlet in Carlisle, 'George McFarlen, drover', was taken up and examined by one of the Carlisle justices, Montague Farrer, better known perhaps as captain of the Carlisle (Cumberland and Eskdale wards) company of militia who had done garrison in the castle last November before it was surrendered to the jacobites. McFarlen the drover was taken into custody—but Farrer's examination of him did not disclose the source of supply.[35] Occurrences of this character made the continued presence of the French officers so objectionable in

the city. Further batches of prisoners and witnesses arrived from
Scotland and the situation in Carlisle grew steadily worse.

In the meantime the business went on of identifying the
prisoners, and sorting out the evidence and witnesses against
them. With regard to identification, it had earlier been provided
that two captains, two lieutenants, two ensigns, ten sergeants, ten
corporals and forty private men of Brigadier Bligh's regiment[36]
should 'go into the several prisons and places where the non-
commissioned officers and soldiers belonging to the rebells were,
in order with the utmost caution, to remark every man so as to
be able to know him again'.[37]

It was thought desirable to have some at least of these to
'attend the service of the special commission, and to be in
Carlisle by the 12th September when the trials will begin'. Not
only the prisoners but the witnesses also had to be identified, and
Richard Jackson, one of the bailiffs of Carlisle, was paid out of
crown funds £25 'for his and his clerk's trouble for forty days in
attending four hundred and thirty-five of the witnesses for the
crown at Carlisle, calling them over twice a day [etc]'.[38] Various
other expenses, civil guards for the prisoners, coal and candle and
so forth, he recovered from the county.[39] There were also the
welfare services to be paid for, the 'apothecary for medicines,
given to several of the Witnesses who were sick' (£1 18s 2d),
'Beer sundry times for several of the witnesses' (£4 16s 6d), payments to doctors (10 guineas and 11½ guineas),[40] and so on. Then
there were the 'office' expenses, paper, parchment, postages, post-
horses, tollgates—Webb said he found 'these northern posts
come and go out very irregularly'.[41]

With regard to the lotting procedure at Carlisle, a batch of
forty-one prisoners, sorted and lotted on 20th July, may be taken
as typical. Of these, ten had been originally confined in Carlisle
on the charge of high treason and levying war, but three were
ordered not to be proceeded against owing to the insufficiency of
evidence. A further twenty were brought in from Whitehaven,
of whom two could be charged only with misdemeanours. There
were sixteen further prisoners brought in from Newcastle and
Morpeth, making forty-one in this batch. Of these, it was decided to set five apart as witnesses and nineteen were persons of
sufficient note or who had distinguished themselves by a degree

of guilt in the rising itself or 'by indecent behaviour' in custody since, to warrant their trial. This left seventeen, three from Carlisle, nine from Whitehaven, two from Newcastle, and three from Morpeth, to cast lots for trial.[42] The fatal lot fell upon William Elliott from Morpeth: the certificate as to this lotting is noted: 'present at drawing of lotts: Governor Fleming and Town Mayor'.[43]

This was not the end of the business, however, for the condition of 'lotting' was that the concession was in any case reserved to those who pleaded guilty and petitioned for mercy. They would then be transported for life to the plantations, usually under indentures not far distinguished from slavery. In the present case, however, the precise procedure adopted was not the efficient one, namely of requiring the prisoners to plead and petition before drawing the lots. Hence seven of the sixteen men after they had drawn the blank lot and thus escaped trial, protested their innocence, and refused to plead guilty and petition for mercy solely in order to qualify for transportation. The crown solicitor himself 'questioned whether if they were indicted they could be convicted', for 'the evidence against them is so slight'. In the circumstances, therefore, the prisoners naturally wished 'forthwith to be tried'.[44] So far as the crown solicitor himself was concerned, he managed things otherwise. He says he was 'twenty times in Carlisle gaol'. The prisoners drawing lots that he was concerned with were all fully apprized of what they were doing. The order-in-council was read over to them; they had to own themselves guilty of high treason in levying war against his Majesty; they had to sign a petition submitting themselves to transportation—and then he permitted the lotting to proceed.[45]

The general assembling of the prisoners and the witnesses against them was no simple matter; there were many complications, especially with witnesses from Scotland, where probably language difficulties contributed some confusion. For example, certain witnesses (not otherwise charged) found themselves among the prisoners on the strength of statements they had made as witnesses. When indicted they pleaded they had surrendered themselves and their arms voluntarily in Scotland under the terms of the royal proclamation and could not therefore be charged. They had to be acquitted on these grounds.

Not only did all this business in Carlisle cause a shortage of accommodation, food, forage and so forth, but also a shortage of specie. The crown solicitor in Carlisle, like Charles Edward before him,[46] had recourse to the office of the collector of the land tax and other public moneys. To put himself in funds, Philip Carteret Webb would draw a 14-day bill on his principals in London to the order of the receiver of the land tax, Peter How,[47] who being a Whitehaven tobacco merchant had other access to money and credit. Incidentally, How was one of those who served on the grand jury. Samuel Billingsley acted as expenditor for the receipt and payment of the various moneys and keeping the necessary accounts, for which service he received £44 10s, to cover York as well as Carlisle.[48] Apart from these there were also such petty-cash items as Dr Tenton and Dr Dinkel, both of Lancaster, 'expended at Carlisle twenty-three days', $11\frac{1}{2}$ guineas each, and 'pd Timothy Granham, beer sundry times for seven witnesses', £4 16s 6d.

In due course, the four judges named in the special commission arrived in Carlisle, the lord chief baron Sir Thomas Parker of the Court of Exchequer and Sir Thomas Burnett of the Common Pleas, both for the eastern part of the northern circuit, and Sir Thomas Dennison of the King's Bench and Charles Clarke of the Court of Exchequer, both for the western part.[49] The lord chief baron arrived in his coach and six with one spare horse and five saddle horses for his servants. His brother barons each came in his coach and six, and three or four saddle horses each for their servants. Chief baron Parker and Sir Thomas Burnett were accommodated at the house of Charles Highmore—another lawyer—Earl's Inn, once the town residence of the earls of Egremont, and more recently the lodging of both the duke of Cumberland and Charles Edward. According to the latter's household book, he paid twenty guineas for four nights and kept the family in the meantime.[50] The judges paid sixty guineas for nearly four weeks, and kept their own table.

Sir Thomas Dennison and baron Clarke lodged at John Holmes' house at a more modest cost of forty guineas, the sums in both cases covering 'small beer and firing'. The cost of tea, coffee and chocolate consumed by the judges, their clerks and servants at Carlisle and York came only to £38 14s 6d, but the cost of their wine amounted to £253 15s 7d. Both of these sums are in addition to the money paid to 'two cooks for the expenses of their Lordships' table during forty-five days, the time of the execution of the Commission at York and Carlisle, and for the time and expenes as cook to the Judges'. The sum was £415.[51]

At the end of the first week in August—the commission was due to open the following Tuesday—the situation was near chaos. It had been planned to open the commission on the afternoon of Tuesday 12th August. On the Wednesday the bishop of Carlisle was to preach his sermon, and the lord chief baron would give his charge to the grand jury. On Wednesday, Thursday and Friday they would hear the arraignments, find the bills and give copies of the indictments to those indicted, adjourn the court on Friday 15th August until Tuesday 9th September, and set out for York on the Saturday where they were opening on the following Wednesday, and at Lincoln on the Wednesday week.[52] Events were to show that such a programme was impossible. About 140 of the prisoners from Scotland did not come into Carlisle until 13th August and a further 100 witnesses came in on the 13th and 14th August. The crown solicitor and the trial judges were much distressed by the prisoners not coming in a timely manner. As the solicitor said on 14th August—two days after the commission opened—'I am an utter stranger to the evidence against these prisoners from Scotland, which consists of many large volumes in folio, which I must begin to read.'[53]

Certainly the prisoners and the witnesses had been sent 'in an irregular manner to Carlisle'. When the slight delay occurred in consequence of the question about the Scottish pleadings, no other bill could be got ready to be presented, for 'if the prisoners were come' the witnesses were not arrived, and if the witnesses had arrived 'the prisoners were not',[54] a misfortune that the lord justice-clerk in Scotland 'did not feel disposed to blame himself for'.[55] Little wonder the Cumberland grand jury became very uneasy.

A further sixty-one prisoners arrived on 17th August,[56] and congestion got worse. The governor consulted with the sheriff and magistrates as to where to put them all, but 'all the assistance I could get from them', he complained in his letter to the secretary of state of 14th August, 'was an old malt-house, . . . and that no place of security'.[57] A quantity of straw—360 'waps', followed by another 200 'waps', with an additional forty-six 'to the sick in the kiln'—was supplied by the magistrates at local cost.[58] The major part of the cost, however, could not be borne by the county.

The crown solicitor warned the secretary of state that 'the expence of maintaining [witnesses and prisoners] is excessive', apart from the expense of getting them to Carlisle. The account relating to subsistence alone is no mean item. For example: 'Paid at several times to Mr Richard Jackson at Carlisle, being what he paid to the four hundred and thirty-five persons who attended at Carlisle as witnesses for the Crown against the Rebels, many of whom attended there forty days and upwards . . . £1,311 13s'.[59]

The item includes not only subsistence as such but also horse-hire, loss of time and 'expenses home', but does not include the cost of bringing to Carlisle the witnesses from Scotland other than that 435; this cost additionally £1,469 15s 10d.[60]

The crown solicitor, in his report from Carlisle to London of 14th August, undertook to reduce the number of these witnesses as soon as he was able, but in the meantime 200 more un-lotted prisoners were expected from Scotland to be in Carlisle on Sunday or Monday 16th or 17th August; 'till they come in, it will not be possible . . . to proceed to the lotts or to know which of the Scotch witnesses may be spared or not'.[61] In consequence of all this, and of the additional fact that 'several Scotch advocates and writers' were arriving for the defence, the delay of the judges and their retinues in Carlisle 'both in finding the bills and going thro' the tryals will be much longer than was expected'.[62] At first the trial judges suggested that they should 'enlarge the time for finding bills here [in Carlisle] to the 20th', but the Cumberland grand jury was already beginning 'to be excessive uneasy at the few bills preferred'. The trial judges were fearful lest they should upset the grand jury at York also, which they would certainly do if they did not open the commission on the date announced, there being now 'not time to give [them] notice to prevent them coming to York . . . from the remote parts of so large a county'.[63]

It was known that the grand jury would be 'out of humour to be disobliged'; therefore, said the lawyers, 'our proceedings could not be delayed at Carlisle'. On this account it was suggested that they should divide forces, two only of the judges hearing the preliminary proceedings at Carlisle, the other two proceeding to York. Ultimately it was decided to cancel all proceedings at Lincoln,[64] since clearly it would be 'impossible for the commission to go to Lincoln as was intended', and the Lincoln prisoners commenced to be transferred to Carlisle for trial.

On Friday 15th August, twenty-two true bills were found at Carlisle, and on Saturday five more, and on the following Monday and Tuesday a further eighteen and fifteen.[65] Next day the crown solicitor reported to London that the grand jury stood adjourned, 'many of the prisoners arrived too late for the sitting of the Judges'.[66] 'As many witnesses as could be spared' were sent away, and the crown solicitor set out for York in the morning, whither the lord chief baron and justice Burnett would follow.[67] During Webb's absence in York his position as solicitor for the crown was filled by Jerome Adderton, a Carlisle attorney. He was 'employed by Mr Webb in examining the Carlisle witnesses and attending on these witnesses during all the times of the tryal at Carlisle and was afterwards employed to make out lists of the names places and residences and occupations of the persons who had drawn lotts at Carlisle'—for which he received the sum of £35.[68]

In the meantime, however, Carlisle had been 'so crowded that many of the witnesses who attended on behalf of the Crown had not a bed to lye on. The service will suffer when we come to proceed to the tryals. Unless this can be remedied the witnesses will many of them, as they declare, not attend unless they can be lodged.'[69] The situation was relieved somewhat by a further lotting of Carlisle prisoners on Sunday 17th August and more on Tuesday, to the total of 180; but it could be eased more if the French prisoners 'were removed to Brampton, Penrith or any other neighbouring town'.[70] The point still rankled: the friction between the civil and military sides had in no way abated.

Joseph Backhouse, the mayor, told the secretary of state after the August adjournment and before the September trials, that 'this is but a small place for to entertain the number of them that are in it, so that the soldiers wanting that convenience they ought to have makes an uneasiness at present'. The corporation, however —in general terms—had 'always acted and shown their loyalty upon all occasions for his Majesty's Service', and—to be more specific—had 'furnished the Commandant for the Castle with quantities of meal and tatoes, and what else he thought necessary to order'. The magistrates had gone through the city with the brigadier 'and let him see all the conveniences of this Town'.[71] About the best they could do was to make over 'an old malt house, which might contain about a hundred and twenty prisoners or witnesses'.

All this overcrowding in Carlisle, however, caused deep concern on another account. The judges who had left Carlisle wrote to the secretary of state from York on 23rd August that the overcrowding at Carlisle was not only dangerous to the health of the prisoners: it was also a menace to the health of the city.

> The gaol is so crowded with the prisoners that have cast Lotts that there is danger of contagious disease breaking out among them if they are not immediately removed to Whitehaven or some other more convenient place.[72]

An epidemic of fever in the town might be truly tragic. Furthermore—this may have been even more important to the gentlemen of the long robe—it 'will make it highly inconvenient for the councel and sollicitors to resort to the prisoners, as by law they ought, to do under proper restriction'.[73] In order to make some additional space, the French prisoners should be removed out of the city, where in any case it was legally improper for them to be, where they 'probably inter-mix with jurymen and witnesses and corrupt their minds'.[74]

On 23rd August the governor reported from Carlisle that at last the French prisoners had been removed. That morning the last of them (save only the marquis D'Eguilles, France's ambassador to Charles Edward, and two French officers, Captain Cusack and Captain Stack) had set out under an escort from Howard's regiment for Penrith, where they were to remain until further orders.[75] As regards witnesses, by the time the trials had started 'many hundred came into this place from Scotland'. In this they ran some risk, for as the crown solicitor said, he himself 'detected two of them to be themselves rebels, and they are [now] committed for high treason in levying War'.[76]

It is natural if in all this confusion locally the crown solicitor was apprehensive that some prisoner or prisoners might somehow or other slip through the official mesh. However, after the trials, he was bold enough to report to the secretary of state that 'we have had the good fortune that not one hath escaped thro' any slip or mistake in the proceedings'.[77] In fact, however, their good fortune was not quite so good as that. For example, of two of the Manchester men who surrendered at Carlisle, Seton and Arnot say nothing at all about Ralph Carter, and of William Cooper merely that he was 'taken at capture of Carlisle. No further reference to him.'[78] From other sources it is known that both of them were among those who refused to sign the petition for mercy. They were removed to Lancaster castle, and could not be indicted at the assizes in the following year for want of evidence, and eventually they were discharged by the court without entering into recognizances, notwithstanding that the crown opposed that course.[79]

There was a gruesome reminder of the trials, when, during the adjournment, the sheriff of the county received a warrant from the secretary of state dated 22nd August 'for putting up the heads . . . on one of the gates of the city' of Thomas Chadwick[80] and John Berwick,[81] two of the Carlisle garrison, tried and condemned at the trials in London.[82] Christopher Pattinson the sheriff replied that he was unable to do so, for although he had received the warrant safely, he had not received the heads. It was a month later—20th September—that he was able to report that he had 'yesterday' received the heads, which he had 'caused to be set up on the English Gate of this city'.[83]

In the meantime the trial judges arrived back in Carlisle from York on Monday 8th September. 'Our Grand Battle will be at Carlisle, which is already swarming with Jacobite Scots.'[84] The court assembled at the town hall on Wednesday 10th September to proceed with the arraignment of those who stood indicted. The grand jury found true bills against a further batch of prisoners —the late arrivals—and were then discharged. At the opening of the proceedings a number of prisoners refused to plead in English fashion. Furthermore, the same 'scruple of conscience . . . seized our Scotch witnesses'. It was certainly 'a concocted thing', said the crown solicitor. 'It was certainly a scandalous combination,' commented the lord chancellor.[85] After legal argument, however, pleas in the Scottish form had to be admitted.

On Friday 12th September nine prisoners were either tried or pleaded guilty, and the trial then continued each weekday until 26th September, in the morning of which day ten prisoners were disposed of. By noon that day all the trials had been finished, and the judges and their retinue set out for York[86] next morning where the trials were due to open the following Thursday.[87]

The daily totals of prisoners who were tried or who pleaded guilty ran as follows: Friday 12th September, 9; Saturday 13th, 7; Monday 15th, 7; Tuesday 16th, 19; Wednesday 17th, 13; Thursday 18th, 11; Friday 19th, 12; Saturday 20th, 15; Monday 22nd, 1; Tuesday 23rd, 6; Wednesday 24th, 3; Thursday 25th, 12; Friday 26th, 10; Total 125.[88]

Even with the trials over, there was plenty of excitement in Carlisle. Scarcely were the trials closed than some of the most notorious of the prisoners staged an escape effort. The notorious Thomas Cappock and two other prisoners 'endeavour'd to corrupt the centree and had filed off their Irons'. Upon this news, said the crown solicitor, 'I apply'd to the Brigadier Fleming and Lieut.-Colonel Howard, and the guard is just now doubled.[89] The trouble was that eighty-nine of the ninety-one condemned men were confined 'in one long room in the Castle', and the gaol was filled with prisoners who had drawn blank lots. The gaoler in whose custody the prisoners were was 'a very bad man of whom anything ill may be expected'. Webb reported to the secretary of state that he had 'frequently applied to the High Sheriff to remove him, but without effect'.[90]

Probably as a result of this the secretary of state wrote to Christopher Pattinson, the sheriff, on 3rd October informing him that it had been reported that the keeper of Carlisle gaol was 'suspected of being very negligent of his office'. To this the sheriff replied that he had now 'thought it his duty to discharge him, and appoint a new gaoler'. The sheriff and his under-sheriff 'alternately have made Carlisle our residence ever since the Assize, by the Judge's recommendations', and would continue to do so until after the executions.[91]

According to the crown solicitor's final report to the secretary of state, eleven of the prisoners had pleaded guilty, forty-nine were tried and convicted, and thirty-one pleaded not guilty but retracted and pleaded guilty. Thus a total of ninety-one were sentenced. Of those acquitted (by consent of the crown counsel) eight were on account of being entitled to the benefit of the proclamation about surrender, and the remainder 'on account of youth, old age or other favourable circumstance'.[92]

The ninety-one condemned men were now divided by the trial judges into three categories, namely 'those who appeared to be most worthy of Royal clemency', those who merely 'partook of the general guilt', and 'those who appeared upon their trials to be most guilty'. In respect of those in the first category to the number of eleven, no date of execution was fixed. In respect of the second category, to the number of fifty, later dates of execution were fixed in order to provide fuller opportunity to examine into the circumstances of their several cases. In respect of the third category, to the number of thirty, executions were fixed in various towns of Cumberland, namely Carlisle, Penrith and Brampton, on forthcoming market days, in Carlisle on Saturday 18th October, in Brampton the following Tuesday 21st October, and because the market day at Penrith was on a Tuesday also, the executions were fixed there for the following Tuesday 28th October.

Finally, the high and grand juries of the county of Cumberland were informed 'of his Majesty's satisfaction with their good conduct, and of the King's commands . . . to return his Majesty's thanks for the same'.[93] The crown solicitor informed the secretary of state of 'the zeal and readiness of the people of this town [of Carlisle] in comeing in to give testimony',[94] and the trial judges were told that 'in all your proceedings nothing could be more proper'.[95]

The king himself felt—as he put on a minute[96] under the report of the trial of the last of the rebel lords—'I am glad this tedious affair is over.'

Notes

[1] The figures from various sources are not easy to reconcile.
[2] As to which, see below, pp. 258–9 and 264–5.
[3] 1 Geo. I, stat. 2 (1716), cap. 33.
[4] 19 Geo. II, cap. 9.

5 19 Geo. II, cap. 1.

6 19 Geo. II, cap. 19; and 20 Geo. II, cap. 1.

7 SP Scot. 31/71 and SP Dom. 83/270 (or 274). (This reference seems to be misquoted at *S & A*, vol. i, p. 94.) For letters from the secretary of state to the sheriffs of Cumberland and Northumberland, see SP Dom. 86/103 (or 262).

8 SP Dom. 86/57 (or 145–8), and 61 (or 95).

9 *Ibid*. 86/23.

10 *Ibid*. 85/93.

11 *Ibid*. 12.

12 *Ibid*. 86/289–90.

13 *Ibid*. 85/3.

14 *Ibid*. 86/290.

15 *Ibid*. 229.

16 *Ibid*. 85/253.

17 *Ibid*. 86/291.

18 *Ibid*. 85/14.

19 *Ibid*. 108.

20 Raised 1745 (SP Dom. (Entry Books, Dom.) 44/186, p. 216) and disbanded 1746 (WO 4 (out-Letters—Sec.-at-War) 42, pp. 126–7 and 135–6).

21 SP Dom. 84/127.

22 *Remarks on the Pretender's Declaration* and *Commission*, and *Remarks on the Pretender's Eldest Son's Second Declaration* (1745).

23 Stowe MSS, 255, p. 5.

24 Pelham–Holles MSS.

25 SP Dom. 85/242.

26 Add. MSS 30170, f. 47, and SP Dom. 85/427.

27 SP Dom. 86/23.

28 Pelham–Holles MSS.

29 SP Dom. 86/23.

30 Stowe MSS, 255, pp. 10 and 6–7.

31 SP Dom. 86/36.

32 Hardwick MSS, f. 317, and SP Dom. 86/23.

33 SP Dom. 86/235.

34 A copy of this pamphlet is filed among the state papers, marked at the various offending passages.

35 SP Dom. 87/143.

36 Brigadier Bligh's regiment, 1740–6; Lord George Sackville's, 1746–9; later the 20th Foot, later the Lancashire Fusiliers.

37 SP Dom. 86/73.

38 Pelham–Holles MSS.

39 Cumb. QSMB, Easter 1746, p. 328 (Jarvis, *Jac. Risings*, 363).

40 Pelham–Holles MSS.

41 SP Dom. 86/31.

42 *Ibid*. 92 and 177.

43 *Ibid*. 177.

[44] *Ibid.* 223.

[45] *Ibid.* 90/18.

[46] *Ibid.* 80/315.

[47] Whose bankruptcy in 1763 occasioned the noted Lowther–Portland conflict (*Lonsdale MSS*, 126).

[48] Pelham–Holles MSS.

[49] Stowe MSS, 255, p. 2.

[50] R. Forbes, *Jacobite Memoirs*, 149–50.

[51] Pelham–Holles MSS.

[52] Stowe MSS, 255, pp. 3–4.

[53] Hardwick MSS, f. 300.

[54] *Ibid.* f. 332.

[55] *Ibid.* f. 325.

[56] *Ibid.* f. 311.

[57] SP Dom. 36/86.

[58] Cumb. QSR, Epiphany 1746–7, petitions 22 (Jarvis, *Jac. Risings*, 371–2).

[59] Pelham–Holles MSS.

[60] *Ibid.*

[61] SP Dom. 86/235.

[62] *Ibid.* 237.

[63] Hardwick MSS, f. 332–3.

[64] The commission was superseded by writ of *supersedeas* under the great seal (Stowe MSS, 255, p. 5).

[65] SP Dom. 86/239 (or 273).

[66] Hardwick MSS, f. 325.

[67] Baron Dennison went off to Scarborough and Clark to Godmanchester (Hardwick MSS, f. 332).

[68] Pelham–Holles MSS.

[69] SP Dom. 86/287.

[70] *Ibid.* 290.

[71] *Ibid.* 316.

[72] *Ibid.* 287.

[73] Hardwick MSS, f. 319, and SP Dom. 86/329.

[74] SP Dom. 86/329.

[75] *Ibid.* 324.

[76] *Ibid.* 87/145.

[77] *Ibid.* 434.

[78] *S & A*, 568.

[79] SP Dom. 97/146.

[80] *S & A*, 463.

[81] *S & A*, 155.

[82] SP Dom. 87/156.

[83] *Ibid.* 288.

[84] Hardwick MSS, f. 323.

[85] *Ibid.* f. 325.

[86] Newcastle MSS: Add. MSS 32708, f. 139.

[87] Stowe MSS, 255, pp. 20–38.
[88] SP Dom. 87/400.
[89] *Ibid.* 434.
[90] *Ibid.* 88/1.
[91] *Ibid.* 72, and Hardwick MSS, f. 346.
[92] SP Dom. 87/434.
[93] *Ibid.* 88/16.
[94] *Ibid.* 87/217.
[95] *Ibid.* 88/47.
[96] Add. MSS 32708, f. 2.

23 *Trial Proceedings*

The principal contemporary printed sources for the trial proceedings in 1746 are the various editions of the trials of the jacobite lords, namely, Lovat, Kilmarnock, Cromartie and Balmarino, and certain of the commoners, such as Francis Towneley, jacobite governor of Carlisle, Archibald Stewart. lord provost of Edinburgh, Thomas Cappock, usually referred to as 'bishop' or 'mock bishop' of Carlisle, and Thomas Syddall, together with the 'Lives, Behaviour and Dying Speeches', often completely unreliable and sometimes demonstrably false. There were also the various more or less contemporary omnibus volumes, for example, Wilkinson's *Complete History of the Trials*—not complete, of course—and in addition a number of contemporary and later secondary accounts. *The Report of Some Proceedings of the . . . Trial of the Rebels* by Sir Michael Foster, relating primarily to the proceedings at Southwark, contains some 'added discourses' dealing with the crown law relating to treason (and some other capital offences) which is a valuable and highly authoritative exposition.[1] Howell's *State Trials*[2] contains only those relating to the jacobite lords, Charles Ratcliffe (on a conviction and attainder in respect of 1715), Archibald Stewart and eleven others. The *State Trials* explains that it includes no trials of commoners in respect of 1715, but it would however furnish in respect of 1745 a short account of a few of the trials of 'the principal commoners concerned . . . to show they were persons of no consequence or estate . . . being either men of small fortunes or had run out of what they had, or tradesmen'—no estate, small fortune and trade being, presumably, increasing degrees of ignominy. However the series, notwithstanding the deference and respect usually

---

The notes and references are on pages 300–302

paid to it, has no specific official warrant and the word 'state' in the title in fact confers no authority whatsoever. D. Murray Rose transcribed some trial pleadings for Allardyce's volumes for the New Spalding Club in 1896.[3] The principal printed authority for the prisoners, as distinct from the trials, is Seton and Arnot's volumes for the Scottish History Society.[4] In general the literature is well known.

The principal manuscript sources are the *baga de secretis*[5] and the various papers scattered throughout the state papers at the time,[6] both in the Public Record Office; the correspondence and other papers of the lord chancellor, among the Hardwick papers in the British Museum;[7] the notes of Sir John Strange, counsel for the crown, also in the British Museum;[8] an account 'of the legal proceedings against the prisoners at York and Carlisle, August and September 1746', including witnesses' depositions, etc., among the collection of Thomas Astle, a late-eighteenth century antiquary and palaeographer;[9] and certain other miscellaneous collections of papers.[10] Certain of the letters of Sir Thomas Parker, later Lord Macclesfield, chief justice of the king's bench during 1715, and lord chancellor during the rising of 1719 and the affair of 1722, are among the Stowe manuscripts.[11] There is also a very informative notebook kept by Charles Clarke, one of the judges of the special commission, now in Tullie House, Carlisle.[12] Most of these various sources have, of course, been fairly well worked, but—exceptionally—the Clarke notebook has been most neglected and certainly deserves to be better known. The greater part of this Paper, therefore, is based upon it.

The notebook measures about $8\frac{1}{2}$ in by 5 in, and its pages are gathered up into five sections (or 'gatherings'), one small, three large and one small. Because the blank pages, where they occur, are found at the end of one or other of these gatherings, I assume (and the assumption is confirmed by other evidence) that it was the judge's practice to take his notes during the various trials on the assize circuits, in a particular gathering of plain leaves, and thus be able later to bind up (or bundle together) the various batches of gatherings relating to a particular circuit or series of trials. The first of the five gatherings, as they are bound up in the book, relates to the northern circuit assize trials at Lancaster; the second is in respect of the normal circuit trials at Carlisle; the third and fourth are of the special—that is to say, the jacobite—trials at St Margaret's Hill (Southwark), York and Carlisle; and the fifth is in respect of St Margaret's Hill, consisting entirely of legal arguments in arrest of judgement (regarding discharge of jury). The five gatherings were (apparently later) bound together into a single volume in quarter leather and paper board.

The commission of oyer and terminer and gaol delivery which opened at Carlisle on 12th August and closed on 27th September 1746 consisted of the lord chief baron (Sir Thomas Parker), Sir Thomas Burnett, Sir Thomas Dennison and baron Charles Clarke. Apart therefore from the jacobite trials proper, the portions of the volume dealing with the northern circuit trials at Lancaster and the ordinary circuit business at Carlisle are routine, but nevertheless quite interesting. In the Carlisle section, a number of noted Cumberland families and estates, both old and new, are mentioned, e.g. the Hudlestons, Nicolsons, Pattersons, Nevinsons, Penningtons, Lutwidges and Speddings. One cannot help noticing how much of this legal business was remitted by the judge of assize to Richard Gilpin, the noted recorder of Carlisle, who as we know from the lieutenancy papers[13] and the quarter sessions rolls,[14] was so active in Carlisle during the course of the rising in his dual capacity of deputy lieutenant and justice of the peace. Indeed, he alone of the civil and civic arm added his signature to those of the commanders of the horse and foot of the militia of Cumberland and Westmorland, to the important letter to the lord lieutenant in the critical days in October and November before Carlisle was besieged, urgently requesting instructions from the lord lieutenant, in the legal and constitutional doubt as to whether or not—and if so, how—at that critical juncture the militia could be legally held embodied.[15]

It is very interesting to notice how local (and apparently relatively insignificant) information in the Clarke notebook can be made to blend in with information from either local or central sources to tell a more complete story. For example, in the Cumberland quarter sessions rolls one may find an imperfect justice's warrant, produced by the keeper of the Carlisle gaol, committing a certain man on the somewhat vague charge of 'being concerned in the Rebellion'.[16] Although part of the warrant is torn off, it clearly refers to a 'Lancelot ——', the surname being in doubt.

Later, a Lancelot Hall, who had been taken up 'for further Examination &c for being concerned in the Rebellion' by a 'Commitment dated the first of February last', submits a petition to the effect that he 'has laid in Prison since the date of Commitment to this time to the great prej[udice] of his Health and Circumstances', and 'has never yet been able to obtain a hearing'.[17]

Lancelot Hall remains, in the quarter sessions rolls, a completely shadowy character, and one wonders what the story behind it all might be. Had someone locally a motive for making an accusation against Hall, which could not be brought home? Baron Clarke's notebook may supply the answer. There is a reference there to a trover action (i.e. a process to recover possession of property found by another and converted to his own use) which tells a good story about Lancelot Hall. It seems fairly clear that after the action at Clifton one of the English dragoons stole a gelding belonging to Hall, and sold it for a guinea to a Penrith ostler by the name of Henry Turner. Turner took the horse to be shod and 'having him to a Smith, he [the smith] said "'twas Lanty Hall's" '. Turner the ostler took the horse to the inn in Penrith where he worked, but Lancelot Hall, the real owner, recognized his horse, whereupon John Watson, the Penrith innkeeper, said they had 'bought the Horse of a Soldier for a Guinea—and if Hall would pay the Guinea he might have the Horse'. Hall said, 'No,' he would have him and pay nothing. Poor Lancelot Hall who sued the innkeeper—and not the ostler— was non-suited by baron Clarke, apparently because he had not shown that the innkeeper ever had the horse 'but as in his Stable in a Common Inn'.

Incidentally, it is interesting to note that in the (unpublished) excise records relating to the duties collected in Cumberland by the jacobites,[18] the innkeepers' excise duty collected in Penrith amounted to £63 17s 3d of which John Watson the innkeeper in this case accounted for the modest sum of 1s 8½d. The entry in the Clarke notebook then is interesting, not only as illustrating the local repercussions of armies living on the country (the regulars, be it noted—not the invaders), but also as sketching in the more shadowy character of the Lancelot Hall of the quarter sessions rolls.

Or again, it would be interesting to know whether the Isaac

Brown who gave evidence against Thomas Lawson[19] ('a poor wretched mortal'), was the Isaac Brown of Fenton quarter, Hayton, who was a sergeant in the company (Eskdale and Cumberland wards) of the local militia. He describes himself as 'Prisoner in their Hands, and had Centinels set over him, and amongst others the Prisoner was set over him several times'. The accused, however, 'was himself afterwards commited to a Guard for some Misdemeanor as he told me, but s[aid] twas a false charge'. We know that Isaac Brown was local, for he testified against another prisoner, John Henderson of Edinburgh,[20] that he saw him 'With his Cockade and broad sword—he took a Horse and Cart of Hay from me at Scotch Gate'. We know from the quarter sessions rolls that sergeant Isaac Brown did not draw certain of his militia pay, and that he had to petition the sessions to get it from the county.[21] One wonders therefore whether he missed the pay parade by being in the enemy's hands at the time.

Once it was decided, however, to hold the trials by special commission at Carlisle, however fortuitously, it was clear that (if only to reduce the cost of producing witnesses) the various indictments would be drawn in respect of some act of treason alleged in Carlisle itself, and local witnesses depended upon to secure conviction. In the generality of cases, therefore, the Crown seems to have relied upon the somewhat haphazard method of removing various prisoners from a number of Scottish prisons to Carlisle and then parading Carlisle inhabitants, in batches of fifteen a time, before the prisoners, to see which could be identified to particular acts of overt treason locally, e.g. marching with the jacobites, wearing the plaid or cockade, appearing under arms, patrolling the walls, occupying the castle, guarding the gates, and so on.

This sort of evidence, however, could not always be produced, as we find for example in the case of John (*alias* James) MacLaring[22] who was indicted not for high treason merely, but more specifically, 'for H[igh] Treason *at Carlisle*'. His case is endorsed 'No evidence in Cumberland—not Guilty'. Incidentally, MacLaring's case is one of those in which the Clarke notebook produces the name of a prisoner who is not known[23] to Seton and Arnot's usually very reliable standard work. Because, however, many of the prisoners had been quartered in private billets, or had been in one of the licensed houses in Carlisle, and as there had naturally been 'incidents' of one sort and another during the occupation, it does not seem to have been so very difficult to find some sort of evidence of identification. All that was wanted from a witness was an obliging 'he wore a sash and cockade', 'he bore arms on the walls', or 'he was with the rebels as one of them'; and here was a heaven-sent opportunity of paying off any old score. The Isaac Brown mentioned above, who had had his cart of hay taken away from him at the Scotch Gate; the Carlisle gaoler who had been sent packing by his erstwhile prisoner; the recorder of Carlisle, whose goods had been stopped at the gate on an unofficial evacuation of the town; Dr Waugh's curate who had had to entertain a very unwelcome guest; the chancellor's maidservant who had had to provide 'a Gown and Cassock', 'A Band and Common Prayer Book'; the clerk of St Mary's, who had been ordered 'to ring the Bells as usual' and to provide choirmen and choirboys as well; these and many others in and about Carlisle probably felt that after all they had managed to get their laugh in last.

Had the trials been staged at Lancaster, Manchester or Derby, doubtless the self-same prisoners would have been charged with very similar offences provable by local (i.e. Lancaster, Manchester or Derby) witnesses. For example, Richard Morrison, a barber and wigmaker of Edinburgh, who had acted throughout as *valet de chambre* to Charles Edward, escaped from Culloden but was taken up four weeks later at Leven in Fife. The offence alleged against him was high treason in Edinburgh, but he was transferred from the Canongate to Carlisle in August of 1746, and among the witnesses produced against him was Charles Highmore the attorney-at-law of Carlisle, at whose house in English Street[24] Charles Edward—and hence Richard Morrison—had lodged. In the results, therefore, the trials provide a number of interesting sidelights upon the occupation of Carlisle, garrisoning the place, life under the occupation, holding the castle, town walls and gates, and of course life at the inns and taverns. Of these last-named, we read of the 'Turk's Head', the 'Bush', the 'Crown & Mitre', the 'Duke's Head' and so on. Robert Threlkeld, servant to William Eddison at the 'Crown and Mitre', swore against John Cappock, a tailor of Manchester, younger brother of 'parson' Cappock, that he 'was quartered at his

master's, the Crown and Mitre in Carlisle among the other Rebels
—Tartan sash and don't remember cockade'. Anne Ecles testified
that she saw the other Cappock—'parson' Cappock[25]—'in a
Cockade and Sash Plad tied with a White Ribband—in Compa[ny]
at the Turk's Head with the Rebels and was one of them'. The
'Bush' was kept by Thomas Pattinson, the deputy mayor, very much
acting as mayor, and the 'Crown and Mitre' by that other character of doubtful conduct, William Addison. Adam Elliott swore
against Thomas Warrington, a 'Boy of 14 or 15', that he 'lived at
the Duke's Head in Carlisle—in a Tartan Sash and a Cockade—
he was running after a Chicken'.

Of the 385 prisoners already in Carlisle or later brought in,
251 drew lots and thus (in mitigation of the presumed penalty)
received punishment, e.g. slavery or transportation, without any
form of trial. Of the 134 to be brought before the commission,
about seventy of the indictments were in respect of offences
alleged in Carlisle or Cumberland; about seventy of the eighty
indictments at York were likewise in respect of Cumberland; as
were also about forty of the seventy at Southwark: thus, of a total
of about 300 indictments, about 180 were in some respect relating
to Cumberland. Baron Clarke provides notes in respect of only
seven of the Southwark prisoners, forty-nine of the Carlisle, and
fifteen of the York: total, seventy-one.

According to the Clarke notebook, the court was already in
difficulties on the very first day of the trials proper in Carlisle,
because some of the panel for the jury were holders by tenant
right of customary estates,[26] baron Clarke notes:

Friday—12th. Sept—1746—the first day of the Trials.
> Jury called over by the Pannell—and appear to a man except in
> two or three Instances of sickness
> Pannell consists of 110.

I. THOMAS HAYES[27] indicted for High Treason &c.
> Special Jurymen challenged peremptorily.
> Several challenged for not being Freeholders.
> Several have customary Estates in this County, but they are not
> Freehold, nor Copyhold—these not qualified to be Jurors.

Certainly some interesting human stories—if it is stories that
are looked for—can be pieced together from some of the most

scrappy notes of the most scrappy evidence, regarding life in
Carlisle during those critical times. One of the most notorious of
the Carlisle prisoners must have been Thomas Cappock of the
Manchester regiment, who figures so frequently in the prints of
the time as jacobite 'bishop of Carlisle'. The charge preferred
against him was 'High Treason in levying war against the King
at Carlisle—and taking and holding the castle and City against the
King'. Even Mounsey, who was not always very critical in his
treatment of material,[28] and sympathetic as he was towards the
clerical faction in Carlisle, could see that a great deal of nonsense
had already been talked about 'this young Clergyman'. For
example, at his trial it was sworn against him, and corroborated,
that with his brother (also charged) he joined them, and the
Manchester regiment, at Manchester; and also that 'Mr Hamilton,
the Pretender's Governor of the Castle of Carlisle, made him
Bishop, and that was done by order of the young Pretender *soon
after the city of Carlisle surrendered to the Rebels*'. Certainly the
testimony was not only false—it was inconsistent with itself, for
if he did not come in until they arrived at Manchester, he could
not have been made bishop of Carlisle *soon after that city surrendered*, whatever the pamphlets and cartoons might have to say.
We are a little surprised then to see in baron Clarke's notes,

> N.B. this is a Young Clergyman who affected the character of Bishop
> of Carlisle among the Rebels as Report says—

entered after the terms of the indictment *and before the evidence*.
There is in fact no evidence there that he ever affected the character of bishop of Carlisle. It is of particular interest that he
stayed at Dr Waugh's[29] house while in Carlisle, and hence it was
the chancellor's domestics and Robert Wardale, the curate whom
he left in charge,[30] who testified against Cappock at the trials;
but although certain church and cathedral matters are touched
upon, there is not the slightest hint in Clarke's notes or the evidence to suggest that he ever 'affected the character of Bishop of
Carlisle'. Dorothy Tiffin, the Waughs' maidservant, gave evidence
for the crown, as did also Lancelot Beck, the clerk of St Mary's,
and John Gardiner (who may very well have been the Gardener
who 'got safe home with the little mare last Friday'), as John
Nicolson—who later collaborated with Richard Burn in the

History and Antiquities of the Counties of Westmoreland and Cumberland—wrote to Chancellor Waugh during the course of the occupation.[31]

Baron Clarke writes:

> Mr. Robert Wardall: lives in Carlisle and saw P[risoner]s come to Dr. Waugh's House Friday before Xmas [20th December]. When Rebels were in [their *deleted*] Poss[ess]ion and the Main Body were gone forward to Scotland—I went in and found him sitting in Drs Study—

> Maid gave me a Billet on which was written 'Th. Cappock'—I showed it him and told him it was very inconvenient, no body being at the House—and the Rebels having taken all provisions &c—he said he knew how to make his Quarters good—I laid in the House till the Town was taken—he often came there and he lay at the House all the time.

There is in the evidence quite a deal of information about borrowing a gown and cassock ('My master's was too big,' said the maidservant); about the orders 'to ring the Bell as usual' (it is to be noted that 'parson' Cappock wanted the bells *rung*—not confiscated); about the 'Xmas Day *Service*'—corrected to read '*Sermon*'; about the prayers for 'K[ing] James—P[rince] Charles, Regent of England—Duke of York and Albany and rest of Royal Family'; about the choir—'to order bringing Men and boys as usual'; but nothing about 'affecting the character of Bishop of Carlisle'.

It ought not to be necessary to say that not all the evidence is to be taken at its face value. It must be approached critically. A single example should suffice: John Mason testified against Thomas Lawson[32] (a prisoner who had earlier been a chapman of Alyth in Perth) that he had

> seen the prisoner often in Carlisle—in white Cockade—and in arms—both Gun and Sword—one night took him lurking about his house—carried him before their Gov[erno]r who committed him.

This might be read as implying that the jacobite governor committed him for an offence at the complaint of a Carlisle citizen. We might assume from another source,[33] however, that it is more likely that Lawson was loitering about the back streets of Carlisle after dark, not to commit some offence against a whig inhabitant, but rather to make good his escape from the jacobite garrison—and that his governor knew it. In any case although he was found guilty and sentenced to death, the sentence was (presumably on these grounds) commuted to transportation; and as a matter of fact the prisoner was later pardoned and released, presumably because of ill health.

Although the evidence presented piecemeal, in some of the longer cases, serves to unfold some interesting stories, the shorter cases also are not without their own interest. There is for example the story of Thomas Barton, 'indicted for High Treason at Hesketh in the Forest in this county', for carrying to Carlisle Charles Edward's summons to surrender. The case was taken by the lord chief baron; but Charles Clarke has a brief note:

acquitted for want of p[ro]ducing the written Message which he was carrying to the Rebel Gov[erno]r—which was delivered over to the Justice at Hexham.

There is the even briefer case of

James Barithwaite a sadler at Peroith, nothing made out ag[ains]t him.

Not Guilty.

Just that, and no more.

The notes of a trial judge, jotted down during proceedings, may be of special interest when he records the impression any particular prisoner may have had upon the court. For example, of Thomas Hayes[34] baron Clarke says: 'Guilty. NB. A poor miserable Fellow'; of Thomas Lawson,[35] 'a poor wretched mortal'. Thomas Turner[36] he finds guilty on the evidence, but notes, 'a poor boy, an object of mercy, recommended by the Jury for mercy', and it is interesting to notice that although sentenced to death, Turner was in fact reprieved and pardoned (on condition of enlistment). Of James Millar[37] he notes, 'Tried by L[ord] c[hief] B[aron]. A com[mon] man—in the Manch[ester] Regiment. Of no Consequence one way or the other—Guilty.' Of Buchanan of Arnprior[38] he said, 'He is laird of good estate and is called Arne Prior. His trial last 8 hours and all 4 Judges present.' Of Peter MacEwen[39] he says, 'Not guilty—because when he came to England he would have quitted the service if he could.'

One of the briefest notes of the trials is that of John Thoirs,[40] noted as 'a little deformed Boy'. All it says is: 'The Pretender ask'd this boy what use he could be of—to which he answered, "Sir, tho' my body is small my Heart is as big as any Man you have".' The judge notes: 'acquitted by favour of the King's Counsel'.

There is an interesting entry of general import in the trial notebook, under the name of John Wallace.[41]

John Wallace, being called on to Trial, Desires by his Counsel, Mr Ferguson and Mr Lockhart, to withdraw his Plea, and plead Guilty—&c &c.

Intimation that they expect to lay Affidavits before the judges for them to represent a favourable case to the Crown—on which we all—Lord ch[ief] Baron, My Bro[ther] Denison and myself—Bro[ther] Barret being ill at home with the Gaol [fever] declared to the Counsel that we cannot at all interpose in cases where the parties plead guilty—and we desire it to be understood generally that the Prisoners may not think we deceive them.

However, the De[fence] did persist and withdrew his Plea and pleaded Guilty.

But apart from these brief entries, there are some interesting stories to be pieced together from the evidence as jotted down by the trial judge. There is also in the evidence occasionally the hint of much intrigue or of some dark underplot. There is, for example, the case of Patrick Stuart[42] of Innerbaik in Perthshire, of Tullibardine's regiment. This man, having returned safely home after the great adventure, 'went to surrender his arms to the Minister of the Parish acc[or]d[in]g to the Declaration of the D[uke] of Cumberland'. He was indeed, as another witness swore, 'the first Man in Blair Athol who offered his Arms to the Minister of that Place'. But there were much more important considerations in Blair Athol than mere insurrection and capital charges. Unfortunately for this same Patrick Stuart who offered his arms to the minister, *he owed the same minister some money.* Why then should the minister accept the surrender of his arms, and thus relieve the man of a capital charge—until he had paid him his money! 'He refused to take the arms, and would not take them.' 'He would take others', but not Patrick Stuart's who owed him money. 'Other two or three went in and gave up their arms—some time in the Spring but cannot tell when exactly.' The minister was apparently pressed to accept Patrick Stuart's also, but 'told him he wouldn't receive the arms from him if he was his Brother'. Patrick Stuart had therefore to skulk 'in the country'. He had the misfortune, however, to be taken up, and consequently was now indicted and must stand his trial. It does not seem to be going too far to say that poor Patrick Stuart was being tried for his life for owing the minister money. He now must needs plead guilty, at least to the charge of bearing arms, for his whole point was that he had been prevented from surrendering them. If he now pleaded guilty, the jury were compelled to find him guilty, and the law prescribed one penalty only—that of death—which is a lot, at least for owing the minister money. If was therefore hoped that the minister might at last relent, and one witness testified that he (the witness) 'went to Mr Alexander Stuart, the minister, to come hither and prove it on the Man's behalf—but he [the minister] said he could say no more—*and is not come*'. Baron Clarke notes: 'Confessed the Indictment before the Jury—So Guilty'. But a little farther down: ''Tis admitted by Mr Webb [the crown solicitor for the trials] that there is no evidence of any fact done by him after the time.' The verdict: 'Jury find Guilty—but desire this may be represented on behalf of the prisoner to the Crown.' This was presumably done, for the man was pardoned—but only for treason—on condition of enlistment, against which (as we know from other sources) he later appealed, as having been 'forced' in the first instance.

Nor was every case at the trials by any means a straightforward one of producing witnesses to prove treason, finding the verdict, and then pronouncing sentence. Some of the cases provided curious instances of conflict of evidence, mistaken identity, and so forth. Such a curious case was that of John Petrie,[43] alehousekeeper of Edinburgh, charged with high treason at his home at Edinburgh. The curtain-raiser to the little drama in which John Petrie played the principal part was in the Edinburgh Volunteers and their standing down on the approach of Charles Edward in September. The main piece was played on the day of Prestonpans with the horses of Hamilton's Dragoons—without Hamilton's dragoons—supplying the noises off, clattering up and down the streets of Edinburgh. After the heroics (and the playing to the gallery) comes the villain of the piece (and the boos), some sneak laying information against a—shall we say?—merely indiscreet fellow-citizen. And the epilogue to this piece was played out at Carlisle.

John Petrie was charged with treason on the day of Prestonpans. David Lyon (*not* in mourning) came forward as witness and swore that on the morning of the battle he 'saw the prisoner at the Gate coming into Edinburgh, riding on a Dragoon Horse and leading another in his hand'. It is perhaps amusing that the trial judge's note of the evidence says that the prisoner 'flourished his broad sword and called aloud, "God bless K[ing] G[eorge]",' —but the note is immediately altered to read 'called aloud God bless *Prince Charles*', and the 'Prince Charles' is underlined. George Porteous, another witness, corroborated.

He saw the P[risone]r up the Cannongate, day of[44] battle—riding one Dragoon Horse and leading two. He had a Dragoon sword in his hand drawn—there was a great Huzzaing, but can't say he hear. Believes they were Hamilton's Dragoons Horses by the livery.

Asked, apparently, about what arms the prisoner carried, the witness answered there were 'Pistols on the Horse he rode'. Another witness swore he wore a cockade and arms. 'He came to me and told me, G[od] d[amn] me for a scoundrel—Go bid the Ministers pray for Cope. They prayed for him last Sunday, let them pray for him now'. After further evidence of a similar nature baron Clarke notes:

Defence:
1. Words not treason.
2. he is a loyal man.
3. no facts but on this day. I thought he had from all this been at the Battle of Preston Pans, but you will find he was not, nor ever associated with them.

Alexander Bosville and Charles Mackie testified on the prisoner's behalf that he had been in the 'Volunteer Company associated to defend the Town a[gainst] the Rebels'—and now comes the real story! 'Prisoner keeps a public House', and the witnesses said they 'saw the Rebels at his House charging him that he had 5 Dragoon Horses and had d[elivere]d them but 3— and if he had 40l in the Earth he should pay it for the two Horses'. James Hunter and Andrew Somerville corroborated. The evidence was quite dramatic and the underplot begins to emerge.

Prisoner was angry when orders came to bid them [the Volunteers] deliver up their arms.
Rebels at the Door—he found his wife crying, for these Ruffians would ruin him—and it was about the Horses of Dragoons he had found.
Several Declarations aga[inst] people who had been Volunteers.
X[45]
All the time the Highlanders were in the Town he appeared openly, but afterwards he didn't—for one, Steenson, who had a falling-out with the Prisoner went and told the soll[icito]r he had joined the Rebels and a warrant was out ag[ains]t him,

Baron Clarke analysed the evidence as follows:

1. here are facts which Treason if satisfied of the intent, and if he was at Preston Pans or helped them after—or marched with them—it would explain his mind to be traitorous.
2. but here is only this Day's facts, he lived at his own House after— and the Rebels from that time used him ill.
3. his acting openly at home while the Rebels there and keeping house after was doubtful at first—but last witness accounted for it. A quarell with one Steenson had occasioned an Information ag[ains]t and a warrant out.
Design must be judged by a men's former Behaviour and after Behaviour—
The Proof is not weak. But the fact is weak and renders the Treason doubtful—If he had consulted with them, Regimented himself, carried their money or any other act of assent—tho for a moment—'tis treason, but not this sort of Noises Tumult &c.

Result: 'Not Guilty'.
Such analyses of evidence and summings-up as these are of considerable interest and assist us in getting to understand the trial issues at the time. Another case that might be cited is that of Archibald McLauchlane,[46] 'shopkeeper to Mr McLauchlan at Inverlochy', who was charged with treason in that he attempted

to enlist recruits from the prisons at Crieff, Perth and Edinburgh. The crown relied principally upon three witnesses, one civil and two military prisoners. John Lune, a soldier in Lee's regiment, had been at the barracks at Inversnaid at the head of Loch Lomond, when the modest garrison of a corporal and six men was captured by the nameless ones in the earliest days of the rising. The present witness was then brought prisoner to Perth. The trial judge notes that this soldier of Lee's testified that he

saw the P[risone]r and others with the D[uke] of Perth come into Gaol at Perth where we were prisoners. In arms—Rebels—a broad sword and White Cockade. Their Business was to desire us to list with the Pretender. Saw him at Dunblane in the same dress—Highland—walking the streets with D[uke] of Perth's servants. It was the 15th or 16th of September—4 or 5 days before the battle of Preston Pans.

John Davidson, one of Hamilton's Dragoons, taken prisoner at Prestonpans and placed in the Cannongate, swore the prisoner 'came to me in Gaol and would have me list'. He had no doubts whatever as to identity. 'Saw him every day for nine weeks that I was prisoner.' John Hammond and John McDougal, civil prisoners at Crieff and Edinburgh, testified to much the same effect. They too had no doubts as to identity and none as to date: 'is sure of the Man—2nd Monday in September'.

The case for the defence was simple: mistaken identity. 'One, Alex[r] MacLauchlane of Greenhaugh is very like this man and was in the Rebellion'. McLauchlane, the prisoner, was of Inverlochy, and at the very time sworn against him was in fact in the service of Archibald Campbell, the governor of Fort William. Duncan Mac-Fie, giving his evidence in gaelic through an interpreter, said he

lived at Inverloch[y] in Sept last—prisoner was there and 2 Sept went with witness and ano[the]r Post from Fort William to Cufferstarff.[47] They couldn't go the Road for the Rebels—so they went over the Ferry by Boat—Prisoner was one of the Hands—Gov[erno]r of Fort William sent him for that purpose—returned to Fort William 5th or 6th of Sept . . . Six Hand and prisoner was one—by order of Gov[erno]r. He left the prisoner at Bonah[48] and the other 5 at the Boat—the witness went to Inverary for his Letters—the Boat went to Dunstaffnitch to wait for witness who came to them the 15th and prisoner there, and returned with them to Inverlochy.

The 'X' in the trial judge's notes marks (presumably) where the cross-examination commences: Yes, the witness identifies the prisoner as the shopkeeper of Inverlochy. Yes: he is certain of the date.

remembers the day because they rec[eive]d part of their pay at setting out and were to receive the rest when they [arrived] back.
which is all he remembers it by—main body of the Rebel army he heard was then North—it was after they ferried over there that they took Edinburgh.

The point arises: could the accused have been in the Fort William boat, as Duncan MacFie swears, on 15th September and also, as the soldier of Lee's regiment swears, at Dunblane 'walking the streets with the Duke of Perth's servants' on the 15th or 16th of September—'4 or 5 days before the battle of Preston Pans'? In further cross-examination MacFie swears it is '84 miles the short way from Inverlochy to Edinburgh—he was the Land Post—is sure this was in Sept.' The judge inserts a hurried note—'The Interruption must be sooner to the Post, for the Rebels must be at Inverlochy and post it before Sept, and if . . .'
The sentence is left unfinished and there are a couple of lines left blank in the manuscript. The notes then continue:

Witness prisoner 16th August near Inverlochy till 20 by the Rebels—and 26 went forward to Inverary—returned *28*. 16 Sept was the last day he saw the prisoner.

Incidentally, there are one or two interesting points here with regard to the current lack of news from the west. The *Du Teillay* fetched up at Eriskay on 23rd July (old style), and made the mainland on the 25th. Yet no news of the landing arrived in Edinburgh until as late as 8th August. This fact is usually attributed to the great loyalty of the common people of the western clans to the Stuart cause. It is clear that the local clansmen by holding the strategic passes and ways could—and did—throttle all communication from the west, save perhaps that by water, and therefore any intelligence that might get through by land would have necessarily to be by a very circuitous route, at a sacrifice not only of distance, but of time—and it was time that was so valuable. Thus, from so important a station as Fort William, the principal

government post north of the highland line, even as late as 2nd
September, as we see from MacFie's evidence, the land post
'couldn't go the Road for the Rebels—so went over the Ferry by
Boat'. From Fort William the post could not go forward to
Inverary, the whig Campbell stronghold in the west, until as
late as 26th August. MacFie returned on the 28th and when he
went again on 2nd September the roads were still closed: 'they
couldn't go the Road for the Rebels'. The significance of the
arrival of news, by ship, in the port of Liverpool as late as 15th
August[49] should be seen in this light.

To return, however, to the prisoner, Archibald McLauchlane, of
Inverlochy: John McCormack, servant to old Alexander Campbell, the governor of Fort William, came now to the court with
the governor's leave, to testify that they had employed the
prisoner in the Fort William boat as a local man with six soldiers
of the garrison.

Returned 6th—went again 11th Sept to carry Engin[ee]r Campbell
with post—ordered to go from thence to Dunstaffnitch to wait for the
Post and returned the 15th Governor ordered me to come here on this
occasion.

There is a deal of other evidence, all tending in the same direction and furnishing, incidentally, some interesting side-lights
on communications and life generally in the west during the time
of the trouble. Baron Clarke's analysis and summing-up of the
evidence in this simple but interesting case reads as follows:

1. Treason clearly proved if this is the Man.
2. the difficulty is the Contariety of evidence.
1. Man who swears he saw him 9 weeks together at Edinb[urgh] must
   be either perjured wilfully—or man must mistake the Man—which
   gives ground for the Defence.
2. King's witnesses all agree he could not be at Edinb[urgh] 9 weeks. . .
   Consistent evidence of his being at other places from 2 to 18 Sept which
   takes in both the times mencond ag[ains]t him at Crieff by Lune—who
   swears to 15th or 16th. Hammond who says 2nd Monday in September
   which was the 9th September. ERGO? Whether the King's witnesses
   are not mistaken. . . . King's witnesses strangers, Def[endan]ts knew
   him.

A verdict of 'Not guilty' was returned.

Occasionally we have a note informing us of the grounds for the verdict, as for example in the case of Thomas Collingwood.[50] According to an entry in the state papers this prisoner was acquitted because of the 'Town Clerk of Newcastle suppressing or at least not producing the prisoner's examination'.[51] The trial notes expressed it differently. They say that Thomas Collingwood 'was the man who was carrying 100l to one Sanderson to pay the Colliers'. The letter was produced and read, but he was found 'Not guilty' because they could not clearly 'prove him acting with the Rebels'.

There was, as might be expected, the usual crop of confused cases. There was, for example, the curious case of John Porteous[52] who confessed his guilt, but said 'he was tried for Desertion and convicted at Carlisle, and pardoned by the Duke [of Cumberland]'. Baron Clarke marked this case 'Query', but he was in fact found guilty, and sentenced to death, although he was afterwards reprieved. There was also the curious case of William Beard[53] (or Baird, 'coalhewer to Kilmarnock') 'a serj[eant] in Lord Ogilvie's Regiment', indicted 'for High Treason at Carlisle', and tried by the lord chief baron, and found guilty. He produced a certificate from a major in Lord Cobham's Dragoons to show that he had surrendered under the terms of Cumberland's declaration. He was nevertheless taken up by the lord justice-clerk, but afterwards discharged. He had come now 'as a witness from David Lyon',[54] but was somehow or other himself taken up and charged. This was indeed hard upon a man who had attended merely in the capacity of a witness, as he himself naturally 'had no witness, because he had no expectation of being indicted'. Being unable to answer the charge, he was accordingly found guilty. Certainly it was a hard case, and we learn from other sources that he was later reprieved and ordered to be transported, and later still, pardoned on condition of enlistment.

Sometimes there is a considerable contrast, not to say dramatic contrast, between the evidence for the prosecution and the evidence for the defence. Not that the facts as such were disputed, but they were often presented in a different light. The charge against William Home[55] was treason at Edinburgh. George Irwin, one of Hamilton's Dragoons, testified he saw Home in

Edinburgh with the rebels and with a white cockade. Andrew Jackson swore that he

saw the Prisoner at the Abbey at Edinburgh with the Rebels—was in the Pretender's Life Guard Habit—Blue mounted with Red—he had a broad sword—and Pistols when he rode—saw him riding in England, riding with the Rebel Army.

Saw him at Falkirk and he was at the Battle and in it armed—likewise at Cullonden (*sic*)—and at Falkirk—carried the Standard as Cornet in Lord Balmerino's Troop—and so at the Battle of Cullonden too.

Another of Cope's men swore he 'saw P[risoner] at Fort George when he himself was prisoner there'. He saw him 'carry the Standard when the Pretender came to Forres—he was then in a Tartan Plad'. Another witness corroborated saying he 'saw P[risone]r at Fort George after the Rebels took it—and we carried thither as Prisoners. Was at Forres when the Pretend[e]r came in. Riding with a Party—Prisoner carried the standard and drums beat.' And so the crown, stroke by stroke, completed its portrait, and at this length of time we may picture this stalwart lifeguardsman, in 'blue mounted with Red' or his tartan plaid, this standard-bearer who with drums beating and colours flying, from Holyrood Abbey rode into England; this man of war, whose defeated adversaries now came forward to testify he had been at Fort George, and had fought at Falkirk and at Culloden. Baron Clarke notes only one item in his defence: John Leach swears he knew him; 'saw him every day for 12 years'. He 'was born 2nd November 1731—was at the Christening', and so the judge notes 'he was at that time under 14 years of Age'. Nevertheless, the child was found guilty. There is no record, however, that he was recommended for mercy, but it is known from other sources that his kinsman, the earl of Home, petitioned on his behalf, and asked for him to be excused from serving abroad as a common soldier. The prisoner himself absolutely refused to serve with the East India Company, and in the end the boy received a free pardon.

There can be little doubt that there was often some hard swearing especially on the subject of 'forcing'. It had all along been a sound point in the whig party line that the common men had been 'forced' by their chiefs and superiors. It was therefore a good card for the accused to play, particularly if fate had dealt no other. But some of the testimony sounds a bit thin. Let us take the case of John Ballantine, 'piper to one of the Athol Regiments, commanded by S[ir] Rob[ert] Mercer of Aldie: the regiment was given to Lord George Murray who had pipers of his own'. The first two witnesses for the Crown were John Marr and the Manchester renegade Samuel Madox. John Marr identified the prisoner at Carlisle 'before the Rebels as they marched out southward. Saw him as far as the English Gate.' Madox testified he saw him 'walking in the street among the Rebels—White Cockade in his Hat—and none but Rebels wore them'. At this point the judge entered the name of the third witness, but finding that he was a fellow prisoner, deleted the name and inserted the comment: '2 witnesses as slight as possible. 2nd only White Cockade'. The prisoner's master later testified that he and the prisoner lived '3 miles east of Dunkeld in Kinkardine'. He came to prove the piper had been 'forced'.

P[risone]r was my servant in Harvest of 1745, and about midnight Rebels came to my House, and because I wouldn't let them in they threaten'd to fire my house. When I let them in they asked for the P[risone]r and took him out of bed. Bid him rise and go with them or they would kill him, and drew a sword at his Breast. He cried and took on much—didn't allow him time to dress scarce. Made him play his pipes with them.
About 8 days after he came back, for violin.

The weakness in the story was how the insurgents knew that Ballantine was at Kay's house when they demanded him, and how they knew he was a piper. After baron Clarke's notes on the evidence there comes the cross-examination, and the witness's reply could not have sounded very convincing to the court.

X
can't tell how they knew he was a piper or that he was there.

Clarke's closing note on this particular trial is a pleasing one of unaffected joy and gratitude:

Not Guilty—on his acquittal this poor Piper bless'd K[ing] George and shewed such honest unaffected Signs of Joy on his Delivery as I never saw—he jumped and danced in the Bar with his Irons and couldn't be contained by any means from expressing his Joy and Gratitude.

One gets the impression, however, in going over some of these trial notes and jottings that not everything at the trials was quite so unaffected, so genuine and so spontaneous as this poor piper's joy. There seems (if one must strike a distasteful note) a rather larger proportion than one would perhaps have expected of utterly pathetic cases and instances of mere boys, some of them no more than children, having to stand their trial.

Of Thomas Turner[56] of the Manchester Regiment (a shoe-maker's lad from Bury) the judge says, 'A poor boy—an object of mercy.' It is to be noted that although he was convicted and sentenced to death, the jury recommended him for mercy and the boy was in fact reprieved. Of Thomas Hayes[57] he says, 'a poor miserable fellow'; of Thomas Lawson[58] an Alyth chapman, 'a poor wretched Mortal'; of Simon Lugdown (or Lugton)[59] an Edinburgh tailor, 'a poor silly fellow'; of William Hargrove,[60] 'defence: Lunacy . . . sent to a madhouse by his father. . . . He was mad'. Apart from these, there were the young boys: Thomas Williamson[61] 'a Boy of Manch[este]r who was witness to Cop-pocks Force, he being very young, Not Guilty'. The reference here is to John Cappock the Manchester tailor, not 'parson' Thomas, his more notorious brother. Of John Cappock baron Clarke remarks, 'Defence: only a drummer, very young, not active. Hid himself in a Garrett'. At the close of the case he added the remarks, 'Guilty, but the Jury Desire he may be recommended to the crown to save his Life, and we have promised it'. He was indeed sentenced to death, but pardoned on the usual condition of enlistment. There was David Wilkie[62] from Correfie in Forfar for whom John Farquarson swore 'don't think he is 16—saw a party of L[or]d Ogilvie's men take him away by Force and he cried when he went'. Wilkie was found guilty on the evidence, but the trial notes read: 'but the jury having some doubt, re-commended him for Mercy'. David Ogilvy[63] was a 'boy of about 17, a poor boy, and seems worthy of mercy. Guilty—recom-mended for mercy by the Jury': the mercy, however, could do him no benefit for he died in prison. Thomas Harvey, described in Seton and Arnot[64] as 'or Harvie, or Hervey . . . Soldier in Col

Lascelle's Regt and therefore a deserter', is described by Clarke as '17 years old . . . was Servant to Capt. Fletcher of the Manch[este]r Regiment—Guilty—N.B. Jury desire he may have Mercy &c'. Neal MacLarins[65] 'A young Highlander of 18—proved to be taken by force and kept so from Edinburgh &c. Not Guilty'. Thomas Warrington,[66] 'for High Treason. N.B. Boy of 14 or 15. not Guilty by consent'. John Thors,[67] the 'little deformed boy' we have already met.

James Creighton (or Crichton) whom Seton and Arnot identify as a mason of Edinburgh,[68] aged twenty-five, baron Clarke describes as 'about sixteen years old'; and Alexander Goodbread[69] whom Seton and Arnot show as Alexander Goodwin or Goodbread, a carpenter of Banff, aged '30 (?17)', the judge describes quite definitely as 'about sixteen years old'. Presumably Charles Clarke was experienced enough a judge to know the difference between sixteen and twenty-five in James Creighton and between seventeen and thirty in Alexander Goodbread. John Forrest,[70] elsewhere described as a common man of Elgin, is 'not 15 yet—for H[igh] Treason at Elgin', for whom John Scot testified he 'saw him at Elgin in arms—marching with them—ignorant, and an infant under 14'. Result: 'Not Guilty'.

This factor of the extreme youth of some of the prisoners is common to Carlisle, York and Chester. Naturally not all these young persons could be indicted. At York among those who were indicted and confessed the indictment were a number of youths of sixteen, seventeen and eighteen; James Creighton who was fifteen, John Duncan, 'not 15 years old', William Smith who 'says he is 15', and David Webster who 'seems very young . . .'. Of the four prisoners at York who were condemned but recommended for mercy and in fact reprieved, two were sixteen, and one was 'between 15 and 16'.[71] A list of prisoners held at Chester 'on account of the Rebellion', forwarded from Carlisle, consisted of a boy of fifteen, three of fourteen, one of thirteen and two of eleven, two children of six and eight, and Clementine Macdonald, aged twelve, and Margaret Douglas, aged three.[72] Incidentally, we know from the Ogilvy orderly book that specific orders were at least sometimes given with regard to the children. Just before the action at Clifton, for example, when the duke of Cumberland's advanced elements had come almost into contact with the jacobite rearguard, a specific order was given that all the women and children were to be sent to the van of the retreat.[73]

Certainly many people in England were struck by the very high proportion of young boys accompanying the invading army. This could be illustrated from a variety of contemporary sources. A particular letter from Manchester,[74] from one private person to another, found to be quite reliable in a number of other details, estimated that the army as it entered Manchester included as many as three thousand 'boys of 10, 12 or 14 years old'. It goes on: 'the boys are armed with a Musket, Sword and Target [i.e. the round shield] and one or two brace of Pistols'. The current news-sheets had it that some of the boys 'were not as long as the Swords they carried'.[75] This does seem to leave open the possibility that not all the boys were enlisted soldiers or rebel volunteers. The clan and family dignity of many of the chiefs, chieftains, lairds and other gentlemen in the army might have required them to have their own servants to save them from certain menial tasks and they may, therefore, have taken their own household boys or younger family retainers. If, therefore, these boys are seen to carry 'Musket, Sword and Target and one or two brace of Pistols' it is at least possible that the boys are merely carrying their masters' arms on the line of march—much as the squire of old bore the arms of his knight—rather than that these mere boys, not to say sometimes children, were in fact *armed* with such an array of weapons.

In these circumstances it is not, perhaps, that one should be surprised at the *number* of young prisoners: what is apt to surprise one, however, is the seemingly unduly high proportion of prisoners young and feeble-minded *on whom the lot fell*, and whether therefore some of the elder and less simple-minded had not found a way of 'arranging' the lots. One should perhaps hasten to add that this might conceivably be done with the best of motives, for it would thus leave to the mercy of the jury those with no family or other responsibilities and at the same time those upon whom the lenity of the court or the clemency of the crown might possibly fall—if it fell upon any at all. There can be no doubt that some of the poor, dejected, simple boys, bewildered doubtless by what was going on around them, *did* excite the sympathy of the court. If the lots did in fact fall unduly upon these poor boys *by a management of the lotting*, it is difficult to believe that this could have been brought about without the connivance, or at least the knowledge, of both sides.

But let the point be not pursued—lest some of the romance of the selfless loyalty for the yellow-haired laddie should seem to fade.

Notes

1 Oxford, 1762. Later editions, 1766 and 1792.

2 Vol. xviii (1743–53), 1813.

3 *HP Jac. Per.*, volume ii, 339–486. Francis Watt's paper 'Treason trials at Carlisle after 1745', *Juridical Review XXV* (1913), pp. 124–35, is without any value.

4 *S & A.*

5 As to which, see the fifth Report of the Deputy Keeper (1844), Appendix II, pp. 172–93; and C. A. Ewald, *Life and Times of Prince Charles Stuart* (new edition, 1883), Appendix, pp. 430–40.

6 SP Dom., mostly bundles 83–90.

7 Add. MSS 35886 (= Hardwick DXXXVIII).

8 Egerton MSS, 2000.

9 Stowe MSS, 255.

10 E.g. Stowe MSS, 158.

11 Stowe MSS, 750.

12 CW2, liii, 116.

13 Cumb. LMB, 16th and 28th September, and 9th October 1745.

14 See, for example, Christmas 1745–6, petitions 14, 21 and 24, and Christmas petitions 1746–7, 23.

15 SP Dom. 72/34 (enc.). And see Papers 5, 6 and 10, volume I.

16 Petition of Richard Goodman, Easter sessions 1746 petition roll, 85 and 93.

17 Easter 1746, petition 32 (this petition also slightly damaged).

18 See Paper 9, volume I.

19 *S & A*, 1533.

20 *S & A*, 1288.

21 Easter 1746, petitions 81–2; and Midsummer 1746, petitions 31 and 50–1.

22 Given by Ewald as 'John Mac Claren' (relying upon the *baga de secretis*, *Life and Times of Prince Charles Stuart*, new edition, 1883, Appendix, p. 437).

23 But query No. 1726, 'John Mc Camel . . . Taken at Capture of Carlisle. There is no further reference to him.' (SP Dom. 79/26).

24 For a plate of his house see G. G. Mounsey, *Carlisle in 1745: Authentic Account* (1846), p. 101.

25 See below, pp. 254–5.

26 Cf. statute, Ric. III (1483), cap. 4.

27 *S & A*, 1276.

28 For example, when Mounsey did not himself know the whereabouts of certain manuscript sources he had the bad habit of implying by ambiguous phrasing that they were not in existence. He says that besides the private letters, Dr Waugh wrote official letters also, 'it is believed, to the Duke of Newcastle then Minister of the Crown. The [private letters] have been preserved; those to the Duke of Newcastle are not forthcoming' (Mounsey, preface, viii). They are in fact 'forthcoming' exactly where one would expect, namely in the state papers, domestic series, in the Public Record Office. In another ambiguous passage regarding the manuscript sources of the trials, he says, 'though it is *much to be wished that a report of the trials of the two Macdonalds had been preserved*, yet possibly had it been so we might have to pronounce the affecting narrative by Sir Walter Scott . . . to be merely a fiction' (*ibid.* 257).

29 Chancellor Waugh was present at the trials; see note above.

30 The curate's letters to the chancellor during the occupation are printed in Mounsey.

31 Mounsey, 162.

32 *S & A*, 1533.

33 SP Dom. 92/225.

34 *S & A*, 1276.

35 *S & A*, 1533.

36 *S & A*, 3306.

37 *S & A*, 2485.

38 *S & A*, 272.

39 Not noted by *S & A*. Ewald, relying upon the *baga de secretis*, calls him McEwan (*Life and Times of Prince Charles Stuart*, new edition, 1853, Appendix, p. 437).

40 *S & A*, 3265.

41 *S & A* have 'Wallace, also Wallas' (No. 3342). Ewald has 'Wallas'.

42 *S & A*, 3176.

43 *S & A*, 2727.

44 Afterwards amended from 'day *after* battle'.

45 Throughout the notebook the 'X' at the end of any item of evidence seems to indicate the commencement of the cross-examination.

46 *S & A*, 2224.

47 Amended to 'Dustaffnitch'—for Dunstaffnage, which serves to illustrate the court's difficulties with proper names.

48 Banavie.

49 See Paper 10, volume I. In London the *General Advertiser*, for example, remarked that 'Edinburgh had not received letters from Lochaber for 13 Days' (31st August 1745).

50 *S & A*, 537.

51 Cf. J. Macbeth Forbes, *Jacobite Gleanings from State Manuscripts* (1903), 20.

52 *S & A*, 2751.

53 *S & A*, 88.

54 *S & A*, 1615.

55 *S & A*, 1320.

56 *S & A*, 3306.

57 *S & A*, 1276.

58 *S & A*, 1533.

59 *S & A*, 1612—'almost an idiot'.

60 *S & A*, 1255—'of distempered brain'.

61 *S & A*, 3417 (age not stated).

62 *S & A*, 3406 (age not stated).

63 *S & A*, 2665 (age not stated).

64 *S & A*, 1261 (age not stated).

65 *S & A*, 2238.

66 *S & A*, 3359.

67 *S & A*, 3265.

68 *S & A*, 600.

69 *S & A*, 1058.

70 *S & A*, 933.

71 SP Dom. 88/48 (or 127).

72 *Ibid.* 92/163.

73 Sir Bruce Seton, *Orderly Book of Lord Ogilvy's Regiment* (Society of Army Historical Research, 1923), 14th–16th December 1745, p. 27.

74 R. C. Jarvis, 'Manchester in the Forty-Five: a letter from an eye-witness', *Manchester Review*, viii (1958), 181–6.

75 *General Advertiser*, and *True Patriot*, 3rd December 1745.

24 *The Administration of the Anti-Catholic Laws*

A study of contemporary manuscript sources, as distinct from a study of the text of the statutes, provides a more agreeable picture than is usually presented of mid-eighteenth-century religious toleration in England. There was, in other words, a greater contrast than has hitherto been fully realized between the law of the land as it was enacted in the capital and the law as it was administered and enforced in the country. The extent of this toleration in the eighteenth century can best be illustrated from the period of the two jacobite risings, in 1714–15 and 1745–6; that is to say, at the very times when such tolerance might quite reasonably be expected to be least.

When the legal position and the general condition of the catholics in England during these times are considered, it will be found that some of the more familiar issues—more clearly discernible in the earlier period—had by now lost something of their edge. In any case, too much has occasionally been argued from the exact text of the law, in which the issues are unduly simplified. It will be best, therefore, to look firstly at the harsh strictness of the law as it was *enacted*, and then to see, in great contrast, the liberal and tolerant manner in which often that law was administered and enforced. More than one contrast will be found between the well-thumbed pages of the statutes and the less often disturbed volumes and bundles of the relevant records.

As regards the text of the law, during the whole of this period catholics generally in England lay under serious legal disadvantages. Any person who acknowledged the Pope as supreme head of the church, and hence denied the royal supremacy; who could not bring himself to deny belief in the doctrine of transubstantiation;

The notes and references are on pages 323–5

who admitted allegiance *de jure* to the catholic house of Stuart rather than to the protestant (*de facto*) house of Hanover—such a person was shorn of many civil liberties. This attitude of the law to catholics generally, or more precisely, this attitude of the *legislature* (from which, of course, the catholics had been absolutely excluded), is perhaps most clearly stated in the discriminatory legislation of 1715.

After the suppression of the rising, an act was passed to register catholics' estates in order that they should be subjected to a discriminatory tax.[1] The preamble of this act recited that it was only in consequence of the many provocations they had given and of 'the horrid designs they [had] framed for the destruction of this kingdom and the extirpation of the Protestant Religion' that 'the many penal laws [had] been made against them'. Nevertheless, out of the 'tender regard' that had been shown by the crown for many years last past, these penal laws had not in fact been put into execution.

Notwithstanding this 'tender regard' and restraint, however, the catholics within this kingdom, 'all or the greatest part of them', so the preamble recited, had recently been concerned in 'stirring up and supporting the late unnatural Rebellion for the dethroning and murdering his most Sacred Majesty; for setting up a Popish Pretender upon the Throne of this kingdom; for the Destruction of the Protestant Religion and the cruel murdering and massacring its Professors'. Therefore, the act went on:

It manifestly appears by their behaviour that they [the catholics] take themselves to be obliged by the Principles they profess, to be enemies to His Majesty and to the present happy Establishment, and watch for all opportunities of fomenting and stirring up new Rebellions and Disturbances within the Kingdom and of inviting Foreigners to invade it.

The law held it highly reasonable, therefore, that the justices of the peace (all of them, of course, conforming protestants) should be instructed to tender the statutory oaths of allegiance, supremacy and abjuration to all known or suspected catholics. Any of them who refused, declined, neglected or otherwise omitted to take these standard oaths within a stipulated period (and thereby became known as 'refusers') were required to register their names and the details of their estates, with the intention of facilitating the levy of a discriminatory tax. Thus only could the catholics be made to contribute any 'large share to all such Extraordinary Expenses as are and shall be brought upon this Kingdom by their Treachery and Instigation'.

If one bears in mind the regular fiscal practice and orthodox constitutional theory of the time, this course was much less unreasonable than it might be judged today. Before Pitt instituted the consolidated fund in 1787,[2] it was quite orthodox practice for a restricted 'service' (particularly an unbudgeted cost) to be met by a restricted 'charge' (or differential tax), and for the tax to be both charged and appropriated by the same act. For example, in 1666 money was required for a particular unforeseen cost, namely, the rebuilding of London after the Great Fire and in particular the rebuilding of the City churches and St Paul's cathedral. No grant-in-aid could be expected from the crown; no tax directly on the nation could be expected from parliament. The restricted 'service' was therefore met by a restricted 'charge': a duty was placed upon coals carried coastwise into the port of London,[3] the charge limited to London and the yield appropriated to the rebuilding of the City.[4] Along similar lines it seemed unobjectionable constitutional practice in 1715 that the exceptional expenses incidental to suppressing the jacobite rising should be met (at least in part) by a charge upon the confessed jacobites. The most convenient way—incidentally, already legal—to identify a confessed jacobite for this purpose was to equate him with a 'refuser' of the existing statutory oaths.

Under the 1715 scheme of discriminatory taxation, clerks of the peace were statutorily required to register the 'refusers' on 'Parchment Books or Parchment Rolls at some notorious place in the county', and to carry these books or rolls 'to the next and every Quarter Sessions of the Peace to be held'.[5] Copies of these registries were required to be sent to the commissioners, who had been appointed under an earlier act to manage the forfeited estates. Land and estates to a total annual rental of about £400,000 were so registered. The original local books or rolls usually survive in the counties, and the commissioners' copies also survive in the Public Record Office.[6]

The preamble of the charging act of 1715 referred to 'the many

Penal Laws made against [the catholics]'. By these penal laws
catholics or suspected catholics could already be summoned by
any two justices to make the standard oath and declarations.
These were the oath of allegiance to the crown as it had been
conveyed away from the catholic—and senior—line of Stuart by
the Revolutionary settlement of 1688,[7] and as it had been settled
in 1714 (by the Act of Settlement of 1701[8]) away from the catholic
Stuarts altogether, upon the protestant house of Hanover; and the
declaration abjuring all belief in the doctrine of transubstantiation.

At the Revolution the oath of supremacy and allegiance laid
down at the accession of Elizabeth I[9] had been abrogated, and
oaths were prescribed[10] in a new form, in effect re-enacting the
tests for office under the Test Acts of 1673[11] and 1678.[12] The
intention of the first Test Act (1673) had been to exclude from
all offices, civil or military, any who did not (i) take the oath of
supremacy and allegiance, (ii) receive the sacrament according to
the usage of the anglican church, and (iii) positively aver a
disbelief in transubstantiation. It was aimed to draft a declaration
against transubstantiation in terms that would make it impossible
for any conscientious catholic to subscribe. In this first Test
Act the declaration was brief:

I A.B. doe declare That I doe beleive that there is not any Transubstantiation in the Sacrament of the Lords Supper, or in the Elements
of Bread and Wine, at, or after the Consecration thereof by any person
whatsoever.[13]

The second Test Act (1678), passed in the rising excitement of
the Titus Oates affair, was drawn in much stronger terms, in
terms that could not be evaded, even by direct dispensation, royal
or papal:

I A.B. doe solemnely and sincerely in the presence of God professe
testifie and declare That I doe believe that in the Sacrament of the
Lords Supper there is not any Transubstantiation of the Elements of
Bread and Wine into the Body and Blood of Christ at or after the
Consecration therof by any person whatsoever; And that the Invoca-
tion or Adoration of the Virgin Mary or any other Saint, and the Sacrifice of the Masse as they are now used in the Church of Rome are
superstitious and idolatrous, And I doe solemnely in the presence of
God professe testifie and declare That I doe make this Declaration and

every part thereof in the plaine and ordinary sence of the Words read unto me as they are commonly understood by English Protestants without any Evasion, Equivocation or Mentall Reservation whatsoever and without any Dispensation already granted me for this purpose by the Pope or any other Authority or Person whatsoever or without any hope of any such Dispensation from any person or authority whatsoever or without thinking that I am or can be acquitted before God or Man or absolved of this Declaration or any part thereof although the Pope or any other Person or Persons or Power whatsoever should dispence with or annull the same, or declare that it was null and void from the beginning.[14]

In 1696, after the death of Mary, a plot was alleged to have been discovered for the murder of William and the invasion of England under the catholic duke of Berwick. By the act passed that year 'for the security of the crown'

all and every Person and Persons who shall refuse to take the Oaths mentioned and appointed to be taken . . . shall until he or they have duly taken the said Oaths, be liable to incurr forfeit pay and suffer all and every the Penalties Forfeitures Sums of Money Disabilities and Incapacities which by the Laws and Statutes of this Realme now in Force or any of them are inflicted upon Popish Recusantes duely convict of Recusancy.[15]

It is particularly to be noticed, with special reference to what follows, that records of refusal were to be transmitted through the assize judges *to the Court of Exchequer*, which was authorized to proceed against lands and goods as in the case of a popish recusant convict.

This provision, that any catholic or suspected catholic refusing or omitting to take the oaths of allegiance, supremacy and abjuration should be adjudged a popish recusant convict, was re-enacted and confirmed immediately upon the outbreak of the rising of 1715.[16] Other acts also were in force against them. For example, 'refusers' of the oath could be disarmed, immobilized (by the loss of their horses) and confined to the neighbourhood of their normal abode.

By an act of 1688 a 'refuser' was prohibited from having or keeping

in his House or elsewhere, or in the Possession of any other person to his use or at his disposition any Arms Weapons Gunpowder or Ammunition[17] other than such as was allowed to him by the sessions. He was liable ('on notice to him, given or left at his usual place of abode') to have his place ransacked by 'the constable or his deputy or the Tythingman or Headborough' or any other person authorized by the justices. Any arms, etc. so found, whether concealed or not, would be forfeit to the crown. Nor could any 'refuser' be left in possession or custody of any horse or horses 'which should be above the value of Five Pounds to be sold', and his premises and lands were open to search.[18]

The year 1593, of course, produced penalties against 'puritans' as well as catholics, but by an act still in force during the period of the jacobite risings a catholic 'refuser' could still be required to repair to the place of his usual abode or dwelling, and not at any time to remove above five miles thence unless licensed.[19]

By the act of 1593 such licence could be obtained only under the hands of 'two Justices of the Peace of the same county, with the privity and assent in writing of the Bishop of the Diocese or the Lieutenant or of any Deputy Lieutenant of the same county'.[20] By a later act of the year of the Gunpowder Plot—but still unrepealed—any papist or popish recusant who should have any necessary occasion or business to travel out of the compass of the five miles was required to state on oath before four justices of his own county the particular cause of his proposed journey and how long he proposed to be absent, travelling, attending and returning; upon his obtaining in writing the assent of the bishop of the diocese or the lieutenant of his county, a licence could be granted.[21]

Thus, by what the law itself called 'the many penal acts made against them', catholics could by a simple process be made subject to penalties which Blackstone described as 'little, if anything, short of those of praemunire'—an incapacity to hold office, to prosecute any suit in law, to be a guardian or executor, to accept a legacy or deed of gift, to vote at any parliamentary election, and penalties generally 'which in the end amount to the alternative of abjuring the realm or suffering death as a felon'.[22]

All this, however, is but the dry text of the law which never comes to life unless we know how the law was in fact administered and enforced. In any case, the day-to-day routine records of the grant of licences to the catholic to travel 'out of the compass of five miles' from his usual abode, the summonses to take the oaths, the search of various catholic premises for arms, ammunition, 'concealed horses', and so forth, certainly help to sharpen the focus of our picture of the times.

Outside London, it was at York, perhaps—under the active campaigning of the archbishop—that most effort was made to arouse the civic authorities to 'put the laws into execution against the catholics'. Yet even at York the surviving records, for example those relating to confining the catholics 'within the compass of five miles of their usual abode', seem necessarily to imply a degree of toleration quite surprising in the circumstances. At the very time when the jacobite invaders were marching southwards through England 'Mr. Saml. Thornton and Mr. John Metcalf' are permitted 'to go about [their] lawful business in Yorkshire, Derbyshire and Staffordshire', which seems vague enough. Between 25th September 1745 and the following 9th July, thirty-four licences were granted at York to 'popish recusants' varying from three days to two months, with an average of twelve days each. Sometimes a 'date of return' is noted in the record, sometimes not. In no case is there any account of any action taken when no return is recorded. The whole seems to suggest an administration very liberal—or very lax.[23]

Searching for arms 'on information received' seems also to be often somewhat half-hearted. A good many of the pieces of information upon which the searches for arms were founded were stories conforming to a familiar pattern. For example, there was information in November of 1745 that at Thorndon near Brentwood in Essex 'three coaches with six horses each'[24] were 'observed to go' late at night up to the Hall—'it has been for some time past uninhabited'. Furthermore, 'several waggons came to that house in the night, which the waggoners themselves had some apprehension were laden with arms'. The house was lately in the possession of Lady Petre, of a noted Essex catholic family, and herself related to the tragic Derwentwaters. The secretary of state directed Lord Fitzwalter the lord lieutenant therefore to make 'immediate and strict search in the said House for arms'.

In less than a week there is a report from Chelmsford. The search of 'these very large and extensive buildings' had employed them 'from sun-rising to sun-setting'. Two deputy lieutenants, a commissioned officer of the militia, and others had 'made very diligent search in all and every part of the house . . . with all the numerous offices and outhouses, with the chapel, barns, stables, and granaries thereto belonging'. They had found no horses nor arms nor ammunition 'except a few fowling pieces, one turkish sabre, five swords and a few pistols, all hanging in a Press in a bed chamber of the late Lord Petre'.[25] A separate report from Lord Fitzwalter himself said that they had also conducted 'a proper and thorough inquiry in the village of Thorndon of some honest and very well intentioned people there' whether they had any reason to suspect 'that any arms had, in waggons or by other means, been conveyed to the house of my Lord Petre' or even into the village.

Their answer was that from the first report of a thing of that kind they had diligently watch'd and observ'd what had pass'd in their parish, and had not the least reason to apprehend that either loaded waggons or coaches and six horses had come to the place as represented.[26]

Particular attention was occasionally paid to those houses which were 'known to be Popish Schools or Seminaries'. In the county of Middlesex, for example, the deputy lieutenants 'attended themselves in person' when in November of 1745 the high and petty constables 'with the assistance of a Guard of Soldiers', searched such a place on the basis of information received.

They

searched a house, commonly call'd 'The Nunnery' and went through every part of the said house (and particularly where the information directed, at the top of the house, between the ceiling and the garrett and the roof) with a lighted candle, where, as well as in all other parts of the said house [they] made a most diligent search,[27]

but found no arms or weapons of any kind, although on other premises they found an old musket and a sword.

From the county of Rutland the justices reported to the privy council that only three houses were due to be searched and this had in fact been done.

On searching we found neither arms nor horses or any correspondence carried on that we think worth troubling [you] with. But in one of the cottages we found a large chest of drawers full of dresses of all sorts, as we suppose used by the Priests Saying Mass, together with pictures, Mass books, Beads, Crosses and other things.[28]

The justices ordered the drawers to be sealed by the constables and waited for orders from the council as to whether anything further was to be done; but they did nothing themselves.

In November of 1745 one of Lord Malton's tenants in North Derbyshire brought him a curious note:

Memorandum:

There are two persons in the parish of Hathersay that are able to depose if compelled to it, their sight of a great number of arms concealed in the private rooms at the Duke of Norfolk's. . . . They saw the same at Worksop Manor.[29]

The memorandum was underwritten 'Report to Lord Malton' and continued on the back:

Be cautious in the search—for the within mentioned rooms have no passage into them but from the top of the leads, the taking up of some part of which will discover the stare case into them.

The information had not been in Wentworth House a quarter of an hour before Lord Malton was writing out a copy of the memorandum for the secretary of state, a copy for the duke of Devonshire as the appropriate lord lieutenant ('that he might keep a watchful eye')[30] and another copy for himself. He then sent the original off to the duke of Kingston, the officer commanding the nearest troops, which were at Nottingham. The duke of Kingston communicated with the secretary of state the same day: 'as it is an affair of great consequence', he for his part 'would not venture to do anything' till he received more explicit instructions. 'If it should be thought proper to make a search' his grace thought the place ought to be firstly surrounded by troops and the architect taken along. In any case his troops would be marching out of Nottingham in a couple of days.[31]

On the purely formal and legal side, the duke of Devonshire thought the situation quite 'difficult'. It might be best to take the information in the form of a deposition and 'thus make them liable to examination'. The secretary of state, however, gave him prompt instructions: 'As the persons therein mentioned lived pretty near Chatsworth' his grace was to direct a convenient justice to take their affidavit and transmit it to the council. If, however, he should think the information was so strong as to warrant it, no time was to be lost but a proper search made with the high sheriff and the deputy lieutenants.[32]

To this the duke of Devonshire replied that he had now directed his own steward to go over to Worksop, but to the best of his own recollection 'the Gallery is built upon the top of the house so as to have nothing on the sides of it but the steps of the leads'. He, too, thought they ought in any search to get the assistance of the builder.[33] The ducal steward, however, replied to the duke: 'I am afraid in this severe weather [it was now 24th November] I dare not undertake a journey over the cold moors.' In any case, so far as he (the steward) could remember, there was 'no "private room" and no arms except two or three arms in the kitchen'.[34]

However, the affidavit was in fact taken, and it was dated 24th November. In it the deponent swore that he had been shown over the house by another servant:

At last coming upon the leads of the house, the other servant raised up the edge of a sheet of lead with her knife till she got her fingers under it . . . and then under that she took up a trap door where there was a pair of stairs which they went down into a little room which was all dark. . . . There was a fireplace a bed and a few chairs in the said room, and asking her what use that room was for she said it was to hide people in troublous times. [She] asked then if they could find a way out of the room into the next, upon which they looked around and could find none. Then [she] went to the side of the room next to the stair foot and opened a door of the height of the room which they looked into, but it being dark they cou'd not see any thing, but [she] said they cou'd not go into it, it was so full of arms.[35]

At this they went back and up the steps, shut the trap-door, laid down the sheet of lead in its place again so that it could not be discerned, so much so in fact that the deponent believed he would be unable to find it again. All this was nine years previously.

In general, there is much evidence of a liberal and tolerant line in a number of counties. For example, from Cheshire it is reported to London that 'the papists are inconsiderable, but they have given it under their hands that they will nor stir'.[36] The route from north-west England into North Wales, where it was commonly stated the jacobites were ready to rise, might very well be crucial. Yet Sir Thomas Mostyn reported from Mostyn: 'I am well assured the Principal Catholicks here have no inclination to give any disturbance, and as they are in my neighbourhood, I think I can answer for them'37—that is to say, no horses, arms or persons were taken up, and none need be taken up.

Some who felt themselves rather more removed from the immediate scene of action, treated the whole affair with a combination of petty annoyance and casual boredom. The sudden need to muster the militia in the various counties had brought to light a curious imperfection in the militia laws which, when parliament legislated to remove it, seemed only to be confirmed. Alternative methods had therefore to be resorted to, one of which was to form 'associations' for the defence of the crown 'and the present happy establishment'. Some counties would have 'associations', others would not.38 Earl Poulett, lord lieutenant of Somerset, writing from Hinton on 18th November 1745—the jacobite army crossed the border on the 8th—reported to the secretary of state that 'the Principal gentlemen of the county' were all of them against any 'association'. 'Their arguments were that the Rebellion was begun in the North and was likely to be exterminated there.' Associations 'were contrary to the nature of Parliament, unparliamentary and unconstitutional'. His lordship had talked to the assembled gentry of the county, but 'there was a bull baiting, wch made a good deal of noise at the time of our meeting, and was supposed by some to have been contrived on purpose'. Doubtless the rebellion could find jobs for the 'great number of unemployed'.39

This very casualness, however, and the general complaisance of the justices, so it was argued by the more ardent whigs, could itself become a danger to the peace. And there was always the mob to be worked on. In Yorkshire, for example, according to an account enclosed by the archbishop to Lord Malton, the catholics at Egton (about eight miles behind Whitby) 'made great rejoicings' on the government defeat at Prestonpans, and furthermore they 'used the Curate with great Insolence'. When this news got as far as Whitby, the 'Brave Ship carpenters of Whitby . . . took there Axes and Cleavers to hack and hew the said papists in pieces'. It was only after 'they had marched two miles towards their Enemies' that they could 'with extreme difficulty' be 'brought back to Whitby'.[40] The moral of this story was said to be that 'if the Justices of the Peace, will persist in their complaisance to the Papists, and not execute the laws of this country against them', one could 'not be sorry if the common people take up their axes'.

Already before the rising of 1715 the counties had had the advantage of some rehearsals of putting the laws into execution against the catholics. In 1696, for example, in the face of the threat of invasion already referred to, it was essential that the Scottish border should be held, and that the English jacobites in the north (and particularly in the north-west) should be prevented from joining hands with the jacobites across the border—which was *not* prevented in 1715—with tragic results.

In 1696, therefore, the king hurried instructions to the earl of Carlisle, lord lieutenant for Cumberland and Westmorland, ordering him forthwith to secure the horses, arms and persons of all the disaffected. The earl of Carlisle would have to rely upon his principal deputy lieutenant, Sir Daniel Fleming of Rydal Hall, and he wrote therefore to him to secure the border. The earl mentioned the orders he had received from the king and added:

I think it will be convenient to secure the Borders by seizeing some of the disaffected there. . . . You must be careful to leive no armes or horses that may be serviceable to them upon such an occasion as this in any Roman Catholick's hands,[41]

but, with a judicial touch that surely does him credit, 'you wil also be careful to return theme their horses againe when this matter is over'. Clearly, it was not a matter of victimizing the catholics: it was a matter merely of complying with orders from London.

Within about a fortnight the council inquired from the lord lieutenant what number of papists he had to report, how many of them were absent from their homes, and what numbers of horses, etc., had been seized.[42] The lord lieutenant had heard from his deputy merely that the orders had been passed on, but now he had to inquire (from London) for 'more precise information that he might answer the council'. This clerk of the peace reported:

> I have not met with any arms or horses I could seize under the warrant. Most of the gentlemen whose houses I searched were not to be found, but I did not inquire how long they had been absent. I did not do so because I had had no such particular commands from the Deputy Lieutenants before.[43]

Fleming of Rydal Hall, when pressed to reply, excused the county by saying that 'the Papists are so few and inconsiderable . . . that they are not dangerous'. In any case, 'the mob' is so averse to them that the odds 'would be twenty to one against them'. However, some sort of account was at last extracted for the privy council. Of the eight persons named for the whole of the county, three lived outside the county and one was dead; of the other four, none had any arms or horses, and two had nothing at all but the gout.[44] This kind of thing, surely, is evidence of toleration in a positive sense, rather than of apathy in a negative way.

To come to the fatal year of 1715, as soon as information was received in London in July—from Lord Stair, the ambassador in Paris—that James Francis Edward was preparing to invade this country, the orders of the privy council were despatched to the lords lieutenant and *custodes rotulorum*[45] to put at once into execution the laws against the catholics. The Habeas Corpus Act had been suspended,[46] the statutory oaths were to be tendered, houses and premises to be searched, arms, weapons, gunpowder and ammunition to be seized, horses to be taken up, 'refusers' to repair to the place of their usual abode to remain confined there, and exact accounts of these proceedings—important in what is to follow—to be returned to the council board in London.[47]

To return to the border—which, as experience was to show, was the one crucial theatre—little enough seems to have been done locally until a couple of months later, until after James had been proclaimed in Scotland, Edinburgh Castle attacked, and further instructions had been received from the council (as we know from the relative lieutenancy minute books) to raise the militia for the country's defence, and (again) 'to seise . . . the persons and all arms of the Papists'.[48] That something was now at last done about it we know from the petitions later on the various quarter-sessions rolls and the entries in the various sessions order-books.

In Cumberland, for example, the high constables of wards (hundreds) were 'put to a great deal of trouble and expenses in riding about to summon the Papists etc. and issuing for the warrants pursuant to the orders of the court', and in executing the warrants, 'summoning the Papists and other disaffected persons to appear before the Justices of the Peace . . . to take the oaths required by Act of Parliament'.

The lord lieutenant had told his deputy lieutenants (on 22nd September) that they should 'take care to secure the horses, arms and persons of all Roman Catholicks and other disaffected people', adding, more precisely, that 'the City of Carlisle will be the safest and proparest place to send the persons you take into custody to'.[49] This was apparently what was done. A 'bill of charges' of the petty constables of Alston Moor, for example, claims the items (1st February 1716):

Selves and Assistances	o.	6s.	od.
One of us, Expenses, myself, Thomas Robinson, Speciall			
Assistance, and the prisoner to and att Carlisle	o.	11s.	6d.

Three days later comes the intriguing item:

In expectation that the rest of the disaffected persons			
might not know how the prisoner was disposed of			
from Carlisle that day and evening, with strong assist-			
ance, with encouragement and Refreshments.	o.	10s.	od.[50]

During the absence of the lord lieutenant from the county, the young Lord Lonsdale (himself to be the lord lieutenant of the Forty-five) was acting in the capacity of vice-lieutenant. A stout young whig peer of a stout old whig family, he no sooner had some, at least, of the catholics safe under lock and key than he was moving to get them released, at least at 'liberty upon their parole'; this notwithstanding the fact that in neighbouring Northumberland Foster had risen, had proclaimed James III, and was riding across the county. As Lonsdale said, 'the Northumberland men, who were all their friends, were very near'.[51] Within a week he was writing again in thanks for the care taken 'in providing for those persons I was desired to recommend . . .; they are all placed to their utmost satisfaction, and the obligation shall always be acknowledged by me, as I am confident it will be by them'.[52] His own brother-in-law, William Howard of Corby ('my brother Howard'), and Howard's cousin, John Warwick of Warwick Hall, were among them. Robert Patten, chaplain to Forster's forces, inserted a paragraph in the second edition of his *History of the Late Rebellion* to the effect that the reason why 'none of any account had yet join'd them on the march' was that 'Mr Howard of Corbee-Castle, Papist, Mr Warwick of Warwick-Hall, a Papist converted to that church some years ago' had been 'secured before-hand in the Castle of Carlisle'.[53]

To come now to the affairs of the Forty-five, on 9th January 1744 Charles Edward left Rome secretly and posted for Paris. British government agents in France forwarded this information to London—his mere presence in France constituted a breach of treaty—and as soon as such firm information was received in this country the council sent out its orders and directions to the lords lieutenants:

His Majesty hath received undoubted intelligence of the arrival of the Pretender's eldest son in France, and that preparations are making at Dunkirk for an invasion of this kingdom in concert with disaffected persons here.[54]

It ought to be easier for present generations than for any earlier to understand this fear regarding the 'disaffected persons here'—the enemy within, the 'fifth column'. Particular steps had to be taken about the 'disaffected persons here', and hence lords lieutenants were expressly commanded and required to tender the statutory oaths to catholics and suspected catholics, and then search the premises of the 'refusers'. It is not surprising, therefore, that one may find, either on the respective quarter-sessions rolls or in the relative lieutenancy minute books, the justices' certificates (or copies of the certificates) as to the 'subscribers' or 'refusers', that is to say, that of the persons summoned 'the following took the statutory oath', or 'none did so except . . .'.[55]

On 19th August 1745 Charles Edward raised his standard in the western highlands, and by the beginning of September it could be said that 'a considerable number of traitorous and rebellious persons' were already in arms and 'in an audacious manner' had 'resisted and attacked [and, it might have been inserted, "completely defeated"] some of His Majesty's Forces'. A proclamation was therefore issued on 5th September for putting into execution the laws against the catholics. The statutory oaths were to be tendered, houses and premises searched, arms, weapons, gunpowder and ammunition seized, horses taken up, 'refusers' to repair to the places of their usual abode, and be there confined. Exact accounts of proceedings taken locally against the catholics were to be again, it is to be noted, reported to the council board.

When in time it became clear, after the jacobites had defeated the only government army in Scotland, that England would be invaded, it was taken for granted, as a letter from London, to the lord lieutenant of the West Riding stated, that the invaders would be 'certain of assistance in Lancashire and North Wales, which counties we expect to hear every day are risen in arms'.[56]

A letter from Manchester among the Newcastle papers states that 'the Disaffection of some in this part of the country is but too notorious, and shu'd the Rebels reach this city (which I hope will be prevented) I fear they will meet with too many friends'. From Lancashire itself the justices and deputy lieutenants reported to the secretary of state that they were informed 'that the rebels are now in motion towards this county'. The arms that had been taken up were few 'and those of little or no value'.

We are apprehensive there are many in this part of the country, as we are surrounded by Papists, some of whom are of good family and large estates; but altho' the strictest search has been made in those houses we have met with no sort of success.[57]

Apart altogether from the proclamations of the orders of the council, the secretary of state sent private letters to certain selected substantial gentlemen in the north, exhorting them to be specially on the watch. Sir Henry Hoghton of Hoghton Tower, justice, deputy lieutenant, colonel of the militia, a baronet of the 1611 vintage and pillar of the whig cause in the north-west, replied from Lancashire to such a letter that though the whigs had '*some* friends' they were 'few in comparison to those against us'. In 1745 the catholics were as strong as they had been in 1715, 'and I know of no converts to be depended on'.[58] In York the archbishop had said at an early stage that certain at least of the catholics were 'upon the point of rising' and it was therefore 'necessary to take immediate and vigorous measures against the Roman Catholiks without distinction'.[59]

With all this exhortation and rousing of enthusiasm for the law, one might expect that it would not have been so very difficult to 'put the laws into execution'. In fact, however, it was found not so easy to effect the searches stipulated in the law, the proclamations and the orders of the council. Some of the justices, petty-constables and head-constables were not so easily moved. As Hoghton reported from the north-west, 'One who was to put into execution has refused, and the other has made excuses.'[60] Yet, as we know from petty-constables' accounts and various petitions on the quarter-sessions rolls, such warrants were drawn, searches effected, horses and arms seized, persons taken up, and returns made as directed.

In the township of Bickerstaffe in the catholic county of Lancashire, the accounts of Benjamin Stockley, 'one of the constables of the township' have the item

Sp[en]t at the summoning of the Papists to appear before the Justices	o. 2s.	od.

and the account of George Rotherham, another constable of the township

Sp[en]t at search of Papists arms etc.	o. 4s.	od.[61]

Or again, in Aughton the constable's accounts show:

1745. Oct. 5th. Going to Ormskirk	o. 1s.	od.
making search for arms and horses— meat and drink	o. 1s.	10d.
Nov. 12th. Spent at delivering in the horses	o. 2s.	od.
Dec. 8th. Spent at bringing the horses in	o. os.	4d.[62]

Not only, therefore, were houses occasionally searched for arms and horses taken up, but also the catholics were 'summoned to appear' and the oaths tendered. Another item in the

Bickerstaffe parish records shows that warrants were served, proofs made and returns transmitted to quarter sessions.

1745
sp[en]t at the Session Returning the Papists names
and copies of the last years Poore and lay Book   o. 1s. od.
sp[en]t when I serv'd the Papists with warrants to
take the oath   o. 2s. od.
Sp[en]t when I made Proof of serving the warrants o. 1s. od.[63]

From all this it might seem that everything was working strictly in accordance with the terms of the acts. On closer examination, however, it seems more likely that the above is not so much evidence of timely concern and general willingness and efficiency on the part of the justices and constables (high and petty) in putting into execution the laws against the catholics, as it is rather a positively modern and topical preoccupation with their expense accounts.

At the news of the first setbacks the ardent Lancashire whig, Hoghton of Hoghton Tower, replied to hints from the secretary of state about taking other country gentlemen into his confidence that he, for his part, knew of no one of his neighbourhood who was not (in current terms) a 'security risk'. 'I have not one gentleman I can discourse freely with on the subject but it would soon be as common as a newspaper.' They were surrounded with papists and other disaffected. Sir Henry Hoghton, at least, and a few other justices had been dutiful in tendering the statutory oaths and making returns of the 'refusers' to quarter sessions. It had, however, been the common talk in that part of the country for more than a year past that the ministry in London had not wanted to hear anything about convicting the 'refusers'; that the duke of Newcastle himself had hinted to the clerk of the peace that the country at large had not gone very far in this matter, and that official requirements would be complied with if any return were made merely to Whitehall rather than into Chancery.[64]

By September of 1745 news was coming through of the increase of the jacobite force and its advance on Edinburgh. Hoghton's surprise can be imagined, at about the time of the fall of Edinburgh and when he was thinking of taking some really effective steps in the north-west of England, when he found that none of the convictions he and others of the ardent whigs had secured the year before had ever been recorded in the Court of Chancery or the King's Bench. He wrote, disgruntled as well as concerned, to the secretary of state.

We have rec'd the orders of Council for putting the laws in execution agst the Papists reputed Papists and non-jurors. We convicted 3000 last year. [The clerk of the peace] promised to record them in the Court of Chancery or King's Bench, but upon enquiry last week says he has not done it. Our laws say we can't proceed neither as to horses, arms nor anything else untill recorded.[65]

He went on to say that because he and his fellow-justices had done all they could, and because these men were known as papists, it ought to be right for the justices to proceed.

But the generality of this county are ready to catch at any thing rather than do any thing of this kind. 'Tis hard that in this disaffected county and at this time o' day, the whole is [stopt] by the wilful neglect of the clerk of the peace, who was obliged by his office to have done it a year agoe, indeed now says he will do it, but may be too late.[66]

Nothing gets done 'against that interest' unless it is forced. When taxed by some of the more ardent of the whig justices, the clerk of the peace pleaded, vaguely enough, that he was 'not a judicial but a ministerial officer' and therefore did as he was instructed. Also, he hinted that what they demanded 'has not been done in other counties'.[67] The advanced whig faction thereupon notified the clerk of the peace in writing that they expected shortly to 'have an account that you have recorded the convictions'. He was reminded he was 'obliged to observe the plain direction of the Act of Parliament', and he was now called upon to do so. Neither neglect nor what is alleged to go on in other counties will excuse him.

There was not such a tenderness shewed to the popish interest, the last rebellion, and as the expectation of the rebells now must be from the support they expect from the popish interest, there is the same reason and necissity to record the convictions now as there was then.[68]

Rightly or wrongly the moderates took an entirely different point of view. They held that the proclamations authorized and required them to tender the oath and to take up the horses and arms of 'refusers'. It was not, however, the intention of the proclamations (as distinct from the statute), nor indeed of the ministry, that the county justices should take it upon themselves to judge whether it was fit to proceed to a final conviction. They should report not to the *high court* but, as they had been asked, merely to the *council board*. In any case, to proceed against the papists 'to a complete conviction' 'would not disable, but rather exasperate' them, 'and be a means to drive them into rebellion, or at least furnish them with a plausible pretence for taking so desperate a step'. 'Instead of disabling, it will irritate and provoke, and make them the more desperate.'[69]

By the time Hoghton, the leader of the extreme whig interest, could get another communication to the clerk of the peace, the jacobite invaders were amongst them, and the clerk on his way (with his family) to Wales 'for fear of the visitors'. The threads of the argument could not be resumed until the new year, when the 'visitors' were north of the Border again. Hoghton then demanded that details of the 'refusers' should be returned in the King's Bench or Chancery. The clerk, however, offered again to make the return to the council board. He pleaded that the moderates had thought theirs was 'the most prudent way', but he himself would 'have been glad the privy council would have given their orders'. He was conscious he had 'been a good deal blamed about it' and could not think it prudent for him 'to stand in the gap in an open breach of an Act of Parliament to screen others from the law'.

In February a form of 'order' was drawn up by certain of the justices, stating that they thought it proper

especially at this time, when there [is] a most unnatural rebellion against his Majestie's person and Government, that the convictions of the papists, reputed papists, and nonjurors, which were returned to the Quarter Sessions [in 1744] be without delay returned to the High Court of Chancery or King's Bench, ... in order there to be recorded, according to an Act of Parliament in that case made and provided.[70]

The matter therefore came up at the next quarter sessions.

WHEREAS at the General Quarter Sessions of the Peace held by adjournment at Manchester aforesaid the twenty-second day of January last it was then and there ordered that the Clerk of the Peace of the said County should on or before the first day of March next certify into the High Court of Chancery of the King's Bench the names of all such persons as were convicted within the said county in pursuance of the Order of Council to put the laws in execution against Papists, reputed Papists and non-jurors etc. . . . .

WHEREAS the said Clerk of the Peace has neglected to report to the Court what he has done in pursuance of the Order.

THIS COURT doth therefore Order that the said Clerk of the Peace do not fail at the General Quarter Sessions of the Peace here to be held by adjournment after Easter next to report to that Court that he has done in pursuance of the said order.[71]

Even this, however, seems not to have been the end of the matter, for in the adjourned session held in Manchester on 14th March a further order had to be made directing the clerk

to certify into the High Court of Chancery and King's Bench the names of all such persons as were convicted . . . in order that the said names may be recorded in one of the courts according to the statute in the case made and provided.

The return to be made 'on or before the first day of March next', that is, 1st March 1747. By then it was all over.

The distinction has been well made between the sort of toleration which is negative, and is perhaps to be condemned, and a more positive kind of toleration which is to be commended; that is to say, between the tolerance which results from a mere indifference and that which grows out of a respect for natural rights to freedom of belief exercised by fellow human beings. There can be little doubt that much of the tolerance referred to in this paper is of the more positive, more commendable, character.

Notes

[1] 1 Geo. I, cap. 55.

[2] 27 Geo. III, cap. 13, sec. 47 and 52.

[3] 18–19 Car. II, cap. 8.

[4] When in 1710 funds were required to build 'fifty new churches in and about the Cities of London and Westminster and suburbs thereof', another tax was placed upon coals brought into the port of London, and confined to

London (9 Anne, cap. 17 (cap. 22 in Ruffhead)). The tax was later extended to all England and in 1727 appropriated as a security for a bank loan (1 Geo. II, stat. 2, cap. 8). This practice of specific appropriation led to great complications. In 1704, for example, a state loan was secured by certain additional duties upon spices, tea and pictures; in 1709 the prizes in a state lottery were guaranteed by additional duties upon pepper, spice and raisins (3-4 Anne, cap. 14 (cap. 4 in Ruffhead)); and 8 Anne, cap. 12 (cap. 7 in Ruffhead)).

[5] 1 Geo. I, cap. 55, sec. 1.

[6] Commissioners of Forfeited Estates, F.E.C. 1/43. In 1745 James Cosin, a son of a former secretary of the commission, published a list of the 'refusers' (*The Names of the Roman Catholics Non-Jurors and Others, who Refused to take the Oaths . . .*). In 1746 Charles Cosin, apparently a brother of James, issued a second edition.

John Orlebar Payne said Cosin was in error in describing these catholics as those 'who refused to take the oaths'. They were, he said, 'persons who complied with the act' (Estcort and Payne, *The English Catholic Non-Jurors of 1715* (1855), preface, p. v). It is Payne himself, however, who is mistaken, for those 'who complied with the act' as regards registering their estates were precisely those who had refused, declined, neglected or otherwise omitted to take the legal oath.

[7] 1 W. and M., cap. 1.

[8] 12-13 Wm. III, cap. 2.

[9] 1 Eliz. I, cap. 1.

[10] 1 W. and M., cap. 8.

[11] 25 Car. II, cap. 2.

[12] 30 Car. II, stat. 2, cap. 1.

[13] 25 Car. II, cap. 2, sec. 8.

[14] 30 Car. II, stat. 2, cap. 1, sec. 1.

[15] 7-8 Wm. III, cap. 27, sec. 1.

[16] 1 Geo. I, cap. 55.

[17] 1 W. and M., cap. 15, sec. 4.

[18] *Ibid.*

[19] 35 Eliz. I, cap. 2.

[20] *Ibid.* sec. 7.

[21] 3 Jac. I, cap. 5, sec. 7 (iv).

[22] *Commentaries*, Bk. IV, ch. iv, III, 2.

[23] York Guildhall, E. 41 B., ff. 82-4.

[24] SP Dom. 75/70 (30th November 1745).

[25] *Ibid.* 27th November 1745.

[26] SP Dom. 75/70 (30th November 1745).

[27] *Ibid.* 73/132.

[28] *Ibid.* 73/23.

[29] MLB, ii, 305-6 and SP Dom. 74/23.

[30] MLB, 305-6.

[31] SP Dom. 74/23.

[32] *Ibid.* 74/27.

[33] *Ibid.* 75/4.

[34] *Ibid.* 75/10.

[35] *Ibid.* 75/4.

[36] *Ibid.* 74/62.

[37] *Ibid.* 74/66.

[38] See Paper 5, volume I.

[39] SP Dom. 74/12.

[40] MLB, ii, 265.

[41] *Rydal MSS*, 340.

[42] *Ibid.* 341.

[43] *Ibid.*

[44] *Ibid.* 341–2.

[45] For the precise difference between the two classes of order see Jarvis, *Jac. Risings*, 143–7.

[46] 1 Geo. I, stat. 2, cap. 8.

[47] Orders of council, 20th July 1715.

[48] Orders of council, 16th September 1715.

[49] Cumb. LMB, f. 4.

[50] Cumb. QSR, Easter 1716 (Petitions, f. 38).

[51] *Carlisle MSS*, 17 (22nd October 1715).

[52] *Ibid.* (29th October 1715).

[53] Pp. 86–7 (not in first edition).

[54] Orders of council, 24th July 1744.

[55] Cf. e.g. Jarvis, *Jac. Risings*, 217–21.

[56] MLB, ii, 302.

[57] SP Dom. 73/73.

[58] Hoghton MSS, Hoghton to Pelham, 11th September 1745.

[59] MLB, ii, 264–5.

[60] Hoghton MSS, 1st October 1745.

[61] Lancs CRO : PR 414.

[62] *Ibid.* PR 56.

[63] Lancs. CRO: PR 414.

[64] *Kenyon MSS*, 471.

[65] Hoghton MSS, 18th September 1745.

[66] *Ibid.*

[67] *Kenyon MSS*, 473.

[68] *Ibid.*

[69] *Ibid.* 473.

[70] *Ibid.* 475–6.

[71] Lancs. QSO, 2/115.

Index

Aberdeen, 153
Act of Settlement, 184
Adams, Elizabeth, 8
  Roger, 7, 8
Adderton, Jerome, 269
Addison, William, 283
Agreeable Miscellany, 6
Allardyce, James, 278
Alston Moor, 316
Altrincham, 10, 20, 35
Alyth (Perth), 285, 297
Annan, 42, 45, 46, 54, 57, 63–4
Annandale, 41
Appleby, 64
Argyll, Archibald, third duke, 85
Arisaig, 128
Arms/ammunition/artillery, *see*
  'Army'
Armstrong, John, 76
Army,
  jacobite,
    arms and ammunition, 41–2,
      247, 298
    artillery, 9, 10, 41, 47, 63
    baggage, 9, 41–2, 47, 62, 64
    bagpipes, 18, 296
    billeting, 17, 18, 20, 27, 242–3
    depredations, 27–30, 64, 120
    dress, 18, 24, 30, 283, 295
    horse (Elcho's, Pitsligo's), 21,
      35, 242, 244, 247
    invasion of England, 9–10, 18,
      24, 38, 42–6
    Manchester regiment, 25, 83,
      251, 271, 282, 284, 286, 296,
      297, 298

quartermasters, 15, 44, 47, 48,
  63
recruiting, 17, 20
supplies, 64
units named, 9, 296
regular,
  artillery, 217, 221, 222
  baggage, 62, 242
  numbers, 215
  postings, 206, 212, 216, 217, 222,
    244–5
  units named, 11, 16, 25, 35, 70,
    77–9, 153, 156, 221, 222, 226,
    251, 259, 270, 274, 289, 291–
    292, 294, 297
  withdrawn from Flanders, 216–
    217, 221, 222
Ashbourne, 10
Ashburner, Thomas, 6
Ashton, Sir Willoughby, 17
Assize circuits, 257, 266, 272, 278–9
Associations, 182, 229–30, 313
Astle, Thomas, 278
Athol brigade, 296
  posts, 204
Atterbury, Francis, bishop, 52
Attorney-General, 246, 258
Aughton, 319

Backhouse, Joseph, 262, 269
Baga de secretis, 278
Baird (or Beard), William, 294
Ballantine, John, 296
Balmerino, Lord, 277, 295
Banavie, 291
Banerji, H. K., 165, 172, 174, 178

2—z

Banff, 298
Bank of England, 185
Barithwaite, James, 286
Barnard Castle, 48, 56, 64
Barra, 127–8, 161
Barrymore, earl, 71, 85–93
Bartholomew, Mrs, 241
Barton, Thomas, 286
Bateman, John, 57
Bath, 154
Baty, Rev., 58, 68
Beard (or Baird), William, 294
Beggar's Opera, 110, 113, 123
Bell, George, 42–3, 45, 59
   Richard, 76
Bellman, 18, 21, 28, 65
Bells, church, 243–4
Bernera, 204
Berwick, 43–5, 77, 133–4, 259
Berwick, duke of, 207
Berwick, John, 271
Bettesworth, Dr, 55
Bickerstaff, 319–20
Bield, 44
Bill of Exchange, 74
Billingsley, Samuel, 266
Blackburn, 7
Blackburn, Sarah, 49, 57, 60–1, 63
Blackstone, Sir William, 308
Blackwell, Captain, 218–19
Blair, Bryce, 42, 45, 46, 57, 63–4
Blakeney, General, 41
Bligh, Brigadier, 93
Bolton, 7, 19
Boroughbridge, 53, 63
Boston, J., 42, 44, 47, 57
Bosville, Alexander, 289
Boswell, James, 113
Bower, Mr (mercer), of Stockport, 26
Bowker, Benjamin, 238, 240, 246, 249
Bow'ness, 46
Boyse, Samuel, 4, 146
Bradbury, Thomas, 8
Bradshaw, justice, 245

Bradstreet, Dudley, ix–xii, 72, 94–106
Braithwaite, James, 286
Brampton, 71–2, 74, 76, 84, 87–8, 91, 92, 262, 269, 273
Brest, 212
Bridge of Don, 70
Bristol, 154–5, 212
Bristol Journal, 154
Brough, 40, 58, 62–3, 65
Broughton, 41, 241
Brown, Isaac, 281–2
   Robert, 154–5
Buccleuch, duke of, 42, 47, 57
Buchanan of Arnprior, 286
Buckley, Samuel, 32
Bullets, casting, 35, 244, 247–8
Burn, Richard, 284–5
Burnett, Sir Thomas, 266, 269
Burton (Lancs), 9, 15, 32
Bury (Lancs), 7
Buttevant, Lord, 86–93
Byram (Yorks), 43, 48, 61, 63
Byrom, Elizabeth, 19, 240

Caledonian Mercury, 9
Callaghan, Father, 127
Cambridge Bibliography of English Literature, 148–9, 151
Cameron, Donald, younger, of Locheil, 101, 136
   Jenny, 31–2, 36, 158, 162, 167
Campbell, Alexander, 136, 292
   David, 72–7, 92
Canonbie, 46, 47
Cape Breton, 183–4
Cappock, John, 282, 284, 297
   Thomas, 252, 272, 277, 284–5
Carlisle, 72, 85, 238, 273, 282, 286, 316
   bailiff, 264
   bishop, 267
   'Bush' inn, 55, 282, 283
   capitulation, 9, 15, 56, 79, 271
   Carlisle Journal, 6
   Castle, 76, 78, 259, 262, 284
   chancellor, 41–3, 75–6, 79–82, 282

'Crown and Mitre', 282–3
'Duke's Head', 282, 283
Earl's Inn, 266
Eden Bridge, 80
friction in, 55–6, 260, 269
gaol, 79–80, 82, 84, 272
garrison, 77–9, 261–2
gates, 81, 281, 282, 296
governor, 43, 45, 55, 73, 255, 261–262, 267, 270
heads on gates, 71, 82, 271
jacobite occupation, 9–10, 15–80, 282, 284
justices, 73–5, 79, 238, 243, 245, 247–60, 263, 267
intelligence/information,
    about, 14, 38, 45
    from, 44, 53, 56–7
    to, 42, 43–5, 46, 47, 54, 58–9
kiln, 268
malt-house, 267–8
mayor/deputy mayor, 42–4, 48, 55, 59, 73, 240, 260–1, 269, 283
operations around, 15, 47, 49, 59, 71, 286
postmaster, 43–4, 55–6, 261
prisoners, 246, 255–300
public houses, 267–8
ramparts, 18
recorder, 74–5, 79–82, 260, 262, 282
'Red Lion', 77–8
relief, 204
sheriff, 255, 260, 267
trials, 255–99
'Turk's Head', 282, 283
Carlisle, earl of, 47, 314
Carriages, 250, 259, 266
Carrington, Nathan, 253
Carter, Ralph, 271
Carteret, John (Earl Granville), 120
Castle Lyon, 86
Castlemains, 71
Catholics,
    arms, 213, 307, 309–10, 314, 319, 322

custos rotulorum, 315
discriminatory tax, 304
five-miles rule, 308–9
gunpowder, 307
horses, 213, 215, 307, 309, 310, 314 319, 322
laws against, 212, 203–23
lords lieutenant, 315
oaths, 213, 306–8, 316, 317–18
parole of, 316–17
recusancy, 307, 309
'refusers', 304–5, 307, 317, 318, 322
registry of estates, 304–5
schools and seminaries, 310
search of houses, 308, 309, 312
transubstantiation, 306–7
travel permits, 308
vestments, 310
Chatsworth, 312
Cheetham, Edward, 242
Chelmsford, 309
Chester, 212, 246
    bishop, 16
    Castle, 16, 20, 22, 23–4
    city, 21–2, 24
    gates, 22
    intelligence/information,
        from, 11, 12, 14, 19–20, 23
        to, 48, 60–1
    newspapers:
        Chester Mercury, 8–33 *passim*
        Chester Weekly Courant, 8–33 *passim*
    prisoners, 25, 255, 259
    threats to, 18, 20, 22
    trade, 22–4, 35
Chadwick, Thomas, 271
Chambers, Walter, 60
Chancery, court of, 320–3
Charles Edward,
    Brampton, 47, 83
    Carlisle, 266, 282
    Derby, 100–1
    Edinburgh, 127, 288
    Forth, 137.

Charles Edward,—*contd.*
 highlands, 5
 invades England, 9–10
 landing, 4, 126–8, 133
 Manchester, 9–10, 237, 243–4
 Perth, 5, 126
 withdrawal, 10, 202, 203, 205, 226
Cholmondeley, earl of, 16, 34, 48, 87, 246
Cibber, Colley, 113, 122
Clarke, Charles, 266, 278–9
 notebook cited, 82, 279–98
Cleggs, Lieutenant, 246
Clifton, 280, 298–9
Cockades, 17, 80–2, 242, 281, 282, 283, 285, 289, 291, 295, 296
Cockbridge, 87
Coldstream, 39, 42
Colehill, 100
Collier, J., 131
Collingwood, Thomas, 294
Compleat and Authentick History, 5, 123, 143–52, 158–62, 177, 179, 207
Compleat History of the Trials, 33
Compleat Journal . . . Cope's Expedition, 157
Congleton, 10
Consolidated fund, 305
Cooper, Mary, 143, 145, 158, 160, 164, 172, 175–7, 206
 Thomas, 164
 William, 271
Cope, Sir John, 5, 37–8, 132–4, 136, 157, 289
Copyhold, 16, 34, 283
Corby, 317
Corby Castle, 83
Correfie, 297
Cosin, Charles, 324
 James, 324
Cotton, Thomas, 6
County assemblies, 16
Court leet, 237, 239
Coventry, 38, 49, 99, 225, 259
Creighton (or Crichton), James, 298

Crichton (or Creighton), James, 298
Crieff, 291, 293
Cromartie, earl of, 277
Cross, W. L., 144–5, 151, 169, 171, 173–4, 176, 178
Crossford bridge (Stretford), 25
Culloden, 13, 50, 70, 153, 159, 204–5, 295
Cumberland, duke of, 10, 12, 18, 20, 23, 26, 84, 93, 98, 287, 294
 operations, 20, 22, 100–2, 160, 204, 220–1, 240
Cummins, John, 241
Cusack, Captain, 270
Customary estates, 283
Customs, H.M., 50–1
 duties, 184

Dacre, James, 76
Daily Advertiser, 11
Dalkeith, 39–40, 42–5
Dalston, Sir Charles, 260
Davidson, John, 76
Davinson, John, 291
Dean, John, 76
Dean of the Arches, 56
Declaimer, writs of, 247, 257
Defoe, Daniel, 143, 146, 149, 158–61, 237
D'Eguilles, Marquis, 270
Dennison, Sir Thomas, 266, 275, 287
Depredations,
 jacobite, 26–30, 35
 regular army, 244–5
Derby, 24, 100, 220, 259
 earl, 48, 238–9, 242
Derby Mercury, 7
Derwentwater, earl of, 104, 277
Devonshire, duke of, 34, 311–12
Dickenson, Serjeant, 17
Dinkel, Dr, 266
Disarming acts, 37
Dix, Thomas, 251
Dodsley, Robert, 5, 143, 146, 149–50, 158–60, 177
Don, Bridge of, 70

Douglas, Margaret, 298
Douglas, Rev., 43
Drummelzier, 44
Drummer, beat for recruits, 70
Drummond, Lord John, 201
Drury Lane, 123
Dukinfield, Sir Robert, 242
    Robert, 27, 242, 245, 248–9, 252
Dudden, H., 148, 151, 169, 172,
    178
Dumfries, 41, 47, 74
    information from, 40–2, 44–7, 54,
        58–9, 63–4
    to, 42, 44
Dumfries-shire, 45, 47
Dunblane, 291–2
Duncan, John, 298
Dunham Massey, 16
Dunkeld, 296
Dunkirk, 214, 224
Dunstable, 99
Dunstaffnage, 291, 293
Durrand, Colonel, 43, 45, 55
Du Teillay, 127–9, 161, 292

Eamont, river/bridge, 15, 62–3
Earl's Inn, Carlisle, 266
East India Company, 227, 295
Ecclefechan, 54
Edinburgh, 41, 52, 288–9, 291–2, 295
Edinburgh Evening Courant, 9
Egmont Diary, 138
Egton (Yorks), 313–14
Elcho, Lord, 9, 14, 20, 27, 35, 201
Elcock, Mr (an attorney), 26
Elgin, 298
Elliott, Adam, 283
Elliott, William, 265
Eriskay, 292
Espionage, 24, 70–106
Essays Against Popery, 155
Evacuation of towns, etc., 15, 17–18,
    21–2
Excise, 20, 27–8, 50, 157, 280
    ale/candles/leather/malt, 27–8
Expresses, 14, 19, 20, 41–4, 53

Falkirk, 295
    battle, 31, 152, 204
Fallowfields bridge, 62–3
Farley, S. and F., 154–6, 162
Farquarson, John, 297
Farrer, Montague, 76, 263
Fawkener, Sir Edward, 53, 102
Fenton quarter, 281
Ferryhill, 19
Feudal casualties, 16, 34
Fielding, Henry:
    and the law, 117, 119–20, 147, 173,
        206–7
    life:
        controversialist, 118–21, 170–1
        dramatist, 111–17
        journalist, 117–18, 170
        pamphleteer, 121–38, 170–1
    views:
        constitutional, 180–2
        political, 111–19, 124–5, 169–70,
            180–2, 193–200, 208–10
    and Walpole, 111–18, 172, 186,
        198
    works:
        pamphlets:
            *Dialogue between the Devil,
            the Pope and the Pretender*,
                121, 123, 131, 135, 170,
                176
            *History of the Present Rebel-
            lion*, 121, 123–5, 131, 135–
                138, 143–9, 170, 173–4,
                178, 179
            Serious Address, 121, 131,
                170–1, 175–6, 178–9
            other, 171–4, 178, 179
        plays, 111–16, 121–2, 123,
            135, 170, 172
        newspapers:
            Jacobite's Journal, 170, 174,
                198
            True Patriot, 11, 12, 23–4,
                27–32, 124, 147, 149–50,
                170, 189–210, 220
            other, 117, 118

Fielding, Henry, works—*contd.*
   other works, 118, 123–4
   improperly ascribed,
     Calm Address . . ., 174–9,
      182–5
     see also '*Compleat and Authentick . . .*'
   (Robert?), 238
   Sarah, 173–4
Fitzjames, 232
Fitzwalter, Lord, 310
Flanders, troops from, 216–17, 221, 222
Fleming, Sir Daniel, 314–15
   Brigadier James, 261–2, 265, 272
Fletcher, Captain, 298
   I. K., 148
Forage, 247, 250
Forbes, Duncan, 136
'Forcing out', 81, 251, 286–7, 288, 297–8
Ford, John, 122
Forfeited estates, Commissioners of, 305, 324
Forrest, John, 298
Fort Augustus, 136, 163, 204
Fort George, 295
Fort William, 136, 163, 204, 291–3
Forth, river, 137
Foster, Sir Michael, 277
Fowden, William, 238–41, 243–4, 246–7, 249
Fowke, Brigadier, 133–4
Frankpledge, view of, 237, 239
French arms and forces, 40–1, 104–5, 221, 224–5
   trade, 183–4

Gaol delivery, 279
   fever, 270, 287
Gardiner (or Gardener), John, 284
Garstang, 10, 11, 12
General Advertiser, 9, 21, 22, 29, 301, 302
General Evening Post, 9, 15
Gentleman's Magazine, 16, 176

Genuine Intercepted Letter, 130–2
Gibraltar, 152, 183–4
Gibson, Roger, 83
Gilcrist, James, 45
Gilpin, J. B., 76–80
   Richard, 92–3, 260, 262, 279
Glenfinnan, 126, 135
Goldie, John, 42, 47
Goodbread (or Goodwin), Alexander, 298
Goodman, Richard, 300
Goodman's Fields, 123
Goodwin (or Goodbread), Alexander, 298
Gordon, John of Glenbucket, 9
Gorton, Robert, 29–30
Government moneys, 20, 27–8, 50, 65, 157, 280
Gower, Lord, 85
Graften, Lieutenant, 156
Graham, John, 42
   Father Patrick, 130–1, 135
   Colonel William, 62
   Timothy, 266
Grave, Robert, 82
Gravesend, 216
Greenhaugh, 291
Grey, Major (of Manchester), 26–7
Grinsdale, 57
Grosvenor, Sir Robert, 16
Gunpowder, 242

Habeas Corpus Act,
   suspensions, 84, 93–4, 256
Hackney, 96
Halifax, 17
Hall, Lancelot, 279–80
Hamilton, John, 255, 284
Hammond, John, 291
Hampstead, 96
Handasyde, Roger, 45–6
Hardwick, earl of, 52, 271, 278
Hargrove, William, 297
Harvey (or Harvie or Hervey), Thomas, 297
Hathersage, 311

Hawick, 42, 47, 58
Hawkins, G., 151
Hawley, General Henry, 101, 204
Hayes, Thomas, 283, 286, 297
Henderson, Andrew, 4, 6, 54, 143-4, 152-3
John, 71-2, 77-82, 281
Herbert, Lord (earl of Pembroke), 16, 34
Hereditary principle, 180-4, 198-9
Herring, T., Archbp., 131
Hervey, Lord John, 111
Hervey (or Harvey or Harvie), Thomas, 297
Hesketh-in-the-Forest, 286
Hewit, Francis, 44, 57
Hexham, 88, 91, 286
High Bridge, 136-7
Highgate, 69
Highlanders, clothing, 24, 30, 157, 283, 295
Highmore, Charles, 266, 282
Hint to the Wise, 120, 131
Hinten, 313
Hippesley, John, 114
History of the Present Rebellion, see 'Fielding, works' and 'Marchant'
Hogarth, 'March of the Guards', 221
Hoghton, Sir Henry, 48, 242, 245, 252, 318-23
Holland, George, 241
Holmes, John, 266
Home, William, 294-5
Horse-hire, 19
Horses, 30, 52, 259, 280, 284, 290
post, 19, 52, 242
pressing for, 21, 64, 242, 244, 247
quartering of, 244-5
Horton, of Chadderton, 27, 242
How, Peter, 76, 266, 275
Howard, Lieut.-Colonel, 272
Lord William, 83
William, 317
Howell's *State Trials*, 277
Hudleston family, 279

Hughes, Michael, 70, 84, 106, 143-4, 153
Hull, 259
Hunter, James, 290
Huske, Major-General John, 16

Innkeepers, 28, 51, 288, 290
Intelligence/Information, 19, 20, 37-66
to duke of Cumberland, 18, 45
expresses, 14, 19, 20, 41-4, 53, 56-62
to general post office, 48-9, 53, 64
horse-hire, 242
to the lieutenancies, 43, 45, 48, 50
per mayors, 44, 45, 48, 50
to military, 18, 37-8, 42-3, 45-6, 48, 49, 50, 58, 292-3
per postmasters, 18-19, 43, 45, 47-50, 53-65
per provosts, 39-42, 45-6, 59
rate of passage, 48-50, 61-2, 65
to secretary of state, 18, 43, 45, 46, 51, 54, 56, 58, 60, 68
spies, 24
per travellers, 41, 45
to Wade, 18, 42-3, 45, 48, 58, 62
Innerbaik, 287
Inveraray, 292
Inverlochy, 291-2
Inversnaid, 204, 291
Ireland, troops from, 212
Irwin, George, 294

Jackson, Andrew, 295
Francis, 76
John, 154, 156, 162
Richard (of Carlisle), 82, 264, 268
(of Manchester), 71, 72-7, 92
Jedburgh, 40, 43-4, 47, 54
Johnstone, Provost, 42, 46
Justices of the peace, 55, 73, 84, 213, 238, 243, 245, 247-9, 260, 263, 267, 279, 286
catholics, 304-23

Justices of the peace—*contd.*
  consultation before jacobite occu-
    pation, 243, 248–9
  examinations, 73–5, 79, 83, 87–91,
    247, 263, 280

Kelso, 39–42
  information from, 47, 54, 58
Kendal, 9–10, 18, 19, 44–5, 48, 57,
  59–62, 64, 87–9, 157
  Courant, 6
  information from, 15, 59–60
  newspapers, 6, 7
Kenyon papers, 240
Keswick, 89
Killing No Murder, 96
Kilmarnock, Lord, 100, 277
Kiln (Carlisle), 268
King's Bench, court of, 321–2
Kingston, duke of, 311
Kinloch-moidart, 129
Knutsford, 18, 20

Lancashire, 44, 48, 318
  assizes, 247, 271
  newspapers, 7
  route through, 9, 11, 38
Lancashire Journal, 7
Lancaster, 12, 15, 18, 45, 48–9, 64–5,
  89, 246–8, 252, 255, 259
  information from, 15, 18, 29, 58,
    60–1
  newspapers, 7
Land tax, 67
Langholm, 40, 42, 44, 47
Lascelles, Colonel Peregrine, 77,
  133–4
Lauder, 42–4, 77, 133–4
Lawson, Sir Gilfrid, 83, 92
  Thomas, 285–6, 297
Lay book, 320
Leadbetter, Peter, 21
Lee, Nathaniel, 122
Lee — (of Stockport), 25
Legh, Charles, 20
Leicester, Peter, 17

Leigh, 10, 17
Leith, 153
Leven (Fife), 282
Licensing Act (theatre, 1737), 110
Lichfield, 99–100, 225
Lieutenancies, 55, 87, 243, 279, 315
  catholics, 315, 317
  deputy lieutenants, 65, 73, 83, 241–
    242, 245, 260, 279, 308, 309–10,
    314, 318
  finance, 16
  intelligence/information, 43, 45,
    48, 50
  lords lieutenant, 17, 50, 65, 308
  militia, *see* 'Militia'
  of:
    Cheshire, 16–17, 43, 45, 47, 48,
      55, 58, 314
    Cumberland, 43, 45, 47, 48, 55,
      58, 314
    Derby, 16–17, 48
    Lancashire, 48, 238, 241–2
    Shropshire, 16, 48
    Somerset, 313
    Staffordshire, 48
    Westmorland, 45, 48, 55, 58,
      314
    Yorkshire, 45, 48, 53, 58, 318
  subscriptions, 16, 313
Ligonier, Sir John, 20, 48, 57, 61,
  101, 215, 217, 225
Lincoln, 259, 267, 269
Liverpool, 6, 21, 62, 293
Livery stables, 223
Lloyd, Richard, 60
Local newspapers, 6–9
Local officials, viii, 51
  bailiff, 82, 264
  beadle, 237
  bell-ringers, 243–4
  bellman, 18, 21, 28, 65
  borough reeve, 237
  churchwarden, 67, 244
  clerk of the peace, 7, 315, 320–3
  constable, 26, 34–5, 67, 226, 237–
    253, 319

high, 73, 74, 316
  petty, 316, 319
  grand jury, 268, 271, 273
  headborough, 308
  keeper of gaol, 272
  market looker, 237
  mise gatherer, 237
  mise layer, 237
  officer for . . . dogs, 237
    for tasting . . . ale, 237
  overseer of the poor, 67
  recorder, 92–3, 260, 262, 267, 271,
    272, 279
  scavenger, 237
  sheriff, 27, 255
  surveyor of the highways, 67
  tythingman, 308
  under-sheriff, 272
Lochmaben, 71, 81
Locke, Miriam A., 190
Lockerbie, 46
Lockhart, Mr (counsel), 287
London, 212–34
  alarm signals, 223, 225
  arms specification, 213
  Artillery Ground, 217–20
  associations, 228–32
  Bank of England, 226
  civil disorder, 222–3, 225–6
  Cripplegate Grenadiers, 228
  defence, 220–1, 223, 225
  Elsing Hospital, 224
  fire, 1666, 305
  Gates and bars, 217, 218, 223
  Garraway's Coffee House, 227
  Guildhall, 220
  horses, saddle and coach, 223
  lieutenancy, 213
    procedure, 213, 217, 220, 223
  lord mayor, 223, 225, 228
  Ludgate, 218–19
  magistrates, 223
  Merchant Taylors, 228
  merchants, 226–8
  Mile End, 226
  militia tax, 213

Minories, 217
newspapers, 5–33, 228, 231, 232–
    234
  London Courant, 12, 32
  London Evening Post, 9, 15, 17,
    18, 21, 22–4, 28
  London Gazette, 9, 15, 17, 18, 20–
    21, 27–8, 30, 50, 127–8, 132,
    143, 152
panic, 220, 224–5, 226
Putney Bridge, 225
royal review, 219
St Thomas's Hospital, 219
'Swan', Holborn, 99
Theatres:
  Covent Garden, 122, 123
  Drury Lane, 123
  Goodman's Fields, 123
  Haymarket, 112, 114, 116
  Lincoln's Inn Fields, 217
trained bands/militia, 212–32
  arms, 213, 218, 230
  defaulters, 219
  fines, 214, 219
  postings:
    Aldersgate church, 224
    Bakers' Hall, 224
    Devonshire Square House,
      218, 224
    Fishmongers' Hall, 224
    Guildhall Yard, 225
    Jewry Street, 224
    London Workhouse, 224
    Mile End, 226
    Old Fish Street, 225
    Poor Jury Lane, 224
    Royal Exchange, 218, 224,
      225
    St Bartholomew's, 218, 224
    St Dunstan's in the West, 218,
      224
    St Paul's Churchyard, 225
    St Sepulchre, 218, 224
    Scotts Hall, 224
    Sion College, 224
    Staple Inn, 224

London, trained bands/militia, postings—*contd.*
  Sun Tavern Fields, 226
  Tower, 212, 215, 217, 222, 225
  Tower Hill, 225
  West Smithfield, 224, 225
  Woolwich, 217, 221
  wounded, 219
  Tower Hamlets, 212–13, 225
  Tower Hill, 219
  Westminster, 214–15
'Long Preston Peggy', 34
Longtown, 47, 54
Lonsdale, Lord, 43, 48, 58, 61, 63
Lord Advocate, 37
Lord Chancellor, 52, 271, 278
Lord Justice-Clerk, 37, 258, 267, 294
Lord President, 37
Lotting (of prisoners), 92, 246, 255, 258–9, 264–5, 269, 283, 300
Lovat, Lord, 277
Lowther House, 9
Lugdown (or Lugton), Simon, 297
Lune, John, 291–3
Lutwidge family, 279
Lyon, David, 289, 294

Macclesfield, 10, 20, 240
McCormack, John, 293
MacDonald, Alastair, younger, of Glengarry, 201
  Alexander of Keppock, 136
  Donald of Tiendrish, 136
  Clementine, 298
  Sir John, 84, 92
McDougal John, 291
MacEvan, Peter, 286–7
McFarlen, George, 263
MacFie, Duncan, 291–3
Mackie, Charles, 289
Mackintosh, William, of Borlum, 11
Maclaren (or MacLaring), John (or James), 281
Maclarins, Neal, 298
MacLauchlane, Alexander, 291

McLauchlane, Archibald, 290–3
Macmillan, John, 61–2
  Robert, 49, 60–2
Macpherson, James, 125–9, 187
Madox, Samuel, 296
Malpas, Lord, 246
Malt-house (Carlisle), 267–8
Malton, Lord, 53, 58, 311, 313
Manchester, 238, 323
  Artillery Ground, 247
  'Bull's Head', 239, 241
  constables, 237–8, 239, 240–1
    trial, 237–52
  Dangerous corner, 243
  disaffection, 318
  gunpowder, 242
  information from, 19, 57
  jacobite occupation, 10–11, 14, 17–21, 26–8, 57, 238–9, 243–5, 247–50, 299
  volunteers, 25
  levy of £2,500, 249
  Manorial records, 34–5, 237–40
    rights (purchase), 239–40, 253
  Market Cross, 244
  Market Street Lane, 26, 253
  moulding of bullets, 35, 244, 247–8
  newspapers, 6
    Manchester Magazine, 6, 7, 8, 15, 16, 20–1, 154, 241
    Manchester Weekly Journal, 7, 33
  Old Coffee House, 242
  plundering, 26–7
  prisoners, 25, 27
  proclamation, 244, 247
  public moneys, 27–8
  regiment (jacobite), *see* 'Army, jacobite'
  reports from, 13
Mann, Sir Horace, 35
Marbury, 85–6, 92
March, William, 29
Marchant, John, 4, 35, 143–4, 152, 158–9
Marr, John, 296
Martin, Colonel (author), 206

Martin, Colonel (City of London), 219
Martin, Vice-Admiral, 5
Mason, John, 285
'Massacre of Paris', 122
Maxwell, James, of Kirkconnel, 84
Mercer, Sir Robert, of Aldie, 296
Mercury (Derby), 7
Mersey, 27
Messenger (state), 245, 253
Metcalf, John, 309
Middlewich, 18
Militia, 205–6, 310
  Cumberland, 45, 47, 76, 263, 279, 281
  Lancashire, 48
  laws, 6, 55, 206, 279, 313
  light horse, 47, 55, 65, 76, 92
  London, see 'London, militia'
  Manchester, 238–9
  raising, 16–17, 83
  statutory liability, 83
  Westmorland, 45, 76, 279
Millar, Andrew, 173–4, 175–7, 186, 187, 206
  James, 286
Mise, 237
Moffat, 44
  information from, 41–2, 44, 46, 47, 54, 57–8
  to, 44, 54
Moidart, 126
Montague, Lady Mary Wortley, 172
Montrose, 41
Morgan, Councillor, 35
Morpeth, 88, 91, 255, 259, 264–5
Morrison, Richard, 282
Mostyn, Sir Thomas, 313
Mounsey, G. G., 83, 284, 301
Mull, 127
Murphy, Arthur, 171–2
Murray, Lord George, 9–10, 13–14, 15, 35, 60, 201, 203, 296
  John, of Broughton, 4, 13, 36, 41
Museum, The, 143, 146–7, 149–50, 158–61

Nairn, 106
Nantes, edict of, 181
Nantwich, 18
Nassau, Count, 215
National debt, 183–5
Naworth, 83
Nevinson family, 279
New Theatre, Haymarket, 112, 114, 116
Newbattle, 43
Newby, Thomas, 24, 87, 89
Newcastle, 92, 256–7, 259, 264–5, 294
  gaol, 83
  information to, 62, 63
  newspapers, 3, 32, 51, 301, 302
  operations round, 15, 38, 43, 49, 62
  Wade at, 55
Newcastle, duke of, 55, 99, 112, 245, 301, 320. *See also* 'Secretary of state'
Newspapers, 3–32, 51, 301, 302
Nicolson, John, 284–5
  family, 279
Nocks, John, 49, 61
Northallerton, 19
Northampton, 99–100, 220
Northwich, 56–7, 89–90
Nottingham, 24, 311

Oaths of office, 51, 303
  abjuration/allegiance/supremacy, 306, 317
Ogilvy, David, 297
  Lord, 294, 297, 298
Ogilvies, 9
Old England, 228
Oliver, John, 175–6
Ormskirk, 319
Orton, 10
Osborn, Mr (of Stockport), 26
O'Sullivan, J. W., *see* 'Sullivan'
Oyer and terminer, commission of, 279

Parker, Sir Thomas, 266–7, 269, 278
Patten, Robert, 317

Patterson family, 279
Pattinson, Christopher, 271, 272
   Peter, 24, 87–94
   Thomas, 43, 55–6, 73–6, 261, 283
Peebles, 29–41, 44, 54
Peebles-shire, 45
Pendleton, 57
Pennington family, 279
Penrith, 57, 82, 255–6, 259, 262, 269,
   270, 273
   information from, 58, 61, 62–5
   to, 44, 45, 48
   jacobite occupation of, 9–10
Peploe, Samuel (bishop), 16, 34
Perkin Warbeck, 122
Perth, 291
Perth, duke of, 9, 13, 43, 79, 88, 100,
   126, 201, 291–2
Petre, Lord, 310
Petrie, John, 288–9
Pevensey Bay, 224
Pewter, 35
Pitsligo, Lord, 9, 13, 35
'Players Last Refuge', 113
Poor book, 320
Popish Idolatory . . ., 34
Port Mahon, 183–4
Porteous, John, 294
Post houses, 51, 67
Post Office:
   expresses, 19, 56
   flying packets, 56
   London, 18, 50–3, 64
   post-boys, 51
   postal services, 50, 51, 53, 59, 60–
      61, 67, 292–3, 301
   Postmaster-General, 48, 49, 53, 61,
      64
   secretary, 53
   surveyor, 60
Postmasters:
   Boroughbridge, 53, 63
   Brough, 58, 61, 62, 63, 65
   Carlisle, 48, 55–6
   Chester, 60
   Coventry, 49, 60

Dumfries, 43, 45, 47, 58, 64
Kendal, 59, 60, 61, 64
Lancaster, 48, 49, 57, 60, 61,
   64
Manchester, 19
Penrith, 48, 58, 61, 62, 64, 65
Preston, 18, 49, 61
Stone, 49, 60
Warrington, 49, 57, 60–1, 63
York, 53
Poulett, Earl, 313
Prescot, 7
Preston, 89
   'defeat', 11–14
   information from, 14, 27–8, 49,
      61
   newspapers, 7
   occupation, 10, 18, 19
Prestonpans, 14, 38, 40, 55, 74–5, 77–
   79, 156–7, 288–90, 313
   contemporary account of, 71, 73
Priestbeck bridge, 6–7
Princess Mary, 129
Printers' ornaments, 154–5
Prisoners:
   at
      Berwick, 59
      Carlisle, 256, 257
      Chester, 259
      Coventry, 250
      Crieff, 291
      Derby, 259
      Edinburgh, 282, 291
      Hull, 259
      Lancaster, 259
      Lincoln, 259
      Morpeth, 259, 264
      Newcastle, 257, 259, 264
      Penrith, 259
      Perth, 291
      Whitehaven, 259
      York, 257, 259
   to Carlisle, 262, 264, 267, 269
   civil, 258, 279–80, 291, 263
   French, 262, 265, 269, 270
   gaol fever, 270, 287

identification, 251, 256–7, 264, 281
lotting, 92, 246, 255, 258–9, 264–5,
    268, 269, 283, 300
medical provisions, 266
named, 263, 271, 279–300
numbers, 255, 272, 273, 283
quartering, 259, 260, 281–2
royal mercy, 258–9, 273
transportation, 265
transports, 257
youth of, 283, 286–7, 295, 297–
    300
Propaganda, 110–38
Public moneys, 20, 27–8, 50, 65, 157,
    280. *See also* 'Excise'
Pulteney, William, 112

Quarter sessions, catholics, 305. *See
    also* 'Justices of the peace'
Quartering, of troops, 17, 18, 20, 27,
    242–3, 244–5

Raby Castle, 63
Radcliffe, Charles, 277
Rapin-Thoras, Paul de, 4
Rawsthorne, John, 243
Ray, James, 5, 26, 84, 143–4, 146–7,
    149, 153–64
Reasons for Giving up Gibraltar, 152
'Refusers', 304–5, 307, 317, 318,
    322
Religious toleration, 303–23
Revolution (1688), 306
Ribble bridge, 11–14
Rich, John, 125
Richardson, Samuel, 149, 158–60
    Thomas, 48
Richmond, duke of, 100
Roads and bridges, 48
'Roast Beef of Old England', 112
Robinson, Thomas, 316
    Mr (grocer of Stockport), 26
Rochdale, 18
Rocheford, 212
Rochester, 212

Rose, D. Murray, 277
Rotherham, George, 319
Route into England (1745), 9–10, 38,
    39–47
Rowanburn, 47
Royal family, prayers, 285
Roxburghshire, 45
Ruthven-in-Badenoch, 204
Ryder, Sir Dudley, 246, 258

St James's Evening Post, 9, 11–12, 17,
    19–21, 23–4, 27–8, 32
Sale, 10
Salford, 244–5
    bridge, 243
Salkeld, Henry, 82–94
    Thomas, 91
Saxby, R., 60
Saxe, Marshal de, 212
Scarborough, 162–3
Scot, John, 298
Scott, John, of Scotstarvet, 136–7
Secretary of state, 16, 52, 55, 101–2,
    105, 223, 229, 245, 247–8, 257–8,
    269, 270–1, 316
Seditious matter, 53
Selkirk, 40–2, 44, 47
    information from, 43, 54, 58
    to, 43, 54, 58
Selkirkshire, 45
Seymour, M., 150
Shap, 9–10
Sharpe, John, 247, 248
Shaw, John, 34, 59–60
Sheerness, 212
Shelvocke, George, 53
Sheridan, Sir Thomas, 88, 92
Short Account, A, 14, 35
Siddal, Thomas, 25–6
Sim(s), Anthony, 82–3, 87, 92
Simpson, Thomas, 77
Skye, 127
Smith, William, 298
Solway, 46
Somerset, 313
Somerville, Andrew, 290

Spain, 183–4
Specie, 266
Spedding family, 279
Spencer, Alexander, 64
Spey, river, 205
Spithead, 212
'Sporus', 111
Stack, Captain, 270
Staffordshire, 48
Stainmore, 40
Stair, earl of, 215, 315
Standish, 101–2
Stanwix, Colonel, 262
State of the Nation for 1748, 152
Staves of office, 237, 244
Steenson (or Stevenson), an in-
    former, 290
Stewart, Archibald, 277
Stirling, 41
    castle, 137
    information from, 41
Stockley, Benjamin, 319
Stockport, 10, 25–6
Stone, 25, 49, 60
Stone, Andrew, 95, 98, 103–5
Strange, Sir John, 278
Stretford, 25
Strickland, Francis, 84
Stuart, Alexander, 287–8
    John Roy, 9, 100
    Patrick, 287–8
Sub-vassal status, 16, 34
Sullivan, J. W., 84, 100–1, 201
'Swan', Holborn, 99
Syddall, Thomas, 277

Tate, Alderman, 262
Tayler, H. and A., 84
Taylor, G. S., 84
Tenantries, 16, 34
Tenton, Dr, 266
Terry, Sir C. S., 162
Test Acts (1673, 1678, 1696), 306
Thames, defences, 212, 225, 226
Theatre—political propaganda, 110–
    117

Theatre Royal, Covent Garden, 122,
    123
Thoirs, John, 286, 298
Thorndon, Essex, 309–10
Thornton, Samuel, 309
Threlkeld, Robert, 282
Tiffin, Dorothy, 284
Tilbury, 212
Tour of the Whole Island, 143, 149, 158
Tower Hamlets, 212–13, 225
Tower of London, 212, 217, 222, 225
Towneley, Francis, 35, 83
Trained bands, *see* 'London, trained
    bands'
Transport,
    baggage, 7, 9, 23, 41–3, 47, 62, 64,
        242, 247, 250
    carriages, 250, 259, 266
    forage, 247, 250
    horses, 259, 290
    pressing, 21, 30, 64, 242, 244,
        247
    quartering, 244–5
    riding post, 19, 52, 242
Transubstantiation, 303, 306–7
Treason, 247, 277–96
Trials, 237–53, 255–300
    accommodation, 259, 260–2, 266–
        267, 268, 269–70
    at
        Carlisle, 256, 257–74, 277
        Lancaster, 247–8, 252, 278
        Lincoln, 267, 269
        Newcastle, 259
        Southwark, 277, 279, 283
        York, 256, 270, 271–2, 277–8,
            283
    bills, 267, 269, 271
    French prisoners, 260, 262–3, 269,
        270
    grand jury, 256, 260, 262, 263,
        269, 271
    high jury, 256, 263
    identification, 251, 256–7, 264, 281
    indictments, 247, 257, 267, 283
    location, 255–62, 266–71

Trials, numbers, 255, 272, 273, 283
officials, 248, 257, 258-62
prisoners, named, 255-73, 277
youth of, 283, 286-7, 295, 297-300
procedure, 247-8, 250, 258, 267, 268, 271-2, 283
sources, 277-8
verdicts, 256
witnesses, 248, 250-2, 256-8, 260, 262, 264-5, 267-70, 277, 280-281, 289
Trover action, 280
True British Courant (Preston), 7
True Patriot, see 'Fielding, Henry, works'
Truncheon, 'borough', 277
Tullibardine, Marquis of, 24, 35, 126, 135, 163
Turner, Henry, 280
Thomas, 286, 297
Turnpike, 54, 67
Tweeddale, 39, 41

Uist, 127-8, 161

Vassal status, 16, 34
Vaughan —, 25, 35
Vere, 'Captain', 101
Vernon, Admiral, 224
Violin, 296

Wade, Marshal George, 47
information to, 18, 42-3, 45, 48, 58
operations, 15, 19, 22, 38, 40, 49
Wales, route into, 18, 38, 40, 312-13, 318
Wallace (or Wallas), John, 287
Walley, Thomas, 238, 240
Walpole, Horace, 35
Sir Robert, 111-18, 171-2, 198
Walsh, Captain A. V., 129
Wardale, Robert, 284-5
Warrington, 7, 12, 89, 90
postmistress, 49, 57, 60-1, 63

Warrington, earl of, 16, 34
Thomas, 283, 298
Warwick bridge, 10
Warwick, John, 317
Watson, John, 280
Waugh, John,
chancellor, 133, 282, 284-5, 301
information/intelligence, 41-2, 45, 54-6
justice, 73, 77, 81
Webb, Philip Carteret,
crown solicitor, 94, 259, 260-3, 264-6, 268-73, 288
pamphleteer, 259
Webster, David, 298
Weekly Courant (Whitehaven), 6
Weekly Mercury (Kendal), 6
Wentworth, General, 19
Wentworth House, 311
Westminster,
St Martin's, 228
Thatched House, 229-30
Westminster Journal, 231
Whalley, 25
Whalley, Thomas, 238-41, 244, 246-247, 249
Whitby, 313
Whitehall (Cumberland), 83
Whitehaven, 44-5, 63-4, 74, 76, 82, 156, 255, 259, 264-6, 270
newspapers, 6, 7
Whitworth, Robert, 6, 7, 8, 14, 154, 162
Manchester Advertiser, 8
Manchester Gazette, 7-8, 154
Manchester Magazine, 6-8, 16, 20-1, 25-6, 29, 154-5
Wigan, 10, 17, 29, 90, 102
Wigton, 74, 82, 92
Wilkie, David, 297
Wilkinson, John, 277
Williamson, Thomas, 297
Wilson, Roger, 59
Wilson, Sarah, 200
Wirral, 21

Wooller, 39, 42, 47
Worksop manor, 311–12
Wright, Captain, 246

York, 53, 155–61, 309, 319

trials, 25, 256–7, 259, 266–9, 271–272, 283
York Gazette, 7, 154
York Journal, 7
'Young Patriots', 169